SQ2R

a quick guide to reading <u>nonfiction</u>

Scan

- ❖ Read any titles, headings, subheadings, and captions.
- ❖ Write 3 things you notice about any chart, picture, graph, or map.
- ❖ Review any reading questions given to you.

Question

- ❖ Turn all titles, headings, and subheadings into questions and write them down.
- ❖ Write open ended questions that are not answered with a yes/no response.

Read

- ❖ Look for answers to questions and underline them.
- ❖ BOX vocabulary words.
- ❖ LOOK UP any words you don't know.
- ❖ Re-read unclear passages (put a ? if you're still unclear)

Respond

- ❖ For every 2 paragraphs, write 3-5 key words that will help you remember the passage.
- ❖ Answer any review questions you've been given.

History Alive!®
The Medieval World and Beyond

TCi™

Chief Executive Officer: Bert Bower
Chief Operating Officer: Amy Larson
Director of Curriculum: Liz Russell
Managing Editor: Laura Alavosus
Editorial Project Manager: Nancy Rogier
Project Editor: Marie Norris
Copyeditor: Ava Hayes
Editorial Associates: Anna Embree, Sarah Sudano
Production Manager: Lynn Sanchez
Art Director: John F. Kelly
Senior Graphic Designer: Christy Uyeno
Graphic Designer: Don Taka
Photo Edit Manager: Margee Robinson
Photo Editor: Elaine Soares
Production Project Manager: Eric Houts
Art Editor: Mary Swab
Audio Director: Katy Haun

Teachers' Curriculum Institute
P.O. Box 1327
Rancho Cordova, CA 95741

Customer Service: 800-497-6138
www.teachtci.com

ISBN 978-1-58371-916-9
7 8 9 10 11 12 -WC-19 18 17 16 15

Manufactured by Webcrafters, Inc., Madison, WI
United States of America, September 2015, Job# 125387

Program Director
Bert Bower

Program Author
Wendy Frey

Creative Development Manager
Kelly Shafsky

Contributing Writers
Lillian Duggan
Marisa A. Howard
Barbara Johnson
Christopher Johnson
Rena Korb
Joan Kane Nichols
Joy Nolan

Curriculum Developers
Joyce Bartky
April Bennett
Nicole Boylan
Terry Coburn
Sarah Cook
Julie Cremin
Erin Fry
Amy George
Anne Maloney
Steve Seely
Nathan Wellborne

Reading Specialist
Kate Kinsella, Ed.D
Reading and TESOL Specialist
San Francisco State University

Teacher Consultants
Terry Coburn
Brookside School
Stockton, California

Randi Gibson
Stanford Middle School
Long Beach, California

Jana Kreger
Hanover Middle School
Hanover, Massachusetts

Dawn Lavond
SC Rogers Middle School
San Jose, California

Michal Lim
Borel Middle School
San Mateo, California

Alana D. Murray
Parkland Middle School
Rockville, Maryland

Stevie Wheeler
Rincon Middle School
San Diego, California

Scholars
Dr. William H. Brennan
University of the Pacific

Dr. Philippe Buc
Stanford University

Dr. Eun Mi Cho
California State University
Sacramento

Dr. Tom Conlan
Bowdoin College

Dr. Thomas Dandelet
University of California, Berkeley

Dr. James A. Fox
Stanford University

Gloria Frey
Ethical Culture Schools,
New York

Christopher Gardner
George Mason University

Dr. Bruce Grelle
California State University Chico

Dr. Kan Liang
Seattle University

Mahan Mirza
University of Notre Dame

Dr. Merrick Posnansky
University of California,
Los Angeles

Dr. John Rick
Stanford University

Dr. Melinda Takeuchi
Stanford University

Dr. Allen Wittenborn
San Diego State University

Assessment Consultant

Julie Weiss
*Curriculum and Assessment
Specialist*
Elliot, Maine

Music Consultant

Melanie Pinkert
Music Faculty
Montgomery College, Maryland

Cartographer

Mapping Specialists
Madison, Wisconsin

Internet Consultant

Amy George
Weston, Massachusetts

Diverse Needs Consultants

Erin Fry
Glendora, California

Colleen Guccione
Naperville, Illinois

Cathy Hix
Swanson Middle School
Arlington, Virginia

UNIT 1

Europe During Medieval Times

UNIT 2

Islam in Medieval Times

UNIT 3

The Culture and Kingdoms of West Africa

UNIT 4

Imperial China

UNIT 5

Japan During Medieval Times

UNIT 6

Civilizations of the Americas

UNIT 7

Europe's Renaissance and Reformation

UNIT 8

Europe Enters the Modern Age

Maps

Diagrams and Tables

Selected Primary Source Quotations

Europe During Medieval Times

Castles built by medieval monarchs still stand in Europe today. Their thick walls gave protection against invaders. Castles were also homes for royalty and people of high rank, although they were built for defense rather than for comfort.

ICELAND

Arctic Circle

Norwegian
Sea

FAROE ISLANDS
(Den.)

SHETLAND ISLANDS
(U.K.)

Ben Nevis
(4,406 ft., 1,343 m)

ATLANTIC
OCEAN

North
Sea

BRITISH
ISLES

Thames
River

Celtic
Sea

English Channel

Seine River

Bay of
Biscay

Loire River

PYRENEES

IBERIAN
PENINSULA

Corsica

Sardinia

BALEARIC
ISLANDS

Strait of Gibraltar

S C A N D I N A V I A

Baltic Sea

N O R T H E R N   E U R O P E A N   P L A I N

Elbe River

Danube River

CARPATHIAN MOUNTAINS

A L P S

Mont Blanc
(15,781 ft., 4,810 m)

Po River

APENNINES

Adriatic Sea

Tiber
River

ITALIAN
PENINSULA

Tyrrhenian Sea

Sicily

Ionian
Sea

PELOPONNESUS

Aegean Sea

Crete

Mediterranean Sea

BALKAN MTS.

BALKAN
PENINSULA

Bosporus

Black Sea

A S I A

AFRICA

Elevation

Feet	Meters
Over 10,000	Over 3,050
5,001–10,000	1,526–3,050
2,001–5,000	611–1,525
1,001–2,000	306–610
0–1,000	0–305
Below sea level	Below sea level

▲ Mountain peak

〰 Present-day
      boundary

0   250   500 miles

0   250   500 kilometers

Lambert Azimuthal Equal-Area

Europe During Medieval Times

The title of this unit has two key words—*Europe* and *medieval*. You probably recognize one of them. Europe—that's the continent east of North America across the Atlantic Ocean. But *medieval*—what does this word mean? Why is it important?

The period of time we call medieval began with the fall of Roman Empire and lasted until about 1450. This long period of time is also known as the Middle Ages. It is the period between ancient and modern times.

Historians divide the Middle Ages into three parts—early, middle, and late. The Early Middle Ages lasted from about the year 476 to 1000 C.E. The High Middle Ages lasted from about 1000 to 1300. The Late Middle Ages lasted from about 1300 to 1450.

You will begin your study of the medieval world with Europe. The physical geography of Europe has remained largely unchanged since medieval times. But the political geography of this region—such as place names and boundaries—have changed a great deal.

Europe is part of the huge landmass called Eurasia. Look at the physical map of Europe on the opposite page. Europe is a giant peninsula attached to Eurasia. Oceans and seas border Europe to the north, south, and west. Much of its land lies on the Northern European Plain. This plain is one of the largest expanses of flat land on Earth. Several mountain ranges extend across Europe, separating different regions. The Alps, for example, form a barrier between central and southern Europe.

Now look at the map of medieval Europe on this page. Some place names, such as England and France, will be familiar to you. Other names refer to political features that no longer exist but live on as present-day names. For example, Castile, Leon, and Navarre were kingdoms in medieval Spain. Now they designate regions in present-day Spain.

Why is it important to study the medieval period? Events in the past have helped to shape the present. For example, in the year 1295 an English king created a governing body that centuries later influenced the creation of modern democratic institutions—including our own Congress.

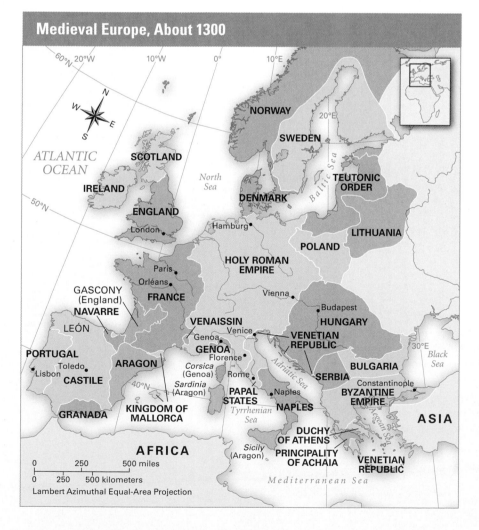

Medieval Europe, About 1300

ATLANTIC OCEAN

SCOTLAND

IRELAND

ENGLAND
London

NORWAY

SWEDEN

North Sea

Baltic Sea

DENMARK
Hamburg

TEUTONIC ORDER

LITHUANIA

POLAND

HOLY ROMAN EMPIRE

Paris
Orléans
FRANCE
GASCONY (England)
NAVARRE
LEÓN
PORTUGAL
Lisbon Toledo
CASTILE
GRANADA

Vienna

Budapest

HUNGARY

VENAISSIN
Venice
Genoa
GENOA
Florence
Corsica (Genoa)
Rome
Sardinia (Aragon)
PAPAL STATES
Naples
KINGDOM OF MALLORCA
ARAGON
Tyrrhenian Sea
Sicily (Aragon)

VENETIAN REPUBLIC

SERBIA

BULGARIA

NAPLES

DUCHY OF ATHENS
PRINCIPALITY OF ACHAIA

Constantinople
BYZANTINE EMPIRE

VENETIAN REPUBLIC

Adriatic Sea

Aegean Sea

Black Sea

ASIA

AFRICA

Mediterranean Sea

0   250   500 miles
0   250   500 kilometers
Lambert Azimuthal Equal-Area Projection

60°N 20°W   10°W   0°   10°E   20°E   30°E   40°N   50°N

Chapter 1

The Legacy of the Roman Empire

To what extent have the contributions of ancient Rome influenced modern society?

1.1 Introduction

"All roads lead to Rome," boasted the ancient Romans. For 500 years, from about 27 B.C.E. to 476 C.E., the city of Rome was the capital of the greatest empire the world had ever seen. Road markers for thousands of miles showed the distance to Rome. But the empire's 50 million people were connected by more than roads. They were also connected by Roman law, Roman customs, and Roman military might.

At its height, around 200 C.E., the Roman Empire spanned the whole of the Mediterranean world, from northern Africa to the Scottish border, from Spain to Syria. During this time, the Roman world was generally peaceful and prosperous. There was one official language and one code of law. Roman soldiers guarded the frontiers and kept order within the empire's boundaries. Proud Romans believed that the empire would last forever.

But the empire did not last. By the year 500, the western half of this great empire had **collapsed.** For historians, the fall of Rome marks the end of the ancient world and the beginning of the Middle Ages.

As one historian has written, "Rome perished, yet it lived on." The medieval world would pass on many aspects of Roman culture that still affect us today.

In this chapter, you will discover how and why the Roman Empire fell. Then you will learn how Rome's influence lives on in so many ways today—in art, architecture and engineering, language and writing, and philosophy, law, and citizenship.

The Roman emperor Constantine appears on this coin. He made major changes to the empire, including moving its capital to Byzantium, later called Constantinople.

◄ The oldest of ancient Rome's great roads, the Appian Way, ran from Rome to southern Italy.

Roman Empire an empire that, at its height, around 200 C.E., spanned the Mediterranean world and most of Europe

empire a large territory in which several groups of people are ruled by a single leader or government

corruption a pattern of illegal or immoral activities by government officials

decline a slow breakdown or failure

1.2 The End of the Roman Empire in the West

Rome's first emperor, Caesar Augustus, ended 100 years of civil war and expanded the boundaries of the **Roman Empire**. When he died in 14 C.E., few Romans could imagine that their **empire** would ever end. Yet by the year 500, the western half of the empire had collapsed. What caused the fall of the mighty Roman Empire?

Problems in the Late Empire There was no single reason for the end of the Roman Empire. Instead, historians point to a number of problems that combined to bring about its fall.

Political Instability Rome never solved the problem of how to peacefully transfer political power to a new leader. When an emperor died, ambitious rivals with independent armies often fought each other for control of the empire.

Even when the transfer of power happened without **conflict,** there was no good system for choosing the next emperor. Many times, the Praetorian Guard, the emperor's private army, chose the new ruler. But they frequently chose leaders who would reward them rather than those who were best prepared to be emperor.

Economic and Social Problems Besides political instability, the empire suffered from economic and social problems. To finance Rome's huge armies, its citizens had to pay heavy taxes. These taxes weakened the economy and drove many people into poverty. Trade also suffered.

Unemployment was a serious problem. Wealthy families used slaves and cheap labor to work their large estates. Small farmers could not compete with the large landowners. They fled to the cities looking for work, but there were not enough jobs for everyone.

Other social problems plagued the empire, including growing **corruption** and a **decline** in the spirit of citizenship. Notorious emperors like Nero and Caligula wasted large amounts of money. A rise in crime made the empire's cities and roads unsafe.

Weakening Frontiers A final problem was the weakening of the empire's frontiers. The huge size of the empire made it hard to defend. It sometimes took weeks for leaders in Rome to communicate with generals. By the 300s C.E., Germanic tribes were pressing hard on the western borders of the empire. Many of these peoples went on to settle inside the empire and were recruited into the army. But often these soldiers had little loyalty to Rome.

In 410 C.E., a Germanic tribe attacked Rome, by then the capital of only the western part of the Roman Empire.

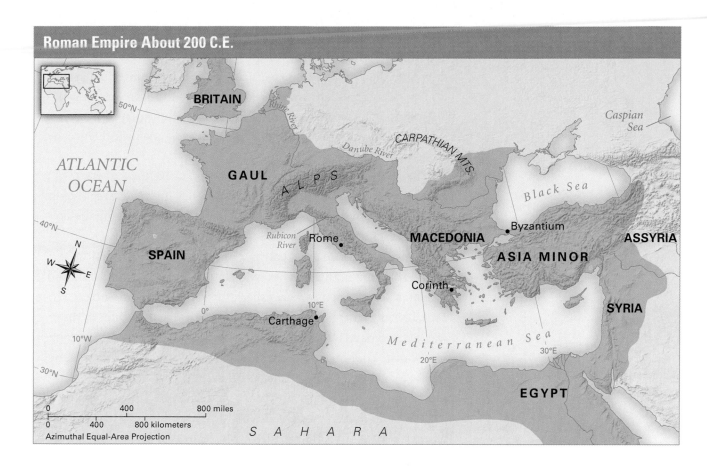

The Fall of Rome In 330 C.E., the emperor **Constantine** took a step that changed the future of the Roman Empire. He moved his capital 850 miles east, to the ancient city of Byzantium. He renamed the city New Rome. Later, it was called Constantinople. In modern times it was renamed yet again. Today, it is known as Istanbul, Turkey.

After Constantine's reign, the vast empire was usually ruled by two emperors, one based in Rome and one based in Constantinople. Rome became the capital of just the western part of the empire. Constantinople was the capital of the eastern part of the empire.

The emperors in Rome soon found themselves threatened by invading Germanic tribes. In 410 C.E., one of these tribes attacked and looted Rome itself. Finally, in 476, the last emperor in the west was driven from his throne. The western half of the empire began to dissolve into separate kingdoms.

In the east, the empire continued for another 1,000 years. Today, we refer to this eastern empire as the Byzantine Empire, after Byzantium, the original name of its capital city.

In western Europe, Rome's fall did not mean the end of Roman civilization. The influence of Rome lived on through the medieval period and all the way to our time. As you read about the legacy of the Romans, think about how ideas and events from the distant past still affect us today.

At its height, the Roman Empire controlled territory all around the coast of the Mediterranean, most of Europe, and large parts of the Middle East.

Constantine Roman emperor who, in 330 C.E., moved the capital to Byzantium and later renamed it Constantinople

1.3 The Legacy of Roman Art

The Romans adopted many features of other cultures and blended them into their own, **unique** culture. This was true of Roman art. The Romans were especially influenced by the art of the Greeks. In fact, historians often speak of "Greco-Roman" art. Rome played a vital role in passing on this tradition, which has had a major influence on western art.

The Romans added their own talents and tastes to what they learned from other cultures. For example, they imitated Greek sculpture, but Roman sculptors were particularly good at making lifelike busts and statues.

Romans were also great patrons, or sponsors, of art. Wealthy families decorated their homes with statues and colorful murals and **mosaics**. Roman artists were especially skilled in painting frescoes, scenes painted on the moist plaster of walls or ceilings with water-based paints. Roman frescoes often showed three-dimensional landscapes. Looking at one of these frescoes was almost like looking through the wall at a view outside. You've probably seen similar murals in restaurants, banks, and other modern public buildings.

The Romans also brought a sense of style and luxury to everyday objects. For example, they made highly decorative bottles of blown glass. A wine bottle might be shaped as a cluster of grapes. The Romans also developed the arts of gem cutting and metalworking.

mosaic a picture made up of small pieces of tile, glass, or colored stone

American artists often adopted a Roman style to add nobility to sculptures and paintings of heroes. Here you see a Roman statue of the emperor Augustus (left) and an American statue of general and first president George Washington (right). How are the statues alike?

One popular art form was the cameo. A cameo is a carved decoration showing a portrait or a scene. The Romans wore cameos as jewelry and used them to decorate vases and other objects. You can find examples of all these art forms today.

About a thousand years after the fall of the empire, Roman art was rediscovered during the period called the Renaissance. During the Renaissance, great artists, such as Michelangelo, revived the Greco-Roman style in their paintings and sculptures.

A good example is the famous ceiling of the Sistine Chapel in Rome. Painted by Michelangelo in the 1500s, the ceiling shows scenes from the Bible. A Roman would feel right at home looking up at this amazing creation. Tourists still flock to Rome to see it.

Roman art has continued to influence painters and sculptors. Roman styles were especially popular during the early days of the United States. Americans imitated these styles to give their art dignity and nobility. Today, you can see a number of statues in Washington, D.C., that reflect a strong Roman influence.

Mosaics, such as this one from the Roman city of Herculaneum, decorated the walls in wealthy homes. This art form often showed scenes of Roman life or landscapes, such as this hunting scene.

1.4 The Legacy of Roman Architecture and Engineering

The Romans were skilled and clever builders. In their architecture and engineering, they borrowed ideas from the Greeks and other peoples. But the Romans improved on these ideas in ways that future engineers and architects would imitate.

Architecture The Romans learned how to use the arch, the vault, and the dome to build huge structures. A vault is an arch used for a ceiling or to support a ceiling or roof. A dome is a vault in the shape of a half-circle that rests on a circular wall.

Roman baths and other public buildings often had great arched vaults. The Pantheon, a magnificent temple that still stands in Rome, is famous for its huge dome. The Romans used concrete to help them build much bigger arches than anyone had attempted before. Concrete is made by mixing broken stone with sand, cement, and water and allowing the mixture to harden. The Romans did not invent the material, but they were the first to make widespread use of it.

The Romans also invented a new kind of stadium. These large, open-air structures could seat thousands of spectators. The Romans used concrete to build tunnels into the famous stadium in Rome, the Colosseum. The tunnels made it easy for spectators to reach their seats. Modern football stadiums still use this feature.

The Pantheon still stands in Rome as an immense tribute to the legacies of Roman architecture.

The grand style of Roman buildings has inspired many architects through the centuries. Early medieval architects, for example, frequently imitated Roman designs, especially in building great churches and cathedrals. You can also see a Roman influence in the design of many modern churches, banks, and government buildings. A fine example is the Capitol building, the home of the U.S. Congress in Washington, D.C.

Another Roman innovation that has been widely copied is the triumphal arch. This is a huge monument built to celebrate great victories or achievements. A famous example is the Arc de Triomphe (Arch of Triumph) in Paris, France. This monument celebrates the victories of the French emperor Napoleon in the early 1800s. Today, it is the national war memorial of France.

Engineering The Romans changed engineering as well as architecture. They were the greatest builders of roads, bridges, and **aqueducts** in the ancient world.

More than 50,000 miles of road connected Rome with the frontiers of the empire. The Romans built their roads with layers of stone, sand, and gravel. Their techniques set the standard of road building for 2,000 years. People in some parts of Europe still drive on highways built over old Roman roads.

The Romans also set a new standard for building aqueducts. They created a system of aqueducts for Rome that brought water from about 60 miles away to the homes of the city's wealthiest citizens, as well as to its public baths and fountains. The Romans built aqueducts in other parts of the empire as well. The water system in Segovia, Spain, still uses part of an ancient Roman aqueduct. Roman arches from aqueducts can still be found in Europe, North Africa, and Southwest Asia.

The ruins of the Roman Colosseum (left), where gladiators fought for the entertainment of spectators, still stand in Rome today. What features of Roman architecture can you spot in the U.S. Capitol building (right)?

aqueduct a pipe or raised channel built to carry water over a long distance

Romans wrote in all capital letters, as seen on this Roman distance marker from 217 C.E.

scribe a person trained to write or copy documents by hand

1.5 The Legacy of Roman Language and Writing

An especially important legacy of Rome for people in medieval times was the Romans' language, Latin. After the fall of the empire, Latin continued to be used by scholars and the Roman Catholic Church. Church **scribes** used Latin to create important **documents.** Educated European nobles learned Latin so they could communicate with their peers in other countries.

Latin remains extremely influential. Several modern European languages developed from Latin, including Italian, Spanish, and French. English is a Germanic language, but it was strongly influenced by the French-speaking Normans, who conquered England in 1066 C.E. English has borrowed heavily from Latin, both directly and by way of French. In fact, we still use the Latin alphabet, although Latin has 23 letters and English has 26.

You can see the influence of Latin in many of the words we use today. For example, our calendar comes from the one adopted by the Roman ruler Julius Caesar. The names of several months come from Latin. August honors Caesar Augustus. September comes from Latin words meaning "the seventh month." (The Roman year started in March, so September was the seventh month.) October means "the eighth month." Can you guess the meanings of the words *November* and *December*? Latin also remains very important in the subjects of the law, medicine, and religion, as well.

Many English words start with Latin prefixes. A prefix is a word part placed at the beginning of a word that carries its own meaning.

Latin Prefixes Used in English Words

Latin Prefix	Meaning	English Word(s)
in, im, il	not	inactive, impossible, illogical
inter	among, between	international
com, co	together, with	communicate, cooperate
pre	before	precede
post	after, behind	postpone
re	back, again	recount
semi	half	semicircle
sub	under, less than, inferior to	submarine
trans	across, through	transportation

Attaching a prefix to a root word creates a new word with a new meaning. In fact, the word *prefix* was formed this way. It comes from *pre-* ("in front of") and *-fix* ("fasten" or "attach"). The chart on the previous page shows other examples.

As you can see from the chart below, other English words come from Latin root words. For instance, the words *manual* and *manipulate* are derived from the Latin word *manus,* meaning "hand."

Even Latin **proverbs** are still in use. For example, look at the reverse side of a U.S. penny. There you'll see the U.S. motto *E pluribus unum* ("Out of many, one").

Finally, we still use Roman numerals. The Romans used a system of letters to write numbers. In the Roman numeral system, the letters I, V, X, L, C, D, and M represent 1, 5, 10, 50, 100, 500, and 1,000. You may have seen Roman numerals used on clocks, sundials, and the first pages of books. You might also spot Roman numerals on buildings and in some movie and television credits to show the year in which they were made.

Roman influence is still important today. For example, this public clock was designed with Roman numerals.

proverb a popular saying meant to express something wise or true

Latin Roots Used in English Words

Latin Root	Meaning	English
anima	life, breath, soul	animal, animate
civil	citizen, community	civic
lex, legalis	law, legal	legislature
manus	hand	manual, manipulate
militare	to serve as a soldier	military
portare	to carry	portable
unus	one	united
urbs	city	urban, suburb
verbum	word	verbal

1.6 The Legacy of Roman Philosophy, Law, and Citizenship

Roman **philosophy**, law, and ideas about citizenship were greatly influenced by the Greeks. But the Romans made contributions of their own that they passed on to future generations.

A Philosophy Called Stoicism A Greek school of thought that was especially popular in Rome was Stoicism (STOH-ihk-ism). Many upper-class Romans adopted this philosophy and made it their own. Stoics believed that a divine (godly) intelligence ruled all of nature. A person's soul was a spark of that divine intelligence. "Living rightly" meant living in a way that agreed with nature.

To the Stoics, the one truly good thing in life was to have a good character. This meant having virtues such as self-control and courage. Stoics prized duty and the welfare of their community over personal comfort. Roman Stoics were famous for bearing pain and suffering bravely and quietly. To this day, we call someone who behaves in this way "stoic."

Law and Justice Roman law covered marriages, inheritances, and contracts (agreements) between people, as well as countless other areas of daily life. Modern legal codes in European countries like France and Italy are based in part on ancient Roman laws.

Another legacy of the Romans was the Roman idea of justice. The Romans believed that there was a universal law of justice that came from nature. By this natural law, every person had rights. Judges in Roman courts tried to make just, or fair, decisions that respected people's rights.

Like people everywhere, the Romans did not always live up to their ideals. Their courts did not treat the poor or slaves equally with the rich. Emperors often made laws simply because they had the power to do so. But the ideals of Roman law and justice live on. For example, the ideas of natural law and natural rights are echoed in the Declaration of Independence. Modern-day judges, like judges in Roman courts, often make decisions based on ideals of justice as well as on written law. Similarly, many people around the world believe that all humans have basic rights that no written law can take away.

> **philosophy** the study of wisdom, knowledge, and the nature of reality

The emperor Marcus Aurelius was a devoted Stoic. He wrote about this philosophy of life in his *Meditations*. Many people are still inspired by the ideas in this book.

Citizenship When Rome first began expanding its power in Italy, to be a "Roman" was to be a citizen of the city-state of Rome. Over time, however, Rome's leaders gradually extended citizenship to all free people in the empire. Even someone born in Syria, in Southwest Asia, or in Gaul (modern-day France) could claim to be Roman. All citizens were subject to and protected by Roman law, enjoyed the same rights, and owed allegiance (loyalty) to the emperor.

The idea of citizenship as both a privilege and a responsibility has descended from Roman times to our own. While most people in the United States are citizens by birth, many immigrants become citizens by solemnly promising loyalty to the United States. Regardless of where they were born, all citizens have the same responsibilities. For example, they must obey the law. And all enjoy the same basic rights spelled out in the Constitution and its amendments, including the Bill of Rights.

U.S. citizens enjoy the right to vote for government leaders, thanks to the ideas of citizenship that began in Roman times.

Chapter Summary

In this chapter, you explored the rich legacy of ancient Rome. The Roman Empire fell more than 1,500 years ago. But it left a lasting influence throughout Western culture that you experience nearly every day.

Art, Architecture, and Engineering Artists still follow Roman styles in sculpture, mosaics, glass, and other art forms. Roman influences are seen in the arches, domes, and vaults of many modern churches, banks, and government buildings. The Romans also were talented engineers, whose construction methods and standards lasted thousands of years.

Language and Writing Many words and word parts in modern languages, including English, French, and Spanish, developed from the Roman language, Latin. Roman numerals appear today on clocks, in books, and in TV and movie credits.

Philosophy, Law, and Citizenship Roman ideals, such as the philosophy of Stoicism, rule of law, and justice, shaped the law codes and government structures of many nations today. Examples of the continuing influence of Roman ideas include today's law courts, written law, such as the U.S. Constitution, and our representative government.

Chapter 2

The Development of Feudalism in Western Europe

How well did feudalism establish order in Europe in the Middle Ages?

2.1 Introduction

The fall of the Roman Empire in 476 C.E. marks the beginning of the period in Europe known as the Middle Ages. In this chapter, you will learn about a political and economic system that developed during the Middle Ages.

Historians divide the Middle Ages into three periods. The Early Middle Ages lasted from about 476 to 1000 C.E. The High Middle Ages lasted from about 1000 to 1300. The Late Middle Ages lasted from about 1300 to 1450.

The Early Middle Ages began with the fall of Rome. The Roman Empire had unified much of Europe for about 500 years. After the empire collapsed, life was dangerous and difficult in Western Europe. People worked hard simply to survive and to have enough to eat. They also needed to protect themselves from conquest by invading barbarians and neighboring kingdoms.

These challenges gave rise to the economic and political system historians call feudalism (FEWD-ahl-ism). In the feudal system, people pledged loyalty to a lord—a ruler or powerful landholder. In return, they received protection from that lord. Warriors fought on behalf of their lords. Peasants worked the land. At the bottom of the system were serfs, peasants who were not free to leave the lord's land without permission.

In this chapter, you will learn more about the difficulties people faced during the Early Middle Ages. Then you will learn about the rise of feudalism and how it helped to establish order and security after the fall of Rome. Finally, you will explore what daily life was like for people living under feudalism.

This pyramid shows the basic social structure in the Middle Ages. The monarch was at the top, followed by the nobles, and then knights. Peasants were at the bottom.

◀ This page from an illuminated manuscript shows a typical day on a feudal manor.

2.2 Western Europe During the Middle Ages

For 500 years, much of Europe was part of the Roman Empire. The rest of the continent was controlled by groups of people the Romans called "barbarians" because they did not follow Roman ways. When Rome fell to invading barbarians in 476 C.E., Europe was left with no central government or system of defense. Many invading groups set up kingdoms throughout Western Europe. These kingdoms were often at war with one another. The most powerful rulers were those who controlled the most land and had the best warriors.

In 800 C.E., Charlemagne was crowned Holy Roman emperor by Pope Leo III.

Charlemagne's Empire One powerful group during this time was the Franks (from whom modern-day France takes its name). The Franks were successful because they had developed a new style of warfare. It depended on troops of knights, heavily armed warriors who fought on horseback. To get and hold power, a ruler needed the services and loyalty of many knights. In return for their loyalty and service, the ruler rewarded knights with land and privileges.

One of the early leaders of the Franks was an ambitious young warrior named Clovis. In 481 C.E., at the age of 15, Clovis became leader of the Franks. Five years later, he defeated the last great Roman army in Gaul at Soissons. During his 30-year **reign,** he led the Franks in wars that greatly extended the boundaries of the Frankish kingdom.

Clovis also helped lead the Franks into **Christianity**. Clovis married a Christian woman, Clotilda, and eventually was baptized into the Roman Catholic Church. Many of his followers became Christians, as well.

The most important leader of the Franks was **Charlemagne** (SHAR-luh-main), which means "Charles the Great." This impressive king ruled for over 40 years, from 768 to 814. Writings from that period say that he was six feet four inches tall—extremely tall for his time—and "always stately and dignified." Legend has it that he read very little and couldn't write, yet he loved to have scholarly works read to him. He encouraged education and scholarship, making his court a center of culture. Most important, he unified nearly all the Christian lands of Europe into a single empire. One of the poets at his court called him the "King Father of Europe."

Christianity the religion based on the life and teachings of Jesus

Charlemagne the leader of the Franks from 768 to 814 C.E., who unified most of the Christian lands of Europe into a single empire

Charlemagne built his empire with the help of a pope Leo III, the leader of the Roman Catholic Church. The Church was a central part of society during this time. For Charlemagne, the blessing of the Church sent the message, "God is on my side." For his part, Leo needed the support of someone with an army. In return for Charlemagne's help, the pope crowned him Holy Roman emperor in 800 C.E.

Charlemagne's empire survived many attacks. After his death in 814, however, it quickly fell apart. The weak rulers who followed him could not defend the empire against new waves of invasions. Still, these kings helped prepare the way for the system of **feudalism** by following Charlemagne's example of rewarding knights with land and privileges in return for military service.

A Need for Order and Protection In the 9th and 10th centuries, Western Europe was threatened by three main groups. Muslims, or the followers of the religion of Islam, advanced from the Middle East and northern Africa into what is now Spain. The Magyars, a central Asian people, pressed in from the east. Vikings swept down from present-day Norway and Denmark.

The Vikings were fierce warriors who struck fear in the people of Europe. At times, the Vikings' intent was to set up colonies. But they were best known for their terrifying raids on towns and religious centers.

Picture a Viking attack. The people of the town are at early morning church services when an alarm bell starts to peal. Vikings! Long, shallow wooden boats have brought the Vikings close to shore. Now they leave their boats and run toward the town with swords and axes raised over their heads. People are running in all directions. Several villagers who try to resist are killed. Others are seized by the Viking raiders and taken back to the ships.

Clearly, the people of Western Europe needed to figure out new ways to defend themselves. To protect themselves and their property, they gradually developed the system we call feudalism. Let's find out how it worked.

feudalism the economic and political system of medieval Europe in which people exchanged loyalty and labor for a lord's protection

A raiding party of Vikings attacked the walled city of Paris in 885 C.E.

The Granger Collection, New York

2.3 Feudalism: Establishing Order

By the High Middle Ages (about 1000 C.E.), Europeans had developed the system of feudalism. Feudalism provided people with protection and safety by establishing a stable social order.

Under this system, people were bound to one another by promises of loyalty. In theory, all the land in the kingdom belonged to the monarch (usually a king, but sometimes a queen). A great deal of land was also owned by the Church. The king kept some land for himself and gave **fiefs** (FEEFS), or land grants, to his most important lords, who became his vassals. In return, each lord promised to supply the king with knights in times of war. A lord then enlisted lesser lords and knights as his vassals. Often, these arrangements were written down. Many of these contracts **survive** to this day in museums.

At the bottom of the social system were peasants. Lords rented some of their land to the peasants who worked for them. However, some peasants, called **serfs,** were "tied" to the land they worked. They could not leave the lord's land without permission, and they had to farm his fields in exchange for a small plot of their own.

Most lords and wealthier knights lived on manors, or large estates. A manor included a castle or manor house, one or more villages, and the surrounding farmland. Manors were in the country, far from towns. That meant the peasants had to produce everything the people on the manor needed. Only a few goods came from outside the manor, such as salt for preserving meat and iron for making tools.

During the Middle Ages, people were born into a social class for life. They had the same social position, and often the same job, as their parents. Let's take a closer look at the social classes in feudal society.

fief land granted by a lord to a vassal in exchange for loyalty and service

serf a peasant who could not leave the lord's land on which he or she was born and worked

Knights fought on horseback, along with foot soldiers and archers, to defend their king's or their lord's castle and land.

2.4 Monarchs During Feudal Times

At the very top of feudal society were the monarchs, or kings and queens. As you have learned, medieval monarchs were also feudal lords. They were expected to keep order and to provide protection for their vassals.

Most medieval monarchs believed in the divine right of kings, the idea that God had given them the right to rule. In reality, the power of monarchs varied greatly. Some had to work hard to maintain control of their kingdoms. Few had enough wealth to keep their own armies. They had to rely on their vassals, especially nobles, to provide enough knights and soldiers. In some places, especially during the Early Middle Ages, great lords grew very powerful and governed their fiefs as independent states. In these cases, the monarch was little more than a figurehead, a symbolic ruler who had little real power.

In England, monarchs became quite strong during the Middle Ages. Since the Roman period, a number of groups from the continent, including Vikings, had invaded and settled England. By the mid-11th century, it was ruled by a Germanic tribe called the Saxons. The king at that time was descended from both Saxon and Norman (French) families. When he died without an adult heir, there was confusion over who should become king.

William, the powerful Duke of Normandy (a part of present-day France), believed he had the right to the English throne. However, the English crowned his cousin, Harold. In 1066, William and his army invaded England. William defeated Harold at the Battle of Hastings and established a line of Norman kings in England. His triumph earned him the nickname "William the Conqueror."

When William of Normandy conquered England, he brought feudal institutions from Europe with him. Supported by feudalism, strong rulers brought order to England. In fact, by the start of the High Middle Ages, around 1000 C.E., the feudal system had brought stability to much of Europe.

William, Duke of Normandy, became known as "William the Conqueror" after he seized the English throne. He is shown greeting English leaders in this modern illustration.

Lords and ladies were served elaborate meals at feasts or banquets. Often, musicians and jesters entertained them while they ate.

2.5 Lords and Ladies During Feudal Times

Like monarchs, lords and ladies were members of the nobility, the highest-ranking class in medieval society. Most of them lived on manors. Some lords had one manor, while others had several. Those who had more than one manor usually lived in one for a few months and then traveled with their families to another.

Manor Houses and Castles Many of the people on a manor lived with the lord's family in the manor house. Built of wood or stone, manor houses were surrounded by gardens and outbuildings, such as kitchens and stables. They were protected by high walls.

The manor house was the center of the community. In times of trouble, villagers entered its walls for protection. Its great hall served as the lord's court. It was also a place for special celebrations and feasts, such as those given at Christmas or after a harvest.

Kings and queens, high-ranking nobles, and wealthy lords lived in even grander structures: castles. Castles were built for many purposes. One of a castle's main **functions** was to serve as a home. Castles were also one of the most important forms of military technology. With their moats, strong walls, and gates, they were built for defense. Finally, their large size and central locations made castles visual reminders of the social hierarchy and the power of the ruling classes.

The earliest medieval castles were built of wood and surrounded by high wooden fences. The strongest part, the *motte,* was built on a hilltop. A walled path linked the motte to a lower enclosed court, the *bailey,* where most people lived. After about 1100 C.E., most castles were built of stone to resist attacks by more powerful siege weapons.

Castles gradually became more elaborate. Many had tall towers for looking out across the land. The main castle building had a variety of rooms, including storerooms, kitchens, a library, a dining hall, sleeping quarters for distinguished guests, and the lord and lady's quarters.

The Responsibilities and Daily Life of Lords and Ladies It was the lord's responsibility to manage and defend his land and the people who worked it. The lord appointed officials to make sure villagers carried out their duties, which included farming the lord's land and paying rent in the form of crops, meat, and other foods. Lords also acted as judges in manor courts and had the power to fine and punish those who broke the law. Some lords held posts in the king's government. In times of war, lords fought for their own higher-ranking lords, or at least supplied them with a well-trained fighting force.

In theory, only men were part of the feudal relationship between lord and vassal. However, it was quite common in the Middle Ages for noblewomen to hold fiefs and inherit land. Except for fighting, these women had all the duties that lords had. They ran their estates, sat as judges in manor courts, and sent their knights to serve in times of war.

Noblewomen who were not landowners were still extremely busy. They were responsible for raising and training their own children and, often, the children of other noble families. Ladies were also responsible for overseeing their household or households. Some households had hundreds of people, including priests, master hunters, and knights-in-training called *pages* and *squires,* who assisted the knights. There were also cooks, servants, artists, craftspeople, and grooms. Entertainment was provided by musicians and jesters who performed amusing jokes and stunts.

When they weren't hard at work, lords and ladies enjoyed hunting and hawking (hunting with birds), feasting and dancing, board games such as chess, and reading. Ladies also did fine stitching and embroidery, or decorative sewing.

Although nobles and monarchs had the most privileged lives in medieval times, they were not always easy or comfortable by modern standards. Lit only by candles and warmed only by open fires, manor homes and castles could be gloomy and cold. There was little or no privacy. Fleas and lice infected all medieval buildings. People generally bathed only once a week, if that. Clothes were not washed daily either. Diseases affected the rich as well as the poor. And, of course, warfare was a great and ever-present danger.

A lady had servants to help her with her personal needs, as well as with the care of her large household.

2.6 Knights During Feudal Times

Knights were the mounted soldiers of the medieval world. In general, knights had to have a good deal of wealth, since a full suit of armor and a horse cost a small fortune. Knights were usually vassals of more powerful lords.

Before a joust or tournament, knights received gifts, or tokens of support, from the ladies of the manor.

Becoming a Knight The path to becoming a knight involved many years of training. A boy started as a page, or servant. At the age of seven, he left home and went to live at the castle of a lord, who was often a relative. Nearly all wealthy lords had several pages living in their castles and manors. A page learned how to ride a horse and received religious instruction from the local priest or friar.

During this first stage of training, pages spent much of their time with the ladies of the castle. They were expected to help the ladies in every way possible. During this period, the ladies taught pages how to sing, dance, compose music, and play the harp. These skills were valued in knights.

After about seven years as a page, a young boy became a squire. During this part of his training, he spent most of his time with the knight who was his lord. He polished the knight's armor, sword, shield, and lance. He helped care for his horse. He even waited on him at mealtime, carrying water for hand washing, carving meat, and filling his cup when it was empty.

Most importantly, squires trained to become warriors. They learned how to fight with a sword and a lance, a kind of spear that measured up to 15 feet long. They also learned how to use a battle-axe and a mace (a club with a heavy metal head). They practiced by fighting in make-believe battles. But squires also went into real battles. A squire was expected to help dress his lord in armor, care for his weapons and horses, follow him into battle, and look after him if he was wounded.

In his early 20s, if deserving of the honor, a squire became a knight. Becoming a knight could be a complex religious event. A squire often spent the night before his knighting ceremony in prayer. The next morning, he bathed and put on a white tunic, or long shirt, to show his purity. During the ceremony, he knelt before his lord and said his vows. The lord drew his sword, touched the knight-to-be lightly on each shoulder with the flat side of the blade, and knighted him. Sometimes, if a squire did particularly well in battle, he was knighted on the spot.

Knights in a joust tried to knock each other off their horses.

The Responsibilities and Daily Life of Knights Being a knight was more than a profession. It was a way of life. Knights lived by a strong code of behavior called **chivalry**. (*Chivalry* comes from the French word *cheval,* meaning "horse.") Knights were expected to be loyal to the Church and to their lord, to be just and fair, and to protect the helpless. They performed acts of gallantry, or respect paid to women. From these acts, we get the modern idea of chivalry as traditional forms of courtesy and kindness toward women.

Jousts and tournaments were a major part of a knight's life. In a joust, two armed knights on horseback galloped at each other with their lances extended. The idea was to unseat the opponent from his horse. Jousts were held as sporting events, for exercise, or as serious battles between rival knights. A tournament involved a team of knights in one-on-one battle.

Knights fought wearing heavy suits of armor. In the 11th century, armor was made of linked metal rings, called chain mail. By the 14th century, plate armor was more common and offered better protection.

The medieval style of knighthood lasted until about the 17th century, when warfare changed with the growing use of gunpowder and cannons. Knights, who fought one-to-one on horseback, were no longer effective against such weapons.

But knights were only a small group in medieval society. Next, let's turn to daily life for the vast majority of the population: the peasants.

chivalry the medieval knight's code of ideal behavior, including bravery, loyalty, and respect for women

2.7 Peasants During Feudal Times

Most people during the Middle Ages were peasants. They were not part of the feudal relationship of vassal and lord, but they supported the entire feudal structure by working the land. Their labor freed lords and knights to spend their time preparing for war or fighting.

During medieval times, peasants were legally classified as free or unfree. These categories had to do with the amount of service owed to the lord. Free peasants rented land to farm and owed only their rent to the lord. Unfree peasants, or serfs, farmed the lord's fields and could not leave the lord's manor. In return for their labor, they received their own small plot of land to farm.

The daily life of peasants revolved around work. Most peasants raised crops and tended livestock (farm animals). But every manor also had carpenters, shoemakers, smiths (metalworkers), and other skilled workers. Peasant women worked in the fields when they were needed. They also cared for their children, their homes, and livestock.

Along with the work they performed, peasants and serfs might owe the lord numerous taxes. There was a yearly payment called "head money," at a fixed amount per person. The lord could demand a tax, known as *tallage,* whenever he needed money. When a woman married, she, her father, or her husband had to pay a fee called a *merchet.*

Men and women worked side by side in the fields.

Peasants were also required to grind their grain at the lord's mill (the only mill on the manor). As payment, the miller kept portions of the grain for the lord and for himself. Lords could keep any amount they wanted. Peasants found this practice so hateful that some of them hid small handmills in their houses.

Most peasants lived in small, simple houses of one or two rooms. A typical house was made of woven strips of wood covered with straw or mud. Peasants had little furniture or other possessions. There was a hearth fire in the middle of the main room, but often there was no chimney, so it was dark and smoky inside. An entire family might eat and sleep in one room that sometimes also housed their farm animals.

Peasants ate vegetables, meat such as pork, and dark, coarse bread made of wheat mixed with rye or oatmeal. Almost no one ate beef or chicken. During the winter, they ate pork, mutton, or fish that had been preserved in salt. Herbs were used widely, to improve flavor and reduce saltiness, or to disguise the taste of meat that was no longer fresh.

Peasants' homes were small and crowded with people and animals.

Chapter Summary

In this chapter, you learned about life during feudal times. The fall of the Roman Empire led to a period of uncertainty and danger. Europeans developed the system of feudalism to help provide economic and social stability and safety.

Feudalism The feudal system arose as a way of protecting property and creating stability. It was based on loyalty and personal relationships. Monarchs gave fiefs to lords, their most important vassals. In exchange, vassals promised to supply monarchs with soldiers in war.

Monarchs and Lords At the top of the feudal social structure was the monarch. Below the monarch were his vassals, the lords, or nobles. Monarchs and nobles oversaw their lands and the people who worked them. They lived in manor houses or castles.

Knights and Peasants Below the lords were the knights, heavily armored warriors on horseback who provided service in war in return for land and protection. At the bottom of the social hierarchy were free peasants and then serfs. Serfs were peasants bound to the land. Peasants farmed the land and made most of the necessary articles of life.

Chapter 3

The Roman Catholic Church in Medieval Europe

How influential was the Roman Catholic Church in medieval Europe?

3.1 Introduction

In this chapter, you will explore the influence of the Roman Catholic Church in Europe during the High Middle Ages, from about 1000 to 1300 C.E.

The Church was the center of life in medieval western Europe. Almost every community had a church building. Larger towns and cities had a cathedral. Church bells rang out the hours, called people to worship, and warned of danger.

The church building was the center of community activity. Religious services were held several times a day. Town meetings, plays, and concerts were also held in churches. Merchants had shops around the square in front of the church. Farmers sold their produce in the square, and markets, festivals, and fairs were held there, as well.

During the Middle Ages, the Church provided education for some and it helped the poor and sick. It was a daily presence from birth to death. In fact, religion was so much a part of daily life that people even said a certain number of prayers to decide how long to cook an egg!

Christian belief was so **widespread** during this time that historians sometimes call the Middle Ages the "Age of Faith." People looked to the Church to explain world events. Storms, disease, and famine were thought to be punishments sent by God. People hoped prayer and religious devotion would keep away such disasters. They were even more concerned about the fate of their souls after death. The Church taught that salvation, or the saving of a one's soul, would come to those who followed the Church's teachings.

In this chapter, you will learn how the Church began and how it grew. You will also discover how much the Church influenced people's daily lives during the High Middle Ages.

The interiors of medieval cathedrals, with their soaring arches and beautiful stained-glass windows, inspired and reinforced religious belief.

◀ *The Mass of Saint Giles* was painted in about the year 1500.

The pope is the most powerful official of the Roman Catholic Church. This painting of the procession of Pope Lucius III was created in the year 1183, and shows the pope, cardinals, archbishops, bishops, and priests in their various garments and finery.

religion a set of spiritual beliefs, values, and practices

persecute to cause a person to suffer because of his or her beliefs

Roman Catholic Church the Christian church headed by the pope in Rome

clergy the body of people, such as priests, who perform the sacred functions of a church

3.2 The Christian Church Takes Shape

The Christian **religion** is one of the most important legacies of ancient Rome. Christians are followers of Jesus, who, according to Christian scripture, was put to death on a Roman cross in the 1st century C.E. Christians believe that Jesus was the son of God, that God sent him to Earth to save people from their sins, and that he rose from the dead after his death by crucifixion.

Initially, the Romans **persecuted** Christians for their beliefs. Yet the new religion continued to spread. In 313 C.E., the Roman emperor Constantine issued a decree allowing Christians to practice their religion freely. In 395 C.E., Christianity became the official religion of the Roman Empire.

At the start of the Middle Ages, all Christians in western Europe belonged to a single church, which became known as the **Roman Catholic Church**. After the collapse of Rome, the Church played a vital role in society. In part, it was one of the few ties that people had to a more stable time. The Church provided leadership and, at times, even organized the distribution of food. Monasteries, or communities of monks, provided hospitality to refugees and travelers. Monks also copied and preserved old texts, and in this way helped keep both new and ancient learning alive. The spread of monasteries and the preaching of missionaries helped bring new converts to the Christian faith.

The Organization of the Roman Catholic Church Over time, Church leaders developed an organization that was modeled on the structure of the old Roman government. By the High Middle Ages, they had created a system in which all **clergy** members had a rank.

The pope, who was the bishop of Rome, was the supreme head of the Roman Catholic Church. He was assisted and counseled by high-ranking clergymen called cardinals. Cardinals were appointed by the pope and ranked just below him in the Church **hierarchy**.

Archbishops came next. They oversaw large or important areas called archdioceses. Below them were bishops, who governed areas called dioceses from great cathedrals. Within each diocese, priests served local communities, called parishes. Each parish had its own church building.

The Increasing Power of the Church During the Middle Ages, the Church acquired great economic power. By the year 1050, it was the largest landholder in Europe. Some land came in the form of gifts from monarchs and wealthy lords. Some land was taken by force. The medieval Church added to its wealth by collecting a tithe, or tax. Each person was expected to give one-tenth of his money, produce, or labor to help support the Church.

The Church also came to wield great political power. Latin, the language of the Church, was the only common language in Europe. Church officials were often the only people who could read. As a result, they kept records for monarchs and became trusted scribes and advisers.

In the winter of 1077, the Holy Roman emperor, Henry IV, traveled to Italy to the castle of Canossa to beg forgiveness from Pope Gregory. Legend has it that the pope made Henry stand barefoot in the snow for three days before he forgave him.

At times, the Church's power brought it into conflict with European monarchs. One key struggle involved Pope Gregory VII and Henry IV, the Holy Roman emperor.

Gregory was elected pope in 1073. An ambitious leader, he undertook several reforms, such as forbidding priests to marry and outlawing the selling of Church offices (official positions). He also banned the practice whereby kings could appoint priests, bishops, and the heads of monasteries. Only the pope, said Gregory, had this right.

Gregory's ruling angered Henry IV. Like rulers before him, Henry considered it his duty (and privilege) to appoint Church officials. He called a council of bishops and declared that Gregory was no longer pope. Gregory responded by excommunicating Henry. This meant Henry was thrown out of the Church and, therefore, could not gain salvation. Gregory also said that Henry's subjects were no longer obliged to obey him.

The pope's influence was so great that Henry begged forgiveness and was readmitted to the Church. For the moment, his action amounted to recognizing the pope's **authority,** even over an emperor. But future rulers and popes would resume the fight over the rights of the Church versus those of the state.

The sacrament of baptism welcomes a person into a Christian church. Baptism is the first sacrament of a Christian's life. It is required to receive the other sacraments.

sacrament a sacred rite of the Christian religion

3.3 Sacraments and Salvation in the Middle Ages

Most people in medieval Europe believed in God and an afterlife, in which the soul lives on after the body's death. The Church taught that people gained salvation, or entry into heaven and eternal life, by following the Church's teachings and living a moral life. Failing to do so condemned the soul to eternal suffering in hell.

To believers, hell was a real and terrifying place. Its torments, such as fire and demons, were pictured in vivid detail in many paintings.

The Church taught its members that receiving the **sacraments** was an essential part of gaining salvation. Sacraments were sacred rites that Christians believed brought them grace, or a special blessing from God. The sacraments marked the most important occasions in a person's life.

The Seven Catholic Sacraments

Baptism	Entry into the Church; to cleanse a person of sin, a priest pours water gently over the person's head at the baptismal font, the basin that holds the baptismal water.
Confirmation	Formal declaration of belief in God and the Church
Eucharist	A central part of the mass, the Church service in which the priest consecrates (blesses) bread and wine. In Catholic belief, the consecrated bread and wine become the body and blood of Jesus.
Matrimony (marriage)	A formal union blessed by the Church; after being married by a priest, a couple signs their names in a registry, or book of records.
Holy Orders	The sacrament in which a man becomes a priest
Penance	Confession of sins to a priest in order to receive God's forgiveness; today, Catholics call this sacrament *reconciliation*.
Extreme Unction	A blessing in which a person in danger of death is anointed (blessed with holy oil) by a priest; today, this rite is known as the sacrament (or anointing) of the sick.

3.4 Pilgrimages and Crusades

During the Middle Ages, religious faith led many people to perform extraordinary acts of devotion. For example, most Christians hoped to go on a **pilgrimage** at some point in their lives. Pilgrims traveled long distances to visit holy sites, such as Jerusalem (where Jesus was killed) and Rome. They also visited churches that housed relics, the body parts or belongings of saints. Canterbury Cathedral in England was a major destination for pilgrims.

Pilgrims went on these journeys to show their devotion to God, as an act of penance for their sins, or in hopes of being cured of an illness. A pilgrimage required true dedication, because travel was difficult and often dangerous. Most pilgrims traveled on foot. Because robbers were a constant threat, pilgrims often banded together for safety. Sometimes they even hired an armed escort. Along the routes of popular pilgrimages, local rulers built special roads and bridges. Monks and nuns set up hostels, or special guest houses, spaced a day's journey apart.

Geoffrey Chaucer wrote a popular narrative poem about pilgrims called the *Canterbury Tales*. Chaucer lived in England from about 1342 to 1400. His amusing "tales" are stories that a group of pilgrims tells to entertain each other as they travel to the shrine of Saint Thomas Becket at Canterbury. Among Chaucer's pilgrims are a knight, a miller, a cook, and a prioress (the head of a convent, or community of nuns).

A second type of extraordinary service involved fighting in the Crusades. The Crusades were a series of military expeditions to the land where Jesus had lived, which Christians called the Holy Land. During the 7th century, this part of the Middle East had come under the control of Muslims. Jerusalem, which was a holy city to Jews, Christians, and Muslims alike, became a Muslim city. Between 1095 and 1270, Christians in western Europe organized several Crusades to recover Jerusalem and other sites of pilgrimage in that region.

Some people went on Crusade to seek wealth, and some to seek adventure. Others went in the belief that doing so would guarantee their salvation. Many Crusaders acted from deep religious belief.

> **pilgrimage** a journey to a holy site

Pilgrims believed that their journeys of devotion earned them grace in the eyes of God. Beliefs such as this served to strengthen the power of the Church.

The construction of Chartres Cathedral in France began in 1194 and took 66 years to complete. Further additions spanned 300 years.

3.5 Art and Architecture

During the Middle Ages, most art was made for a religious purpose. Paintings and sculptures of Jesus and Christian saints were placed in churches to help people worship. Since most people did not know how to read, art helped tell the story of Jesus's life in a way that everyone could understand.

Medieval art and architecture found their most glorious expression in cathedrals, the large churches headed by bishops. (The word *cathedral* comes from the Latin word *cathedra,* meaning "the throne upon which a bishop sits".) Cathedrals were built to inspire awe. For centuries, they were the tallest buildings in any community. Often they were taller than a 30-story building of today. Most were built in the shape of a cross, with a long central section called the *nave* and shorter side sections called *transepts.*

The cathedrals built between 1150 and 1400 were designed in the Gothic style. Gothic cathedrals were designed to look like they are rising to heaven. On the outside are stone arches called *flying buttresses*. The arches spread the massive weight of the soaring roof and walls more evenly. This building **technique** allowed for taller, thinner walls and more windows.

Gargoyles are a unique feature of Gothic cathedrals. Gargoyles are decorative stone sculptures projecting from the rain gutters or edges of a cathedral roof. They were usually carved in the form of mythical beasts. In medieval times, some people thought gargoyles were there to remind them that devils and evil spirits would catch them if they did not obey the teachings of the Church.

The immense space inside a Gothic cathedral was lined with pillars and decorated with religious images. Beautiful stained-glass windows let in colorful light. Stained-glass windows are made from pieces of colored glass arranged in a design. The pictures on medieval stained-glass windows often taught people stories from the Bible.

Cathedrals were visible expressions of Christian devotion. They were mostly constructed by hand by hundreds of workers and craftsmen over many years. On average, it took from 50 to 100 years to complete a cathedral. In some cases, the work took more than 200 years.

The gargoyles on Gothic cathedrals were often carved in the shape of hideous mythical beasts.

The invention of flying buttresses was a crucial step in the development of medieval cathedral design. They helped to make the soaring, thin stone arches and vast stained-glass windows possible by carrying the load of the building on the outside.

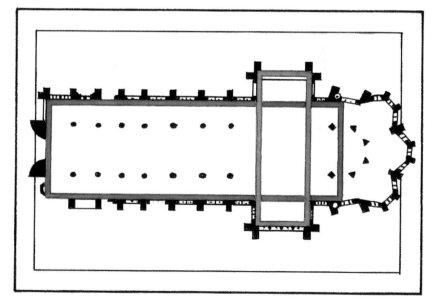

Most cathedrals were built in the form of a cross, the main symbol of Christianity. The longer, central section of the building is called the *nave* (outlined in orange). The shorter, section that crosses the nave is called the *transept* (outlined in green). Although it was not always possible, builders tried to construct a cathedral so that it faced east, toward Jerusalem.

3.6 Education

During the Middle Ages, most schooling took place in monasteries, convents, and cathedrals. This pattern was established under Charlemagne, who encouraged the Church to teach people to read and write. During his reign, scholars developed a new form of writing that helped make reading easier. Instead of writing in all capital letters, as the Romans did, scholars began to use lowercase letters, too. We still use this system today.

In medieval times, the clergy were the people most likely to be educated. Most of the students in Church schools were sons of nobles who were studying for careers in the clergy. They spent much of their time memorizing prayers and passages from the Bible in Latin.

Students at the University of Paris wore scholars' caps and gowns. This illustration from 1400 shows some students carrying scepters of the Church.

natural law the concept that there is a universal order built into nature that can guide moral thinking

Starting in the 1200s, cathedral schools gave rise to universities. Students in universities studied Latin grammar and rhetoric, logic, geometry, arithmetic, astronomy, and music. Books at that time were hand copied and very rare, so teachers often read to students.

Ancient texts were greatly respected in the universities, but the Church was sometimes uneasy about them. The Church taught people to be guided by faith. Ancient writers like the Greek philosopher Aristotle taught that reason, or logical thinking, was the path to knowledge. Church leaders feared that studying such writers might lead people to question its teachings.

Thomas Aquinas (uh-KWINE iss), an Italian scholar of philosophy and theology, tried to bridge the gap between reason and faith. Aquinas greatly admired Aristotle. He saw no conflict between faith and reason, because he believed that both were gifts from God. Reason, he believed, helped people discover important truths about God's creation. Faith, meanwhile, revealed its own truths about God.

Aquinas wrote logical arguments in support of his faith to show how reason and religious belief worked together. For example, his concept of **natural law** stated that there was an order built into nature that could guide people's thinking about right and wrong. Natural law, he said, could be discovered through reason alone. Since God had created nature, natural law agreed with the moral teachings of the Bible.

Aquinas's teachings unified ancient philosophy and Christian theology. His teachings were later accepted and promoted by the Church.

3.7 Holidays

Medieval Europeans enjoyed many festivals and fairs that marked important days of the year. Most of these celebrations were connected in some way to the Church. Almost every day of the year was dedicated to a Christian saint, an event in the life of Jesus, or an important religious idea. In fact, our word *holiday* comes from "holy day."

Two of the main medieval holidays were Christmas and Easter. Christmas is the day when Christians celebrate the birth of Jesus. During the Middle Ages, Christmas celebrations lasted for 12 days. On Christmas day, Christians attended church. Then they enjoyed a great feast, which was often held for everyone on the manor by its lord.

Easter is the day when Christians celebrate the Resurrection. In Christian belief, the Resurrection is Christ's rising from the dead. For medieval Christians, Easter was a day of church services, feasting, and games. Often the games involved eggs, a symbol of new life.

Music, dancing, and food were all part of medieval holidays and festivals. People sang folk songs and danced. They drank their favorite beverages and they ate baked and fried foods.

Other favorite holiday entertainments included bonfires, acrobats and jugglers, and dancing bears. Plays were also popular. During religious services on special days, priests sometimes acted out Bible stories. By the 13th century, plays were often held outdoors in front of the church so more people could watch. In some English villages, mummers (traveling groups of actors) performed with masks, drums and bells, dances, and make-believe sword fights.

In the Middle Ages, Lent and Carnival were important holidays. Lent is a period of 40 days before Easter when Christians are especially pious and give up luxuries. Before the start of Lent, medieval Christians celebrated with a three-day festival, Carnival, shown here in a painting by Pieter Brueghel (BROY-gel) the Elder. Today, many Christians still celebrate Carnival and Lent before Easter.

3.8 Monks, Nuns, and Friars

Religion was important to all Christians in the Middle Ages. Some men and women, however, solemnly promised to devote their lives to God and the Church.

The Monastic Way of Life Monks were men who joined monasteries, communities devoted to prayer and service to fellow Christians. This way of life is called monasticism.

Men became monks for many reasons. Some were seeking refuge from war, sickness, or sinfulness. Some came to study. Some were attracted by a quiet life of prayer and service.

The man who developed the monastic way of life in western Europe was Saint Benedict. In the 6th century, he founded a monastery in Italy. His followers became known as the Benedictines. They followed Benedict's "Rule," or instructions. Benedictines made three solemn vows, or promises: poverty (to own no property), chastity (never to marry), and obedience (to obey their leaders).

Monks spent their lives in prayer, study, and work. They attended eight church services every day. Other duties included caring for the poor and sick, teaching, and copying religious texts. Since most monasteries were self-sufficient, monks spent much of their time working. They farmed their land, tended their gardens, raised livestock, and sewed clothing.

Most monasteries were laid out around a *cloister,* a covered walkway surrounding an open square. On the north side was the church. On the south side were the kitchen and dining hall. On the third side was the *dormitory,* or sleeping quarters. Monks slept in small cells, often on beds of wood.

The library writing room, called the *scriptorium,* was on the fourth side of the cloister. Here the monks copied books by hand and created beautiful illuminated manuscripts. By copying rare documents, monks kept knowledge of the past alive. Much of what we know today, about both the Middle Ages and ancient times, comes from their important work.

Both monks and nuns joined **religious orders**. Each order had its own distinctive rules and forms of service. The Benedictines were only one such group.

Work was especially important to Saint Benedict, who once wrote, "To work is to pray."

religious order a brotherhood or sisterhood of monks, nuns, or friars

Monastic life was one of the few opportunities open to medieval women who did not wish to marry. Women who became nuns lived in convents. These communities were run in the same way as monasteries. Nuns did most of the same types of work that monks performed.

Many nuns became important reformers and thinkers. For example, in Germany, Hildegard of Bingen founded a convent and was an adviser to popes and other Church officials. She also wrote books in which she criticized some of the practices of the Church.

Friars Some people wanted to live a religious life without the seclusion of the monastery. A famous example is Saint Francis of Assisi. Francis was born to a wealthy Italian family, but he gave up his money to serve the poor. He founded the Franciscans, an order that is also called the Little Brothers of the Poor.

Instead of living in monasteries, Franciscan friars traveled among ordinary people to preach and to care for the poor and sick. They lived in complete poverty and had to work or beg for food for themselves and the poor. For this reason, they were also called *mendicants,* a word that means "beggars." With his friend Clare, Francis founded a similar order for women called the Poor Clares.

Francis, who loved nature, believed that all living things should be respected. He is often pictured with animals. To many, his example of faith, charity, and love of God represents an ideal of Christian living.

St. Francis of Assisi lived a simple life, with great love and respect for all living things. Here he is shown preaching to the birds.

Chapter Summary

The Roman Catholic Church emerged from the fall of Rome to play a central role in daily life in medieval western Europe.

The Church Takes Shape More than just a religious institution, the Catholic Church was the center of community life and acquired great political and economic power. All clergy had a rank in the hierarchy, from priests to bishops, archbishops, to the pope.

Sacraments, Pilgrimages, and Crusades The Church's sacraments marked all the most important occasions of life, from birth to death. Many people expressed their faith by going on pilgrimages or fighting in the Crusades.

Art, Architecture, Education, and Holidays The importance of the Church to medieval people was seen in the art and architecture of churches, in education, and in holidays.

Monks, Nuns, and Friars During the Middle Ages, Saint Benedict developed his "Rule" for religious communities of monks and nuns. Other religious orders were founded, too, including groups of friars, such as the Franciscans, and the nuns called the Poor Clares.

Chapter 4

Life in Medieval Towns

What was life like in medieval European towns?

4.1   Introduction

In this chapter, you will find out about daily life in the Late Middle Ages. This period lasted from about 1000 to 1450 C.E.

At the start of the Middle Ages, most people lived in the countryside, either on feudal manors or in religious communities. But by the 12th century, towns were growing up around castles and monasteries and along trade routes. These bustling towns became centers of trade and industry.

Almost all medieval towns were protected by thick stone walls. Visitors entered through gates. Inside, homes and businesses lined unpaved streets. Since few people could read, signs with colorful pictures hung over the doorways of shops and businesses. Open squares in front of public buildings, such as churches, served as gathering places.

Most streets were very narrow. The second stories of houses jutted out, blocking the sunlight from reaching the street. Squares and streets were crowded with people, horses, and carts—as well as cats, dogs, geese, and chickens. There was no garbage collection, so residents threw their garbage into nearby canals and ditches or simply out the window. As you can imagine, most medieval towns were filled with unpleasant smells.

In this chapter, you will first learn about the growth of medieval towns. Then you will look at several aspects of daily life. You will explore trade and commerce, homes and households, disease and medical treatment, crime and punishment, and leisure and entertainment.

In the late Middle Ages, towns such as Paris in France grew around castles and monasteries and along trade routes. Most were protected by walls, with only a few entry gates.

◀ Merchants offer their wares to shoppers in a 13th-century marketplace.

4.2 The Growth of Medieval Towns

In the ancient world, town life was well established, particularly in Greece and Rome. Ancient towns were busy trading centers. But after the fall of the Roman Empire in the west, trade with the east suffered, and town life declined. In the Early Middle Ages, most people in western Europe lived in scattered communities in the countryside.

By the High Middle Ages, towns were growing again. One reason for their growth was improvements in agriculture. Farmers were clearing forests and adopting better farming methods. As a result, they had a **surplus** of crops to sell in town markets. And because of these surpluses, not everyone had to farm to feed themselves. Another reason for the growth of towns was the revival of trade. Seaport towns, such as Venice and Genoa in Italy, served as trading centers for goods from the Middle East and Asia. Within Europe, merchants often traveled by river, and many towns grew up near these waterways.

Many merchants who sold their wares in towns became permanent **residents**. So did people practicing various trades. Some towns grew wealthier because local people specialized in making specific types of goods. For example, towns in Flanders (present-day Belgium and the Netherlands) were known for their fine woolen cloth. The Italian city of Venice was known for making glass. Other towns built their wealth on the banking industry that grew up to help people trade more easily.

At the beginning of the Middle Ages, towns were generally part of the domain of a feudal lord—whether a monarch, a noble, or a high-ranking Church official. As towns grew wealthier, town dwellers began to resent the lord's feudal rights and his demands for taxes. They felt they no longer needed the lord's protection—or his interference.

In some places, such as northern France and Italy, violence broke out as towns struggled to become independent. In other places, such as England and parts of France, the change was more peaceful. Many towns became independent by purchasing a royal **charter**. A charter granted them the right to govern themselves, make laws, and raise taxes. Free towns were often governed by a mayor and a town council. Power gradually shifted from feudal lords to the rising class of merchants and craftspeople.

The trade routes shown on this map carried a constant flow of goods among European cities and from distant Asia and Africa. Towns of the Hanseatic League cooperated to form a powerful trade group in northern Europe.

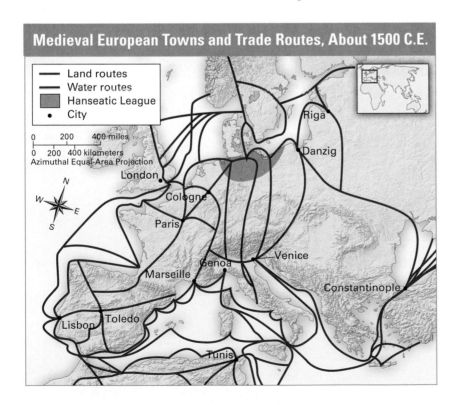

Medieval European Towns and Trade Routes, About 1500 C.E.

Land routes
Water routes
Hanseatic League
• City

0   200   400 miles
0   200   400 kilometers
Azimuthal Equal-Area Projection

Riga
Danzig
London
Cologne
Paris
Genoa
Venice
Marseille
Constantinople
Lisbon
Toledo
Tunis

4.3 Guilds

Medieval towns began as centers for trade, but they soon became places where many goods were produced, as well. Both trade and the production of goods were overseen by organizations called **guilds**.

There were two main kinds of guilds: merchant guilds and craft guilds. All types of craftspeople had their own guilds, from cloth makers to cobblers (who made shoes, belts, and other leather goods), to the stonemasons who built the great cathedrals.

Guilds provided help and protection for the people doing a certain kind of work, and they maintained high standards. Guilds controlled the hours of work and set prices. They also dealt with complaints from the public. If, for example, a coal merchant cheated a customer, all coal merchants might look bad. The guilds therefore punished members who cheated.

Guild members paid dues to their guild. Their dues paid for the construction of guildhalls and for guild fairs and festivals. Guilds also used the money to take care of members and their families who were sick and unable to work.

It was not easy to become a member of a guild. Starting around age 12, a boy, and sometimes a girl, became an **apprentice**. An apprentice's parents signed an agreement with a master of the trade. The master agreed to house, feed, and train the apprentice. Sometimes, but not always, the parents paid the master a sum of money. Apprentices rarely got paid for their work.

At the end of seven years, apprentices had to prove to the guild that they had mastered their trade. To do this, an apprentice produced a piece of work called a "master piece." If the guild approved of the work, the apprentice was given the right to become a master and set up his or her own business. Setting up a business was expensive, however, and few people could afford to do it right away. Often they became journeymen instead. The word *journeyman* does not refer to a journey. It comes from the French word *journee,* for "day." A journeyman was a craftsperson who found work "by the day," instead of becoming a master who employed other workers.

The cobblers working in this shop were probably journeymen working for the master cobbler.

guild an organization of people in the same craft or trade

apprentice a person who works for a master in a trade or craft in return for training

During the Late Middle Ages, marketplaces provided townspeople with food and goods from local farmers and faraway lands.

4.4 Trade and Commerce

What brought most people to towns was business—meaning trade and commerce. As trade and commerce grew, so did towns.

At the beginning of the Middle Ages, most trade was in luxury goods, which only the wealthy could afford. People made everyday necessities for themselves. By the High Middle Ages, more local people were buying and selling more kinds of products. These included everyday goods, such as food, clothing, and household items. They also included the specialized goods that different towns began producing, such as woolen cloth, glass, and silk.

Most towns had a market, where food and local goods were bought and sold. Much larger were the great merchant fairs, which could attract merchants from many countries. A town might hold a merchant fair a couple of times a year. The goods for sale at large fairs came from all over Europe, the Middle East, and beyond.

With the growth of trade and commerce, merchants grew increasingly powerful and wealthy. They ran sizable businesses and looked for trading opportunities far from home. Merchant guilds came to **dominate** the business life of towns and cities. In towns that had become independent, members of merchant guilds often sat on town councils or were elected mayor.

Not everyone prospered, however. In Christian Europe, there was often prejudice against Jews. Medieval towns commonly had sizable Jewish communities. The hostility of Christians, sometimes backed up by laws, made it difficult for Jews to earn their living. They were not allowed to own land. Their lords sometimes took their property and belongings at will. Jews could also be the targets of violence.

One opportunity that was open to Jews was to become bankers and moneylenders. This work was generally forbidden to Christians, because the Church taught that charging money for loans was sinful. Jewish bankers and moneylenders performed an essential service for the economy. Still, they were often looked down upon and abused for practicing this "wicked" trade.

4.5 Homes and Households

Medieval towns were typically small and crowded. Most of the houses were built of wood. They were narrow and could be up to four stories high. As wooden houses aged, they tended to lean. Sometimes two facing houses would lean so much they touched across the street!

Rich and poor lived in quite different households. In poorer neighborhoods, several families might share a single house. A family might have only one room where they cooked, ate, and slept. In general, people worked where they lived. If a father or mother was a weaver, for example, the loom would be in their home.

Wealthy merchants often had splendid homes. The first level might be given over to a business, including offices and storerooms. The family's living quarters might be on the second level, complete with a solar, a space where the family gathered to eat and talk. An upper level might house servants and apprentices.

Even for wealthy families, life was not always comfortable compared to life today. Rooms were cold, smoky, and dim. Fireplaces were the only source of heat, as well as the main source of light. Most windows were small and covered with oiled parchment instead of glass, so little sunlight came through.

Growing up in a medieval town wasn't easy, either. About half of all children died before they became adults. Those who survived began preparing for their adult roles around the age of seven. Some boys and a few girls attended school, where they learned to read and write. Children from wealthier families might learn to paint and to play music on a lute (a stringed instrument). Other children soon began work as apprentices.

In general, people of the Middle Ages believed in an orderly society in which everyone knew their place. Most boys grew up to do the same work as their fathers. Some girls trained for a craft. But most girls married young, usually around the age of 15, and were soon raising children of their own. For many girls, their education was at home, where they learned cooking, cloth making, and other skills necessary to care for a home and family.

As with many medieval families, this family in Italy probably conducted most of their indoor activities in this one main room. Here, two women are preparing wool for weaving, while the men at the table enjoy a meal.

4.6 Disease and Medical Treatment

Unhealthy living conditions in medieval towns led to the spread of disease. Towns were very dirty places. There was no running water in homes. Instead of bathrooms, people used outdoor privies (shelters used as toilets) or chamber pots that they emptied into nearby streams and canals. Garbage, too, was tossed into streams and canals or onto the streets. People lived crowded together in small spaces. They usually bathed only once a week, if that. Rats and fleas were common, and they often carried diseases. It's no wonder people were frequently ill.

Many illnesses that can be prevented or cured today had no cures in medieval times. One example is leprosy, a disease of the skin and nerves that causes open sores. Because leprosy can spread from one person to another and can cause death, lepers were ordered to live by themselves in **isolated** houses, usually far from towns. Some towns even passed laws to keep out lepers.

Common diseases for which there was no cure at this time included measles, cholera, small pox, and scarlet fever. The most feared disease was bubonic plague, known as the Black Death.

No one knew exactly how diseases were spread. Unfortunately, this made many people look for someone to blame. For example, after an outbreak of illness, Jews—often a target of unjust anger and suspicion—were sometimes accused of poisoning wells.

Although hospitals were invented during the Middle Ages, there were few of them. When sickness struck, most people were treated in their homes by family members or, sometimes, a doctor. Medieval doctors believed in a combination of prayer and medical treatment. Many treatments involved herbs. Using herbs as medicine had a long history based on traditional folk wisdom and knowledge handed down from ancient Greece and Rome. Other treatments were based on less scientific methods. For example, medieval doctors sometimes consulted the positions of the planets and relied on magic charms to heal people.

Another common technique was to "bleed" patients by opening a vein or applying leeches (a type of worm) to the skin to suck out blood. Medieval doctors believed that this "bloodletting" helped restore balance to the body and spirit. Unfortunately, such treatments often weakened a patient further.

This doctor is treating patients by "bleeding" them. It was believed that this removed contaminated blood from the body, restoring health.

4.7 Crime and Punishment

Besides being unhealthy, medieval towns were noisy, smelly, crowded, and often unsafe. Pickpockets and thieves were always on the lookout for travelers with money in their pouches. Towns were especially dangerous at night, because there were no streetlights. In some cities, night watchmen patrolled the streets with candle lanterns to deter, or discourage, criminals.

People accused of crimes were held in dirty, crowded jails. Prisoners had to rely on friends and family to bring them food or money. Otherwise, they might starve or be ill-treated. Wealthy people sometimes left money in their wills to help prisoners buy food.

In the Early Middle Ages, trial by ordeal or combat was often used to establish an accused person's guilt or innocence. In a trial by ordeal, the accused had to pass a dangerous test, such as being thrown into a deep well. Unfortunately, a person who floated instead of drowning was declared guilty, because he or she had been "rejected" by the water.

The introduction of a court system to judge crimes and decide punishments was a great improvement over trials by ordeal and combat.

In a trial by combat, the accused person had to fight to prove his or her innocence. People believed that God would make sure the right party won. Clergy, women, children, and disabled people could name a champion to fight for them.

Punishments for crimes were very harsh. For lesser crimes, people were fined or put in the stocks. The stocks were a wooden frame with holes for the person's arms and sometimes legs. Being left in the stocks in public for hours or days was both painful and humiliating.

People found guilty of crimes, such as highway robbery, stealing livestock, treason, or murder, could be hanged or burned at the stake. Executions were carried out in public, often in front of large crowds.

In most parts of Europe, important nobles shared with monarchs the power to prosecute major crimes. In England, kings in the early 1100s began setting up a nationwide system of royal courts. The decisions of royal judges contributed to a growing body of **common law**. Along with an independent judiciary, or court system, English common law would become an important safeguard of individual rights. Throughout Europe, court trials based on written and oral evidence eventually replaced trials by ordeal or combat.

> **common law** a body of rulings made by judges or very old traditional laws that become part of a nation's legal system

4.8 Leisure and Entertainment

Although many aspects of town life were difficult and people worked hard, they also participated in many leisure activities. They enjoyed quite a few days off from work, too. In medieval times, people engaged in many of the same activities we enjoy today. Children played with dolls and toys, such as wooden swords, balls, and hobbyhorses. They rolled hoops and played games like badminton, lawn bowling, and blind man's bluff. Adults also liked games, such as chess, checkers, and backgammon. They might gather to play card games, go dancing, or for other social activities.

Townspeople also took time off from work to celebrate special days, such as religious feasts. On Sundays and holidays, animal baiting was a popular, though cruel, amusement. First, a bull or bear was fastened to a stake by a chain around its neck or a back leg, and sometimes by a nose ring. Then, specially trained dogs were set loose to torment the captive animal.

Fair days were especially festive. Jugglers, dancers, and clowns entertained the fairgoers. Minstrels performed songs and recited poetry and played harps and other instruments. Guild members paraded through the streets, dressed in special costumes and carrying banners.

Guilds also staged mystery plays in which they acted out Bible stories. Often they performed stories that were appropriate to their guild. In some towns, for instance, the boat builders acted out the story of Noah. In this story, Noah had to build an ark (a large boat) to survive a flood that God sent to "cleanse" the world of sinful people. In other towns, the coopers (barrel makers) acted out this story, too. The coopers put hundreds of water-filled barrels on the rooftops. Then they released the water to represent the 40 days of rain described in the story.

Mystery plays gave rise to another type of religious drama, the miracle play. These plays dramatized the lives of saints. Often they showed the saints performing miracles, or wonders. For example, in England it was popular to portray the story of St. George, who slew a dragon that was about to eat the king's daughter.

Mystery and miracle plays were put on by guild members to entertain townspeople with dramatizations of stories from the Bible or from the lives of saints.

As medieval towns grew, farmers brought crops to sell at the marketplaces.

Chapter Summary

At the beginning of the Middle Ages, most Europeans lived in the countryside. By about 1200, however, towns were growing.

Guilds, Trade, and Commerce Many towns were wealthy enough to purchase a charter that made them independent from feudal lords. An economy based on trade and commerce significantly changed daily life. Guilds became leading forces in their communities. Farmers brought crops and merchants brought many goods to sell in town marketplaces.

Homes and Households Homes varied, depending on how wealthy or poor a family was. Most families had small, crowded homes with only a fireplace for heat. Few children were educated. Girls married relatively early and boys began work as early as age seven.

Disease and Treatment Medieval towns were crowded, noisy, and dirty. Diseases spread rapidly, and many people could not be cured with the medical knowledge of the time.

Crime and Punishment Crime was a problem in medieval towns, and it was punished harshly. Prisons were filthy, dark places, and many prisoners had to buy their own food.

Leisure and Entertainment Despite the hardships in a medieval town, many types of leisure activities made life more enjoyable for town dwellers, including games, fairs, festivals, and religious plays put on by guilds.

Chapter 5

The Decline of Feudalism

How did events in Europe contribute to the decline of feudalism and the rise of democratic thought?

5.1 Introduction

In this chapter, you will explore key events that contributed to the decline of feudalism. This decline took place in Europe from the 12th through the 15th centuries.

There were many causes for the breakdown of the feudal system. In this chapter, you will focus on three: political changes in England, a terrible disease, and a long series of wars.

In England, several political changes in the 12th and 13th centuries helped to weaken feudalism. A famous document known as *Magna Carta,* or Great Charter, dates from this time. Magna Carta was a written legal agreement that limited the king's power and strengthened the rights of nobles. As feudalism declined, Magna Carta took on a much broader meaning and contributed to ideas about individual rights and liberties in England.

The terrible disease was the bubonic plague, or Black Death. The plague swept across Asia in the 1300s and reached Europe in the late 1340s. Over the next two centuries, this terrifying disease killed millions in Europe. It struck all kinds of people—rich and poor, young and old, town dwellers and country folk. Almost everyone who caught the plague died within days. In some places, whole communities were wiped out. The deaths of so many people led to sweeping economic and social changes.

Lastly, between 1337 and 1453, France and England fought a series of battles known as the Hundred Years' War. This conflict changed the way wars were fought and shifted power away from feudal lords to monarchs and the common people.

How did such different events contribute to the decline of feudalism? In this chapter, you will find out.

In this scene, both women and men work the fields outside a feudal castle. In the late Middle Ages, the bubonic plague and other forces began to change the way people lived.

◀ Life could be difficult and short in the Middle Ages. In this image of the time, the Horseman of Death rides toward a medieval town, driving the dead before him.

King John's acceptance of Magna Carta has been illustrated and painted many times. He is often, as he is here, incorrectly shown signing his name with a pen. In fact, he stamped his royal seal on the document to show his agreement.

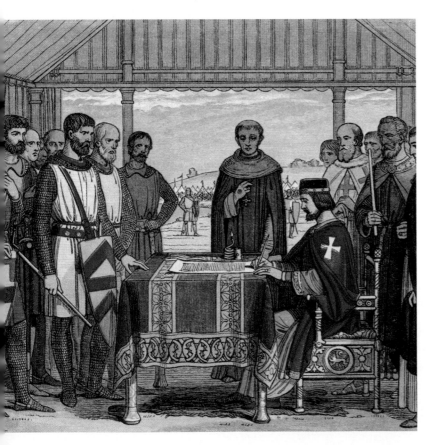

5.2 Political Developments in England

There were many reasons for the decline of feudalism in Europe. In one country, England, political developments during the 12th and 13th centuries helped to weaken feudalism. The story begins with King Henry II, who reigned from 1154 to 1189.

Henry II's Legal Reforms Henry made legal reform a central concern of his reign. For example, he insisted that a jury formally accuse a person of a serious crime. Cases were then tried before a royal judge. In theory, people could no longer simply be jailed or executed for no legal reason. There also had to be a court trial. These reforms strengthened the power of royal courts at the expense of feudal lords.

Henry's effort to strengthen royal authority led to a serious conflict with the Catholic Church. In the year 1164, Henry issued the Constitutions of Clarendon, a document that he said spelled out the king's **traditional** rights. Among them was the right to try clergy accused of serious crimes in royal courts, rather than in Church courts.

Henry's action led to a long, bitter quarrel with his friend, Thomas Becket, the archbishop of Canterbury. In 1170, four knights, perhaps seeking the king's favor, killed Becket in front of the main altar of Canterbury Cathedral. The cathedral and Becket's tomb soon became a popular destination for pilgrimages. In 1173, the Catholic Church proclaimed him a saint. Still, most of the Constitutions of Clarendon remained in force.

King John and Magna Carta In 1199, Henry's youngest son, John, became king of England. John soon made powerful enemies by losing most of the lands the English had controlled in France. He also taxed his barons heavily and ignored their traditional rights, arresting opponents at will. In addition, John quarreled with the Catholic Church and collected large amounts of money from its properties.

In June 1215, angry nobles forced a meeting with King John in a meadow called Runnymede, beside the River Thames, outside of London. There, they insisted that John put his seal on a document called **Magna Carta,** which means "Great Charter" in Latin.

Magna Carta was an agreement between the nobles and the monarch. The nobles agreed that the monarch could continue to rule. For his part, King John agreed to observe common law and the traditional rights of the nobles and the Church. For example, he promised to consult the nobles and the Church archbishops and bishops before imposing special taxes. He also agreed that "no free man" could be jailed except by the lawful judgment of his peers or by the law of the land. This idea eventually developed into a key part of English common law known as **habeas corpus** (HAY-be-us KOR-pus).

In many ways, Magna Carta only protected the rights and privileges of nobles. However, as time passed, the English people came to regard it as one of the **foundations** of their rights and liberties.

King Edward I and the Model Parliament In 1295, Edward I, King John's grandson, took a major step toward including more people in government. Edward called together a governing body called the **Model Parliament**. It included commoners and lower-ranking clergy, as well as high-level Church officials and nobles.

The Impact of Political Developments in England These political changes contributed to the decline of feudalism in two ways. Some of the changes strengthened royal authority at the expense of the nobles. Others weakened feudalism by eventually shifting some power to the common people.

Magna Carta established the idea of rights and liberties that even a monarch cannot violate. It also affirmed that monarchs should rule with the advice of the governed. Henry II's legal reforms strengthened English common law and the role of judges and juries. Finally, Edward I's Model Parliament gave a voice in government to common people, as well as to nobles. All these ideas formed the basis for the development of modern **democratic** institutions.

This 14th-century illustration shows King Edward I attending his Parliament. The King of Scots is seated to his right; the Prince of Wales is seated to his left.

habeas corpus the legal concept that an accused person cannot be jailed indefinitely without being charged with a crime

Model Parliament a governing body created by King Edward I of England that included some commoners, Church officials, and nobles

bubonic plague a deadly contagious disease caused by bacteria and spread by fleas; also called the Black Death

5.3   The Bubonic Plague

You have learned how political developments in England helped to weaken feudalism in that country. Another reason for the decline of feudalism was the **bubonic plague,** which affected all of Europe. The bubonic plague first struck Europe from 1346 to 1351. It returned in waves that occurred about every decade into the 15th century, leaving major changes in its wake.

Historians think the plague began in Central Asia, possibly in China, and spread throughout China, India, the Middle East, and then to Europe. The disease traveled from Central Asia to the Black Sea along the Silk Road (the main trade route between Asia and the Mediterranean Sea). It probably was carried to Italy on a ship. It then spread north and west, throughout the continent of Europe and to England.

The Black Death   Symptoms, or signs, of the plague included fever, vomiting, fierce coughing and sneezing fits, and egg-sized swellings or bumps, called *buboes*. The term "Black Death" probably came from these black-and-blue swellings that appeared on the skin of victims.

The dirty conditions in which people lived contributed significantly to the spread of the bubonic plague. The bacteria that cause the disease are carried by fleas that feed on the blood of infected rodents, such as rats. When the rats die, the fleas jump to other animals and people. During the Middle Ages, it was not unusual for people to go for many months without a change of clothing or a bath. Rats, covered with fleas, often roamed the floors of homes looking for food. City streets were filled with human waste, dead animals, and trash.

At the time, though, no one knew where the disease came from or how it spread. Terrified people falsely blamed the plague on everything from the positions of the planets to lepers and to Jews.

The bubonic plague, or Black Death, most likely originated in Asia. In the 14th century, this disease killed about one-third of the population of Europe and brought about major political and social change.

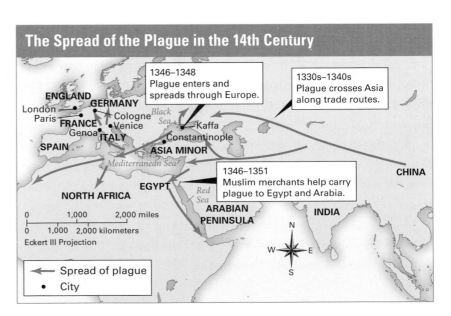

The Spread of the Plague in the 14th Century

1346–1348
Plague enters and spreads through Europe.

1330s–1340s
Plague crosses Asia along trade routes.

1346–1351
Muslim merchants help carry plague to Egypt and Arabia.

ENGLAND
London
Paris
GERMANY
Cologne
Venice
FRANCE
Genoa
ITALY
SPAIN
Black Sea
Kaffa
Constantinople
ASIA MINOR
Mediterranean Sea
EGYPT
Red Sea
NORTH AFRICA
ARABIAN PENINSULA
INDIA
CHINA

0   1,000   2,000 miles
0   1,000   2,000 kilometers
Eckert III Projection

N
W   E
S

→ Spread of plague
• City

Persecution of the Jews did not begin with the plague. Prejudice against Jews had led the English government to order all Jews to leave the country in 1290. In France, the same thing happened in 1306 and again in 1394. But fear of the plague made matters worse. During the Black Death, many German cities ordered Jews to leave.

The Impact of the Plague   The plague took a terrible toll on the populations of Asia and Europe. China's population was reduced by nearly half between 1200 and 1393, probably because of the plague and famine. Travelers reported that dead bodies covered the ground in Central Asia and India.

Some historians **estimate** that 24 million Europeans died of the plague—about a third of the population. The deaths of so many people speeded changes in Europe's economic and social structure, which contributed to the decline of feudalism.

Trade and commerce slowed almost to a halt during the plague years. As Europe began to recover, the economy needed to be rebuilt. But it wouldn't be rebuilt in the same way, with feudal lords holding most of the power.

After the plague, there was a shift in power from nobles to the common people. One reason for this was a desperate need for

During the plague, a dancing mania spread among those who remained healthy—an expression of people's joy of life during those dark times.

workers because so many people had died. The workers who were left could, therefore, demand more money and more rights. In addition, many peasants and some serfs abandoned feudal manors and moved to towns and cities, seeking better opportunities. This led to a weakening of the manor system and a loss of power for feudal lords.

After the plague, a number of peasant rebellions broke out. When nobles tried to return things to how they had been, resentment exploded across Europe. There were peasant revolts in France, Flanders, England, Germany, Spain, and Italy.

The most famous of these revolts was the English Peasants' War in 1381. The English rebels succeeded in entering London and presenting their demands to the king, Richard II. The leader of the rebellion was killed, however, and after his death, the revolt lost **momentum.** Still, in most of Europe, the time was coming when serfdom would end.

Joan of Arc inspired the people of France to fight. To this day, she is honored for her heroism. A late 19th-century artist painted this scene called *Entrance of Joan of Arc into Orleans on 8th May 1429.*

Hundred Years' War a series of battles fought between France and England from 1337 to 1453

heretic a person who holds beliefs that are contrary to a set of religious teachings

5.4 The Hundred Years' War

Between 1337 and 1453, England and France fought a series of battles for control over lands in France. Known as the **Hundred Years' War,** this long conflict contributed to the erosion of feudalism in England and in France.

English monarchs had long claimed lands in France. This was because earlier English kings had actually been feudal lords over these French fiefs. French kings now disputed these claims. When Philip VI of France declared that the French fiefs of England's King Edward III were part of Philip's own realm, war broke out in France.

Early English Successes   Despite often being outnumbered, the English won most of the early battles of the war. What happened at the Battle of Crécy (KRAY-see) shows why.

Two quite different armies faced each other at the French village of Crécy in 1346. The French had a feudal army that relied on horse-mounted knights. French knights wore heavy armor, and they could hardly move when they were not on horseback. Their weapons were swords and lances. Some of the infantry, or foot soldiers, used cross-bows, which were effective only at short ranges.

In contrast, the English army was made up of lightly armored knights, foot soldiers, and archers armed with longbows. Some soldiers were recruited from the common people and paid to fight.

The longbow had many advantages over the crossbow. Larger arrows could be fired more quickly. The arrows flew farther, faster, and more accurately, and could pierce the armor of the time. At Crécy, the longbow helped the English defeat the much larger French force.

The French Fight Back   The French slowly chipped away at the territory the English had won in the early years of the war. In 1415, after a long truce, English King Henry V again invaded France. This time, the English met with stronger resistance. One reason was that the French were now using more modern tactics. The French king was recruiting his army from commoners, paying them with money collected by taxes, just as the English did.

Another reason for increased French resistance was a new sense of national identity and unity. In part, the French were inspired by a 17-year-old peasant girl, known today as Joan of Arc. Joan claimed that she heard the voices of saints urging her to save France. Putting on a suit of armor, she went to fight.

In 1429, Joan led a French army to victory in the Battle of Orléans (OR-lay-uhn). The next year, the "Maid of Orléans" was captured by English allies. The English pushed certain Church leaders to accuse Joan of being a witch and a **heretic** and to burn her at the stake.

Joan of Arc's heroism changed the way many French men and women felt about their king and nation. Twenty-two years after Joan's death, the French finally drove the English out of France. Almost 500 years later, the Roman Catholic Church made Joan a saint.

The Impact of the Hundred Years' War The Hundred Years' War contributed to the decline of feudalism by helping to shift power from feudal lords to monarchs and to common people. During the struggle, monarchs on both sides had collected taxes and raised large professional armies. As a result, kings no longer relied as much on nobles to supply knights for the army.

In addition, changes in military technology made the nobles' knights and castles less useful. The longbow proved to be an effective weapon against mounted knights. Castles also became less important as armies learned to use gunpowder to shoot iron balls from cannons and blast holes in castle walls.

The new feeling of nationalism also shifted power away from lords. Previously, many English and French peasants felt more loyalty to their local lords than to their monarch. The war created a new sense of national unity and patriotism on both sides.

In both France and England, commoners and peasants bore the heaviest burden of the war. They were forced to fight and to pay higher and more frequent taxes. Those who survived the war, however, were needed as soldiers and workers. For this reason, the common people emerged from the conflict with greater influence and power.

At the Battle of Crécy, the English army's lighter armor and longbows triumphed over the French knights' heavy armor and crossbows.

Chapter Summary

In this chapter, you have explored three key events that contributed to the decline of feudalism in Europe in the Late Middle Ages.

Political Developments in England Henry II's legal reforms strengthened English common law and the role of judges and juries. Magna Carta established the idea of rights and liberties that even a monarch cannot violate. It also affirmed that monarchs should rule with the advice of the governed. Edward I's Model Parliament gave a voice in government to common people, as well as to nobles.

The Bubonic Plague The bubonic plague killed about one-third of the people of Europe. After the plague, the need for workers to rebuild Europe led to a slight shift in power from feudal lords to the common people.

The Hundred Years' War This series of battles between England and France caused a rise in national pride and identity in both countries. It strengthened the monarchs and began to reduce the importance of nobles and knights on the battlefield.

Artists all over the world have depicted Joan of Arc. This stained-glass window from a church in New Zealand shows Joan dressed in armor.

The Trials of Joan of Arc

In 1429, a teenage girl named Joan of Arc helped a prince to become king of France. Joan lived at a time when the feudal system in Europe was beginning to weaken. How did Joan's extraordinary life show that new ways were about to replace old traditions in Europe?

The visions and the voices came without warning, like a flash of lighting. In 1425, Joan of Arc, the daughter of northern French peasants, had just turned 13. Until then, she had had a normal childhood. She attended mass regularly and prayed frequently to God.

Then the voices and visions started. Saints Michael, Catherine, and Margaret suddenly came to her. "I was terrified," Joan remembered later. "There was a great light all about." But soon she was reassured by the sweet, kind voices and stopped being afraid.

Joan lived in a religious time. It wasn't unheard of for people to report that saints spoke to them. But Joan's voices set her a daunting task. They directed her to help Charles, the dauphin (DOE-fehn), or French heir to the throne, to become king. They also wanted her to free France from the English, who had conquered parts of the country.

France in Chaos

The year when Joan's voices started, France was in chaos. Since 1337, the English and French had been fighting the Hundred Years' War. In 1420, English king Henry V took the French throne. When Henry died in 1422, the dauphin Charles insisted that he, and not Henry's infant son, was the rightful king. His claim led to even bloodier fighting between the English and French.

France itself was deeply divided. The feudal lords of the powerful province of Burgundy helped the English seize northern France. Those loyal to Charles controlled the southern half of the country. Even though Charles was the dauphin, he hadn't been crowned.

Since the 11th century, all French kings had been crowned in Reims (RAHNZ), but the English controlled land around the city. However, Joan's voices told her that she should lead Charles to Reims and see that he was crowned king.

A Journey to Find a King

At the age of 17, Joan set out to find Charles. It was dangerous for a female to travel alone, so she disguised herself by cutting her hair and putting on men's clothing. Without telling her parents, she rode to a nearby fort to ask the commander for soldiers to protect her.

When she reached the fort, the commander just laughed at her request. But Joan soon convinced him, and he ordered a group of soldiers to ride with her. On February 13, 1429, they set out for Charles' court at Chinon (shee-NOHN).

Charles heard she was on her way. He had heard prophecies, or predictions, that this young peasant woman would rescue France from the English. When she arrived at Chinon, Charles tested Joan's claims by disguising himself. Court officials introduced another man to Joan as the dauphin. However, Joan immediately picked out Charles from the crowd. She knelt before him, announcing, "Very noble Dauphin, I am come and sent by God to bring succor [help] to you and your kingdom." Charles agreed that God had sent Joan to save France.

The Battle to Free Orléans

Joan's first challenge on the way north to Reims was to free the city of Orléans (OR-lay-uhn). Charles had a suit of armor made for her, but she still needed a sword. She predicted that priests would find one for her in a nearby church. Sure enough, they dug behind the altar and found a sword. She also had a banner made. Armed with her sword and carrying her banner, Joan filled the French with hope.

In the spring of 1429, Joan led Charles's troops toward Orléans, which the English had had under siege for six months. The French feared that if they lost that city, they would lose all of France. On May 4, Joan led the French troops into battle for the first time.

At a monastery near Orléans held by the English, French soldiers attacked. They were on the verge of defeat when Joan suddenly galloped into the battle, carrying her banner and flashing her sword. Inspired, the French soldiers soon overwhelmed the English.

In this 19th-century painting, you can see Joan of Arc standing on a ladder as she leads the French army in the battle to free the city of Orléans from the English.

Three days later, the French attacked Orléans itself. In the middle of the battle, Joan was hit by an arrow. Grimacing with pain, she pulled the arrow out and threw herself back into the fight. She then led French troops across a moat and stormed the city's walls. The French soon poured into Orléans, and the English beat a rapid retreat.

After the victory, thirty thousand grateful residents of Orléans cheered Joan as she road with her soldiers through the streets. Forever after, she would be known as the "Maid of Orléans." In the following weeks, Joan's forces freed more surrounding towns from the English.

Crowning King Charles VII

After these victories, Joan returned to Charles and persuaded him to travel to Reims to be crowned. At last, on July 17, 1429, with Joan at his side, the dauphin became King Charles VII. After the coronation, Joan burst into tears of joy.

Unfortunately, the coronation proved to be the high point for Joan. Charles started to distance himself from her, perhaps fearing her enormous popularity. In the fall of 1429, Charles and Joan led troops toward Paris, which the English and their allies controlled. But on his own, Charles reached a ceasefire agreement with the Duke of Burgundy. When Joan learned about it, she was outraged. She had wanted to fight to free Paris. "I am not satisfied with this manner of truce," she fumed.

Joan's Capture

Joan was captured by French soldiers under the command of the Duke of Burgundy and turned over to the English, who put her on trial for witchcraft.

Meanwhile, French troops, now with a king to follow and tired of fighting, were deserting Joan's army. In May 1430, Burgundy's army of 6,000 soldiers prepared to attack Compiègne (komp-YANE), a French-held town near Paris. Joan's army had only 300 soldiers. At five in the evening, she launched a surprise attack.

At first, the French held their own, but thousands of English soldiers soon joined the battle. The French were forced to retreat to Compiègne. When the town's mayor saw English troops approaching, he closed the drawbridge, trapping Joan outside. The Burgundian leaders captured her and threw her into prison. Charles made no effort to rescue or ransom the woman to whom he owed so much. After several months, the English paid the Burgundians a huge ransom for her.

On Trial for Her Life

The English and the Catholic Church put Joan on trial in Rouen (ROO-ahn) for witchcraft and for heresy, or spreading beliefs that violate accepted religious teachings. They hoped that, by proving that God did not guide Joan, they could undermine Charles VII's right to the French throne. Bishop Pierre Cauchon, an ally of the English, led the proceedings. When the trial started in February 1431, Joan boldly warned the bishop, "You say that you are my judge. Take thought over what you are doing. For, truly, I am sent from God, and you are putting yourself in great danger."

The warning did not stop Bishop Cauchon from drilling Joan with questions, such as, "Did God command you to put on men's clothing?" Joan responded, "I did not put on this clothing, or do anything else, except at the bidding of God and the angels." Ordinary people watching the trial loved Joan's courageous answers. She was following her conscience and standing up to the bishop and to the English.

The court made 70 accusations against Joan. In May, to save her life, she signed a confession. But after a few days, she took it back, saying, "What I said, I said for fear of the fire." She had made the brave decision to stay true to her beliefs—even though she faced execution.

A huge crowd gathered in Rouen on May 30, 1431, to watch Joan be burned at the stake, a common death sentence for heretics and witches. Through her horrible ordeal, she showed great courage.

Charles VII remained king for 40 years, forced the English out of France, and united the country. During that time, Joan's life became a legend.

In 1455, Joan's family asked the pope to reopen her case, and Joan was found innocent of all charges. In 1920, Joan was made a Catholic saint. Today, Saint Joan is one of the most beloved of French heroes, the patron saint of the nation and of its soldiers. She inspired her country and helped to restore the throne to a French king. She also proved that women could be brave and effective leaders. Finally, her remarkable life shows that with faith, courage, and determination someone from ordinary beginnings can make history.

At her execution, Joan asked a priest to hold a crucifix high for her to see and to pray loud enough so that she could hear him over the roar of the flames.

Chapter 6

The Byzantine Empire

How did the Byzantine Empire develop and form its own distinctive church?

6.1 Introduction

In this chapter, you will learn about the Byzantine Empire. This great empire lay in two continents, Europe and Asia. It lasted from about 500 to 1453 C.E., when it was conquered by the Ottoman Turks.

At first, the Byzantine Empire was the continuation of the Roman Empire in the east. In 330 C.E., the Roman emperor Constantine moved his capital from Rome to the city of Byzantium. This city was an old Greek trading colony on the eastern edge of Europe. Constantine called his capital New Rome, but it soon became known as Constantinople, which is Greek for "Constantine's City."

Later, control of the huge original empire was divided between two emperors—one based in Rome and one based in Constantinople. After the fall of Rome, the eastern empire continued for another 1,000 years. We call this the Byzantine Empire, after Byzantium, the original name of its capital city.

East and west remained connected for a time through a shared Christian faith. But the Church in the east developed in its own unique ways. It became known as the Eastern Orthodox Church. Over time, Byzantine emperors and Church officials came into conflict with the pope in Rome. The conflict eventually led to a permanent split between the Eastern Orthodox Church and the Roman Catholic Church.

In this chapter, you will learn about the Byzantine Empire, one of its greatest emperors, and its **distinctive** church. Let's begin by exploring the empire's capital—the fabulous city of Constantinople.

In 330 C.E., the emperor Constantine moved his capital from Rome to the city of Byzantium.

◀ This modern drawing re-creates the city of Constantinople during the Byzantine Empire.

6.2 Constantinople

Constantinople the city on the eastern edge of Europe, which Constantine made the capital of the Roman Empire in 330 C.E.

Byzantine Empire the name for the eastern Roman Empire, located at the crossroads of Europe and Asia; it lasted from about 500 to 1453 C.E.

Constantinople was more than 800 miles to the east of Rome. Why did Constantine choose this site to be the capital of the Roman Empire?

One reason was that the site was easy to defend. It was surrounded on three sides by water. The Byzantines fashioned a chain across the city's harbor to guard against seafaring intruders. Miles of walls, fortified by watchtowers, and gates discouraged invasion by land and by sea.

Constantinople also stood at the crossroads of Europe and Asia, and the many sea and overland trade routes linking east and west. During the **Byzantine Empire,** this special location helped to make the city, and some of its citizens, very wealthy. For more than 700 years, Constantinople was the richest and the most elegant city in the Mediterranean region. Ivory, silk, furs, perfumes, and other luxury items flowed through its markets. A French soldier who saw the city in 1204 exclaimed, "One could not believe there was so rich a city in all the world."

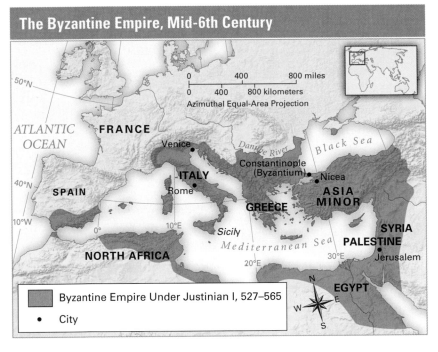

The Byzantine Empire, Mid-6th Century

Byzantine Empire Under Justinian I, 527–565
• City

The eastern Roman Empire, later called the Byzantine Empire, ruled much of the Mediterranean world for several hundred years.

At its height, Constantinople was home to around one million people. The city's language and culture were Greek, but traders and visitors spoke many languages. Ships crowded the city's harbor, loaded with goods. The city streets, some narrow and twisting, some grand and broad, teemed with camel and mule trains.

Life in Constantinople was more comfortable than in Western Europe. The city boasted a sewer system, which was quite rare in medieval times. Social services were provided by hospitals, homes for the elderly, and orphanages.

Despite the luxuries enjoyed by the rich, many people lived in poverty. The emperor gave bread to those who could not find work. In exchange, the unemployed performed such tasks as sweeping the streets and weeding public gardens.

Almost everyone attended the exciting chariot races at a stadium called the Hippodrome. Two chariot teams, one wearing blue and the other green, were fierce rivals. In Constantinople and other cities, many people belonged to opposing groups called the Blues and Greens after the chariot teams. At times the rivalry between Blues and Greens erupted in deadly street fighting. But in 532, the two groups united in a rebellion that destroyed much of Constantinople. You will find out what happened in the next section.

6.3 The Reign of Justinian I

One of the greatest Byzantine emperors was Justinian I, whose long reign lasted from 527 to 565. But Justinian's reign nearly came to an abrupt end much sooner. In January 532, the emperor and his beautiful wife, Theodora, were attending chariot races at the Hippodrome. In the past, Blues and Greens among the spectators had often fought with each other. This time, however, both groups were upset over the arrests of some of their members. To Justinian's horror, they united in denouncing him. Fighting broke out, spilled into the streets, and escalated into a full-scale rebellion.

The rioting continued for a week while Justinian and Theodora hid in the palace. Much of the city was in flames. Justinian's advisors wanted him to flee the city. Theodora, however, urged him to stay and fight. With her encouragement, Justinian put down the **revolt.** According to the official court historian, Procopius (pro-KOH-pee-us), 30,000 people were killed in the fighting. The city of Constantinople lay in ruins.

Justinian was determined to rebuild the city on a grand scale. He put huge sums of money into public works. Soon, Constantinople had new bridges, public baths, parks, roads, and hospitals. The emperor also built many grand churches, including the magnificent Hagia Sophia (AH-ee-yah SOH-fee-uh). Its name is Greek for "Holy Wisdom." Today, this great structure is one of the most famous buildings in the world.

The Granger Collection, New York

During a revolt in Constantinople, the empress Theodora (third from the left) encouraged her husband, Justinian I, to stay and fight for his city.

Besides rebuilding Constantinople, Justinian tried to reclaim some of the Roman Empire's lost territory. He launched military campaigns that, for a time, took back parts of North Africa, Italy, and Spain.

Justinian is most famous, however, for creating a systematic body of law. Under his direction, a committee studied the thousands of laws the Byzantines had inherited from the Roman Empire. They revised outdated and confusing laws. They also made improvements, such as extending women's property rights. The result of their work is known as Justinian's Code. It became the basis for many legal codes in the western world.

Procopius, the court historian, wrote glowing accounts of Justinian's achievements. But he also wrote the *Secret History,* in which he called the emperor "a treacherous enemy, insane for murder and plunder." Throughout Byzantine history, distrust and divisions often plagued the imperial court. Justinian's court was no exception.

Hagia Sophia was built between the years 532 and 537. Its architectural features inspired the design of many later Orthodox churches.

Eastern Orthodox Church a Christian religion that developed out of early Christianity in the Byzantine Empire

6.4 The Eastern Orthodox Church

To the Byzantines, Christianity was more than a religion. It was the very foundation of their empire.

When Constantine built his new capital, he intended it to be the religious center of the empire, as well as the seat of government. Constantine himself tried to settle religious disputes by assembling a council of bishops.

Over time, the Byzantine Church separated from the Church in Rome and became known as the **Eastern Orthodox Church**. The word *orthodox* means "in agreement with right belief." The leaders of the medieval Eastern Orthodox Church thought that their church was based on a set of beliefs that they could trace back to Jesus Christ and to the work of bishops in early Christian councils.

The Role of the Eastern Orthodox Church in the Empire

Religion and government were more closely linked in the Byzantine Empire than in the west. The Byzantines viewed the emperor not just as the head of the government but as the living representative of God and Jesus Christ. This meant that church and state were combined into one all-powerful body.

The state religion also united people in a common belief. The Eastern Orthodox Church played a central role in daily life. Most people attended church regularly. Religious sacraments gave shape to every stage of the journey from birth to death. Monasteries and convents cared for the poor and the sick. These institutions were supported by wealthy people and became quite powerful. Let's look at some of the practices of Eastern Orthodoxy.

Church Hierarchy Like Roman Catholic clergy, Orthodox clergy were ranked in order of importance. In Byzantine times, the emperor had supreme authority in the Church. He selected the **patriarch** of Constantinople, who ranked just below him in matters of religion.

Unlike the pope in the west, the patriarch did not claim strong authority over other patriarchs and bishops. Instead, he was "first among equals." The patriarch of Constantinople (modern Istanbul, Turkey) still holds this honor.

Orthodox priests served under patriarchs and other bishops. Unlike Roman Catholic priests, who were not allowed to marry, many Orthodox priests were married. Bishops, however, could rise only from the ranks of unmarried clergy.

Liturgy and Prayer The Orthodox Church service corresponding to the Roman Catholic mass was the Divine Liturgy. Both the clergy and worshippers sang or chanted the liturgy, or form of public worship. The liturgy was conducted in Greek or in the local language.

Orthodox Christians also prayed to saints. Two saints were particularly important. Saint Basil promoted charity and reformed the liturgy. Saint Cyril helped create the Cyrillic (sih-RIL-ik) alphabet, which allowed scholars to translate the Bible for people in Eastern Europe.

Architecture and Art Christian faith inspired magnificent architecture and artwork in the Byzantine Empire. With its square base and high dome, the cathedral Hagia Sophia served as a model for many Orthodox churches. The architecture of the church also reflects Orthodox views. The simple base represents the earthly world. Upon it rests the "dome of heaven." Rich decorations on the inside were meant to remind worshippers of what it would be like to enter God's kingdom.

Building on the Greek love of art, the Orthodox Church used many images in its services and prayers. Byzantine artists created beautiful icons, which were usually painted on small wooden panels. Artists also fashioned sacred images as mosaics and painted them in murals.

An image of Christ as the *Pantocrator,* or ruler of all, gazed down from the domes of all Orthodox churches. Most churches also displayed an icon of Jesus's mother, Mary (called the *Theotokos,* or god-bearer) and the Christ child over the altar.

Many Byzantines believed that sacred pictures brought them closer to God. But later, icons also became a source of violent disagreement.

patriarch in the Eastern Orthodox Church, the bishop of an important city

A feature of Eastern Orthodox churches is an image of Christ the Pantocrator, like this one, watching over Orthodox worshippers from the dome above.

6.5 Conflict Between East and West

Medieval Europe and the Byzantine Empire were united in a single faith, Christianity. Over the centuries, however, cultural, political, and religious differences brought the two parts of the old Roman Empire into conflict.

The two regions had been quite different even in the days of the early Roman emperors. The eastern half of the empire had many cities, much trade, and great wealth. The western half was mostly rural and agricultural, and not nearly as wealthy.

Other differences became more pronounced after the fall of Rome. Byzantine culture was largely shaped by its Greek heritage. The west was influenced by Frankish and Germanic cultures. In the city of Constantinople, people spoke Greek. In the west, Latin was the language of scholars, diplomats, and the Church.

Perhaps most important was the conflict that developed between the churches of east and west. After the fall of Rome, popes gradually **emerged** as powerful figures in western Europe. The popes claimed supreme religious authority over all Christians. The emperors and patriarchs of the east did not claim that power.

Other differences added to the conflict. Let's look at three major disagreements and how they led to a split in the Christian Church.

Iconoclasm The first major disagreement concerned religious icons. Many Christians in medieval times used images of Jesus, Mary, and the saints in worship and prayer. Some Christians in the east, however, believed that people were wrongly worshipping the icons as if they were divine. In 730 C.E., Byzantine emperor Leo III banned the use of religious images in all Christian churches and homes.

This policy of *iconoclasm* ("icon smashing") led to the destruction of much religious art. Throughout Christian lands, people cried out in protest. In Rome, Roman Church leaders were angry because Leo's order applied to parts of Italy that were under Byzantine control. Pope Gregory III even excommunicated the emperor.

The Byzantine Empire lifted its ban on icons in 843. But the dispute over iconoclasm had caused a major split between the east and west. It also helped drive popes in Rome to look for support and protection against enemies.

Byzantine emperor Leo III banned the use of religious images, or icons, in 730 C.E. The ban was lifted in 843. This mosaic of Jesus in Hagia Sophia escaped destruction because it was created after the ban was lifted.

The Crowning of a Holy Roman Emperor Another major disagreement occurred in 800 C.E. At the time, Empress Irene was the ruler of the Byzantine Empire. Because she was a woman, Pope Leo III did not view her as true or strong enough to govern. He wanted the protection of a strong leader to help defend the Church in the west.

Instead, Leo decided to crown Charlemagne, the king of the Franks, as Holy Roman emperor. The pope's action outraged the Byzantines, who felt that their empress was the rightful ruler of the remains of the Roman Empire.

The Final Break Matters between east and west came to a head in 1054. The patriarch of Constantinople, Cerularius, wanted to reassert Byzantine control of the Church. He closed all churches that worshipped with western rites. Pope Leo IX was furious. He sent Cardinal Humbert to Constantinople. The cardinal marched up to the altar of Hagia Sophia. In front of everyone, he laid down a bull (a proclamation by the pope) excommunicating Cerularius.

Cerularius responded by excommunicating the cardinal. This was only a symbolic act, for the patriarch did not have that power. But it showed that the split, or schism, between east and west was complete. Despite future attempts to heal the division, the Eastern Orthodox Church and the Roman Catholic Church were now separate churches.

The division between the Eastern Orthodox and Roman Catholic churches lasted until 1964. In that year, Patriarch Athenagoras (left) and Pope Paul VI (right) met in Jerusalem and made a formal statement that undid the excommunications of 1054.

Chapter Summary

In this chapter, you learned about the founding of the Byzantine Empire and the Eastern Orthodox Church.

Constantinople and the Byzantine Empire In 330 C.E., the Roman emperor Constantine moved his capital to Byzantium, later called Constantinople. After the fall of Rome, the eastern half of the empire continued on there. Today, it is referred to as the Byzantine Empire.

The Reign of Justinian I One of the greatest Byzantine emperors was Justinian I. He rebuilt Constantinople after it was destroyed by rioting in 532 and worked to reclaim some of Rome's lost territory. His most lasting contribution is probably the Justinian Code, which became the basis for many other, later legal codes in the western world.

The Eastern Orthodox Church The Byzantine Empire was a Christian state. The Eastern Orthodox Church was at the center of daily life and inspired distinctive and magnificent art and architecture.

Conflict Between East and West Byzantine emperors and patriarchs in Constantinople clashed with popes in Rome over a number of issues. These disagreements led to a schism between the Roman Catholic Church and the Eastern Orthodox Church in 1054.

Europe During Medieval Times

313
Constantine's Decree
Roman emperor Constantine issues a decree allowing Christians to worship freely, leading to the recognition of Christianity as the official religion of the Roman Empire.

476
Fall of Rome
The last Roman emperor in the west is driven from his throne, and the western half of the empire dissolves into separate kingdoms.

About 500–1453
Byzantine Empire
Straddling two continents, Europe and Asia, the Byzantine Empire gives rise to a new church in the east, the Eastern Orthodox Church.

1 C.E.   200 C.E.   400 C.E.   600 C.E.   800 C.E.

330
New Capital
of the Roman Empire
Constantine moves the capital of the Roman Empire from Rome to Byzantium. The city is renamed Constantinople.

About 476–1450
Middle Ages
The Middle Ages begin after the fall of Rome, continue through the rise and decline of feudalism, and end with the fall of the Byzantine Empire.

527–565
Rule of Justinian I
During his reign over the Byzantine Empire, Justinian I rebuilds the city of Constantinople and creates a systematic body of law known as Justinian's Code.

768–814
Charlemagne's Reign
As ruler of the Franks, Charlemagne unifies nearly all the Christian lands of Europe into a single empire.

1215
Magna Carta
King John of England accepts Magna Carta, under which he agrees to protect the rights and privileges of nobles.

1337–1453
Hundred Years' War
The Hundred Years' War, a series of wars between England and France, shifts power from feudal lords to monarchs and common people.

800 C.E.   1000 C.E.   1200 C.E.   1400 C.E.   1600 C.E.

1076
Excommunication of Henry IV
Henry IV, emperor of the Holy Roman Empire, is excommunicated from the Roman Catholic Church after disputing Pope Gregory VII's decision that kings could not appoint church officials.

1295
Model Parliament
King Edward I creates the Model Parliament, a governing body that includes commoners, church officials, and nobles.

1347
Bubonic Plague Reaches Europe
The bubonic plague, also known as the Black Death, reaches Europe after sweeping across Asia. The plague forces a shift in power from nobles to the common people.

Unit 2

Islam in Medieval Times

Muslims built the Great Mosque of Cordoba in Spain around the late 700s. Shown here is its prayer room. The mosque was converted into a Christian church in the late 1200s.

Physical Features of the Arabian Peninsula and Surrounding Lands

EUROPE

Black Sea

ANATOLIAN PLATEAU

TAURUS MOUNTAINS

Caspian Sea

Amu Darya

ASIA

Mediterranean Sea

ZAGROS MOUNTAINS

Sea of Galilee

Tigris River

SYRIAN DESERT

Euphrates River

Dead Sea

SINAI PENINSULA

Nile River

Gulf of Suez

Persian Gulf

Strait of Hormuz

Gulf of Oman

Tropic of Cancer

ARABIAN PENINSULA

20°N

AFRICA

SAHARA

Red Sea

RUB AL KHALI (EMPTY QUARTER)

60°E

Arabian Sea

20°E

30°E

40°E

50°E

10°N

Gulf of Aden

| 0 | 200 | 400 miles |
| 0 | 200 | 400 kilometers |

Albers Conic Equal-Area Projection

Elevation

Feet	Meters
Over 10,000	Over 3,050
5,001–10,000	1,526–3,050
2,001–5,000	611–1,525
1,001–2,000	306–610
0–1,000	0–305
Below sea level	Below sea level

Present-day boundary

N W E S

Islam in Medieval Times

If you could zoom out a satellite picture of the Arabian Peninsula to see the surrounding land, you would find that it borders on the continents of Africa, Asia, and Europe. Satellite imagery also shows that most of the Arabian Peninsula is a brown, dry land. These two geographic facts about the Arabian Peninsula—its location and its dry climate—have shaped and defined its people and their history. That history centers on trade with northern Africa, Asia, and Europe. It also centers on the religion of Islam.

The people of the Arabian Peninsula learned how to survive in the desert. They raised sheep, goats, and camels and learned to keep moving in search of food and water. Over time, they also learned to earn a living through trade. These skills proved valuable as merchants came to the Arabian Peninsula from surrounding countries, buying and selling. Trade between Africa and Asia passed through the peninsula, as did trade between Asia and Europe. The Arabian Peninsula became a major trading hub for all three continents.

Traders carried silk, jewels, cotton, spices, and other goods from one region to another. But more than merchandise passed between merchants and traders. Ideas, knowledge, and beliefs also passed along trade routes

One belief that spread quickly was the religion of Islam, which began on the Arabian Peninsula and spread outward. Islamic traders from the Arabian Peninsula who traveled to Persian, Egypt, Spain, and elsewhere brought their religion with them. The followers of Islam also won people to their religion through war and conquest. The map below shows the extent of Islamic lands by the year 750.

Today, more than a billion people around the world practice Islam, and the Middle East, which includes the Arabian Peninsula, is one of the most important regions in the world. In this unit, you will take a closer look at this region.

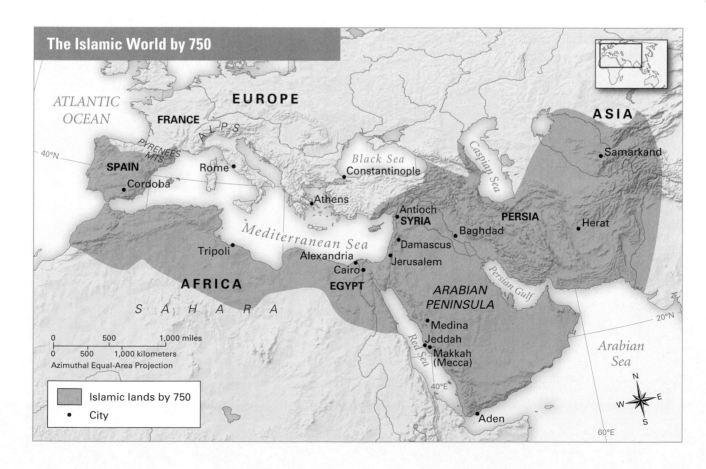

The Islamic World by 750

Islamic lands by 750
• City

Chapter 7

The Origins and Spread of Islam

How did Islam originate and spread?

7.1 Introduction

Muhammad was born around 570 C.E. He taught the faith called Islam, which became one of the major religions of the world. In this chapter, you will learn how Islam was started by Muhammad and how it spread throughout the Arabian Peninsula and beyond, during the 600s and 700s C.E.

Muhammad's birthplace, Makkah (Mecca), was an ancient place of worship. According to tradition, many centuries before Muhammad was born, God tested the prophet Abraham's faith by ordering him to leave Hagar and their infant son Ishmael in a desolate valley. As Hagar desperately searched for water, a miracle occurred. A spring bubbled up at her son's feet. This spring became known as Zamzam. According to the Qur'an (koor-AHN), Abraham built a house of worship at the site, called the Ka'bah. Over time, people settled near it.

By the time of Muhammad's birth, this settlement, Makkah, was a **prosperous** city at the crossroads of great trade routes. Many people came to worship at the Ka'bah. But instead of honoring the God of Abraham's faith, Judaism, and Christianity, the worshippers at the Ka'bah honored the many traditional gods whose shrines were there.

According to Islamic teachings, Muhammad was living in Makkah when he experienced his own call to faith. Just as Abraham did, Muhammad **proclaimed** belief in a single God. At first, the faith he taught, Islam, met with resistance in Makkah. But Muhammad and his followers, called Muslims, eventually gained a great number of followers. Makkah became Islam's most sacred city, and the Ka'bah became a center of Islamic worship.

In this chapter, you will explore how Muhammad started Islam. You will learn how the Islamic faith quickly spread throughout Arabia and beyond. As you will see, within a century of Muhammad's death, a vast Muslim empire stretched from North Africa to Central Asia.

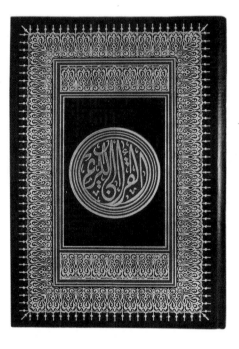

The Qur'an is the holy book of Islam. Its pages record Muhammad's teachings.

◄ The ancient Ka'bah shrine in Makkah is one of the holiest sites of Islam.

The Arabian Peninsula

• Makkah (Mecca)

The holy city of Makkah is located on the Arabian Peninsula. Makkah is the birthplace of Muhammad, the founder of Islam.

Islam the religious faith of Muslims; also the civilization based on the Islamic religion and the group of countries where Islam is the main religion

Muhammad a man born around 570 C.E. who taught the faith of Islam

polytheism belief in more than one god

7.2 Arabia in the 6th Century

Islam has its roots in Arabia, where **Muhammad** was born. To understand Islam's beginnings, we first need to look at the time period in which Muhammad grew up.

The town of Makkah, Muhammad's birthplace, was located in a dry, rocky valley in western Arabia. Makkah did not have agriculture. Instead, it gained wealth as a center of trade. Merchants traveling along caravan routes stopped at the city's market and inns. They bought spices, sheepskins, meat, dates, and other wares from townspeople and nomads.

By the time that Muhammad was born, Makkah was a prosperous city. Merchant families brought goods into Makkah from faraway places. Merchants grew wealthy through trade with Yemen (southern Arabia), Syria, and kingdoms in Africa. Over time, a handful of families, or clans, had come to rule the city. These families would not share their fortune with the weaker, poorer clans who lived there.

Makkah was also a religious center. According to the Qur'an, Abraham had built the cube-shaped shrine, the Ka'bah, centuries before, to honor God. In Muhammad's day, according to Islamic teaching, most Arabs followed **polytheism,** and the Ka'bah housed hundreds of statues of different gods. Pilgrims from all over Arabia came to worship at Makkah.

Many Arabs lived a nomadic life in the desert environment. There was no central government in Arabia. Instead, Arabs pledged loyalty to their clans and to larger tribes. These tribes sometimes fought each other to capture territory, animals, goods, watering places, and even wives. When someone from one tribe was killed during a raid, his family was honor-bound to avenge that death. This led to long periods of fighting among tribes.

Although Arabs on the peninsula were not united as a nation, they shared cultural ties, especially language. Arabic poetry celebrated the history of the Arab people, the beauty of their land, and their way of life. Poets and singers from different tribes competed at gatherings held at the markets and during pilgrimages.

This was the culture into which Muhammad was born. Let's turn now to the story of how he founded one of the world's major religions.

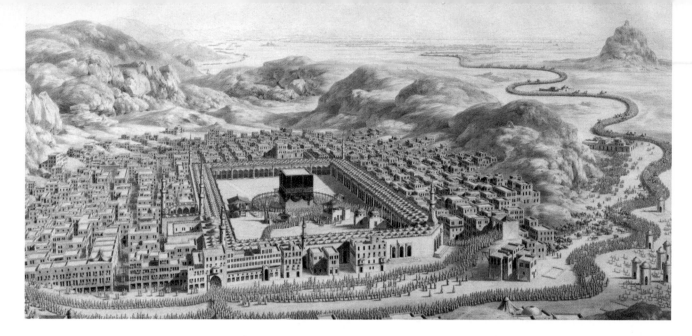

7.3 Muhammad's Early Life

As you have learned, around 570 C.E., a boy named Muhammad was born in Makkah. Muhammad's early life was ordinary. Few people who were not members of his clan, the Hashim, noted his birth. His father was dead, and the clan was not very wealthy. However, the Hashim had prestige, as they belonged to the leading tribe in Makkah.

Following custom, Muhammad's mother sent her baby to live with a family of nomads in the desert. There, the young boy learned about traditional Arab values, such as being kind to strangers and helping orphans, widows, and other needy members of society.

When Muhammad was about six, he returned to the city and his mother. They had little time together, because she soon died. Then Muhammad was left in the care of his grandfather, a highly regarded leader of the Hashim clan. Upon the grandfather's death, Muhammad's uncle, Abu Talib, a respected merchant, took charge of the orphan. Abu Talib also became head of the clan.

As a boy, Muhammad tended his family's flocks of sheep and goats. When he was about 12 years old, he accompanied his uncle on a trading journey. They traveled far north to Syria. On this journey, Muhammad gained his first experiences outside Arabia.

As Muhammad grew up, he took on more duties and made more trading journeys. He became a merchant who enjoyed a reputation throughout Makkah for his honesty. People called him *al-Amin,* which means "the Trustworthy."

Muhammad was still a young man when he began managing caravans for a widow named Khadijah, who ran a trading business. Muhammad earned her great profits. Impressed with his abilities and honesty, Khadijah proposed marriage. Muhammad accepted her offer, and when he was about 25, they married. Muhammad and Khadijah had several children, but only their daughter Fatima had children of her own. She continued the bloodline of Muhammad.

The Ka'bah in Makkah was surrounded by homes. In Muhammad's time, people came from all over Arabia to worship many gods at Makkah.

Muhhamad's clan. Not many outside his clan knew about his birth.

muhhamad sent her young child on a nomadic journey.

7.4   The Call to Prophethood

For the next 15 years, Muhammad made his living as a merchant. Although he enjoyed success in business, he also cared about spiritual matters. He often spent time at prayer and meditation in the mountains around Makkah. He was concerned about the effects of wealth and the worship of idols on his city.

In about 610 C.E., Muhammad went to meditate in a cave in the mountains. There, according to Islamic teachings, Muhammad received the call to be a **prophet,** or messenger of Allah. *Allah* is the Arabic word for God. The same word for God, Allah, is used by Arab Jews and Arab Christians.

Muhammad later described the remarkable events of that night. He told of being visited by the angel Gabriel who brought revelations, or revealed teachings, from God. Gabriel told Muhammad, "You are the messenger of God."

In the Hira Cave, according to Islamic teachings, the angel Gabriel first visited Muhammad.

According to Islamic tradition, at first Muhammad feared that he might be going mad. But Khadijah consoled Muhammad and expressed her faith that God had chosen him as a prophet to spread his words to the people. Khadijah became the first convert to Islam.

Islam is based on **monotheism,** or the belief in a single God. This God, Muhammad taught, was the same God of Abraham, Moses, and Jesus. Through Gabriel, God told Muhammad to teach others to practice compassion, honesty, and justice.

According to Muslim tradition, the angel Gabriel continued to reveal messages over the next 22 years. At first, Muhammad confided these messages only to family and friends, including his cousin Ali and a close friend, Abu Bakr (ah-BOOH BAHK-uhr). Gradually, a small group of followers developed at Makkah. They were called **Muslims,** which means "those who surrender to God." For Muslims, Islam was a way of life and the basis for creating a just society. For example, at the time women had few rights. Muslims granted more rights to women and ensured their equality before God.

Though Muhammad apparently could neither read nor write, he said that the messages from Gabriel were imprinted on his mind and heart. His followers also memorized them. Eventually, some followers wrote down these words and collected them in the Qur'an (also spelled *Koran*), the holy book of Islam. The poetic beauty of this book helped lend **credibility** to Muhammad's claim that it contained the words of God. It also attracted new believers to Islam.

7.5 Muhammad's Teachings Meet with Rejection

Around 613 C.E., Muhammad began to preach to other Makkans. He taught that people must worship the one God, that all believers in God were equal, and that the rich should share their wealth. He urged Makkans to take care of orphans and the poor and to improve the status of women.

Some members of Muhammad's clan became Muslims. People from other clans and social classes also joined him. Most Makkans, however, rejected Muhammad's teachings. Makkah's leaders did not want to share their wealth. They also feared that if Muhammad grew stronger, he would seize political power. Merchants worried that if people stopped worshipping their gods, they might stop their pilgrimages to Makkah. That would be bad for their businesses. Muhammad's monotheistic teachings also disturbed Arabs who did not want to give up their gods.

To prevent the spread of the prophet's message, some Arabs called Muhammad a liar. Some persecuted his followers. Despite this treatment, the Muslims would not give up their faith. Muhammad was also protected by Abu Talib, the head of the Hashim clan. Anyone who harmed a member of the clan would face Abu Talib's vengeance.

As the number of Muslims grew, the powerful clans of Makkah started a **boycott** to make Muhammad's followers give up Islam. For three years, the Hashim clan suffered as Makkans refused to do business with them. Although they were threatened with starvation, the boycott failed to break their will. These difficult years, however, took their toll on Abu Talib and Khadijah. In 619, these trusted family members died.

While these losses were terrible for Muhammad, that year he reported a miraculous event. Muslim tradition tells the story of the Night Journey in which a winged horse took Muhammad to Jerusalem, the city toward which early Muslims had directed their prayers. Jerusalem was already holy to Jews and Christians. There, Muhammad met and prayed with earlier prophets, such as Abraham, Moses, and Jesus. Then the horse guided Muhammad through the seven levels of heaven, and Muhammad met God. To this day, Jerusalem is a holy city for Muslims.

This rock is thought to be where Muhammad ended his Night Journey to Jerusalem and was led to heaven. An eight-sided, domed monument, the Dome of the Rock, now marks the spot.

boycott a refusal to do business with an organization or group

The Prophet's Mosque in Madinah contains Muhammad's tomb.

7.6 From the Migration to Madinah to the End of His Life

With Abu Talib's death, Muhammad lost his protector. As Muslims came under more attacks, Muhammad sought a new home. A group of Arab pilgrims from a town called Yathrib visited Makkah and converted to Islam. They asked Muhammad to move to Yathrib to bring peace between feuding tribes. In return, they pledged to protect him.

In 622, Muhammad and his followers left Makkah on a journey known as the *hijrah* (HEEJ-rah). Yathrib was renamed Madinah (also spelled *Medina*), short for "City of the Prophet." The year of the hijrah later became the first year of the Muslim calendar.

Over the next six years in Madinah, Muhammad developed a new Muslim community as more Arabs converted to Islam. Muslims pledged to be loyal and helpful to each other. They emphasized the brotherhood of faith over the ties of family, clan, and tribe. Even though Muhammad and the Qur'an criticized Jews and Christians on some aspects of their beliefs, Muhammad asked his followers to respect Christians and Jews. Like Muslims, these "People of the Book" believe in one God. Muhammad asked that they be treated as lawful members of society.

The Makkans, however, still felt threatened. In 624, fighting broke out between the Muslims and Makkans, and the Muslims won that battle. A few years later, the Makkans staged a **siege** of Madinah, but failed to capture the city.

siege a military action in which a place is surrounded and cut off to force those inside to surrender

The victory against the Makkan troops—and the ideas of charity, generosity, and forgiveness that Muhammad preached—convinced other tribes to convert to Islam. As Islam spread across Arabia, the Makkans agreed to a truce that would allow the Muslims to make their pilgrimage to Makkah. In 630, however, they broke the truce. In response, Muhammad's army marched on Makkah, and the city's leaders surrendered without a battle. Muhammad and his followers entered the city and destroyed the idols (statues of gods) at the Ka'bah. They rededicated the shrine solely to one God. Muhammad then forgave his former enemies. The war had ended.

In March 632, Muhammad led his final pilgrimage to Makkah. In the town of his birth, he delivered his Last Sermon. He reminded Muslims to treat each other well and to be faithful to their community. Shortly after his return to Madinah, Muhammad died.

7.7 The Four Caliphs

By the time of Muhammad's death, most of central and southern Arabia was under the control of Muslims. Now, his followers had to choose a new leader to preserve the community. They chose Abu Bakr, Muhammad's friend and father-in-law.

Abu Bakr became the first *caliph* (KAY-lif), or Muslim ruler. He and the three leaders who followed him came to be known to a large group of Muslims as the "rightly guided" caliphs. These caliphs were said by this group of Muslims to have followed the Qur'an and the example of Muhammad. The Muslim government led by the caliphs was called the *caliphate*.

When some tribes tried to break away, Abu Bakr used military force to reunite the community. He also completed the **unification** of Arabia. Then Muslims began to carry the teachings of Islam beyond the Arabian Peninsula.

After Abu Bakr died in 634, Caliph Umar (ooh-MAR) continued to expand the Muslim empire by conquest. In addition to spreading the faith of Islam, conquest allowed Muslims to gain new lands, resources, and goods.

By 643, the Muslim empire included lands in Iraq, Persia, the eastern Mediterranean, and North Africa. Umar set up governments and tax systems in all these provinces. Among the taxes was one levied on Jews and Christians and other non-Muslims. But Umar also let Jews and Christians practice their beliefs as they liked within their own homes and places of worship. It was unlawful for Muslims to damage Jewish or Christian holy places. In Egypt, treaties allowed for freedom of worship in exchange for the payment of tribute. Later, Muslims completed similar treaties with the Nubians, a people who lived to the south of Egypt.

The four Muslim leaders, or caliphs, who ruled after Muhammad were known as the "rightly guided" caliphs.

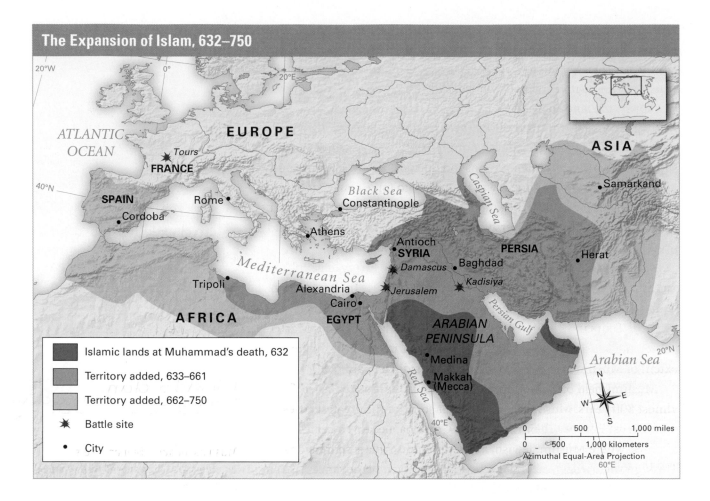

The Expansion of Islam, 632–750

Legend:
- Islamic lands at Muhammad's death, 632
- Territory added, 633–661
- Territory added, 662–750
- ✳ Battle site
- • City

Azimuthal Equal-Area Projection

Muslim leaders, such as Abu Bakr and Umar, spread Islam and Muslim rule across the entire Middle East and as far west as Spain and North Africa.

Upon Umar's death in 644, Uthman became the third caliph. Uthman was a member of the Umayyad (ooh-MY-ed) clan. He helped unite Muslims when he oversaw the creation of an official edition of the Qur'an. But he also awarded high posts to relatives. People in the provinces complained that he ruled unfairly. Discontent spread, and rebels killed Uthman in 656.

Ali ibn Abi Talib (AH-lee i-ben ah-bee TAH-lib), Muhammad's cousin and his daughter Fatima's husband, agreed to become the fourth caliph. Some important Muslims challenged his rule, which led to civil war. Ali sent forces against them, fought two major battles, and won one. But when he ended the other through negotiation, he lost supporters. In 661, one of these former supporters murdered Ali.

7.8 The Umayyad Dynasty

Soon after Ali's death, Mu'awiyah (mooh-AH-wee-YAH), the leader of the Umayyads, claimed the caliphate. Most Muslims, called the Sunnis (SOOH-neez), came to accept him. But a minority of Muslims, known as the Shi'ah (SHEE-ah), or "party" of Ali, refused to do so. They believed that only people directly descended from Muhammad through his daughter Fatima and son-in-law Ali should be caliph. The schism between the Sunnis and Shi'ah lasts to this day.

Mu'awiyah put down a revolt by Ali's supporters. He held on to the caliphate. He also founded the Umayyad dynasty. In 661, the Umayyads moved their capital to Damascus, Syria. From there, the caliphs ruled the huge Muslim empire for close to 100 years.

Slowly, the lands of the Muslim empire took on more elements of Arab culture. Muslims introduced the Arabic language. Along with Islam, acceptance of Arabic helped unite the diverse people of the empire. In addition, Arabs took over as top officials. People bought goods with new Arab coins. While it was not policy to force conversion to Islam, some non-Muslims began to embrace the new faith for a variety of reasons. These included personal belief in the message of Islam and social pressure to join the people of the ruling group.

The Muslim empire continued to expand. The Umayyad caliphs sent armies into central Asia and northwestern India. In 711, Muslim armies began their conquests of present-day Spain. However, at the Battle of Tours in 732, forces under the Frankish king Charles Martel turned the Muslims back in France. This battle marked the farthest extent of Muslim advances into Europe, outside of Spain.

Muslims held on to land in Spain, where Islamic states lasted for almost 800 years. Muslims in Spain built some of the greatest cities of medieval Europe. Their capital city, Cordoba, became a center of learning where Muslim, Jewish, and Christian scholars shared ideas. Through their work, Muslim culture made important advances in arts, science, technology, and literature.

Muslims followed Muhammad's teachings as Islam spread throughout the Middle East and beyond.

Chapter Summary

In this chapter, you learned about the life of Muhammad and the early spread of Islam. Muhammad and his followers unified Arabia and created a great empire.

Arabia in the 6th Century When Muhammad was born, Arabia was not a united country. Arabs did, however, share ties through trade, as well as the Arabic language and culture.

The Life of the Prophet Muhammad Born in Makkah, Muhammad became the prophet of Islam after he received revelations from the angel Gabriel, which were recorded in the Qur'an, the holy book of Islam. However, many in Makkah opposed Islam. In the year 622, Muhammad and his followers moved to Madinah, where they established a Muslim community. By the time Muhammad died in 632, people throughout Arabia had accepted the teachings of Islam and the Qur'an as the words of God.

The Four Caliphs and the Umayyad Dynasty The caliphs who followed Muhammad greatly expanded the lands under Islamic rule, despite struggles over leadership and civil war. In 661, the Umayyad caliphs moved their capital to Syria. By the mid 700s, the Muslim empire included Spain, North Africa, the Middle East, and parts of Asia and India. Along with the Arabic language, the acceptance of Islam helped unify this vast empire.

Chapter 8

Learning About World Religions: Islam

How do the beliefs and practices of Islam shape Muslims' lives?

8.1 Introduction

In this chapter, you will take a closer look at the religion of Islam. It was founded by the prophet Muhammad in the 7th century.

If you visited any city in a Muslim country today, you would notice many things that reflect the teachings of Islam. Five times a day, you would hear a call to prayer throughout the city. While some people hurry to houses of worship, others simply remain where they are to pray, even in the street. You would see people dressed modestly and many women wearing head scarves. You would find that Muslims do not drink alcohol or eat pork. You might learn how Muslims give money to support their houses of worship and many charities. Soon, you would come to understand that Islam is practiced as a complete way of life.

In this chapter, you will explore the basic beliefs and practices of Islam. You will learn more about the holy book called the Qur'an. Together with the Sunnah (SOON-ah)—the example of Muhammad—this book guides Muslims in the Five Pillars of Islam.

The Five Pillars are: declaration of faith, prayer, charity, fasting, and making a pilgrimage to Makkah. You will also study the idea of jihad (jee-HAHD). Jihad represents Muslims' struggle with internal and external challenges as they strive to please God. Finally, you will examine shari'ah (sha-REE-uh), or Islamic law.

Pictured above is the Ortaköy Mosque, built in the mid-1800s in Istanbul, Turkey.

◀ These Muslims are praying during a service at a mosque in Indonesia.

The Islamic community has spread throughout the world. These Muslims in Jerusalem, Isreal, prepare to pray on a sidewalk by facing toward Makkah.

8.2 Background on Islam

Since the time of Muhammad, Islam has had an impact on world history. Islam spread rapidly throughout the Middle East, across North Africa to Spain, and across Central Asia nearly to China. In addition to sharing a common faith, Muslims also belonged to a single Islamic community, called the *ummah* (UH-mah). The Islamic community blended many peoples and cultures.

Islam is the world's second largest religion, after Christianity. One out of five people in the world is Muslim. Most people in the Middle East and North Africa are Muslim, but Muslims live in nearly every country of the world. In fact, the majority of Muslims live in Asia, in nations such as Pakistan, Afghanistan, and the southeast Asian country of Indonesia. Islam is also the fastest-growing religion in the United States.

Islam, Judaism, and Christianity have much in common. Members of all three faiths are monotheists (they believe in one God). All three religions trace their origins to Abraham. Their scriptures, or sacred writings, all include such figures as Adam, Noah, and Moses. Muslims believe that all three religions worship the same God.

Muslims consider Jews and Christians to be "People of the Book." Muslims believe that God **revealed** messages to Moses, Jesus, and others that were compiled into holy books, just as the Qur'an came from God to Muhammad. The Qur'an states that God "earlier revealed the Torah (Judaism) and the Gospel (Christianity) as a source of guidance for people."

For Muslims, however, the Qur'an contains God's final revelations to the world. They believe that its messages reveal how God wants his followers to act and worship. In the rest of this chapter, you will learn more about the ideas that have shaped the Muslim faith.

8.3　The Qur'an and the Sunnah

Two foundations of Islam are the **Qur'an** and the **Sunnah**. Through the Qur'an, God describes his laws and moral teachings, or the "straight path." The Qur'an holds a central position for Muslims everywhere, guiding them in all aspects of their lives.

The Qur'an contains passages that Muslims believe Muhammad received from the angel Gabriel. Muhammad and his followers recited and memorized these verses. Because Muhammad apparently could not read or write, scribes wrote down these passages. The Arabic of the Qur'an is notable for its great beauty.

In about 651 C.E., Caliph Uthman established an official edition of the Qur'an. He asked those with variant versions of the Qur'an to destroy them so that there would be no confusion with these and the official **edition**. The Qur'an used today has remained largely unchanged since then.

Muhammad called the Qur'an God's "standing miracle." Muslims honor the spoken and written Qur'an. Most Muslims today do not let copies of the sacred book touch the ground. They also handle the Qur'an in a state of ritual purity. Most Muslims memorize all or part of the Qur'an in Arabic. Its verses accompany Muslims throughout their lives, from birth to death.

The Sunnah ("practice") is the example that Muhammad set for Muslims during his lifetime. What Muhammad did or said in a certain situation has set a precedent, or guide, for all Muslims. For instance, Muhammad told his followers to make sure that their guests never left the table hungry, underscoring the importance of hospitality. He also reminded children to honor their parents when he said, "God forbids all of you to disobey your mothers." For Muslims, the Sunnah is second only to the Qur'an in religious authority.

About 300 years after Muhammad's death, thousands of reports about the prophet had spread throughout Muslim lands. Scholars looked into each story. They organized the stories they could verify into collections. Called *hadith* ("reports" or "tradition"), these accounts provided written evidence of Muhammad's Sunnah through his own words and deeds. They continue to have this role today.

The most basic acts of worship for Muslims are called the **Five Pillars of Islam**. The Qur'an provides general commands to perform these five duties. The Sunnah explains how to perform them, based on Muhammad's example. Let's look next at each of the Five Pillars.

Qur'an the holy book of the religion of Islam

Sunnah the example that Muhammad set for Muslims about how to live

Five Pillars of Islam the most basic acts of worship for Muslims: declaration of faith, prayer, charity, fasting, and making a pilgrimage to Makkah

These girls in Bangladesh are reading the Qur'an to learn how to perform the basic acts of Muslim worship, called the Five Pillars of Islam.

8.4 The First Pillar: Shahadah

The first Pillar of Islam is *shahadah* (shah-HAH-dah), the profession or declaration of faith. To show belief in one God and in Muhammad's prophethood, a Muslim testifies, "I bear witness that there is no god but God, and that Muhammad is the messenger of God."

The first part of the shahadah affirms monotheism—"There is no god but God." Like Christians and Jews, Muslims believe that one all-powerful God—called *Allah* in Arabic—created the universe. They believe that the truth of that God was revealed to humankind through many prophets. These prophets include Adam, Abraham, Moses, and Jesus, who appear in Jewish and Christian scriptures. The Qur'an honors all these prophets.

A muezzin calls Muslim people to prayer from a mosque's tower, or minaret.

The second part of the shahadah **identifies** Muhammad as God's messenger—"and Muhammad is the messenger of God." According to this statement, Muhammad announced the message of Islam, which was God's final word to humankind.

The meaning of shahadah is that people not only believe in God, but also pledge their submission to him. For Muslims, God is the center of life. The shahadah follows Muslims through everyday life, not just prayers. Parents whisper it into their babies' ears. Students taking a difficult test say the shahadah to help them be successful. To enter into the religion of Islam, a person must pronounce the shahadah aloud in the presence of two Muslim witnesses.

Beyond the shahadah, Muslims also believe in the idea of an unseen world of angels and other beings. According to their faith, God created angels to do his work throughout the universe. Some angels reveal themselves to prophets, as Gabriel did to Muhammad. Other angels observe and record the deeds of each human being. Belief in angels is found in Christianity and Judaism, as well as in Islam.

Muslims also believe that all souls will face a day of judgment. On that day, God will weigh each person's actions. Those who have lived according to God's rules will be rewarded and allowed to enter paradise. Those who have disbelieved or done evil will be punished by falling into hell.

8.5 The Second Pillar: Salat

The second Pillar of Islam is *salat* (SAH-laht), daily ritual prayer. Muhammad said that "prayer is the proof" of Islam. Salat emphasizes religious discipline, spirituality, and closeness to God.

Throughout Muslim communities, people are called to prayer five times a day: at dawn, noon, mid-afternoon, sunset, and after nightfall. A crier, called a *muezzin* (moo-EHZ-en), chants the call to prayer, sometimes through a loudspeaker, from the tall minaret (tower) of the community's **mosque** (MOSK).

Before praying, Muslims must perform ritual washings. All mosques have fresh, flowing water in which worshipers wash their hands, face, arms, and feet. With a sense of being purified, Muslims enter the prayer area. There, they form lines behind a prayer leader called an imam. The worshipers face the *qiblah* (KIB-lah), the direction of Makkah. A niche in a wall marks the qiblah. People of all classes stand shoulder to shoulder, but men stand in separate rows from women.

The imam begins the prayer cycle by proclaiming "Allahu akbar!" ("God is most great!"). The worshipers then recite verses from the Qur'an and kneel before God.

While praying at a mosque is preferable, Muslims may worship anywhere. In groups or by themselves, they may perform their prayers at home, at work, in airports, in parks, or on sidewalks. A qiblah compass may help them locate the direction of Makkah. Some Muslims carry a prayer rug to have a clean spot on which pray. Some make additional prayers by using prayer beads and reciting words describing God's many characteristics.

Unlike Christians and Jews, Muslims do not observe a sabbath, or day of rest. On Fridays, however, Muslims gather at a mosque for midday congregational prayer. The worshipers listen to a Qur'an reading and the sermon. After saying prayers together, some return to their regular business. For others, Friday is a special day when people meet with family and friends.

This mosque in Dubai has two minarets. Muezzins climb to the top of the tall towers to chant their calls to prayer out over the city.

mosque a Muslim house of worship

8.6 The Third Pillar: Zakat

The third Pillar of Islam is *zakat,* or charity. Muhammad told wealthy people to share their riches with the less fortunate. This practice remains a basic part of Islam.

The word *zakat* means "purification." Muslims believe that wealth becomes pure by giving some of it away, and that sharing wealth helps control greed. Zakat also reminds people of God's great gifts to them.

According to the teachings of Islam, Muslims must share about one-fortieth (2.5 percent) of their surplus wealth each year with their poorer neighbors. They are encouraged to give even more. Individuals decide the proper amount to pay. Then they either give this sum to a religious official or **distribute** it themselves.

Zakat helps provide for many needs. In medieval times, zakat often went to constructing public fountains, so everyone had clean water to drink, or to inns so pilgrims and travelers had a place to sleep. If you walk down a busy street in any Muslim town today, you will see the effects of zakat everywhere. Zakat pays for soup kitchens, clothing, and shelter for the poor. It supports the building and running of orphanages and hospitals. Poorer Muslims may receive funds to pay off their debts. Zakat provides aid to stranded travelers.

Zakat also helps other good causes that serve the Muslim community. For instance, zakat can cover the school fees of children whose parents cannot afford to send them to Muslim schools. It can be used to pay teachers.

Zakat is similar to charitable giving in other religions. For instance, Jews and Christians also ask for donations, called tithes (TYTHZ), to support their houses of worship and charitable activities.

8.7 The Fourth Pillar: Siyam

The fourth Pillar of Islam is *siyam* (see YAM), or fasting (going without food). Muslims were not the first people to fast as a way of worshipping God. The Bible praises the act. But the Qur'an instructs Muslims to fast for an entire month during **Ramadan,** the ninth month of the Islamic calendar.

According to Islamic teachings, Ramadan was the month when God first revealed his message to Muhammad. Muslims use a lunar calendar (one based on the phases of the moon). A year on this calendar is shorter than a 365-day year. As a result, over time, Ramadan cycles through all the seasons of a standard year.

During Ramadan, Muslims fast from daybreak to the setting of the sun. Pregnant women, travelers, the sick, the elderly, and young children do not have to fast.

During the daylight hours on each day during the month of Ramadan, Muslims do not eat any food or drink any liquid, including water.

Through zakat, Muslims give to the poor or needy.

Ramadan the ninth month of the Islamic calendar, during which Muslims are required to fast

At sunset, Muslims then break their fast, often with dates and other food and beverages—as Muhammad did—and perform the sunset prayer. After a meal shared with family or friends, Muslims attend special prayer services. Each night, a portion of the Qur'an is read aloud. By the end of Ramadan, devout Muslims who attended mosque regularly would have heard the entire holy book.

The holy month of Ramadan encourages generosity, equality, and charity within the Muslim community. Fasting teaches Muslims self-control and makes them realize what it would be like to be poor and hungry. Well-to-do Muslims and mosques often provide food for others. During Ramadan, Muslims also strive to forgive people, give thanks, and avoid gossip, arguments, and bad deeds.

Toward the end of Ramadan, Muslims remember Gabriel's first visit to Muhammad. It is supposed to have occurred during one of the last ten odd-numbered nights of the month. Worshippers seek out this night because, according to the Qur'an, prayer during this "night of power" is equal to a thousand months of devotion. A celebration called Eid al-Fitr (eed-AL-fitter) takes place when Ramadan ends. People attend prayers. They wear new clothes, decorate their homes, and prepare special foods. They visit friends and family, exchange gifts, and give to the poor.

The holy month of Ramadan ends with a celebration that includes a feast of special foods.

8.8 The Fifth Pillar: Hajj

The fifth Pillar of Islam is *hajj* (HAJZH), the pilgrimage to the holy city of Makkah. In the twelfth month of the Islamic year, millions of believers from all over the world come together at Makkah. All adult Muslims who are able to make the journey are expected to perform the hajj at least once during their lifetime. By bringing Muslims from many places and cultures together, the hajj promotes fellowship and equality.

In Makkah, pilgrims follow what Muslims believe are the footsteps of Abraham and Muhammad, and so draw closer to God. For five days, they dress in simple white clothing and perform a series of rituals, moving from one sacred site to another.

Upon arrival, Muslims announce their presence with these words: "Here I am, O God, at thy command!" They go to the Great Mosque, which houses the Ka'bah. Muslims believe that Abraham built the Ka'bah as a shrine to honor God. The pilgrims circle the Ka'bah seven times, which is a ritual mentioned in the Qur'an. Next, they run along a passage between two small hills, as Hagar did when she searched for water for her baby Ishmael. The pilgrims drink from the Zamzam spring, which, appeared miraculously at Ishmael's feet.

Later, pilgrims leave Makkah to sleep in tents at a place called Mina. In the morning, they move to the Plain of Arafat to pray until sunset, asking God's forgiveness. Some climb Mount Arafat, where Muhammad preached his Last Sermon. After spending another night camped in the desert, they reject evil by casting stones at pillars representing Satan.

Afterward, pilgrims may celebrate with a four-day feast. In honor of Abraham's ancient sacrifice, as recounted in religious scriptures, they sacrifice animals, usually sheep or goats, and share the meat with family, friends, and the poor. Then, having completed the hajj, they dress again in their own clothes. Before leaving Makkah, each pilgrim circles the Ka'bah seven more times. Muslims around the world celebrate this "farewell" day as Eid al-Adha (eed-AL-adh-hah).

Pilgrims to the holy city of Makkah circle the Ka'bah seven times as directed in the Qur'an and the Sunnah.

8.9 Jihad

The word **jihad** literally means "to strive." Traditionally in Islam, it has meant "physical struggle with spiritual significance." The Qur'an tells Muslims to fight to protect themselves from those who would harm them or to right a terrible wrong. Early Muslims considered efforts to protect their territory and conquests to extend their empire as forms of jihad. However, the Qur'an forbids Muslims to force others to convert to Islam. So, non-Muslims under Muslim rule were usually allowed to practice their faiths.

Today, some have used jihad to try to make their government more Islamic or to resist perceived aggression from non-Muslims with acts of terrorism. But most Muslims reject such actions. They agree that to deliberately harm civilians, including non-Muslims, is forbidden in Islam.

Although the Qur'an allows war, it sets specific terms for fighting. Muhammad told his followers to honor agreements made with foes. Muslim fighters must not mutilate (remove or destroy) the dead bodies of enemies, nor harm women, children, the elderly, and civilians. Nor should they destroy property, orchards, crops, sacred objects, or houses of worship.

jihad Muslims' struggle with challenges within themselves and the world as they strive to please God

Jihad originally meant a physical struggle against enemies while striving to please God. Sometimes it may be a struggle within an individual to overcome spiritual challenges.

Jihad represents the human struggle to overcome difficulties and do things that would be pleasing to God. Muslims strive to respond positively to personal difficulties as well as to worldly challenges. For instance, they might work to become better people, reform society, or correct injustice.

Jihad has always been an important Islamic concept. One hadith tells about the prophet's return from a battle. He declared that he and his men had carried out the "lesser jihad," the external struggle against oppression. The "greater jihad," he said, was the fight against evil within oneself. Examples of the greater jihad include working hard for a goal, giving up a bad habit, getting an education, or obeying your parents when you may not want to.

Another hadith says that Muslims should fulfill jihad with the heart, tongue, and hand. Muslims use the heart in their struggle to resist evil. The tongue may convince others to take up worthy causes. Hands may perform good works and correct misdeeds.

A shari'ah court is shown on this page from an illuminated manuscript dated 1334.

The Granger Collection, New York

shari'ah the body of Islamic law based on the Qur'an and the Sunnah

8.10 Islamic Law: Shari'ah

The body, or collection, of Islamic law is called **shari'ah** (sha-REE-ah). It is based on the Qur'an and the Sunnah. Shari'ah covers Muslims' duties toward God. It guides them in their personal behavior and relationships with others. Shari'ah promotes obedience to the Qur'an and respect for others.

In Madinah's Muslim community, Muhammad explained the Qur'an and served as a judge. After his death, the caliphs used the Qur'an and the Sunnah to solve problems. As the Muslim empire expanded, leaders faced new situations. Gradually, scholars developed a body of Islamic law. By the 12th century, several schools of Islamic law had emerged.

Islamic law guides Muslim life by placing actions into one of five categories: forbidden, discouraged, allowed, recommended, and obligatory (required). Sometimes the law is quite specific. Muslims, for instance, are forbidden to eat pork, drink alcohol, or gamble. But other matters are mentioned in general terms. For example, the Qur'an tells women "not to display their beauty to strangers." For this reason, Muslim women usually wear various forms of modest dress. For example, most women cover their arms and legs. Many also wear scarves over their hair. Others cover themselves from head to toe.

Shari'ah also outlines Muslims' duties toward other people. These duties can be broadly grouped into criminal, commercial, family, and inheritance law.

In a shari'ah court, a *qadi* (KAH-dee), or judge, hears a case, which includes witnesses and evidence. Then the qadi makes a ruling. Sometimes the qadi consults a *mufti,* or scholar of law, for an opinion.

Islamic law helped Muslims to live by the rules contained in the Qur'an. By the 19th century, however, many Muslim regions had come under European rule. Western codes of law soon replaced the shari'ah except in matters of family law. Today, most Muslim countries apply only some parts of Islamic law. But shari'ah continues to develop in response to modern ways of life and its challenges.

For the past century, one of the major questions the Muslim world faces is how Islamic law can be made to relate to modern society and government. Turkey has chosen a non-religious legal model. However, Saudi Arabia and Iran have adopted shari'ah as the law of the land, each nation according to its own ideas. Other countries, such as Egypt and Pakistan, have strong Islamist parties and strong non-Islamist parties. Most Muslims feel that democracy and freedom do not **contradict** the teachings and law of Islam. But others feel that the two cannot go hand in hand. The debate continues.

Chapter Summary

In this chapter, you learned about the basic beliefs and practices of Islam. One of the world's major religions, Islam has more followers than any faith except Christianity.

Background on Islam Islam, Judiaism, and Christianity share many similarities. People of these faiths believe in one God and have holy books. Muslims accept the Jewish and Christian scriptures as earlier revelations by God.

The Qur'an and the Sunnah The Qur'an is the Islamic holy book. It contains God's final messages to humanity and guides Muslims on how to live their lives. Additional guidance comes from the Sunnah (practice), the example of Muhammad. The hadith (tradition) provides a written record of sayings and deeds of the prophet.

The Five Pillars of Islam Islam is a way of life, as well as a set of beliefs. Muslims follow the Five Pillars of Islam. The five pillars are: shahadah (declaration of faith), salat (daily worship), zakat (charity), siyam (fasting), and hajj (the pilgrimage to Makkah).

Jihad Muslims also have the duty of jihad, which is a physical or spiritual struggle or striving to please God.

Islamic Law: Shari'ah Shari'ah, or Islamic law, helps Muslims live by the teachings of the Qur'an. It includes practices of daily life, as well as the duty to respect others.

Chapter 9

Muslim Innovations and Adaptations

What important innovations and adaptations did medieval Muslims make?

9.1 Introduction

In the Middle Ages, Muslim people developed a rich culture. In this chapter, you will study many contributions made by Muslims to world civilization.

By 750 C.E., Muslims ruled Spain, North Africa, the Middle East, and much of central Asia. Over the next 500 years, many cultural influences blended in this vast region. Arabs, Persians, Turks, and others all helped to build Islamic civilization.

The Islamic world was rich, **diverse,** and creative. Great cities flourished as centers of culture. Jewish, Christian, and Muslim scholars worked to translate ancient texts from Greece, India, and Persia into Arabic. They preserved old learning. They also improved ways of doing things that influenced the Scientific Revolution in Europe centuries later.

You can still see signs of this influence today. For instance, Muslims introduced many foods to other parts of the world. Among them were sugar (*al-sukkar,* in Arabic), rice (*al-ruzz*), and oranges (*naranj*). The English words *mattress* and *sofa* are both from Arabic. *Pajamas* and *tambourine* are derived from Persian words. The Arabic numerals (1, 2, 3, and so on) we use today were brought to Europe by Muslims.

In this chapter, you will explore Muslim contributions to world civilization. You will study Muslim achievements in city building and architecture, scholarship and learning, science and technology, geography and navigation, mathematics, medicine, literature and bookmaking, art and music, and recreation. Let's begin by looking more closely at the flowering of Islamic civilization following the Arab conquests of the 7th and 8th centuries.

With its ornate arches and other rich details, the Alhambra is considered to be one of the best examples of medieval Muslim architecture in the world.

◀ In the 14th century, Muslim rulers built the magnificent palace complex called the Alhambra in Granada, Spain.

9.2 The Flowering of Islamic Civilization

Islam began on the Arabian Peninsula. By the middle of the 8th century, Arab conquests had created a vast Muslim empire. Spain, North Africa, and much of western and central Asia came under Muslim rule. Over the next 500 years, Islamic civilization flowered over this huge area.

As a political unit, however, the empire did not last. Despite this loss of political unity, Islamic civilization flourished. Muslim rulers built great cities where scholars and artists made **adaptations** and **innovations** in many fields.

Muslims learned from other cultures, and helped spread cultural elements to other places. The spreading of ideas and ways of life is called **cultural diffusion**. Cultural diffusion occurs as different societies interact through trade, travel, or even conflict. Often, these cultural elements are changed, or adapted, in the regions to which they spread.

The Islamic lands were ideally located for cultural diffusion. As you can see on the map of medieval trade routes, several important trade routes linking Asia, Europe, and Africa met in the Middle East. Muslim traders carried ideas, as well as goods, along their routes, spreading learning to and from Asia, Europe, and Africa.

For example, Muslims learned paper making from the Chinese, and they passed this knowledge on to Europeans. Muslims produced new scientific, medical, and philosophical texts based on earlier Greek works. Many of these texts were translated into Latin in the 12th century and became available to western Europeans for the first time.

adaptation a change made to an existing object or way of doing things

innovation something new; an improvement

cultural diffusion the spread of cultural elements from one society to another

Over many connecting trade routes, goods and ideas moved from Asia through Muslim lands, where they were adapted. They then spread as far as North Africa and Europe.

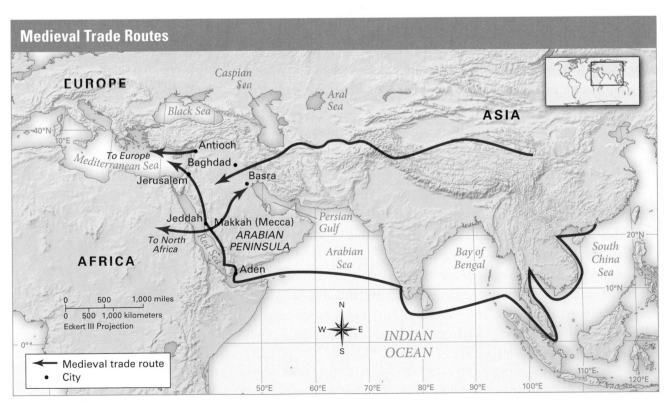

Medieval Trade Routes

Muslim mathematicians were also able to translate and study the work of Babylonian, Indian, Chinese, Greek and Jewish math scholars. They were able to develop innovations in that field, too.

As you read this chapter, keep in mind the great diversity of the Islamic world. Only a minority of Muslims were from the Arabian Peninsula. Persians, Egyptians, North Africans, Turks, and others all contributed to the cultural blending we call Islamic civilization.

9.3 City Building and Architecture

Many large cities developed in Muslim lands. The growth of these cities encouraged new kinds of architecture. Thousands of workers labored to build palaces, schools, orphanages, hospitals, mosques, and other buildings.

The City of Baghdad After the Muslim Abbasid dynasty rose to power in the Middle East, Caliph al-Mansur decided to move his capital from Damascus to a site that was more central to his far-flung empire. The site he chose was Baghdad, a village between the Tigris and Euphrates rivers, in present-day Iraq. This location was a crossroads of trade routes connecting distant parts of the empire.

Baghdad was one of the most glorious Muslim cities. It took 100,000 architects, workers, and craftspeople four years to build the new capital. Because of its shape, people called the capital complex the "round city." At its center were the caliph's palace and the grand mosque. Around them were offices and the houses of court officials and army officers. A double wall with four guarded gates surrounded the inner city. Shops, markets, and residences grew up outside the wall. Soon, Baghdad was one of the world's largest cities. Bridges, palaces, and gardens all added to its splendor. One Arab historian of the 11th century called Baghdad "a city with no equal in the world."

The Mosque Muslims created distinctive forms of architecture. A particularly important type of building was the mosque, the Muslim house of worship.

Mosques usually have at least one minaret (tower) with a small balcony where the muezzin chants the call to prayer. In a courtyard, stands a fountain for washing before prayers. Inside the mosque is the prayer room. Worshippers sit on mats and carpets on the floor. The imam gives the sermon from a raised pulpit called the minbar. Next to the minbar is a niche in the wall that indicates the direction of prayer towards Makkah.

Many design styles and materials went into building mosques, reflecting the great diversity of Muslim lands. Like the cathedrals of Europe, mosques express the religious faith and the artistic heritage of their builders.

The minaret of the Great Mosque of Samarra has a spiral design. Muezzins climb spiral steps around the outside of the tower to the balcony at the top.

Students in Muslim schools discussed and debated philosophical ideas with their teachers.

9.4 Scholarship and Learning

Scholarship and learning were very highly valued in Islamic culture. Muhammad is reported to have said, "The ink of scholars is more precious than the blood of martyrs."

Acceptance of the Arabic language helped promote learning. Beginning in the 8th century, Arabic became the language of scholarship and science throughout Islamic lands. A shared language and love of learning allowed scholars in Europe, North Africa, and the Middle East to exchange ideas and build on one another's work.

Muslim rulers built schools, colleges, libraries, and other centers of learning. As you have read, one of the most important cities was Baghdad. From a small village, Baghdad grew into one of the world's largest cities. It became a major center of learning, where Persian influences combined with the Arabic heritage of Islam. There, Caliph al-Ma'mun founded the House of Wisdom in 830. Scholars from many lands gathered there to do research and to translate texts from Greece, Persia, India, and China.

Other cities also became great centers of learning. In the 10th century, the Fatimid dynasty in Egypt built a capital, Cairo, which rivaled Baghdad. Its university became the most advanced in the Muslim world. In Cairo, the Hall of Wisdom opened in the 10th century. Scholars and ordinary people could visit its library to read books. In Spain, the Muslim capital, Cordoba, became a large and wealthy city. Jews, Christians, and Muslims worked and studied there together. That city's huge library held as many as 400,000 volumes. Buyers traveled far and wide to purchase books for its shelves.

Among the texts studied were the works of ancient Greek thinkers, such as the **philosophers** Plato (PLAY-toh) and Aristotle. Following the example of the Greeks, Muslim philosophers used reason and **logic** to try to prove important truths.

Like thinkers in Europe, thinkers in the Islamic world sometimes wondered how to make reason and logical proof agree with their faith. Al-Kindi, a 9th-century Arab philosopher, tried to resolve this issue. Humans, he said, had two sources of knowledge: reason and revelation by God. People could use reason to better understand the teachings of faith. Some truths, however, could be known only through God's word. For example, no one could prove that there would be a resurrection, or rising from the dead, on the day of judgment.

Ibn Sina (i-ben SEE-na), a Persian, became Islam's most famous philosopher. Known as Avicenna in Europe, he wrote in the early 11th century. He believed that all knowledge came from God and that truth could be known through revelation and reason. For example, he presented an argument that the soul was **immortal**. His writings were widely translated and influenced many thinkers in medieval Europe.

philosopher a scholar, teacher, or thinker who seeks knowledge

immortal able to live forever

9.5 Science and Technology

Muslims showed an endless curiosity about the world. In fact, the Qur'an instructed them to learn more about the world God had made:

Have they not looked at the camel—how it was created?
And at the sky—how it was raised up?

As a result, Muslims made advances in science and technology. They were particuarly interested to learn how things worked.

Zoology A number of Muslim scholars became interested in zoology, the scientific study of animals. Some wrote books describing the structure of animals' bodies. Others explained how to make medicines from animals parts. In the 800s, a scholar named al-Jahiz (AHL-jay-HEEZ) even presented theories about the **evolution** of animals. Muslims also established zoological gardens, or zoos.

Astronomy Muslim scholars did much work in the field of astronomy, the study of objects in the universe. Astronomy had many practical uses for Muslims. For example, navigational tools were improved to locate the direction of Makkah. These instruments allowed worshippers far from the holy city to pray facing in the right direction. Astronomers also figured out exact times for prayer and the length of the month of Ramadan.

Beyond such practical matters, Muslim astronomers simply wanted to learn about the universe. Some realized that Earth rotates, or turns, like a spinning top. Many questioned the accepted idea that Earth was the center of the universe, with the sun and stars traveling around it. In fact, as later astronomers proved, Earth does travel around the sun.

evolution the slow process of change in plants and animals from simpler forms to more complex forms

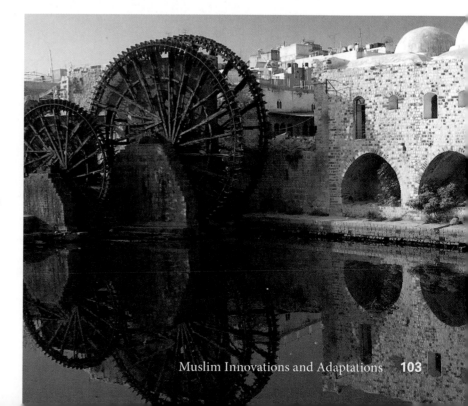

The town of Hama, Syria, has 17 wooden waterwheels from medieval times. These waterwheels scoop water from the Orontes River into aqueducts, bringing it to homes and farms.

Irrigation and Underground Wells Muslims made technological advances to make the most of scarce water resources. Much of the land under Muslim rule was hot and dry. Muslims restored old irrigation systems and designed new ones. They built dams and aqueducts to provide water for households, mills, and fields. They improved existing systems of canals and underground wells. Some wells reached down 50 feet into the ground. Muslims also used water wheels to bring water up from canals and reservoirs.

9.6 Geography and Navigation

Another subject of study for Muslim scholars was geography. Muslim geographers examined plants and animals in different regions. They also divided the world into climate zones.

Most educated people in medieval times believed that Earth was round, but they disagreed about Earth's size. Muslim scientists improved on calculations made by the ancient Greeks to reach a measure of Earth's circumference within nine miles of its correct value.

As with all scholarship, some Muslims studied geography simply out of curiosity. But geography had practical uses, too. For example, Muslims were able to create extremely accurate maps. A scholar in Muslim Spain even produced a world atlas, with dozens of maps of lands in Europe, Africa, and Asia.

A work called *The Book of Roads and Provinces* provided maps and descriptions of the major Muslim trade routes. *The Book of Countries* listed useful facts about the lands under Muslim rule. From this book, travelers could get information about a region's physical features and water resources.

Travelers were another source of knowledge. Some travelers wrote guidebooks to help pilgrims make the journey to Makkah to fulfill the hajj. Others explored and described foreign lands, such as China and Scandinavia. One traveler wrote a 30-volume encyclopedia about all the places he had seen.

As aids to travel, Muslims used navigational instruments. Muslim scientists adapted and perfected the compass and astrolabe. Muslims probably learned about the compass from the Chinese. Compasses allow people to identify the direction in which they are traveling.

The astrolabe is a device for computing time based on the location of the sun or the stars. It was probably invented much earlier by the Greeks. With this instrument, sailors at sea could use the position of objects in the sky, such as the sun or stars, to pinpoint their location by knowing how far they had traveled.

The astrolabe was a navigational tool widely used in the Islamic world and in Europe.

9.7 Mathematics

Muslims greatly advanced the study of mathematics. They based their work in part on ideas from ancient Babylon, India, and Greece. For example, scholars in Baghdad's House of Wisdom translated the works of the Greek mathematician Euclid (YOO-klid). They also translated important texts from India. Then they adapted what they learned and added their own contributions.

One of these Muslim scholars was the astronomer and mathematician al-Khwarizmi (ahl KWAR-iz-mee), who worked in the Hall of Wisdom in Cairo in the 9th century. Al-Khwarizmi is best known as "the father of algebra." In fact, the word *algebra* comes from the title of one of his books. It originated in an Arabic phrase meaning "the reunion of broken parts."

Algebra is used to solve problems involving unknown numbers. An example is the **equation** $7x + 4 = 25$. Using algebra, we can figure out that in this equation, x represents 3. Al-Khwarizmi's famous book on algebra was translated into Latin in the 12th century. It became the most important mathematics textbook used in the universities of Europe.

The translation of another one of Al-Khwarizmi's books helped to popularize Arabic numerals in Europe. Actually, Muslims learned this way of writing numerals, along with fractions and decimals, from Indian scholars. Arabic numerals were a big help to business and trade. Compared to earlier systems, such as Roman numerals, they made it easier for people to do calculations and check their work. We still use Arabic numerals today.

Muslims also spread the Indian concept of zero. In fact, the word *zero* comes from an Arabic word meaning "something empty." Ancient peoples used written symbols for numbers long before anyone thought of using a symbol for zero. Yet zero is very important in calculations. (Try subtracting 2 from 2. Without using zero, how would you express the answer?) Zero also made it easier to write large numbers. For example, zero allows people to distinguish between 123 and 1,230.

The geometric designs in Muslim art and architecture are based on knowledge about advanced mathematical principles.

9.8 Medicine

Muslims made some of their most important innovations in the field of medicine. They learned a great deal from the work of ancient Greeks, Mesopotamians, and Egyptians. Then, as in other fields of study, they improved upon this earlier knowledge.

Muslim doctors established the world's first hospitals. By the 10th century, Baghdad had at least five hospitals. Most cities and towns also had one or two. Many hospitals served as teaching centers for doctors in training. Anyone who needed treatment could get it at these centers. There were also hospital caravans that brought medical care to people in remote villages.

Muslim hospitals had separate wards for men and women, surgical patients, and people with diseases that others could catch. Doctors treated ailments with drugs, diet, and exercise. They gave patients remedies made from herbs and other plants, animals, and minerals. Pharmacists made hundreds of medications. Some drugs dulled patients' pain. Antiseptics (medications that fight infection) cleaned wounds. Ointments helped to heal the wounds.

For some problems, surgeons performed delicate operations as a last resort. Drugs, such as opium and hemlock, put patients to sleep before operations. Muslim surgeons removed limbs, took out tumors, and cleared cataracts (cloudy spots) from the eye. After surgery, doctors used thread made from animal gut to stitch the wounds.

Muslim doctors made many discoveries and helped spread medical knowledge. For example, al-Razi, a Persian doctor, realized that infections were caused by bacteria. He also studied smallpox and measles. His work helped other doctors diagnose and treat these deadly diseases.

The Persian philosopher Ibn Sina (Avicenna), whom you met earlier in this chapter, was also a great doctor. In fact, he has been called "the prince of physicians." His most important medical book, *The Canon of Medicine*, explored the treatment of diseases. It is one of the classics in the history of medical scholarship.

Europeans later translated Ibn Sina's book and many other Muslim works into Latin. Medical schools then used these texts to teach their students. In this way, Muslim doctors had a major impact on European medicine.

Muslim doctors treated patients with herbal remedies, as well as drugs, diet, and exercise. This illustration of a lily plant is from an Arabic herbal encyclopedia of the 10th century.

9.9 Bookmaking and Literature

In the 8th century, Muslims learned the art of making paper from the Chinese. Soon, they were creating bound books. Bookmaking, in turn, encouraged the growth of Muslim literature.

Craftspeople used their talents to produce beautiful books. Bookmakers gathered the sheets of paper and sewed them into leather bindings. They **illuminated** the bindings and pages with designs in gold, as well as with miniature paintings.

Books became a big business in the Muslim world. In Baghdad, more than one hundred bookshops lined Papersellers' Street. In addition to copies of the Qur'an, booksellers there sold many volumes of poetry and prose.

Arabs had a rich heritage of storytelling and poetry. Arab poetry often honored love, praised rulers, or celebrated wit. Persians introduced epic poems, or long poems that tell a story. Prose eventually replaced poetry for recording history, special events, and traditions. Writers also composed stories in prose.

One famous collection of stories is called *A Thousand and One Nights.* Also known as *Arabian Nights,* this book gathered stories that originally came from many places, including India and Persia, as well as elsewhere in the Middle East. In the book, a wife tells her husband a new tale each night. The stories take place in Muslim cities and in places such as China, Egypt, and India. Later, a European translator added tales that were not part of the medieval Arabic collection. Among these added tales are those about Aladdin's magic lamp, Ali Baba, and Sinbad the Sailor, which remain well known today.

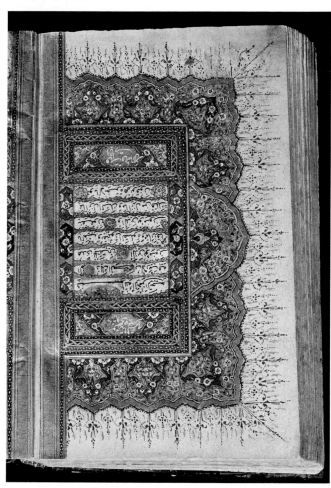

As in medieval Europe, bookmaking was an art in the Muslim world. Copies of the Qur'an were written with elaborate letters and decorated in gold.

Muslim literature was enriched by Sufism, or Islamic mysticism. This type of religious practice involves intense personal experiences of God, rather than routine performance of rituals. Sufis longed to draw close to God in their everyday lives. One way to express their love and devotion was through poetry filled with vivid images and beautiful language. Rabi'a, a poet of the 8th century, shared her feelings in this verse: "But your door is open to those who call upon you. My Lord, each lover is now alone with his beloved. And I am alone with Thee."

A 13th-century Sufi poet, Rumi, had an enormous influence on Islamic mysticism. Rumi wrote a long religious poem in Persian that filled six volumes. Pilgrims still travel to his tomb in Turkey.

9.10 Art and Music

Muslims created many forms of art and music. In this section, you'll look at four types of artistic expression in the medieval Islamic world.

Geometric and Floral Design Muslims earned fame for their decorative arts. Early in the history of Islam, Muslims rejected the use of images of humans or animals in their visual art, especially religious art. Only God, they said, can create something that is alive. Instead, artists turned to shapes and patterns found in nature and geometry to create marvelous designs and decorations.

Art sometimes was religious, as in the beautiful illuminated manuscripts of the Qur'an. But artists and craftspeople also applied their talents to everyday items like plates, candlesticks, glassware, and clothing. They decorated the walls and other features of mosques and palaces with intricate designs.

Arabic calligraphy and arabesque designs are featured in the decoration on the inside of this mosque.

A type of design called *arabesque* took its beauty from the natural world. In arabesque, artists crafted stems, leaves, flowers, and tendrils (threadlike parts of plants) into elegant patterns that were repeated over and over. Artists carved, painted, and wove arabesque designs into objects both large and small. Metal boxes, ceramic bowls, tiles, carpets, and even entire walls displayed intricate arabesque designs.

Artists also used geometric shapes in their designs. Circles, triangles, squares, and hexagons had special meaning to Muslims. Artists used simple tools—rulers and compasses—to create abstract designs from these shapes. This basic design was then repeated and combined to create a complex pattern.

Calligraphy For Muslims, the highest form of decorative art was calligraphy, the art of beautiful handwriting. When Muslims began copying the Qur'an, they felt that only calligraphy was worthy to record the words of God. For this reason, they honored calligraphers above other artists.

Calligraphers used sharpened reeds or bamboo dipped in ink to write on parchment and paper. Some forms of calligraphy had letters with angles. Most featured round letters and cursive writing, in which the script flowed, and letters within words were connected.

In addition to copying the Qur'an, artists used calligraphy to decorate everyday items. They put elegantly written lines of poetry on pottery, tiles, and swords. Bands of calligraphy trimmed the borders of fabric. Calligraphy even adorned coins, which often featured verses from the Qur'an.

Verses of the Qur'an also decorated mosques. Sometimes, the holy verses were engraved along the tops of exterior walls or they circled the inside dome of the mosque.

Textiles Manufactured fabrics, or textiles, had long been important to Arab people as practical items and as trade goods. Muslims in medieval times brought great artistry to making textiles. Weavers wove wool, linen, silk, and cotton into cloth, and then dyed it in vivid colors. Valuable cloths sometimes featured long bands of inscriptions or designs showing important events. Fabrics were also embroidered, often with gold thread.

As is still often the case today, clothes showed rank, and served as status symbols in the Muslim world. The caliph and his court wore robes made of the most valuable materials. Fine textiles served as awnings and carpets in the royal palace.

The lute, or *oud,* shown in this illustration, is a popular instrument in Muslim music.

Music in Muslim Spain There were several centers of music in the Islamic world, including Baghdad and Damascus. Persian musical styles were very influential in the cities of the east. But in Cordoba, Spain, a unique style developed that blended elements of Arab and native Spanish cultures.

A key figure in this cultural innovation was Ziryab, a talented musician and singer from Baghdad. Ziryab re-settled in Cordoba in 822. There, he established Europe's first conservatory, or music school. Musicians from Asia and Africa came to Cordoba to learn from the great Ziryab. Many of his students were then hired as entertainers at royal courts in other parts of the world.

Singing was an essential part of Muslim Spain's musical culture. Musicians and poets worked together to create songs about love, nature, and the glory of the empire. Vocalists performed the songs accompanied by such instruments as drums, flutes, and lutes. Although this music is lost today, it undoubtedly influenced later musical forms in Europe and North Africa.

9.11 Recreation

Recreation was also part of medieval Islamic culture. Two favorite pastimes that Muslims helped popularize were polo and chess.

Polo Muslims first learned about the game of polo from the Persians. Polo is a sport in which teams on horseback use mallets (long wooden hammers) to strike a ball through a goal. Muslims looked at horses as status symbols, and polo quickly became popular among the wealthy. For example, Abbasid rulers began to raise champion Arabian horses to play polo. Muslims adapted and refined the game of polo. Today, the game is enjoyed all over the world.

Chess The game of chess was probably invented in India. Persians introduced the game to the Muslim world in the mid-600s. It quickly became popular at all levels of society. Caliphs invited chess champions, even women and slaves, to their palaces to play in matches. Players enjoyed the **intellectual** challenge that chess presented.

Chess is a battle of wits in which players move pieces on a board according to complex rules. Each player commands a small army of pieces, one of which is the king. The goal is to checkmate the opponent's king. *Checkmate* means that the king cannot move without being captured.

As with polo, Muslims adapted and improved the game of chess. They spread it across Muslim lands and introduced it to Europe. Chess remains one of the world's most popular board games.

This illustration of two men playing chess is from a medieval book. The board is shown flipped up so that readers could analyze the players' positions in the game.

Muslim people greatly influenced the course of history as they traveled from place to place, carrying cultural influences and goods between Asia and Europe.

Chapter Summary

In this chapter, you learned about many contributions Muslims have made to world civilization. In a variety of fields, Islamic culture has left a lasting mark.

The Flowering of Islamic Civilization Arab conquests created a vast Muslim empire. Although the empire did not last as a political unit, Islamic civilization thrived. Muslim rulers built great cities. Cultural diffusion occurred due to the location of Muslim lands where trade routes connected Asia and Europe. This allowed a flow of new ideas.

Architecture, Scholarship, Learning, Science, and Technology Muslims made a number of advances in city building, architecture, technology, and the sciences. Muslim cities became important centers of culture and scholarship, where ancient learning could be preserved and shared. Scientists very accurately measured the circumference of Earth and studied subjects such as logic, zoology, and astronomy.

Geography, Navigation, Mathematics, and Medicine Muslim scientists built on the work of Indians and Greeks, adapting and improving devices such as the compass and astrolabe. Muslim mathematicians developed a new type of math called algebra. Doctors, too, improved on ancient knowledge. Many of these advances had a major influence on Europe.

Bookmaking, Literature, Art, Music, and Recreation Having learned paper making from the Chinese, Muslims created beautiful books. Writers composed works of both poetry and prose. The religious poetry of Sufis celebrated the love of God. Muslim artists and craftspeople created distinctive forms of decorative art. A unique style of music developed that combined Arabic and Spanish influences. Two of medieval Muslims' favorite pastimes, polo and chess, are still enjoyed around the world.

Many of the foods we eat today, as well as spices such as these, originally came from or through the Middle East.

History at the Dinner Table

Books, movies, and even computer games can tell you a lot about past cultures and civilizations. You can also learn from what is on the dinner table. The foods we eat have a unique history. Even the ways we eat have roots in the past. Nearly every culture has contributed to world cuisine, or cooking. Suppose that you checked a world encyclopedia of food. What might you find in the entry for the Middle East?

In an encyclopedia of world foods, under "the Middle East," you might find the story of Ibrahim ibn al-Mahdi. Al-Mahdi was a famous Muslim poet and singer who lived in the 800s. He was also a gourmet, or a person who loves fine food. Al-Mahdi was the uncle of Caliph al-Ma'mun who ruled the Abbasid Empire from the capital city of Baghdad. Al-Ma'mun invited his uncle to live at his court. There, al-Mahdi took charge of planning the caliph's feasts.

The chefs of the court had an amazing variety of meats, grains, fruits, and vegetables in their kitchens and storerooms. The geography of the Middle East was ideal for growing certain kinds of food. The climate was temperate and the growing season was long. Fig and date trees thrived. Their fruits appealed to people because of their natural sweetness and because they kept relatively well. Watermelons, oranges, limes, lemons, bananas, mangoes, apricots, plantains, and apples were abundant. Vegetables, such as eggplants, artichokes, and spinach, were also plentiful.

Foods from Other Lands

The Middle East was at the crossroads of several major trade routes that connected Asia and the Mediterranean world. Because of this, al-Mahdi and the caliph's chefs were able to serve many dishes from other lands. They had melons shipped from Europe in metal boxes filled with snow, like modern coolers, to preserve the fresh fruit. They served jams and fruit preserves from around Southern Asia. They ate eggplant, which came from India. They sweetened many recipes with sugar, which also came from India.

Many of the foods they served at the royal court in Baghdad had arrived there as a result of cultural diffusion. This is the process by which foods, songs, stories, poems, plants, animals, and other cultural features move from one region to another. Cultural diffusion enriches civilizations all over the world.

Caliph al-Ma'mun's table was so varied because, for many years, Muslim merchants imported foods from Africa and Asia. When Muslims conquered Persia, they discovered that the Persians had many delicious recipes. Bit by bit, Muslims adopted them. By the time of Caliph al-Ma'mun, people in Muslim lands ate Persian dishes all the time. They cooked stews that combined lamb with vegetables, herbs, and spices. They baked using a tandoor oven, which is cylinder-shaped and creates a steady, high, even heat.

One imported food that became very important to the Middle Eastern diet was sugar. Muslim merchants brought it from India. Farmers quickly mastered the art of growing sugar cane. By the 13th century, Middle Easterners improved methods of refining sugar cane to make better sugar. Sugar became an essential ingredient in Middle Eastern cooking. Chefs also sweetened stews by adding dates or honey.

In addition to sugar, Muslim merchants brought home from their travels eggplants, bananas, spinach, and watermelons, among other foods. Chefs then included these foods in recipes they developed. For example, during the 9th century, Muslim merchants brought eggplants from India. People hated them at first. They said the odd-looking vegetable had "the color of a scorpion's belly and the taste of a scorpion's sting." However, people in Muslim lands gradually developed a taste for eggplant. Today, it is among the main vegetables used in the region's cuisine.

Popular foods, such as pita bread (left), chick peas (top), and hummus (center), all came from the Middle East.

During a traditional Middle Eastern meal, people may sit on the floor and eat together from a number of dishes.

Arab and Muslim Traditions in Food

It is not only what people eat that can tell us about history. The way people eat can also tell a story. A long-standing tradition in the Muslim world, for example, is for people to eat with their right hands. In the caliphs' time, people held food between their thumbs and first and second fingers. It was very rude to eat with the left hand. People washed the food down with water flavored with mint, roses, or lemons. They did not drink beer or wine, which the Qur'an forbids.

Religion played an important role in deciding how and what Muslims ate. In addition to alcohol, the Qur'an does not allow Muslims to eat pork. Instead, the most common meat was lamb, though people also ate some veal and chicken. Muslim butchers had to cut the meats in certain ways to ensure cleanliness. Meats prepared according to these rules were called *halal,* or "allowed." Halal foods are still important in Muslim culture today.

Caliph al-Ma'mun enjoyed feasts, but he was also wise enough to know that most people in Baghdad couldn't afford the types of food served at court. He took seriously the Third Pillar of Islam, *zakat,* which calls for Muslims to share their wealth. One evening, al-Ma'mun went to al-Mahdi's house for dinner. Al-Mahdi served a dish made with the tongues of hundreds of small fish. The dish was delicious, but the caliph thought it was terribly wasteful. He remembered the prophet Muhammad's words that the wealthy should share with the poor. So, he ordered al-Mahdi's servants to hand out 1,000 silver pieces to needy people in Baghdad. He also gave away the expensive plate on which the dish was served.

Al-Ma'mun wasn't the only Muslim leader to relate issues of food to the Third Pillar of Islam. A later caliph named al-Mutawakkil, who died in 861, lived in a palace next to a canal. One day, the caliph smelled a wonderful aroma. He looked out and saw that a sailor and his cook were preparing a stew on the sailor's small boat. The caliph ordered the sailor to bring the stew to him. He ate it and exclaimed that it was the best meal he had ever eaten, even though it had simple ingredients. To thank the sailor and cook, he directed his servants to fill their stewpot with silver coins.

Cuisine for the World

Stories like this show that food and cooking have been central to Muslim culture for more than a thousand years. Throughout those years, Middle Easterners participated in another kind of cultural diffusion. In addition to importing foods, they sent food to the rest of the world. For example, when Muslims conquered Spain and Portugal during the 8th century, they introduced sugar to Europe. The word *sugar* comes from the Arab word *al-sukkar.* Other words related to sugar also have an Arabic origin, including *syrup, caramel, sherbet,* and *candy.* Muslims also introduced eggplants, watermelons, rice, lemons, and other vegetables and fruits to Europe.

Another food that peoples of the Middle East introduced was pita bread, which is common in the United States today. Pita bread is baked without yeast so that it doesn't rise, remaining flat. In an American restaurant today, you also might eat falafel, which is a fried ball or patty made of chickpeas and flavored with various spices. A popular dip is the Middle Eastern hummus, also made from chickpeas.

The Cultural Diffusion Continues

Today, Middle Easterners still exchange foods with the rest of the world. In 2004, a Jordanian man named Fadi Jaber visited the United States. While here, he ate a cupcake. In 2007, he started selling cupcakes in Jordan, his native country in the Middle East. Fadi had to educate some of his customers, who thought that the cupcakes were muffins. But no matter what people called them, they flew off the shelves. Soon, Jaber opened shops in Dubai in the United Arab Emirates and in Beirut, the capital and largest city in Lebanon. Shops that sell only cupcakes first became popular in the United States and spread to Australia, South Korea, Italy, Germany—and also to the Middle East. Jaber brought a sweet treat back to his homeland, completing a cycle of cultural diffusion that began many centuries ago.

Jordanian businessman Fadi Jaber, shown here in front of one of his stores, brought the cupcake from the United States to the Middle East.

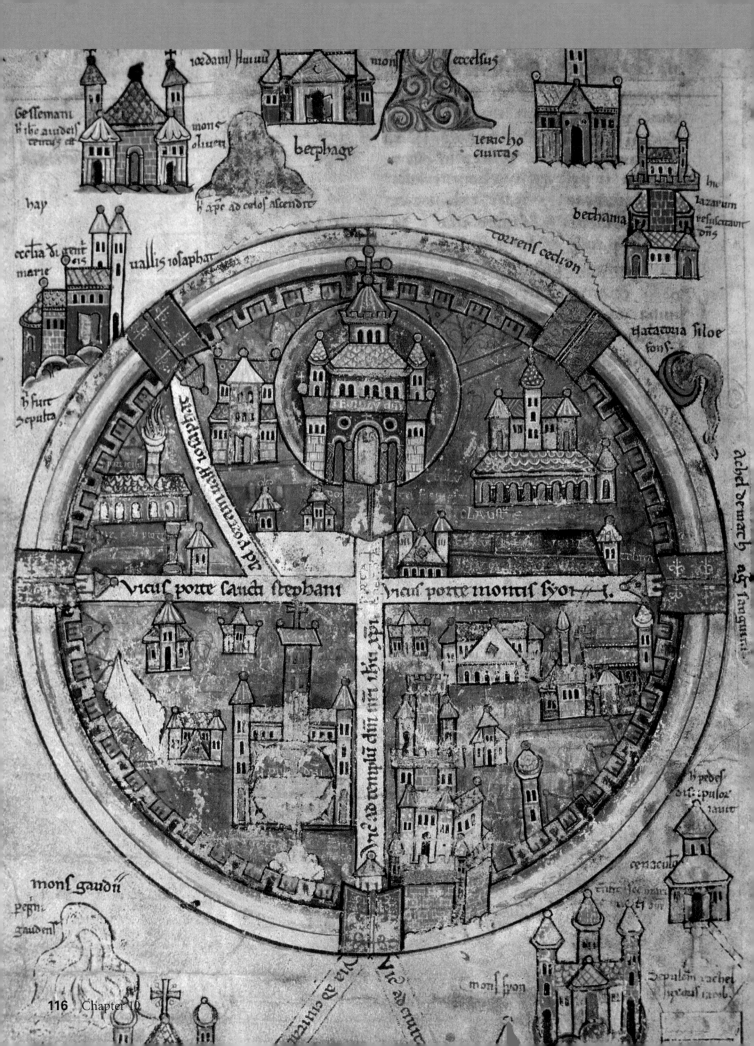

Chapter 10

From the Crusades to New Muslim Empires

How did the Crusades affect the lives of Christians, Muslims, and Jews?

10.1 Introduction

In this chapter, you will learn about a series of religious wars, the Crusades, that took place during the Middle Ages. The Crusades were launched by European Christians to reclaim Jerusalem and other holy sites in the Middle East from Muslims.

Christians mounted these religious wars between 1096 and 1291. A major purpose was to gain control of Palestine. This area is the ancient homeland of Jews and the place where Jesus lived. The spiritual heart of Palestine was the city of Jerusalem. As you will learn, the city was, and is, sacred to Jews, Christians, and Muslims alike.

In the 11th century, Palestine came under the rule of a rising Muslim power, the Seljuk Turks. They were building a huge empire and treating Christians badly. The advances of the Seljuk Turks into Byzantine territory, and their ill treatment of Christians, alarmed the Byzantine emperor. In 1076, the Seljuks took Jerusalem. In 1095, the emperor asked Pope Urban II for help. The pope called on Christians to go on a religious war to turn back the Seljuks and win control of Jerusalem and the surrounding area. The next year, the first armies set out from Europe.

Muslims were not the only targets of these religious wars. Europeans also mounted violent campaigns against Jews and Christian heretics. Religious wars were waged in Europe and North Africa, as well as the Middle East.

In this chapter, you will read the story of these religious wars. You will explore the effects of this warfare on Christians, Muslims, and Jews. You will also learn how new Muslim empires arose after the wars, and how Islam continued to spread to new parts of the world.

Two important religious sites stand near each other in Jerusalem. Muslims believe that Muhammad ascended to heaven at the site of the gold-roofed Dome of the Rock. In the foreground, Jews gather to pray at the Western Wall, the remains of their ancient Temple. It is the holiest place in the world for Jews.

◀ This 12th-century map shows the city of Jerusalem, which is holy to Jews, Christians, and Muslims.

Crusades a series of religious wars launched by European Christians to reclaim Jerusalem and other holy sites from Muslims

sultan the supreme ruler of a Muslim state

Holy Land the area between Egypt and Syria that was the ancient homeland of Jews and the place where Jesus Christ had lived; also called Palestine

10.2 Events Leading Up to the Crusades

Why did European Christians begin the religious wars, or **Crusades**, at the end of the 11th century? To answer this question, we need to look at what was happening in Muslim lands at the time.

During the 11th century, the Seljuk Turks established a new Muslim dynasty. The Turks were a Central Asian people who had been migrating into Muslim lands for centuries. The Seljuks were named for a Turkish chieftain who converted to Islam in the mid-11th century. In 1055, his descendants took control of the Abbasid dynasty's capital of Baghdad in what was then Persia. A Seljuk **sultan** now ruled the old Abbasid Empire.

The Seljuks were eager to expand their territory. Moving westward, they took Syria and Palestine from the Fatimid dynasty. They also overran much of Anatolia (also called Asia Minor), which was part of the Byzantine Empire. In 1071, the Seljuks defeated a large Byzantine army at Manzikert in present-day Turkey.

The Seljuk advance alarmed Christians in Europe. They feared for the safety and property of Christians living to the east. The Seljuks' growing power seemed to threaten the Byzantine Empire itself. Christians also worried about the fate of the **Holy Land,** especially the city of Jerusalem, where the Seljuks treated Christians and their holy sites with intolerance.

As it is today, Jerusalem was a sacred city to Jews, Christians, and Muslims. It was the spiritual capital of the Jews, where their great Temple had once stood. It had also been their political capital in ancient times. For Christians, it was the city where Jesus was crucified and arose from the dead. For Muslims, it was where Muhammad ascended to heaven during his Night Journey.

Jerusalem and the rest of Palestine first came under Muslim rule during the Arab conquests of the 7th century. Muslims built a shrine in Jerusalem, called the Dome of the Rock, to mark the spot where they believed that the Night Journey had occurred. Under Muslim rule, Jews, Christians, and Muslims usually lived together peacefully. People of all three faiths made pilgrimages to Jerusalem and built houses of worship there. Depending on the policies of various Muslim rulers, however, non-Muslims' rights and freedoms varied from time to time. Some Muslim rulers allowed the destruction of important Christian churches.

After the Seljuks took control of Palestine, political turmoil made travel unsafe. Tales began reaching Europe of highway robbers attacking and even killing Christian pilgrims. Christians feared they would no longer be able to visit Jerusalem and other sacred sites in the Holy Land. Together, with concern over the Seljuk threat to Christian lands in Europe, this fear helped pave the way for the Crusades.

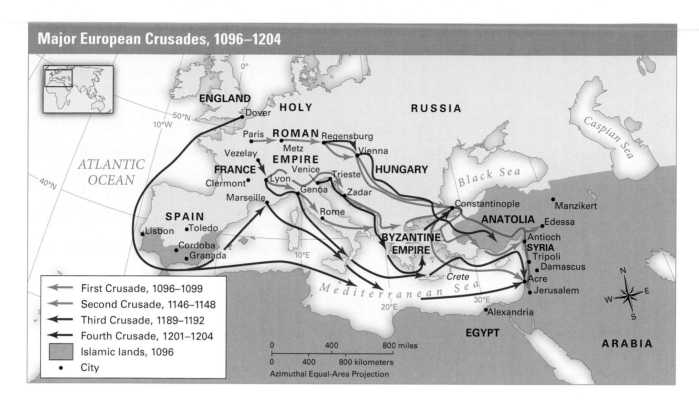

Major European Crusades, 1096–1204

Legend:
- First Crusade, 1096–1099
- Second Crusade, 1146–1148
- Third Crusade, 1189–1192
- Fourth Crusade, 1201–1204
- Islamic lands, 1096
- City

Azimuthal Equal-Area Projection

10.3 The Story of the Crusades

The Crusades began as a **response** to the threat posed by the Seljuks. By 1095, the Seljuks had advanced to within 100 miles of the Byzantine capital, Constantinople. The emperor appealed to Pope Urban II for help.

The pope invited nobles and Church leaders to attend a council in Clermont, France. There, he called for a crusade to drive out the Muslims and reclaim Jerusalem. He promised entry to heaven to all who joined the fight.

French-speaking nobles quickly organized armies to fight in the Holy Land. In addition to trained knights, thousands of townspeople, craftsmen, and peasants joined the crusade.

Throughout the Crusades, the Christian faith inspired many to put on the red cross, worn by Crusaders as a symbol of their mission, and join the fight. But people joined the Crusades for other reasons as well. Merchants saw the chance to earn money through trade. Younger sons of nobles hoped to gain estates in the Holy Land. A person who had fought in the Holy Land also gained respect and prestige at home.

The First Crusade (1096–1099) Four European nobles led the First Crusade. Close to 30,000 Crusaders fought their way through Anatolia, and headed south toward Palestine. In June of 1098, the Crusaders laid siege to the city of Antioch in Syria. Antioch was protected by a ring of walls. After nine months, the Crusaders found a way over the walls. Antioch fell to the Christians.

For more than 200 years, in four major Crusades, Europeans and Muslims clashed over control of the Holy Land and the nearby territory. In the end, Muslims retained control of the area.

In 1099, the Crusaders surrounded Jerusalem and scaled the city walls. After a month of fighting, the city surrendered. The victorious Crusaders killed most of the people who had fought against them. They sold the survivors into slavery. With Jerusalem taken, most of the Crusaders went home. Some, however, stayed behind. They established four Crusader kingdoms in Palestine, Syria, and modern-day Lebanon and Turkey.

The Second Crusade (1146–1148) The Crusaders owed their early victories, in part, to a lack of unity among Muslim groups. When the Crusades began, the Seljuk empire was already crumbling into a number of smaller states. Muslims had trouble joining together to fight the invaders.

When Muslims started to band together, they were able to fight back more effectively. In 1144, they captured Edessa, the capital of the northernmost crusader kingdom. Christians answered by mounting the Second Crusade.

That Crusade ended in failure. An army from Germany was badly defeated in Anatolia. A second army, led by the king of France, arrived in Jerusalem in 1148. About 50,000 Crusaders marched on the city of Damascus, which was on the way to Edessa. Muslims from Edessa came to the city's aid and beat back the Crusaders. Soon after this defeat, the French army went home, ending the Second Crusade.

Richard I, king of England, led the Third Crusade to try to regain Christian control of Jerusalem from Muslims.

The Third Crusade (1189–1192) Over the next few decades, Muslims in the Middle East increasingly came under common leadership. By the 1180s, the great sultan Salah al-Din (SAL-eh ahl-DEEN), called Saladin by Europeans, had formed the largest Muslim empire since the Seljuks. Salah al-Din united Egypt, Syria, and other lands to the east. He led a renewed fight against the Crusaders in the Holy Land. Salah al-Din quickly took back most of Palestine. In 1187, his armies captured Jerusalem.

The loss of Jerusalem shocked Europeans and sparked the Third Crusade. King Richard I of England, known as "the Lionheart," led the European fight against Salah al-Din.

In 1191, Richard's army forced the surrender of the Palestinian town of Acre (AH-kreh). Afterward, arrangements were made between the two sides to exchange prisoners. When Richard lost patience waiting for Salah al-Din to complete the exchange, Richard ordered the deaths of all 2,700 of his Muslim prisoners.

Richard then fought his way toward Jerusalem, but his army was not strong enough to attack the city. Salah al-Din's forces had also grown weaker. In September 1192, the two leaders signed a peace treaty. The Crusaders kept a chain of cities along the coast of Palestine. Muslims agreed to let Christian pilgrims enter Jerusalem.

Later Crusades The Crusades continued for another 100 years. Some Crusades were popular movements of poor people, rather than organized military campaigns. In 1212, for example, thousands of peasant children from France and Germany marched in a Children's Crusade. Few, if any, ever reached the Holy Land. Some made it to European port cities, only to be sold into slavery by merchants. Some returned home. Many disappeared without a trace.

None of the later Crusades succeeded in recapturing Jerusalem. Muslims, meanwhile, were gaining back the land they had lost. In 1291, they took Acre, the last Crusader city. This victory ended some two hundred years of Christian kingdoms in the Holy Land.

The Reconquista Crusaders fought against Muslims in Europe and North Africa, as well as in the Middle East. One important series of wars was called the *Reconquista* (ree-con-KEE-stah), which means "reconquest" in Spanish. Christians launched these wars to retake the Iberian Peninsula from Muslims. The Iberian Peninsula is a region in southwestern Europe that contains Spain and Portugal.

The Umayyads had established a Muslim dynasty in Spain in the 8th century, where Muslims, Jews, and Christians lived together in peace. However, non-Muslims had to pay a special tax.

Over time, Christian rulers in northern Iberia chipped away at Muslim lands. The pace of reconquest quickened after the Umayyad caliphate in Cordoba broke up into rival kingdoms in 1002. In 1085, Christians gained a key victory by capturing Toledo, in central Spain.

Muslims gradually gave up more and more territory, and new Muslim dynasties were intolerant of Jews and Christians. In 1039, Portugal became an independent Christian kingdom. By 1248, only the kingdom of Granada, in southern Spain, remained in Muslim hands.

Many Jews and Muslims remained in areas ruled by Christians. In the late 1400s, Queen Isabella and King Ferdinand wanted to unite Spain as a Catholic country. They used the **Inquisition,** a Roman Catholic court, against Muslims and Jews who claimed to have converted to Christianity. The Spanish Inquisition was extremely harsh. Judges, called inquisitors, sometimes used torture to find out whether supposed converts were practicing their old religion. Thousands of people were burned at the stake.

In 1492, Granada fell to Ferdinand and Isabella, ending Muslim rule in Spain. In the same year, Jews were ordered to become Catholics or leave the country. More than 170,000 Jews left their homes forever. Many found refuge in Muslim lands, including in Constantinople, now called Istanbul, the capital of the Ottoman Empire. Muslims remained in Spain, but many were forced to become Catholics. Spain expelled remaining Muslims beginning in 1609. This expulsion ended centuries of cooperation among these groups and Christians in Spain.

Later Crusades, such as the Children's Crusade, were movements by poor people, rather than organized military events led by monarchs or nobles.

Inquisition a judicial body established by the Roman Catholic Church to combat forms of religious error

10.4 Christians and the Crusades

For Crusaders, the religious wars were a costly ordeal, although they promised rewards in the afterlife. But European Christians also reaped many benefits from the Crusades.

New foods and fabrics from Arabian seaports were introduced to Europe through the travels and trading of the Christian Crusaders.

Impact on Christians as a Group Crusaders suffered all the terrible effects of war. Many were wounded or killed in battle. Others died from disease and the hardships of travel.

The impact of the Crusades reached far beyond those who fought, however. The Crusades brought many **economic** changes to Europe. Crusaders needed a way to pay for supplies. Their need increased the use of money in Europe. Some knights began performing banking functions, such as making loans or investments. Monarchs started tax systems to raise funds for Crusades.

The Crusades changed society, as well. Monarchs grew more powerful, as nobles and knights left home to fight in the Middle East. The increasing power of monarchs weakened feudalism.

Contact with Middle Eastern cultures had a major impact on Christians' way of life. In the Holy Land, Christians learned about new foods and other goods. They dressed in clothing made of muslin, a cotton fabric from Persia. They developed a taste for melons, apricots, sesame seeds, and carob beans. They used spices, such as pepper. After Crusaders returned home with these goods, European merchants earned enormous profits by trading in them.

The Experiences of Individuals You have already learned how Richard I of England led the Third Crusade. Richard was devoted to the Christian cause and to knightly ideals of courage and honor. To pay for his armies, he taxed his people heavily. Both ruthless and brave, Richard spent most of his reign fighting in the Crusades.

Anna Comnena, the daughter of a Byzantine emperor, wrote about her experiences during the First Crusade. She expressed mixed feelings about the Crusaders. She respected them as Christians, but she also realized that many were dangerous. She questioned whether all of the Crusaders were truly fighting for God. She thought that some sought wealth, land, or glory in battle. Her suspicions proved to be justified. During the Fourth Crusade, a force of Crusaders invaded and looted Constantinople, then under Christian control.

10.5 Muslims and the Crusades

The Crusades brought fewer benefits to Muslims than they did to Christians. Muslims succeeded in driving the Crusaders from the Middle East, but they lost their lands on the Iberian Peninsula. In addition, the contact between cultures benefited Muslims less than Christians. At the time, Muslim societies were among the most advanced in the world, so Muslims had less to gain.

Impact on Muslims as a Group The Crusades were a terrible ordeal for many Muslims. An unknown number lost their lives in battles and the conquests of Middle Eastern cities. Crusaders also destroyed Muslim property in Jerusalem and other communities.

Muslims did gain exposure to some new weapons and military ideas during the Crusades. Like Europeans, they began to adopt standing, or permanent, armies. Muslim merchants, especially in Syria and Egypt, earned riches from trade with Europe. This money helped to fund building projects, such as new mosques and religious schools. The Crusades also brought political changes, as Muslims united to fight their common foe. The Ayyubid dynasty founded by Salah al-Din ruled Egypt and parts of Syria and Arabia until 1250.

The Experiences of Individuals Salah al-Din was the greatest Muslim leader during the Crusades. His experiences taught him many valuable lessons. As a boy in Damascus during the Second Crusade, he saw that Muslims needed to defend themselves and Islam. As a soldier, he realized that Muslims had to be organized and to cooperate with one another. He unified Muslim groups under his strong leadership. Along with his military skills, Salah al-Din also was famed for his courtesy.

Usamah ibn-Munqidh also grew up during the time of the Crusades. Believing it was the will of God, Usamah fought against the Crusaders. At the same time, he respected both Christians and Jews because of their faith in one God. Usamah wrote a valuable account of the Crusades from a Muslim viewpoint. He told how Muslims and Christians observed and sometimes admired one another. He also described how the Muslims were willing to give their lives to protect their families, lands, and property from the Crusaders.

Christian Crusaders captured the city of Jerusalem during the First Crusade.

During the Crusades, there was a great deal of violence against Jews in Europe and elsewhere.

anti-Semitism hostility or discrimination against Jews

segregation the forced separation of one group from the rest of a community

10.6 Jews and the Crusades

Violence and intolerance during the Crusades made targets, not only of Christians who did not strictly follow Church teachings, but especially of non-Christians. In this climate, Jews suffered enormously. Some Church leaders spoke out strongly against ill treatment of Jews and warned Christians that the only aim of the Crusades was to reclaim the Holy Land. However, some Crusaders in the Holy Land killed Jews as well as Muslims. The Crusades also **dramatically** worsened the lives of Jews in Europe.

Impact on Jews as a Group During the First Crusade, European Jews suffered a series of violent persecutions. As Crusaders crossed northern France and Germany, some of them murdered whole communities of Jews. They destroyed synagogues and holy books. They looted homes and businesses. Some Crusaders tortured Jews to make them accept Christianity.

In Europe, **anti-Semitism,** or hostility to or discrimination against Jews, spread among non-Crusaders, as well. Religious prejudice was mixed with resentment of Jews who were wealthy bankers and traders. Riots and massacres broke out in a number of cities.

By the end of the Crusades, the Jews' place in European society had deteriorated. Jews could not hold public office. Christians took over trading businesses that had been run by Jews. In 1290, England expelled all Jews. France did the same in 1394. Many Jews relocated to Eastern Europe.

The **segregation** of Jews spread throughout Europe during the 14th and 15th centuries. Jews were forced to live in crowded neighborhoods called ghettos. Typically, walls and gates separated the ghettos from the rest of the town or city.

The Experiences of Individuals A German Jew named Eliezer ben Nathan lived during the First Crusade. He wrote about the violent destruction of his community by Christians. Eliezer told of Jews who killed their families and themselves rather than give up their religion. He admired their intense devotion, but wondered how God could let so many Jews die. He also expressed his hatred for the Crusaders.

Eleazar ben Judah, a Jewish scholar, also lived in Germany. During the Second Crusade, he and other Jews were forced to flee their town. They had to leave behind their belongings, including their holy books.

Several years later, two Crusaders attacked Eleazar's home and killed his wife and children. This horrible event led him to wonder if his people would be able to survive in Europe. As a Jewish leader in the city of Worms, he continued to preach love for all humanity, despite his suffering.

10.7 The Mongol Invasion

As you have learned, Muslims succeeded in driving the Crusaders from the Holy Land. Even as the Crusades were taking place, other changes were happening in Muslim lands. By the mid-1200s, Muslims were facing a greater threat than the European Crusaders—the Mongols.

The Mongols were a nomadic people whose homeland was north of China. In the 13th century, Mongols began wars of conquest under their leader, Genghis Khan (JENG-giss KAHN). After attacking northern China, Genghis Khan turned his sights westward. The Mongols swept across central Asia, destroying cities and farmland. Hundreds of thousands of Muslims were killed. Many were carried off to Mongolia as slaves.

Under Genghis Khan's successors, the Mongols built an empire that stretched across much of Asia. They defeated the Seljuk Turks in Anatolia and seized parts of Persia. In 1258, they destroyed Baghdad and killed the sultan.

This contemporary statue of Genghis Khan is located in Ulaanbaatar, the modern capital of Mongolia.

Farther west, Muslims were able to stop the Mongol advance. The Mamluks, Turks whose capital was at Cairo, Egypt, led the resistance. In the mid-1200s, they had overthrown the dynasty begun by Salah al-Din. In 1260, they defeated the Mongols in an important battle in Palestine. The Mamluks continued to rule Palestine, Egypt, Syria, Arabia, and parts of Anatolia until 1517.

The Mongols still ruled a huge empire in Asia, including China. Toward the end of the 1200s, in some places they began converting to Islam. The adoption of Islam helped bring unity to their empire. The Mongols made Persian the language of government. They rebuilt the cities they had destroyed and encouraged learning, the arts, and trade.

The Mongol empire was one of the largest the world had ever seen. It suffered, however, from in-fighting among rivals. Local rulers controlled different regions. By the mid-1300s, the empire was badly weakened. In the next section, you will learn about new empires that arose in Muslim lands during the next few centuries.

Mongol leader Timur Lang led an invasion of Anatolia in 1402. His armies prevented the Ottoman Turks from advancing eastward.

shah a ruler in certain Middle East lands, especially Persia (modern-day Iran)

10.8 New Muslim Empires and the Expansion of Islam

New empires arose in Muslim lands after the decline of the Mongols' power. Islam also continued its spread to new lands.

The Ottoman Empire In the early 1300s, a Turk named Osman I started the Ottoman dynasty in northern Anatolia. The Ottomans quickly conquered new lands in Anatolia and southeastern Europe.

The Ottomans' advance to the east was stopped for a time by a new enemy—Timur (TEE-moor) Lang, known to Europeans as Tamerlane. Timur came from a Mongol tribe in central Asia. He claimed descent from Genghis Khan.

Timur began building his own empire in the late 1300s. His armies overran much of central Asia, including present-day Iraq. They then invaded India, Syria, and Anatolia. In 1402, Timur defeated an Ottoman army at Ankara in Anatolia. Ottoman rule was on the brink of collapse. But after Timur's death in 1405, the Ottomans regained control of their lands.

Turning back toward Europe, the Ottomans set out to expand their empire. In 1453, they captured Constantinople, bringing an end to the once powerful Byzantine Empire. The city was renamed Istanbul. It became the Ottoman capital.

In the 1500s, the Ottomans destroyed the Mamluk Empire. They conquered Syria, Palestine, Egypt, and Arabia. At its height, the Ottoman Empire also took in parts of southeastern Europe, North Africa, and Persia, as well as Turkey.

The Ottomans allowed their subjects considerable freedom. Jews, Christians, and Muslims had their own local communities, called *millets*. Millets were allowed to govern themselves. A ruling class collected taxes and protected the sultan and the empire. In the empire's European provinces, some young Christian men were drafted and then raised in the sultan's palace. After most of them converted to Islam, they joined an elite corps of soldiers and government officials known as Janissaries.

The Ottoman Empire slowly declined after about 1700. It finally came to an official end, after World War I, in 1922.

The Safavid Empire Later Ottoman expansion to the east was stopped by another Muslim power. In 1501, Muslims in Persia founded the Safavid dynasty. Their **shahs,** or rulers, soon controlled the heartlands of ancient Persia. This included modern-day Iran and parts of Iraq. Unlike the Ottomans, who were Sunni Muslims, the Safavids were Shi'ah. The two groups fought a number of wars.

The Safavids became a great power. They promoted trade, the arts, and learning. Their dynasty lasted until the mid 1700s.

The Mughal Empire A third Muslim empire was founded by Babur, a descendant of both Genghis Khan and Timur Lang. In 1526, Babur invaded India and founded the powerful Mughal [MOOG-uhl] Empire. The word *Mughal* is Arabic for "Mongol." Mughal emperors ruled most of India until sometime after 1700. Muslims make up a significant minority of India's population today.

The Further Spread of Islam Muslim dynasties grew up in other places, as well. Muslims in North Africa carried Islam into the region of West Africa. Pilgrims and merchants also spread Islam among peoples living around the Sahara.

Traders brought Islam across the Indian Ocean to Southeast Asia. By the late 1200s, there were Muslim kingdoms on the islands of Indonesia. Today, Indonesia has more Muslims than any other country in the world.

Major Muslim Empires, 900–1500

0 1,000 2,000 miles
0 1,000 2,000 kilometers
Eckert III Projection

EUROPE

Constantinople

Cairo

Makkah (Mecca)

AFRICA

ASIA

Delhi

20°N

Ottoman Empire
Savafid Empire
Mughal Empire
• City

INDIAN OCEAN

Sumatra

0°

60°E   80°E   100°E   Java

Three Muslim empires dominated eastern and central Asia and the eastern Mediterranean for over six hundred years. The Ottoman Empire lasted longest of all—until the early 20th century.

Chapter Summary

In this chapter, you learned about the series of medieval wars between European Christians and Middle Eastern Muslims over the Holy Land, known as the Crusades.

The Crusades European Christians began the Crusades to repel the Muslims and re-take the Holy Land. Between 1096 and 1291, a number of Crusades were fought in the Middle East. Crusaders won control of Jerusalem and set up Christian kingdoms in the region. In 1187, Muslims won back Jerusalem. By 1291, Muslims had recaptured all the Crusader cities.

Effects of the Crusades on Christians, Muslims, and Jews As a result of the Crusades, European monarchs gained power, weakening feudalism. The use of money increased. Jews suffered great hardship. Many were killed. Others lost their homes and property. Crusaders also waged war against Muslims in North Africa and Europe. During the Reconquista, Christians drove Muslims from Europe.

The Mongol Invasion In the 13th century, the nomadic Mongols under Genghis Khan and his descendants conquered vast areas of Muslim lands and ruled much of Asia.

New Muslim Empires and the Expansion of Islam After the Crusades and Mongol invasion, the Ottoman Turks built a great Muslim empire in the Middle East and southeastern Europe. The Safavid Empire arose in what is now Iran and Iraq. The Mughals brought Muslim rule to most of India. Islam also spread to West Africa and Indonesia.

Islam in Medieval Times

About 613 C.E.
Beginnings of Islam
Muhammad begins to preach Islam, a religion based on monotheism, but he meets much resistance, including a boycott and violence in Makkah.

632 C.E.
The Last Sermon
Muhammad dies shortly after leading his final pilgrimage to Makkah, where he delivers his Last Sermon.

About 570 C.E.
Muhammad's Birth
Muhammad is born in Makkah, an ancient place of worship on the Arabian Peninsula.

500 C.E.   600 C.E.   700 C.E.   800 C.E.   900 C.E.   1000 C.E.

About 610 C.E.
Call to Prophethood
According to Islamic teachings, Muhammad is praying in the Hira Cave when the angel Gabriel calls him to be a prophet, or messenger of God.

622 C.E.
Migration to Madinah
Muhammad and his followers, known as Muslims, move to Madinah and establish a Muslim community.

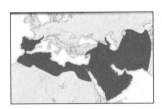

632–750 C.E.
Expansion of Islam
Islam expands as Muslims conquer lands in the Middle East, central Asia, the eastern Mediterranean, North Africa, and Spain.

About 651 C.E.
Official Version of Qur'an
Caliph Uthman establishes an official version of the Qur'an, the holy book of Islam.

About 825 C.E.
Al-Khwarizmi Invents Algebra
Arab scholar al-Khwarizmi invents algebra. His textbook is translated into Latin and becomes the most important mathematics textbook in European universities.

If $y = 6$
Solve for x:
$x + 2y = 20$

1192 C.E.
Peace Treaty
Ends Third Crusade
Richard the Lionheart, King of England and leader of the Crusaders, and Salah al-Din, leader of the Muslim forces, sign a peace treaty ending the Third Crusade.

| 1000 C.E. | 1100 C.E. | 1200 C.E. | 1300 C.E. | 1400 C.E. | 1500 C.E. |

750–1250 C.E.
Flourishing of Islamic Civilization
Islamic civilization flourishes as Muslims build great cities and spread knowledge and ideas to new lands through cultural diffusion.

1096–1291 C.E.
Christians Launch Crusades
European Christians launch a series of Crusades to recapture the Holy Land from Muslims.

1478 C.E.
Spanish Inquisition Begins
Queen Isabella and King Ferdinand begin the Spanish Inquisition, a church court intended to rid Spain of Muslims and Jews who have not fully converted to Christianity.

The Culture and Kingdoms of West Africa

Women dressed in traditional West African clothing stand in front of the Great Mosque of Djenne in present-day Mali. The mosque dates to the 13th century and is the largest mud brick building in the world.

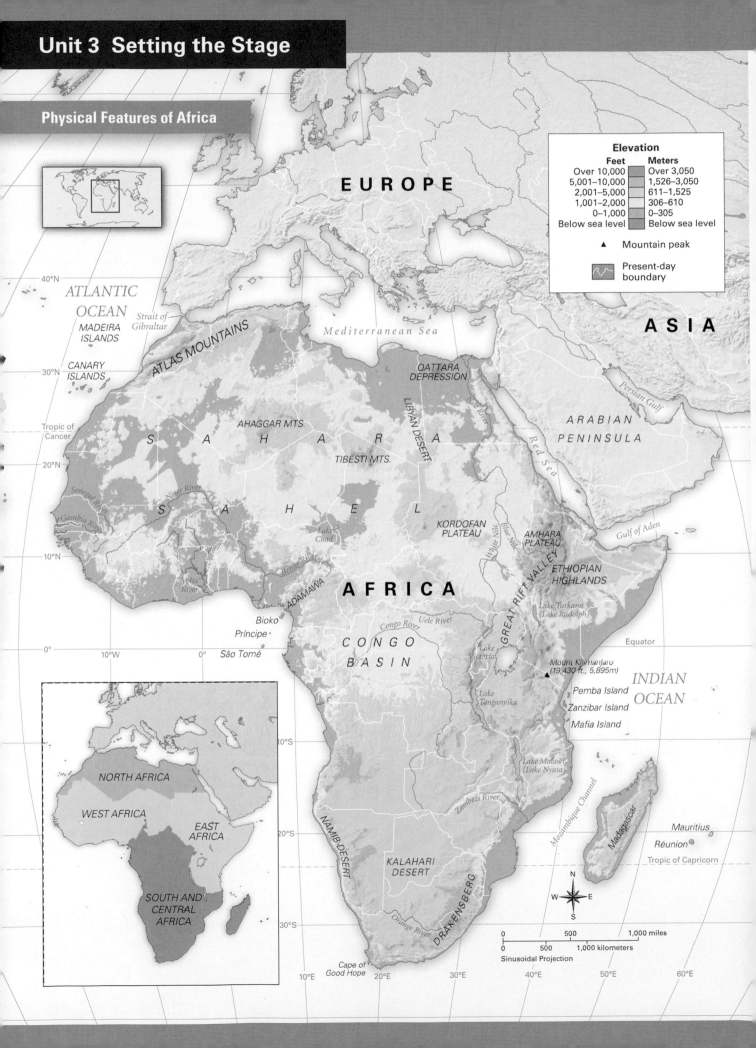

Physical Features of Africa

EUROPE

ASIA

Elevation

Feet	Meters
Over 10,000	Over 3,050
5,001–10,000	1,526–3,050
2,001–5,000	611–1,525
1,001–2,000	306–610
0–1,000	0–305
Below sea level	Below sea level

▲ Mountain peak

Present-day boundary

ATLANTIC
OCEAN

MADEIRA
ISLANDS

Strait of
Gibraltar

Mediterranean Sea

CANARY
ISLANDS

ATLAS MOUNTAINS

Tropic of
Cancer

S A H A R A

AHAGGAR MTS.

TIBESTI MTS.

QATTARA
DEPRESSION

LIBYAN DESERT

Nile River

ARABIAN
PENINSULA

Persian Gulf

Red Sea

Senegal R.

Gambia River

Niger River

S A H E L

Lake
Chad

Benue River

KORDOFAN
PLATEAU

White Nile

Blue Nile

AMHARA
PLATEAU

Gulf of Aden

ETHIOPIAN
HIGHLANDS

Volta
River

ADAMAWA

AFRICA

GREAT RIFT VALLEY

Lake Turkana
(Lake Rudolph)

Bioko

Príncipe

São Tomé

Congo River

Uele River

C O N G O
B A S I N

Lake
Victoria

Equator

Mount Kilimanjaro
(19,430 ft., 5,895m)

Pemba Island

Zanzibar Island

Mafia Island

INDIAN
OCEAN

Lake
Tanganyika

Lake Malawi
(Lake Nyasa)

NAMIB DESERT

Zambezi River

Mozambique Channel

Madagascar

Mauritius

Réunion

Tropic of Capricorn

KALAHARI
DESERT

DRAKENSBERG

Orange River

Cape of
Good Hope

Inset map

NORTH AFRICA

WEST AFRICA

EAST
AFRICA

SOUTH AND
CENTRAL
AFRICA

N

W   E

S

0	500	1,000 miles
0	500	1,000 kilometers

Sinusoidal Projection

40°N

30°N

20°N

10°N

0°

10°S

20°S

30°S

10°W   0°   10°E   20°E   30°E   40°E   50°E   60°E

The Culture and Kingdoms of West Africa

In this unit, you will explore the history of one of the regions to which Islam spread: the region of West Africa. West Africa is part of the continent of Africa, which, after Asia, is the largest continent on Earth. As you can see on the map on the opposite page, Africa is located south of Europe. The Atlantic Ocean borders Africa on the west. The Indian Ocean lies to the east.

Several vegetation zones form belts across Africa. Four zones in West Africa are especially important because of their influence on developing civilizations. These vegetation zones are desert, desert scrub, temperate grassland, and tropical grassland (or savanna). Find them on the map on this page. Listed below the map are definitions of these four vegetation zones.

In ancient times, farming communities developed in the grasslands south of the Sahara. This region is called the Sahel. Rivers, such as the Senegal and the Niger, helped make the land fertile. The rivers also provided fish and served as trade routes within the region.

For centuries, the people of West Africa had limited contact with lands to the north because travel across the Sahara was very difficult. By the late 700s, however, Arab Muslim traders from North Africa were crossing the Sahara. Trans-Saharan trade played a key role in the growth of the three great medieval kingdoms of West Africa: Ghana, Mali, and Songhai.

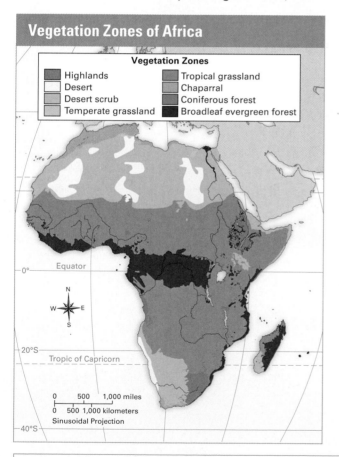

Vegetation Zones of Africa

Vegetation Zones
- Highlands
- Desert
- Desert scrub
- Temperate grassland
- Tropical grassland
- Chaparral
- Coniferous forest
- Broadleaf evergreen forest

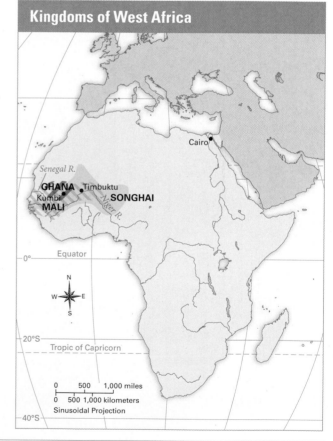

Kingdoms of West Africa

Cairo
Senegal R.
GHANA · Timbuktu
Kumbi · SONGHAI
MALI
Niger R.

West African Vegetation Zones

Desert: dry region with few plants

Desert scrub: small trees, bushes, and other plants adapted to a dry climate

Temperate grassland: short and tall grasses

Tropical grassland: grasses and scattered trees adapted to a tropical wet and dry climate

Chapter 11

Early Societies in West Africa

What was the most significant factor in the development of early societies in West Africa?

11.1 Introduction

In this unit, you will learn about West African cultures between about 500 and 1600 C.E. During this period, three kingdoms arose in West Africa: Ghana, Songhai, and Mali. In this chapter, you will explore how these kingdoms grew and developed.

People have lived in West Africa for hundreds of thousands of years. For most of this time, historians do not have written records to study. Muslim scholars first began writing about the kingdom of Ghana in the 800s. By then, Ghana was perhaps 300 years old, and possibly much older. How did the first kingdoms come to be? Why did they develop where they did?

To answer questions like these, historians and archeologists study many kinds of clues. For example, they look closely at geography. Natural features, such as rivers and vegetation, help explain where people chose to settle and what kind of life they created for themselves. Scholars also try to understand evidence from ancient settlements. How were villages and towns laid out? What can this tell us about life there?

Items left by earlier cultures also provide helpful clues about the past. Iron farming tools, for example, show that agricultural methods improved in West Africa. Scholars have worked to understand how more **efficient** farming affected the growth of towns and cities. Gradually, scholars have pieced together a picture of how complex societies developed in West Africa.

In this chapter, you will explore current thinking about the origins of West African kingdoms. You will discover how early family-based communities developed into villages and how some villages grew into towns and cities. You will see how some cities became great kingdoms.

Early West African societies produced fine crafts, such as pottery, sculpture, and items of iron and gold. This clay sculpture was made in the kingdom of Ghana.

◀ Archaeologists explore settlements like this to learn about early West Africa.

11.2 Geography and Trade

Geography offers many clues about why people settle where they do and how they live. It also helps to explain patterns of trade. As you will see throughout this chapter, trade played a key role in the growth of West African societies. Let's take a look at the geography of West Africa and its influence on trade.

Geography In the north, West Africa begins in the **Sahara**. To the west and south, the region is bordered by the Atlantic Ocean; and to the east, by the mountains of the present-day country of Cameroon. West Africa includes varied vegetation zones of desert, semidesert, savanna, and forest.

The Sahara spreads across approximately 3.5 million square miles in North Africa and the northern part of West Africa. Sand dunes cover one-quarter of the Sahara, but this desert also has bare, rocky plains, and even mountains. The Sahara is very dry except for some scattered oases, or water sources with some vegetation. As you can imagine, the Sahara was not a suitable place for large settlements.

South of the Sahara is a zone of semidesert called the **Sahel**. The Sahel is not as dry as the Sahara. It has enough water for short grasses and some small bushes and trees to survive.

The southern part of the Sahel merges into the **savanna,** an area of tall grasses and scattered trees. The savanna has a long rainy season. Because of the rain, grains such as millet, sorghum, and rice can be grown there. Grasses provide food for cattle, camels, goats, and sheep. Rivers, such as the long **Niger River,** help make nearby land fertile and also provide fish for eating.

The Niger River extends into the forest zone in the southern part of West Africa. This zone is wetter than the savanna. Its northern part is a woodland forest of trees and shrubs. Oil palms, yams, and kola trees grow here. The southern part of the zone is lush rainforest, where rain falls year-round. In the rainforest, tall trees—such as mahogany and teak—grow above swamps and lagoons.

Sahara a large, hot desert in North Africa that covers about 3.5 million square miles

Sahel a zone of semidesert, south of the Sahara, where short grasses, small bushes, and a few trees grow

savanna a vegetation zone of tall grasses and scattered trees, with a long rainy season

Niger River the longest river in West Africa, and a kind of trading highway in early times

As they did in the past, people still use canoes to travel along the Niger River.

Trade The geography of West Africa influenced the patterns of trade that developed there. Different resources are found in each of the vegetation zones. As a result, people living in different zones had to trade to get items they could not provide for themselves. For example, people on the savanna may have traded grains for yams or mahogany from forest dwellers.

Several major rivers served as trading routes in West Africa. The Niger is the region's longest river. It became a kind of trading highway. People in ancient times traveled the Niger and other rivers by canoe to trade goods. Some traders also crossed the Sahara from North Africa, but most early trade was among West African settlements.

Early West African villages might have had homes, such as these, built close together for protection.

11.3 Early Communities and Villages

By about 4000 B.C.E., some people had settled to farm south of the Sahara. The earliest farming communities were made up of extended families. An extended family includes close relatives, such as grandparents, as well as aunts, uncles, and their children.

An extended-family community might have had about fifteen to twenty members. Each community produced most of the things it needed. Family members worked together to clear the fields, plant seeds, and harvest crops. These small communities traded with one another for additional goods. Very likely, one of the male elders made decisions for the family community.

Over time, family-based communities joined together to form villages. A village might contain one- to two-hundred people. The village leader was probably chosen for his wisdom and strength.

Iron tools made farming more efficient. This allowed people to devote more time to weaving, still practiced today, as well as other crafts.

Nok a people living in West Africa in the 500s B.C.E. who mastered ironworking

artifact an item left by an earlier culture

smelting the process of melting ore to produce iron or other metals from it

Extended families usually banded together in villages to get needed help. For example, people might need to work together to control a flooding river or to mine for iron or gold. They may also have united for protection. Archeologists have discovered ruins of high walls and gates at the ancient West African village of Dhar Tichitt, in the present-day country of Mauritania. These structures suggest that the villagers united to defend themselves from attacks by outsiders.

11.4 The Development of Towns and Cities

Some West African villages gradually developed into towns and cities. Ancient cities in West Africa were not as large as modern cities, but some had thousands of residents. Why did villages grow into cities in West Africa? Two important reasons were the growth of ironworking and the expansion of trade.

Ironworking and Trade The Hittites of present-day Turkey mastered ironworking as long ago as 1500 B.C.E. Gradually, knowledge of ironworking spread. Eventually, it reached West Africa, perhaps by way of traders who crossed the Sahara. However, some scholars think that ironworking developed independently among people in the northern part of West Africa.

By the 500s B.C.E., a people called the **Nok** were making iron tools. The Nok lived in what is now central Nigeria. Archeologists have found some **artifacts** of their culture, such as their iron tools and iron-smelting furnaces.

Smelting is the **process** of melting ore to extract iron or other metals. The Nok used enormous amounts of charcoal to fuel their iron-smelting furnaces. The red-hot iron was then hammered and bent into useful shapes by skilled workers called blacksmiths. Nok blacksmiths made axes, hoes, and weapons, such as spears.

The valuable craft of ironworking spread rapidly throughout West Africa. The ability to make tools out of iron brought major changes. With iron tools, farmers could clear land and grow crops more efficiently than with stone tools. The greater abundance of food supported larger villages, where more people were free to work at other trades, such as weaving, metalworking, and pottery making.

More and more, villages produced surplus food and hand-crafted goods. They could then trade their surpluses for goods they could not produce themselves.

As goods traveled across West Africa, villages located along rivers or other easily traveled routes became important trading sites. Villages that controlled the trade routes became market centers, and the inhabitants grew very rich by charging fees for trading activity. These villages also drew many people to work at new jobs, such as supervising trade, learning crafts, and helping to construct public buildings.

Some of the villages grew into sizable towns and cities. Other large settlements grew up around natural resources, such as iron ore and good farmland.

The Ancient City of Jenne-jeno In 1977, archeologists began excavating the ancient West African city of **Jenne-jeno** (jen-NAH jen-OH). Built in the 3rd century B.C.E., Jenne-jeno existed for more than 1,600 years. Before it was rediscovered, historians thought that cities did not exist in West Africa until outsiders arrived and helped local people build them. The discovery of Jenne-jeno proved this theory wrong.

Jenne-jeno was built where the Niger River meets the Bani River. This was an ideal location for farming, fishing, and trade. The people of Jenne-jeno traded their surplus goods—such as catfish, fish oil, onions, and rice—for salt, iron ore, copper, and gold. The iron ore came from 50 miles away and the copper from 600 miles away.

Jenne-jeno grew into a busy city of about twenty thousand people. It was surrounded by a wall 10 feet wide and 13 feet high. The wall may have been built to give the city more status and to make it easier to control the comings and goings of traders.

The people of Jenne-jeno lived in circular houses. At first, they built the houses from bent poles and woven mats. Later, they used mud blocks.

The city's people worked at many crafts. Besides farmers and fishers, there were potters, metalsmiths, weavers, leatherworkers, bead makers, and ivory carvers.

The most respected people in Jenne-jeno were blacksmiths. The people of West Africa prized iron more than gold. They were amazed by blacksmiths' ability to make tools from iron. As in many other early cultures, early West Africans thought blacksmiths had supernatural (magical or godlike) powers. For this reason, blacksmiths had authority and many responsibilities. Blacksmiths acted as political leaders, judges, and doctors. Some were charged with **predicting** the future.

In recent years, scientists have studied the sites of other ancient cities in West Africa. They have found evidence of trade, craftsmanship, and great wealth.

The ancient city of Jenne-jeno was built on this floodplain on the Niger River, less than two miles from the modern city of Jenne.

Jenne-jeno an ancient West African city built along the Niger River

11.5 The Rise of Kingdoms and Empires

Trade was a major factor in the rise of West African kingdoms. Ghana, Mali, and Songhai were all trading powers that ruled over large areas. Historians often refer to them as empires, as well as kingdoms.

How did these first kingdoms develop? The rulers of some trading cities in West Africa became wealthy by collecting taxes from the goods that were bought and sold. With their wealth, they could afford to raise large armies. These armies could conquer other trading areas nearby. Then the ruler could take over the trade of those areas and become even wealthier.

Rulers also collected **tribute** from the people they conquered. The payment of tribute was a sign that the conquered people accepted the king's authority. Tribute could also pay for the king's protection from outside attackers.

West African kings were both the political and the religious leaders of their kingdoms. People believed that they had special powers given to them by the gods. The kings performed religious ceremonies to please the gods.

As a king conquered more territory, the kingdom grew into an empire. Sometimes, a king sent a governor to rule a conquered area. Sometimes, he allowed conquered people to rule themselves.

Becoming part of a kingdom or an empire had disadvantages. One was the obligation to pay tribute. Another was that men had to serve in the king's army. But there were advantages, as well. Kings provided protection for the conquered territory. Armies made sure that trade routes were safe, and they kept out raiders and foreign armies. Wars between small cities ended. Kings collected luxury goods from their subjects and distributed them fairly throughout the kingdom. They also gave expensive presents to their governors.

tribute payment made by one ruler or country to another for protection or as a sign of submission

These modern horsemen from West Africa are a reminder of the armies that rulers were able to raise with the wealth they received from trade.

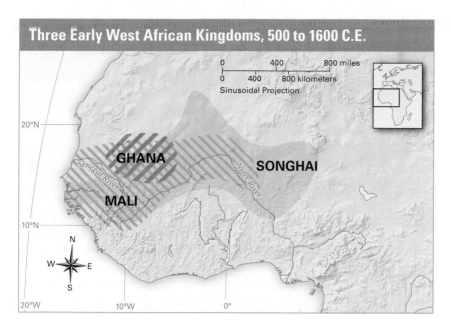

Three Early West African Kingdoms, 500 to 1600 C.E.

Three major kingdoms—Ghana, Songhai, and Mali—arose in West Africa between 500 and 1600 C.E.

The great kingdoms of West Africa did not rely only on local trade. By the time Ghana became an important power, trans-Saharan trade was bringing new wealth to West Africa from other regions, such as the present-day Middle East. Control of trade, particularly in West African gold, was also a key to the power of Mali. Songhai, too, relied on trade with distant lands.

Chapter Summary

In this chapter, you learned how kingdoms and empires grew out of early societies in West Africa.

Geography and Trade Geography was a major factor in the development of West African societies. Settled communities grew south of the Sahara, where the land permitted farming. Geography also influenced trading patterns. Communities traded with one another for items they could not produce locally. Rivers, such as the Niger, served as trade routes.

Early Communities Early societies in West Africa were family-based communities. Some of these communities joined together to form villages. Banding together in villages allowed people to take advantage of natural resources and to defend themselves from attack.

Towns and Cities Ironworking and trade helped some villages grow into sizable towns and cities. Iron tools allowed farmers to grow food more efficiently. As a result, more people could engage in other crafts. Villages traded their surplus goods for items they could not make themselves. Some villages became important trading sites and grew into cities. Others developed into large communities near important resources, such as iron ore or gold.

Kingdoms and Empires Trade brought some cities great wealth. The rulers of the wealthiest cities conquered neighboring areas, leading to the rise of kingdoms and empires. Rulers gained even more wealth through tribute, as well as by controlling trade.

Chapter 12

Ghana: A West African Trading Empire

To what extent did trans-Saharan trade lead to Ghana's wealth and success?

12.1 Introduction

The early West African societies of Ghana, Mali, and Songhai all created empires that gained much of their wealth from trade. In this chapter, you will learn more about the role of trade as you explore Ghana, the first of West Africa's empires.

The kingdom of Ghana lasted from sometime before 500 C.E. until its final collapse in the 1200s. It arose in the semidesert Sahel and eventually spread over the valley between the Senegal and Niger rivers. To the south was forest. To the north lay the Sahara. Today, this region is part of modern nations Mali and Mauritania (maw-reh-TAIN-ee-uh). The modern country of Ghana takes its name from the old kingdom, but it is located far to the south.

The earliest writings about the kingdom of Ghana come from Arab scholars. These scholars recorded information they had gathered from travelers to Ghana. By the time they began writing about Ghana in the 9th century, it was already a flourishing empire.

Historians do not know for certain how Ghana developed into an empire. Possibly, a group of warriors used iron weapons to defeat their neighbors. In fact, the word *ghana* means "war chief." We do know that control of trade, particularly the gold trade, made the king of Ghana and his people very wealthy. West Africans still sing songs about the majesty of ancient Ghana.

In this chapter, you will first learn about Ghana's government and military. Then you will learn how Ghana's people acquired wealth by participating in trans-Saharan trade. You will examine how trade led to Ghana's wealth and success. Finally, you will find out how Ghana declined and a new empire, Mali, arose in West Africa.

The medieval empire of Ghana included several large cities, such as Walata, the remains of which can be seen today.

◄ Camel caravans carried goods across the Sahara to and from medieval Ghana.

12.2 Ghana's Government and Military

Arab scholars described **Ghana** as a fabled "land of gold." Their accounts paint a picture of a rich kingdom with a strong government and a large and powerful army.

The King and His Government Ghana was ruled by a powerful king. The king was the head of the army and had the final say in matters of justice. He also led the people in religious worship.

Ghana's king acquired great wealth through control of the gold trade. Gold was especially plentiful in areas to the south of Ghana. As you will see, Ghana's government collected taxes on the gold that passed through the kingdom.

To preserve his wealth, the king tightly controlled the supply of gold. All the gold nuggets, or chunks, found in the kingdom had to be given to the king. Ordinary people could have only gold dust. One of the king's gold nuggets is said to have weighed almost forty pounds. According to legend, another was large enough to be used as a hitching post for his horse.

Each day, the king held court with his people. The king arrived at court to the beating of royal drums. He was splendidly dressed in colorful robes, gold jewelry, and a cap decorated with gold. His people showed their respect for him by kneeling and throwing dust on their heads as he approached.

Once at court, the king conducted the business of his empire and heard the people's concerns. One Arab historian described the scene at the court like this:

> *Behind the king stand ten pages [young servants] holding shields and swords decorated with gold and on his right are the sons of the vassal kings of his empire wearing splendid garments and their hair plaited [braided] with gold. The governor of the city sits on the ground before the king and around are ministers seated likewise. At the door . . . are dogs of excellent pedigree [ancestry] who hardly ever leave the place where the king is, guarding him. Round their necks, they wear collars of gold and silver.*

A large group of officials was paid from the kingdom's wealth to help the king govern. These officials were probably in charge of different parts of Ghana's society, such as the armed forces, industry, tax collection, and foreigners. The king appointed governors to rule some parts of his empire, such as the capital city and some conquered areas.

When the king died, his son did not inherit the throne. The royal inheritance was **matrilineal**, which means that it was traced through women's bloodlines rather than men's. Therefore, in Ghana, the son of the king's sister was the heir to the throne.

Ghana's kings wore caps like this one, decorated with gold.

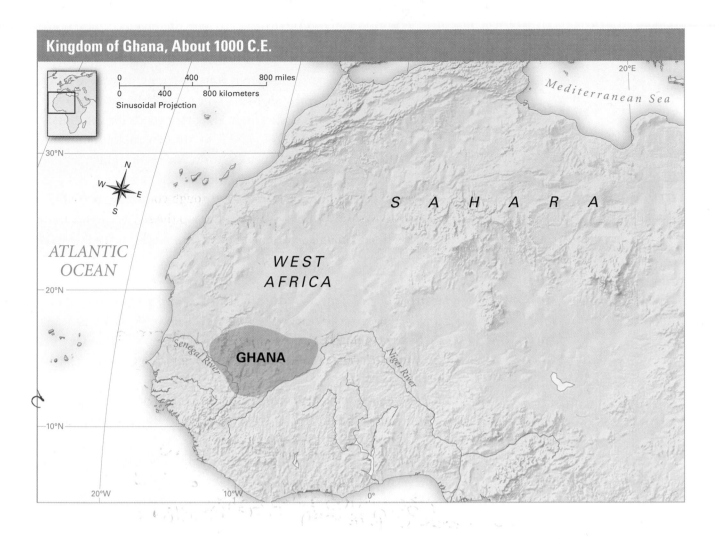

Kingdom of Ghana, About 1000 C.E.

Ghana's Military Ghana's military included a regular army, reserve forces, and elite soldiers. The regular army was made up of several thousand career soldiers. They kept the borders secure, put down minor revolts, and **maintained** peace and order. These soldiers wore knee-length cotton pants, sleeveless tunics (long shirts), sandals, and headdresses adorned with feathers. The color of a soldier's tunic and the number of feathers in his headdress indicated his rank. The soldiers used weapons such as spears, daggers, swords, battle clubs, and bows and arrows. They were well paid and highly respected.

During wartime, the king called up additional reserve forces and the troops of other governors under his rule. Every man in the empire was **required** to complete military training so that he would be ready to serve when called. Stories tell of a king who could call up an army of 200,000 warriors. This number no doubt grew as the story was passed on, but the king certainly could summon a sizable army.

Special groups of soldiers were selected for their courage, honesty, and intelligence. These soldiers served the king as bodyguards, escorts, and military advisors.

Its location at the crossroads of major trade routes south of the Sahara and along the rivers brought medieval Ghana great wealth and power.

12.3 Trade: The Source of Ghana's Wealth

Ghana was located between two areas that wanted to trade—North Africa and West Africa. Traders from North Africa crossed the Sahara with salt, copper, and cowrie shells—a type of seashell that was used as money. The merchants traded these and other goods for kola nuts, hides, leather goods, ivory, slaves, and gold from the southern forests of West Africa. Then they returned to North Africa, bringing the goods from the south to markets at home.

Ghana's location allowed it to control this **trans-Saharan trade**. Traders going to and from the south had to pass through Ghana. Each time, they paid heavy taxes on their goods. These taxes helped to make Ghana rich.

The History of Trans-Saharan Trade Trans-Saharan trade has a long history. Archeologists have found evidence that North Africans brought back gold from the southern forests of West Africa as long ago as 400 to 500 B.C.E. Travel across the Sahara, however, was especially challenging for these early peoples.

Centuries later, two factors led to the growth of trans-Saharan trade. The first was the introduction of the camel to the Sahara. The second was the spread of Islam.

Camels were first brought to the Sahara by Arab traders around 300 C.E. These animals are well suited for desert travel. A camel can drink up to twenty-five gallons of water at a time. As a result, it can travel several days in the desert without stopping. Also, camels have double rows of eyelashes and hairy ear openings that help keep out blowing sand.

The introduction of camels allowed traders to establish caravan routes across the Sahara. By the 4th century C.E., large amounts of gold were being made into Roman coins in North Africa. It is likely that that gold came from West Africa.

Trade expanded even more because of the spread of Islam. In the 7th century, Muslims invaded Ghana's empire. Besides wanting to convert West Africans to Islam, Muslims hoped to control trade in West Africa. Ghana turned back the invaders, but many Muslims settled in West African towns and became merchants.

Control of the trans-Saharan trade made Ghana wealthy and powerful. By the year 1000, Ghana's empire dominated the trade routes between North and West Africa.

The Journey South The traders who traveled to West Africa faced a long, difficult journey. The trans-Saharan caravan routes began in North Africa along the northwestern border of the Sahara. From there they stretched across the desert, passed through Ghana, and continued south to the Gulf of Guinea and east to present-day Chad.

Camels were especially suited for transporting goods across the Sahara.

trans-Saharan trade trade between peoples north and south of the Sahara

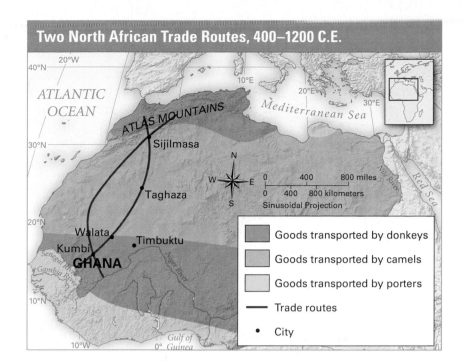

Two North African Trade Routes, 400–1200 C.E.

Goods transported by donkeys
Goods transported by camels
Goods transported by porters
Trade routes
City

Differences in geography led to different methods of transport along the trade routes between North and West Africa.

In 1352, a Muslim historian and traveler named Ibn Battuta (ib-ehn bat-TOO-tah) crossed the Sahara with a trade caravan. Battuta's account of his trip shows what the traders' journeys were like.

Battuta's caravan began at the oasis city of Sijilmasa (see-jeel-MAH-sah), on the northern edge of the Sahara, in the foothills of the Atlas Mountains. Donkeys carried goods from Europe, Arabia, and Egypt to Sijilmasa from the Mediterranean coast. Then camel caravans took the goods south.

Battuta and his caravan stayed in Sijilmasa for a few months, waiting for the rainy season to end. When the watering places were full and there was grass for the animals to eat, the traders set out. The caravan traveled from oasis to oasis. Each day, the traders walked until the afternoon, when the sun was high in the sky. Then they rested until the sun went down.

Walking across the Sahara was challenging and dangerous. Caravans sometimes lost their way, and some traders died in the desert. During one stretch of Battuta's trip, the travelers could not find water, so they slaughtered some of their camels and drank the water stored in the animals' stomachs.

On its way through the desert, the caravan stopped at Taghaza, a village where salt mines were located. There, it took on a load of salt. When the traders reached the town of Walata, at the edge of the desert, they transferred their salt and other goods from the camels to donkeys and to porters, people who carry goods for a living. Then they continued south, passing through Ghana on their way to markets on the Gulf of Guinea, near the southern forests. The entire journey took about two months.

The Romans and people in Muslim lands used West African gold to make their coins.

12.4 The Gold-Salt Trade

Many items were traded between North Africa and West Africa, but the two goods that were most in demand were gold and salt. The North Africans wanted gold, which came from the forest region south of Ghana. The people in the forests wanted salt, which came from the Sahara. Ghana made most of its money from the taxes it charged on the gold-salt trade that passed through its lands.

Wangara: The Secret Source of Gold Gold has long been a source of wealth in much of the world. In the time of Ghana's empire, people in Muslim lands and in Italy made coins from gold. Muslims also needed gold to purchase silk and porcelain from China, which would accept only gold in exchange.

In an area known as Wangara, gold was plentiful. Wangara was located near the forests south of Ghana, but no one except the people of Wangara knew its exact location. The Wangarans kept the locations of their gold mines secret. According to ancient stories, merchants occasionally captured a gold miner and tried to force him to reveal the location of Wangara. The miners would give up their lives rather than reveal the secret.

In one story, after the capture of a miner, the Wangarans stopped trading for three years. They wanted to make sure no one had discovered Wangara's location. To this day, no one knows for certain exactly where Wangara's mines were located.

Taghaza: A Village Built with Salt To West Africans, salt was more precious than gold. Their culture had little use for gold, except as an item for trade. But they craved salt, and for good reason. Salt is an important part of a person's diet. When people and animals perspire, or sweat, they lose salt in their perspiration. People who live in hot climates, like West Africa, perspire a lot and must replace the salt they lose. West Africans also needed salt to keep their food from spoiling and to give to their cattle. In addition, people liked the taste.

West Africans had no local source of salt. They had to obtain it from Taghaza and other places in the Sahara.

Salt was produced in two ways in the Sahara. One method was through **evaporation.** Water was poured into holes in the salty earth. The water slowly drew out the salt and then evaporated in the sun. The salt that remained was scooped out and packed into blocks. The second way to get salt was through mining. At Taghaza, salt deposits were found about three feet below the surface of the earth. Miners, enslaved by Arab merchants, reached the salt by digging trenches and tunnels. Then they cut it out in large blocks.

Taghaza would not have existed without salt. It was a dismal place, without crops or vegetation. People lived there for one purpose only: to mine and sell salt. Even the houses and mosque were built of salt blocks. Trade caravans passed through Taghaza on their way through the Sahara. There, they picked up salt to sell in Ghana and the southern forests. Because no food was produced in Taghaza, the miners had to rely on caravans to bring food, such as camel meat, dates, and a type of grain, called millet. If the caravans didn't come, the miners starved.

Ghana's System of Taxes Traders paid taxes to Ghana on all the goods they carried through the empire. Goods were taxed both when traders entered Ghana and when they left. Ghana charged one-sixth of an ounce of gold for each load of salt that came into the kingdom from the north. It then charged one-third of an ounce of gold for each load the traders took out of the kingdom to the south. The traders also paid taxes for carrying other types of goods. For every load of copper, they were charged five-eighths of an ounce of gold. They paid a little more than one ounce of gold per load of general merchandise.

The taxes enriched Ghana's treasury. They also helped pay for armies that protected the kingdom and allowed the king to conquer other territories. Traders benefited as well, because Ghana secured the trade routes against bandits who might rob the caravans.

In some parts of Africa, salt is made by the evaporation of water in areas called salt flats, such as this one. The salt is then dug out in large blocks.

Even today, salt is an important trade item in West Africa.

12.5 The Exchange of Goods

When trade caravans entered Ghana, they brought their goods to the great marketplace in the capital city of Kumbi. From there, they headed to the southern forests to trade with the Wangarans.

Kumbi had the busiest market in West Africa. Many local crafts-people sold their goods there. Ironsmiths sold weapons and tools. Goldsmiths and coppersmiths sold jewelry. Weavers sold cloth, and leatherworkers sold leather goods. There were blue blouses from Spain and robes from Morocco, in North Africa. People could also buy cattle, sheep, honey, wheat, raisins, dried fruit, ivory, pearls, and slaves. All goods, including slaves, were paid for with gold dust.

Kumbi had one of the largest slave markets in West Africa. The slaves were captured by raiders along the southern border of Ghana. Many were bought at Kumbi by Arab merchants, who took them across the Sahara and sold them to North Africans or Europeans.

Trade with the Wangarans took place along a river in the southern forests. Traders carried out their business using a system of silent barter, or trade. The caravans arrived bringing wool, silk, cotton, dates, figs, grains, leather, and salt. They spread out their goods along the river. The traders beat on a drum to announce that they were making an offer to trade. Then they walked several miles away from the site.

When the Wangarans heard the drum, they traveled to the site by boat. They put some gold dust next to the goods, beat a drum, and left. Later, the traders returned. If the amount of gold dust was acceptable, they took it and left. If not, they went away again and waited for the Wangarans to return and leave more gold dust. The groups bargained back and forth in this way without ever meeting in person.

This system of silent barter had two advantages. First, it allowed people who spoke different languages to trade. Second, it allowed the Wangarans to protect the secret location of their gold mines.

12.6 The Decline of Ghana and the Rise of Mali

Ghana's empire reached its height around the year 1000 C.E. War and the loss of natural resources led to the West African empire's downfall, and the rise of a new power.

In the second half of the 11th century, Muslim warriors known as Almoravids began attacking Ghana's empire. In 1076, they captured the capital city of Kumbi. Ghana's king regained power in 1087, but the old empire had broken apart.

The loss of natural resources further weakened Ghana. The growing population had put great stress on scarce resources, such as trees and water. Trees were cut down to provide charcoal for iron-smelting furnaces. Water became so scarce that farmers could no longer grow crops and keep flocks. People were forced to leave in search of better conditions. The empire came to an end in 1203, when a rival kingdom took over Kumbi.

The end of Ghana's empire opened the way to the rise of a new power, Mali. Around 1240, a group of West Africans called the Mande conquered Kumbi. Their homeland of Mali was south of Kumbi, closer to the Niger River. The Mande built an empire that reached from the Atlantic Ocean to beyond the Niger River, and from the southern forest to the salt and copper mines of the Sahara.

Like Ghana, Mali gained much of its wealth from the control of trade, particularly in gold. Its leaders had accepted Islam, and under their rule, the Muslim faith went on to become even more influential in West Africa.

Natural resources, such as water and trees, are still scarce in areas like the Sahel.

Chapter Summary

Trade played a key role in the growth of kingdoms and empires in West Africa. The first of these was Ghana.

Ghana's Government and Military Ghana was ideally located to control the trans-Saharan trade. It used the wealth from trade to create a strong army, which allowed it to conquer other peoples and build an empire.

Trade: Gold and Salt Ghana became wealthy by charging taxes on goods, especially gold and salt. Gold was mined in secret locations in forests south of Ghana and carried north to trade, while salt was produced in the Sahara and transported south.

The Exchange of Goods The Wangarans used a system of silent barter to trade goods.

The Decline of Ghana and Rise of Mali Years of war and the loss of natural resources led to Ghana's downfall in the 13th century. The next great West African empire, Mali, also built its wealth on trade.

Chapter 13

The Influence of Islam on West Africa

In what ways did Islam influence West African society?

13.1 Introduction

Several important early empires developed in West Africa, such as Ghana. In this chapter, you will explore how Islamic faith and culture influenced West African culture.

During the 7th century, the religion of Islam spread quickly through the Middle East and North Africa. In the 8th century, trans-Saharan trade brought Muslim merchants and traders to West Africa. Over the next few hundred years, Islam spread among West Africans. The new faith left a lasting mark on the culture of the region.

West Africans often blended Islamic culture with their own traditions. For example, West Africans who became Muslims began praying to God in Arabic. They built mosques as places of worship. Yet they also continued to pray to the spirits of their ancestors, as they had done for centuries.

Islamic beliefs and customs affected many areas of life besides religious faith. In this chapter, you will learn about the spread of Islam in West Africa. Then you will look at Islam's influence on several aspects of West African culture. You will explore changes in religious practices, government and law, education, language, architecture, and decorative arts. You can still see the effects of these changes in West Africa today.

The spread of Islam into West Africa changed the way people there lived, worked, and communicated. Many learned Arabic to study the Qur'an.

◀ The Grand Mosque in Mali was built of bricks and mud.

Muslim traders and the missionaries who accompanied them spread Islam to Ghana and beyond.

13.2 The Spread of Islam in West Africa

Trans-Saharan trade brought Islam to West Africa in the 8th century. At first, Muslim traders and merchants lived side by side with the non-Muslims of West Africa. Over time, however, Islam played a growing role in West African society.

Traders Bring Islam to Ghana Between the years 639 and 708 C.E., Arab Muslims conquered North Africa. Before long, they wanted to bring West Africa into the Islamic world. But sending armies to conquer Ghana was not practical. Ghana was too far away, and it was protected by the Sahara.

Islam first reached Ghana through Muslim traders and missionaries. The king of Ghana did not **convert** to Islam. Nor did the majority of the people. But the king did allow Muslims to build settlements within his empire.

Many Muslim merchants and traders settled in Kumbi, the great market city of Ghana. Over time, a thriving Muslim community developed around the trans-Saharan trade with North Africa. The Muslims in Kumbi had 12 mosques and their own imam (spiritual leader). Scholars studied the Qur'an.

In the 11th century, Muslims from the north, the Almoravids, invaded West Africa. In 1076, they captured Kumbi. The Almoravids did not hold power for long in Ghana, but under their rule Islam became more widespread.

Islam in Mali To the south of Ghana, the Mande also accepted Islam. The **tolerance** shown by Muslims toward traditional religious practices helped Islam to spread. For example, West Africans continued to pray to the spirits of their ancestors.

In about 1240, the Mande conquered Kumbi. They took control of the trade routes to North Africa and built the empire of **Mali**.

The early leaders of Mali accepted Islam, but they did not follow all of its teachings. In 1312, a new leader, **Mansa Musa,** took over in Mali. He became the first West African ruler to practice Islam devoutly.

Under Mansa Musa's rule, Mali became a major crossroads of the Islamic world. Muslim merchants, traders, and scholars from Egypt and North Africa came to Mali to do business or to settle.

Like other Muslims, Musa made a hajj, or pilgrimage, to the sacred city of Makkah in Arabia. The hajj was an enormous undertaking. The journey covered some three thousand miles. Officials and servants started preparing for the trip months before Musa left. As many as eighty thousand people may have accompanied Musa on the hajj.

Musa reached Cairo, Egypt, in July 1324, after eight months of travel. A writer from Cairo described Musa's caravan as "a lavish display of power, wealth, and unprecedented by its size and pageantry." Ahead of Musa arrived 500 slaves, each carrying a six-pound staff of gold. He was followed by a caravan of 200 camels carrying 30,000 pounds of gold, along with food, clothing, and supplies.

In Cairo, Musa met the local sultan, or ruler. When Musa was asked to kneel before the sultan, he felt insulted. He was very proud of being the ruler of Mali. After Musa finally agreed to kneel, the sultan invited him to sit beside him as his equal.

Mali a West African empire ruled by the Mande that became a major crossroads of the Islamic world

Mansa Musa the first West African ruler to practice Islam devoutly

The pilgrimage of Mansa Musa to Makkah was so impressive that when news of it reached Europe, mapmakers there produced this map of West Africa with Musa's image prominently displayed.

After leaving Cairo, Musa traveled to Arabia to visit Makkah and Madinah. When word spread that the king of Mali was visiting, people lined the streets to see him. Musa's wealth impressed the people and rulers of Arabia. He paid in gold for all the goods and services he received. He also gave expensive gifts to his hosts.

Because of Musa's hajj, Mali became known as an important kingdom. By 1375, Mali appeared on a European map of West Africa.

Islam in Songhai One of the groups within Mali's empire was the **Songhai** people. In the 1460s, the great warrior Sunni Ali became the new ruler of the Songhai. He built a powerful army that enabled the Songhai to break away from Mali and, eventually, to conquer it.

The early Songhai rulers did not practice Islam seriously. In the 1490s, Muslims in the Songhai empire rebelled. They placed Askia Mohammed Toure, a devout Muslim, on the throne. Toure set up rigid controls to be sure Islam was practiced properly. He also led a series of wars to convert non-Muslims to Islam. Under his rule, the Songhai empire covered a territory as large as western Europe.

13.3 · Religious Practices

As Islam spread in West Africa, the people adopted new religious practices and ethical values. African Muslims learned the Five Pillars of Islam. They prayed in Arabic, fasted, worshipped in mosques, made pilgrimages, and gave alms. They were taught to regard themselves and all other Muslims as part of a single community.

West Africans also began to celebrate Muslim religious festivals. The festival of Eid al-Fitr marks the end of the holy month called Ramadan. Eid al-Adha commemorates a key event in the story of the prophet Abraham. As a test of faith, God asked Abraham to sacrifice his son, Isaac. God spared the boy after Abraham proved his faith through his willingness to offer his son to God.

Alongside these new customs, West Africans preserved some of their old religious practices. Muslim leaders allowed them to continue religious traditions as long as they did not contradict the Five Pillars of Islam. So, for example, West African Muslims continued to show respect for the spirits of dead ancestors. They kept their belief in spirits who could help those who prayed to them or made sacrifices to them. They used amulets, or charms, that they believed helped people or protected them from harm.

Ibn Battuta was an Arab who traveled to Mali in the 14th century. Battuta was upset by some local customs there. For instance, women, including the daughters of rulers, went unclothed in public. Battuta also saw Muslims throwing dust over their heads when the king approached. These customs upset him because they went against the teachings of Islam.

Songhai a people who broke away from the empire of Mali and eventually built their own vast empire in West Africa

With the introduction of Islam, West Africans began praying five times daily, as many still do today.

Yet Battuta was also impressed by how **devoted** West Africans were to Islam. He wrote, "Anyone who is late at the mosque will find nowhere to pray, the crowd is so great. They zealously learn the Qur'an by heart. Those children who are neglectful in this, are put in chains until they have memorized the Qur'an."

13.4 Government and Law

Muslims in the Middle East and North Africa developed Islamic forms of government and law. Muslim rulers in West Africa also adopted some of these ideas.

One major change concerned the line of succession, or inheritance of the right to rule. In West Africa, the succession had traditionally been matrilineal. That is, the right to rule was traced through the mother or female relative, rather than the father or a male relative. As you learned, in Ghana the son of the king's sister inherited the throne. After the arrival of Islam, succession became **patrilineal**. The right to rule now passed from father to son.

With the arrival of Islam, the power of the central ruler increased and local chiefs grew less important.

A second change affected the structure of government. Muslims believed in a highly centralized government. After West African kings converted to Islam, they started to exercise more control over local rulers. The kings also adopted titles used in Muslim lands. Often, the head of a region was now called the sultan, the amir, or emir. *Amir* and *emir* are shortened forms of Amir al-Muminin. This Arabic expression means "Commander of the Faithful."

A third major change was the adoption of shari'ah (Islamic law). In many towns and cities, shari'ah replaced customary law. The customary law of West Africa was very different from shari'ah. Laws were not written, but everyone knew what they were and accepted them from long tradition. A chief or king usually enforced customary law but did not give physical punishments. Instead, the guilty party paid the injured party with gifts or services. The family or clan of the guilty person could also be punished.

> **patrilineal** a family line traced through the father

One example of customary law was "trial by wood." Suppose a man was accused of not paying debts or of injuring another person. The accused man was forced to drink water that had been poured over sour, bitter wood. If the man became ill, he was believed to be innocent.

Unlike customary law, shari'ah is written law. Muslims believe that shari'ah came from God. Shari'ah is administered by judges called *qadis*. The qadis hear cases in a court. They listen to witnesses and rule on the basis of the law and the evidence.

The influence of Islam made the medieval city of Timbuktu a center for learning. Several universities were established there.

13.5 An Emphasis on Education

In West Africa, Muslims encouraged people to get an education. They built many schools and centers of learning.

One key center was the trading city of Timbuktu, on the Niger River. Under Mali and Songhai rule, Timbuktu became famous for its community of Islamic scholars. It remained an important center of learning until the Songhai were conquered by Morocco in the 1500s.

Several universities were built in Timbuktu. The most famous was the University of Sankore. At that time, it was one of the world's great centers of learning.

Sankore was made up of several small, independent schools. Each school was run by an imam, or scholar. The imams at Sankore were respected throughout the Islamic world.

Students at Sankore studied under a single imam. The basic course of learning included the Qur'an, Islamic studies, law, and literature. After mastering these subjects, students could go on to study in a particular field. Many kinds of courses were available. Students could learn medicine and surgery. They could study astronomy, mathematics, physics, or chemistry. Or they could take up **philosophy**, geography, art, or history.

The highest degree a student could earn at Sankore required about ten years of study. During graduation, students wore a cloth headdress called a turban. The turban was a symbol of divine light, wisdom, knowledge, and excellent moral character.

When travelers and traders passed through Timbuktu, they were encouraged to study at one of the universities. Trade associations also set up their own colleges. Students in these colleges learned about the profession of trading, in addition to studying Islam.

Muslims also set up schools to educate children in the Qur'an. Timbuktu had about one hundred fifty Qur'anic schools, where children learned to read and interpret Islam's holy book.

With their love of education, Muslims treasured books. Muslims did not have printing presses, so books had to be copied by hand. Mosques and universities in West Africa built up large libraries of these precious volumes. Some individuals also created sizable collections. One Islamic scholar's private library contained 700 volumes. Many of his books were extremely rare.

13.6 The Arabic Language

Islam is rooted in Arab culture. As Islam spread throughout West Africa, the Arabic language did, as well.

In West Africa, Arabic became the language of religion, learning, commerce, and government. However, West Africans continued to use their native languages in everyday speech.

For Muslims, Arabic was the language of religion. The Qur'an, of course, was written in Arabic. All Muslims were expected to read the Qur'an and memorize parts of it. As West Africans converted to Islam, more and more of them learned Arabic.

Arabic also became the language of learning. The scholars who came to West Africa were mainly Arabic-speaking Muslims. Some of their students became scholars themselves. Like their teachers, they read and wrote Arabic.

Scholars used Arabic to write about the history and culture of West Africa. They wrote about a wide variety of topics. They described how people used animal and plant parts and minerals to cure diseases. They discussed ethical behavior for business and government. They told how to use the stars to determine the seasons. They recorded the history of the Songhai. They also wrote about Islamic law. These writings are an invaluable source of knowledge about West Africa in this period.

Finally, Arabic became the language of trade and government. Arabic allowed West African traders who spoke different native languages to communicate more easily. Arabic also allowed rulers to keep records and to write to rulers in other countries.

Arabic, the language of the Qur'an, became the language of learning, government, and trade in West Africa.

Islamic architects built flat-roofed houses made of sun-dried bricks.

13.7 Islamic Architectural Styles

The influence of Islam brought new styles of architecture to West Africa, too. People designed mosques for worship. They also created a new design for homes.

Traditionally, West Africans had built small shrines to honor the forces of nature. As they converted to Islam, they began to build mosques. The materials that were most available on the savanna were mud and wood. Using these materials, West Africans built mosques that blended Islamic architectural styles with their own traditional religious art. For example, the minaret (tower) of one mosque was designed to look like the symbol of a Songhai ancestor.

After his pilgrimage to Makkah, the Mali ruler Mansa Musa wanted to build more mosques. He convinced al-Saheli, an architect from Spain, to return to Mali with him. Al-Saheli built several structures in Mali. One of them is the most famous mosque in West Africa, Djingareyber (jin-gar-AY-ber). Located in the city of Timbuktu, Djingareyber was built out of limestone and earth mixed with straw and wood. The walls of the mosque have beams projecting out of them. Workers used the beams as scaffolding when the building needed to be repaired.

Al-Saheli also introduced a new design for houses. Most traditional houses in West Africa were round with cone-shaped, thatched roofs. Al-Saheli built rectangular houses out of brick and with flat roofs. The outside walls were very plain and had no windows. Only a single wooden door, decorated with a **geometric** design, interrupted the rows of bricks.

Al-Saheli introduced another feature to houses; clay drain pipes. The pipes improved the quality of people's lives, because during the rainy season they prevented damage to homes from rainwater.

13.8 Islamic Decorative Arts

Muslims used calligraphy (artistic writing) and geometric patterns in their decorative arts. West Africans adopted these designs for their own art and textiles.

Muslims used calligraphy to decorate objects with words or verses from the Qur'an. West Africans adopted this practice. They began using the Arabic word for God to decorate costumes, fans, and even weapons. They also wrote verses from the Qur'an on amulets.

Geometric patterns are an important element in Islamic art. Muslims use these patterns rather than drawing pictures of animals or people. Geometric designs were popular in traditional West African art, as well. West Africans used them to decorate **textiles** and every-day objects, such as stools and ceramic containers. The arrival of Islam reinforced this practice.

Muslims also influenced the way people dressed in West Africa. Arab Muslims commonly wore an Arabic robe as an outer layer. An Arabic robe has wide, long sleeves and a long skirt. Muslims used calligraphy to personalize and decorate their robes. West Africans adopted the Arabic robe. Like Arabs, they still wear it today.

Islam reinforced the West African tradition of using geometric designs in arts and crafts, such as weaving.

textile a woven cloth

Chapter Summary

In this chapter, you learned about the influence of Islam in medieval West Africa. Islam left a deep mark on West African culture.

The Spread of Islam in West Africa Traders and missionaries first brought Islam to Ghana in the 8th century. The influence of Islam increased under the rulers of Mali and Songhai.

Religious Practices Islam changed West African religion. Many continued to show respect for the spirits of ancestors and to follow other traditional beliefs, but they learned to adhere to the Five Pillars of Islam and to celebrate Muslim religious festivals.

Government, Law, and Education Islam brought new ideas about government and law. The royal succession became patrilineal. Government became more centralized. Shari'ah replaced customary law. There was a new emphasis on learning. People studied at Qur'anic schools and Islamic universities. Timbuktu became a center of Islamic and academic study.

Arabic Language and Islamic Architecture and Decorative Arts Arabic became the language of religion, learning, commerce, and government. New styles of architecture developed as West Africans built mosques and changed the designs of their homes. They also adopted new, geometric styles in their decorative arts.

Chapter 14

The Cultural Legacy of West Africa

In what ways do the cultural achievements of West Africa influence our culture today?

14.1 Introduction

Medieval cultures in West Africa were rich and varied. In this chapter, you will explore West Africa's rich cultural legacy.

West African cultures are quite diverse. Many groups of people, each with its own language and ways of life, have lived in the region of West Africa. From poems and stories to music and visual arts, their cultural achievements have left a lasting mark on the world.

Much of West African culture has been passed down through its oral traditions. Think for a moment of the oral traditions in your own culture. When you were younger, did you learn nursery rhymes from your family or friends? How about sayings such as "A penny saved is a penny earned"? Did you hear stories about your grandparents or more distant ancestors? You can probably think of many ideas that were passed down orally from one generation to the next.

Suppose that your community depends on you to remember its oral traditions so they will never be forgotten. You memorize stories, sayings, and the history of your city or town. You know about the first people who lived there. You know how the community grew, and which teams have won sports championships. On special occasions, you share your knowledge through stories and songs. You are a living library of your community's history and traditions.

In parts of West Africa, there are people whose job it is to preserve oral traditions and history in this way. They are talented poet-musicians. For many centuries, they have helped to preserve West Africa's history and cultural legacy.

In this chapter, you will learn about the role of both oral traditions and written traditions in West Africa. You will also explore West African music and visual arts. Along the way, you will see how the cultural achievements of West Africans continue to influence our world.

West African arts, such as this sculpture, have often influenced modern artists.

◀ Kente cloth and hand-carved furniture are traditional arts in West Africa.

14.2 West African Oral and Written Traditions

For centuries, the beliefs, values, and knowledge of West Africans
were **transmitted** orally from one generation to the next. In medieval
times, written traditions also became important. In this section, we
will look at the **oral traditions** and written traditions of West Africa.

Griots: Record Keepers of the People A **griot** (GREE-oh) is a
verbal artist of the Mande people. Griots are poet-musicians who tell
stories, sing songs of praise, and recite poems, often while playing a
drum or stringed instrument. They perform music, dance, and drama.
But griots are much more than skilled entertainers. They also educate
their audiences with historical accounts and **genealogies,** or histories
of people's ancestry. In many ways, they are the record keepers and
historians of their people.

Long before the Mande had written histories, griots preserved the
memory of the past. Every village had its own griot. The griot memorized all the important events that occurred there. Griots could recite
everything from births, deaths, and marriages, to battles, hunts, and
the successions of kings. Some griots could tell the ancestry of every
villager, going back centuries. Griots were known to speak for hours
and, sometimes, even for days.

This rich oral tradition passed from griot to griot. Rulers relied on
griots as their trusted advisors. They used the griots' knowledge of
history to shed light on their current problems.

Modern-day court musicians play
traditional instruments in honor of the
sultan of Cameroon.

The most cherished information in griot history is the story of Sundjata Keita (soon-JAHT-ah KAY-tah). Sundjata was the king who founded Mali's empire in the 13th century. Griot stories were told about him even in his own lifetime. Sundjata remains a hero to many West Africans, who still tell tales about him.

The art of the griots remains alive today. Some of the most famous artists in West African popular music are griots. These artists have changed traditional oral works into modern songs. Poets and story-tellers make recordings and appear on radio broadcasts performing both old and new works.

Folktales West Africa's oral tradition includes hundreds of old stories called **folktales**. West Africans used folktales to pass along their history and to teach young people morals and values.

Many traditional folktales were brought to the Americas by West Africans who were sold into slavery beginning in the 1500s. The tales were spread orally among the enslaved Africans and their descendants. The folktales became part of the culture of North and South America and the West Indies.

One example is a type of folktale known as a "trickster tale." These stories tell of a clever animal or human who outsmarts others. Trickster tales are popular in many cultures. In West Africa, one famous trickster was the hare. West Africans brought tales of the hare to America, where he became known as Brer Rabbit. In the 19th century, a writer named Joel Chandler Harris retold a number of African American stories about Brer Rabbit. These stories have since been woven into American culture.

Proverbs West African oral tradition includes proverbs, or popular sayings. Proverbs are found in all cultures. West African proverbs use images from everyday life to express ideas or give advice. They tell us a great deal about the wisdom and values of West Africans.

One proverb shows how Africans valued their stories. The proverb states, "A good story is like a garden carried in the pocket." Another shows the importance of oral tradition. "Every time an old man dies," the proverb says, "it is as if a library has burnt down." Enslaved West Africans brought proverbs like these to the Americas.

Written Tradition After Islam spread to West Africa, written tradition became more important. Muslims published many works in Arabic. A number of these writings were preserved in mosques and Qur'anic schools. Today, they are a key source of information about West African history, legends, and culture.

Modern writers in West Africa are adding to the literary legacy of the region. Some of them have turned ancient oral traditions into novels and other works.

Griots, or storytellers, continue the oral traditions of West African culture. They also represent the importance of elders in West African society.

folktale a story that is passed down orally and becomes part of a culture's tradition

call and response a song style in which a singer or musician leads with a call, and a chorus responds

14.3 West African Music

Music has always been an important part of life in West Africa. Music serves many functions in West African society. It **communicates** ideas, values, and feelings. It celebrates historic events and important occasions in people's lives. For instance, there are songs for weddings, funerals, and ceremonies honoring ancestors. Among the Yoruba of present-day Nigeria, mothers of twins have their own special songs. In Ghana, there are songs for celebrating the loss of a child's first tooth.

The musical traditions of West Africa continue to influence both African and world culture. Let's look at some key aspects of West African music.

Call and Response A common style of music in West Africa is known as **call and response**. In call-and-response singing, a leader plays or sings a short phrase, known as a call. Then a group of people, the chorus, answer by playing or singing a short phrase, the response. The leader and chorus repeat this pattern over and over as they perform the song.

Enslaved Africans brought call-and-response songs to the Americas. Slaves used the songs to ease the burden of hard work, celebrate social occasions, and express outrage at their situation. This African tradition has influenced many American musical styles, including gospel, jazz, blues, rock and roll, and rap.

The balafon is a traditional musical instrument of West Africa made of wooden bars attached to a horizontal frame. The bars are struck with a hammer, much like a xylophone is.

Musical Instruments Traditional musical instruments in West Africa include three that have been used by griots for centuries. They are called the *balafon* (BAH-la-fon), the *ngoni* (en-GOH-nee), and the *kora* (KOR-ah).

The balafon probably was the original griot instrument. Like a xylophone or marimba, a balafon is made of wooden bars laid across a frame. The musician strikes the bars with a mallet, or hammer, to make melodies. The balafon is used today in popular music in modern Guinea.

The ngoni is a small stringed instrument. It is made of hollowed-out wood carved in a shape similar to a canoe. The instrument's strings are made of thin fishing line. The ngoni is the most popular traditional stringed instrument in Mali today.

The kora is a harplike instrument with 21 strings. The body of the kora is made of a gourd that has been cut in half and covered with cowhide. The kora's strings, like those of the ngoni, are made of fishing line.

People around the world have been introduced to kora music by West African musicians. Some modern musicians in West Africa combine the sounds of the kora with electronic music.

Drumming Drums play an important role in West African culture. Drummers perform at parties, religious meetings, and ceremonies, such as weddings and funerals.

West African drums are made of hollowed-out logs or pieces of wood. The drums are covered with animal skins.

Drummers in West Africa play in ensembles, or groups. The ensembles include different types and sizes of drums, along with bells and rattles. Drumming, singing, and dancing take place together in a circle. Sometimes, drum ensembles use a call-and-response style.

West African slaves brought their drumming traditions to the Americas. Over time, West African drum music **evolved** into new styles, particularly in Cuba. West African drum music and Afro-Cuban drumming are now popular elements of world music.

Drumming is an important element of West African music. Drums of different sizes and shapes often have bells and rattles attached to them.

Dance In West Africa, dance is as much a part of life as singing and drumming are. Traditional West African dances are still performed in Africa and around the world.

West Africans perform dances for all kinds of occasions. They dance during rituals and during ceremonies that mark important events in people's lives. Dances can celebrate a success at work or help educate children. West Africans also perform dances to seek the help of spirits and to connect with dead ancestors.

Dance movements often reflect the conditions people live in. Among forest-dwelling people, for example, dancers move as if they are finding their way through forest undergrowth.

Some dancers wear elaborate masks that represent the spirits of traditional West African religion. For example, to ask the spirits for good hunting for their community, dancers may wear masks of wild animals and imitate their movements.

The Yoruba people of Ife, Nigeria, made brass sculptures of their royalty. Notice the crown on this brass head.

14.4 West African Visual Arts

West African culture includes many forms of visual art. The traditional art of West Africa served a number of functions. Some art objects, such as fabrics and baskets, satisfied everyday needs. Others, such as masks and sculptures, were used in rituals and ceremonies, or to honor ancestors, spirits, or royalty.

Sculpture West Africans of ancient and medieval times used religious sculptures to call upon the spirits to help them in every phase of life. They also used sculptures to honor their leaders.

A wealth of West African sculpture has been discovered in Nigeria. The oldest examples come from the Nok culture (500 B.C.E. to 200 C.E.). The Nok made **terra-cotta** sculptures of human figures. The sculptures tended to have long, narrow heads, unusual hair styles, and dramatic expressions. Scholars believe that they represented ancestors or mythical figures.

The Yoruba people of Ife (EE-fay), Nigeria, also made sculptures of terra-cotta. Later, they used bronze and copper. By the 11th century C.E., they were making brass sculptures of royalty. Later, they taught their neighbors in Benin (founded in 1100 C.E.) how to make brass sculptures. Benin artists produced sculptures in honor of the royal court. By the 16th century, they were making elaborate plaques that showed the king's power and authority.

Masks Wooden masks have been a part of West African life for centuries. Masks were worn during ceremonies, in performances, and in sacred rites. Like sculptures, they were used to bring the spirits of gods and ancestors into the present.

West African masks are detailed and expressive. They have inspired a number of artists around the world. Among these artists is Pablo Picasso, a world-famous Spanish painter of the 20th century.

Textiles West Africans have a long tradition of making textiles that are both beautiful and symbolic. Three well-known types of West African textiles are stamped fabrics, story fabrics, and a particularly colorful kind called **kente** (KEN-tay) cloth.

West Africans make stamped fabric by drawing a grid on a piece of cloth, using a thick dye. They use stamps to fill in the squares with patterns. The stamps represent proverbs, historical figures, objects, plants, or animals.

terra-cotta a baked clay used to make pottery, tiles, and sculptures

kente a traditional form of cloth produced in West Africa

appliqué a technique in which shaped pieces of fabric are attached to a background fabric to form a design or picture

Story fabrics depict events. For example, they might show kings performing great feats, like hunting lions. Some West Africans make story fabrics using a technique called **appliqué**. In appliqué, smaller pieces of fabric are attached to a larger, background piece to make designs or pictures.

Kente cloth is a famous West African textile. To make kente, people sew together narrow strips of silk or other fabrics. The designs of kente cloth have symbolic meanings that reflect the makers' life or family history, values and beliefs, or political or social circumstances.

The influence of West African textiles can be seen in quilts made by African American slaves. Today, commercially made kente cloth is worn around the world.

Everyday Objects West African visual arts also include the design and decoration of everyday objects. Skilled artists turn practical objects into things of beauty. Some examples are ceramic storage containers, utensils, furniture, and baskets.

In many parts of West Africa, baskets are made by the coil method. The basket maker winds fibers into coils and then uses strips of fiber to bind the coils together. Some of these baskets are so tightly constructed that they can hold water.

Enslaved West Africans brought their basket-making tradition to America and taught it to their descendants. This art is still practiced in the American South.

This sculpture was made by the Yoruba people of Ife.

Chapter Summary

In this chapter, you explored the cultural legacy of West Africa. You learned about written and oral traditions, music, and visual arts. The cultural achievements of West Africans are still influential today.

Oral and Written Traditions Storytellers called griots helped to preserve the history and culture of West Africa. Folktales and proverbs are also part of West Africa's rich oral tradition. In medieval times, Muslim scholars added a body of Arabic writings to this heritage, which were preserved in Qur'anic schools and mosques. Modern writers incorporate many elements from West African oral traditions in their novels and other works.

Music Important features of West African music include call and response, traditional instruments, drumming, and dance. West African influences are still heard in world music.

Visual Arts Visual arts include sculptures, masks, textiles, and the design of everyday objects. West African sculpture and mask-making, particularly, influenced many modern artists, one of whom was Pablo Picasso. Kente cloth is still worn today and its influence can be seen in fashions around the world.

Youssou N'Dour: A Modern-Day Griot

Senegalese performer Youssou N'Dour is a best-selling musician and a modern-day griot.

Rolling Stone magazine celebrated him as "perhaps the most famous singer alive." *Folk Roots* magazine named him African artist of the century. For over 30 years, Senegalese singer Youssou N'Dour has made hit albums and performed around the world. N'Dour is a modern-day *griot*. His songs awaken the world to the problems African nations face.

Youssou N'Dour, Senegal's greatest recording artist, sat in his studio in Dakar. He started picking out a series of notes on the keyboard. His guitar player grabbed his guitar and started strumming chords. Then the drummer sat down behind his kit and laid down a rhythm.

N'Dour began to sing in his clear, strong tenor voice. He improvised the lyrics, making them up as he went along. Little by little, the song developed. It was about the tough life of a fisherman. It told how he rose before dawn and went out to sea, but all he caught was a shark. He brought the shark to market, but no one would buy it. The fisherman hoped his luck would change the next day. When N'Dour finished singing, he had just created his newest song. Like so many of his songs, it captured how ordinary people in his native country of Senegal struggle every day to make ends meet.

A Singer Who Tells the Truth

Youssou N'Dour was born in the African nation of Senegal in 1959. He is that nation's most celebrated musician and has been called one of the best African singers. He is also a modern-day griot.

In traditional West African cultures, griots passed along the history of their people through stories and songs. In the past, griots also communicated messages from a king to his people and told stories of the king's triumphs. But griots also told the truth. Sometimes kings would get angry when the griots pointed out royal mistakes.

Telling the truth is one way in which Youssou N'Dour is a modern griot. In one of his songs, titled "Africa," he criticizes the corruption of many of Africa's political leaders. In another song, "Donkaasi Gi," he calls for equality among the people of Senegal. When he sees people perform acts of kindness to one another, he celebrates them in song. A devout Muslim, he also has sung about modern Islamic life.

N'Dour's albums have sold in the millions. He has worked with some of the most popular musicians in the world, including Peter Gabriel, Bruce Springsteen, Sting, Paul Simon, Tracy Chapman, and American jazz musician Branford Marsalis.

His songs have helped make people more aware of Africa's challenges. But he also sings of Africa with hope and pride.

N'Dour performs his music in concerts around the world with his band Super Étoile de Dakar.

A Musical Background

N'Dour was born in Medina, a tough section of Dakar, the capital of Senegal. His mother was a *griotte*—a female griot. His grandparents were talented singers who were much in demand in Dakar.

Yet music also caused some conflict in his family. His father did not come from the griot tradition and forbade N'Dour's mother to sing in public. He also opposed his son's ambitions to be a musician and urged him to go to school and prepare for a more stable career. Yet when N'Dour showed extraordinary musical talent as a child, his mother and grandparents supported him.

N'Dour was lucky to grow up in Dakar during the 1960s and 1970s, because an amazing variety of music made its way there. He grew up listening not only to local and traditional musical styles, but also to African American artists such as Marvin Gaye, James Brown, Michael Jackson, and Jimi Hendrix. He also loved Latin American music. All these styles influenced him.

In 1973, when he was 14 years old, he sang in a talent contest—and won. Brimming with confidence, he went to see the manager of The Miami, a successful nightclub in Dakar, and asked to be hired as a singer. The manager initially turned him down. But N'Dour kept asking until the manager finally gave in. N'Dour became a singer for the Star Band, the best-known band in Dakar.

N'Dour frequently performs at benefit concerts. Here he appears with song-writer and rapper Nena Cherry at a concert held to raise awareness about poverty around the world.

A New Style of Dance Music

The teenage N'Dour was a sensation. The young people of Dakar crowded into the club to dance and listen to his songs. With his silky voice, he expressed what they were feeling. In 1977, in a bold move, Youssou hired away six members of the Star Band for his own group, which he called Étoile de Dakar, French for "Star of Dakar." In 1979, he formed the band Super Étoile de Dakar.

N'Dour and his band gradually developed a new style of dance music. Everybody called it *mbalax* (um-bah-lahks), which means "rhythm" in the Senegalese language *Wolof*. N'Dour and his band also added the sounds of hip-hop, rock, soul, and rhythm and blues to their music.

A Voice of Conscience

Soon N'Dour and Super Étoile de Dakar started to record albums, with N'Dour either writing the songs himself or co-writing them with his bandmates. From 1979 to 1988, they recorded an astonishing 14 albums, which merchants sold on the streets of Dakar. His popularity quickly exploded.

N'Dour was now famous throughout Senegal. For such a young man, he was making a lot of money. Yet he always stayed in touch with his roots. In the lyrics of his songs, he expressed his concern for the problems facing Africa, such as hunger, poverty, and disease. For example, in his song "New Africa," which was released in the mid-1980s, he urged the people of the continent to work together. "Unity," he wrote, "was the traditional strength of Africa."

In other songs, he called for the people of Africa to care for one another, to choose good over evil, and to be honest in their dealings. One song encouraged the Senegalese to remember their roots and learn as much as they can about their country. In the album *Nelson Mandela,* N'Dour celebrated the courage of the South African civil rights leader who later became that nation's first black president.

Keeping the Griot Tradition Alive

By singing about Africa's issues, N'Dour keeps alive a griot tradition that has lasted for centuries. Griots are the voices of their communities. They pass along their people's history from one generation to the next. They tell stories and sing songs that teach lessons so that young people can develop positive values. They make people feel as if they are part of a community.

Some griots have made extraordinary efforts to preserve West African traditions. In the nation of Gambia, the griot Alhaja Papa Susso founded a school where musicians, dancers, and poets can study griot traditions. They take lessons, rehearse, give concerts, make new friends, and exchange ideas. Scholars also visit the school to learn more about griots and their roles in African society.

In recent years, N'Dour has continued to sing about Africa. In a way, he has also become a griot to the world. One night during the mid-1980s, the British rock musician Peter Gabriel went to listen to N'Dour perform. When Gabriel heard the young singer, he was amazed. Gabriel asked N'Dour to sing on his album *So,* which became one of the best-selling albums of the 1980s. They also co-wrote the song "Shaking the Tree—Woman's Day," a remarkable song about women's rights in Africa. Since then, N'Dour has worked with many other musicians to raise money to improve conditions in Africa and around the world.

N'Dour and other modern-day griots are essential voices for the future of Africa. They point out problems, but they also help unify the continent. Most of all, they help Africans face the future with hope and pride.

N'Dour uses his fame to bring attention to important causes. Here he attends a conference on African development with rock musician Bono (right) and pop singer Juanes (left).

The Culture and Kingdoms of West Africa

About 4,000 B.C.E.
Settlements in West Africa
Early farming communities, made up of extended families, farm the area south of the Sahara.

About 250 B.C.E.–1400 C.E.
Jenne-Jeno
Jenne-Jeno thrives on the Niger River, growing to a city of 20,000 people who farmed, fished, and made tools from iron.

1500 B.C.E.	1000 B.C.E.	500 B.C.E.	1 C.E.

About 500 B.C.E.
Trans-Saharan Trade
North Africans bring gold from the southern forests of Africa through the Sahara, a journey that would eventually be made easier by the use of camels.

About 500 B.C.E–200 C.E.
The Nok
The Nok make iron tools in West Africa, fueling the spread of ironworking and helping to begin trade among West African villages.

About 300 C.E
Camels Arrive in West Africa
Camels are introduced to the Sahara region, spurring the growth of trans-Saharan trade.

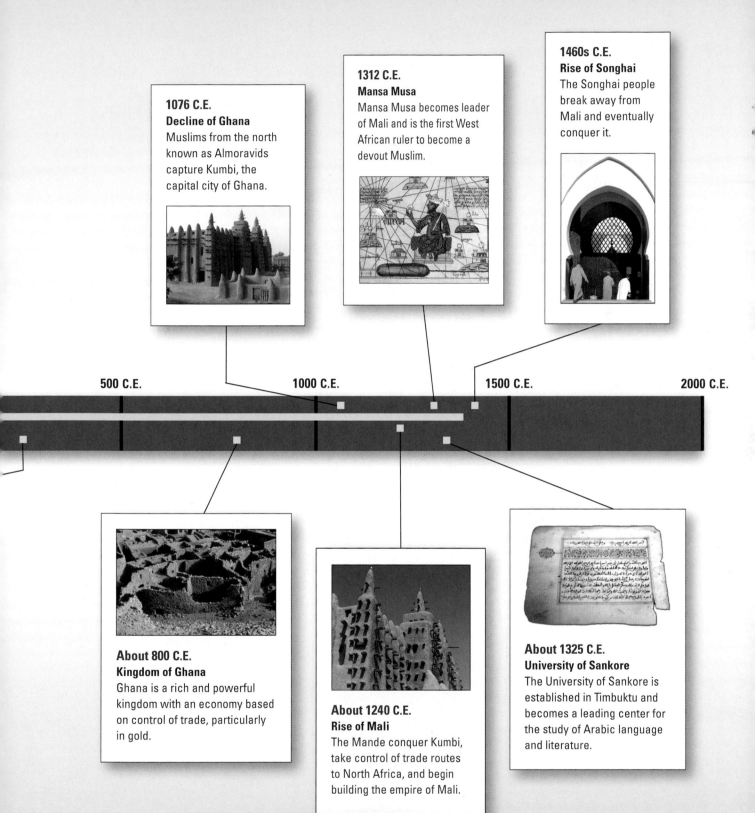

1076 C.E.
Decline of Ghana
Muslims from the north known as Almoravids capture Kumbi, the capital city of Ghana.

1312 C.E.
Mansa Musa
Mansa Musa becomes leader of Mali and is the first West African ruler to become a devout Muslim.

1460s C.E.
Rise of Songhai
The Songhai people break away from Mali and eventually conquer it.

500 C.E.   1000 C.E.   1500 C.E.   2000 C.E.

About 800 C.E.
Kingdom of Ghana
Ghana is a rich and powerful kingdom with an economy based on control of trade, particularly in gold.

About 1240 C.E.
Rise of Mali
The Mande conquer Kumbi, take control of trade routes to North Africa, and begin building the empire of Mali.

About 1325 C.E.
University of Sankore
The University of Sankore is established in Timbuktu and becomes a leading center for the study of Arabic language and literature.

Imperial China

A bronze lion stands guard at the Forbidden City in Beijing, China. A complex of palaces built in the early 1400s, the Forbidden City was the seat of Chinese power for five centuries.

Physical Features of Asia

ARCTIC OCEAN

EUROPE

SIBERIA

East Siberian Sea

Laptev Sea

Kara Sea

Ob River

Yenisey River

Lena River

URAL MTS.

THE STEPPES

Lake Baikal

ALTAY MTS.

Lake Balkhash

Aral Sea

Caspian Sea

Black Sea

CAUCASUS MTNS.

Mediterranean Sea

Euphrates River

Tigris River

ZAGROS MTS.

Red Sea

Persian Gulf

ARABIAN PENINSULA

TIAN SHAN

TAKLIMAKAN DESERT

KUNLUN SHAN

HIMALAYA

PLATEAU OF TIBET

Brahmaputra River

Mount Everest
(29,035 ft., 8,850 m)

Indus River

Ganges River

GOBI DESERT

Huang He (Yellow R.)

NORTH CHINA PLAIN

CHINA

Chang Jiang (Yangtze R.)

CHANG JIANG BASINS

Xi R.

KOREAN PEN.

KAMCHATKA PEN.

Bering Sea

Sea of Okhotsk

Sakhalin

Hokkaido

Sea of Japan (East Sea)

Honshu

Shikoku

Kyushu

PACIFIC OCEAN

Yellow Sea

East China Sea

RYUKYU IS.

Tropic of Cancer

Taiwan

Amur River

INDIAN PENINSULA

DECCAN PLATEAU

WESTERN GHATS

EASTERN GHATS

Arabian Sea

AFRICA

Bay of Bengal

ANDAMAN ISLANDS

MALDIVE ISLANDS

NICOBAR ISLANDS

BATU IS.

MENTAWAI ISLANDS

INDIAN OCEAN

Malay Peninsula

Mekong River

Gulf of Thailand

South China Sea

Hainan

PHILIPPINE ISLANDS

Philippine Sea

Halmahera

New Guinea

Celebes Sea

Ceram

Borneo

Celebes

GREATER SUNDA ISLANDS

Sumatra

Java Sea

Java

Sumbawa

Sumba

Flores

Timor

Equator

AUSTRALIA

Tropic of Capricorn

Elevation

Feet		Meters
Over 10,000		Over 3,050
5,001–10,000		1,526–3,050
2,001–5,000		611–1,525
1,001–2,000		306–610
0–1,000		0–305
Below sea level		Below sea level

▲ Mountain peak

Present-day boundary

0   500   1,000 miles
0   500   1,000 kilometers
Lambert Azimuthal Equal-Area Projection

60°E   80°E   100°E   120°E   140°E

80°N   60°N   40°N   20°N   0°   20°S   40°S

Imperial China

In this unit, you will study imperial China during the period from about 221 B.C.E. to about 1644 C.E. The word *imperial* means "ruled by an emperor." During this time, China was under the control of a series of dynasties, or ruling families.

China is located on the continent of Asia—the largest continent on Earth. China has three distinct elevations: the highlands in western China, the slightly lower plateau in central China, and the lowlands along the eastern coast.

The land is rocky, and the climate is cold in the towering Himalaya and Tian Shan mountains of western China. The Gobi Desert in the northern plateau is very dry. As a result, few people settled in these places. The central and southern part of the plateau were more inviting, but the coastal lands were the real population centers of imperial China. These plains were threaded with life-giving rivers and blanketed with rich soil.

Look at the map on the opposite page. Find the North China Plain, the Huang He (Yellow River), and the Chang Jiang (Yangtze River). This is where Chinese civilization began. People could grow food here, and the rivers made transportation easy. Because of these factors, trade flourished. The bustling market for goods led to the growth of cities. During these years of peace and prosperity, scholars and scientists were able to develop new technologies. Some of these led to new industries. Others helped the Chinese enlarge their trade empire.

The history of China is tied to its geography in other ways as well. Several strong emperors were able to expand China's borders to the west and south. To the north, however, the Gobi Desert stopped Chinese expansion. To the southwest, the cold, high Plateau of Tibet prevented the Chinese from enlarging their empire. At other times, and under other leaders, China was able to protect itself behind its oceans, mountains, and deserts, easily cutting itself off from the world.

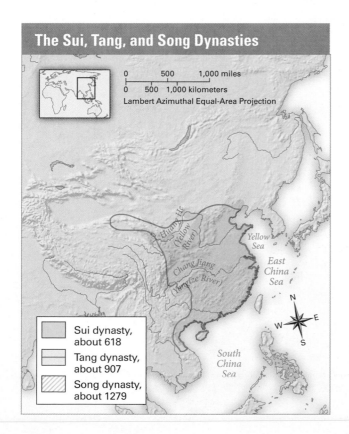

The Sui, Tang, and Song Dynasties

0   500   1,000 miles
0   500   1,000 kilometers
Lambert Azimuthal Equal-Area Projection

Huang He (Yellow River)

Chang Jiang (Yangtze River)

Yellow Sea

East China Sea

South China Sea

N E S W

Sui dynasty, about 618

Tang dynasty, about 907

Song dynasty, about 1279

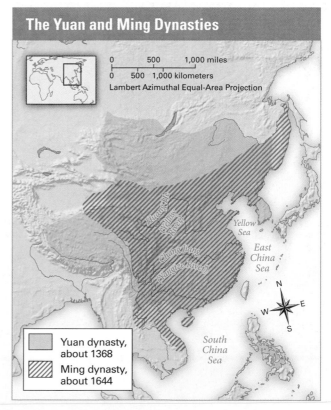

The Yuan and Ming Dynasties

0   500   1,000 miles
0   500   1,000 kilometers
Lambert Azimuthal Equal-Area Projection

Huang He (Yellow River)

Chang Jiang (Yangtze River)

Yellow Sea

East China Sea

South China Sea

N E S W

Yuan dynasty, about 1368

Ming dynasty, about 1644

Chapter 15

The Political Development of Imperial China

Which method of selecting officials led to the best leaders for China?

15.1 Introduction

Welcome to imperial China. Historians divide Chinese history into periods ruled by dynasties, or ruling families. In this chapter, you will learn about China's political development under several dynasties from 220 to 1644 C.E.

China was first unified under an emperor in the 3rd century B.C.E. From the beginning, emperors needed help to rule. Emperor Han Wu Di, for example, once sent out this announcement:

Heroes Wanted! A Proclamation
Exceptional work demands exceptional men. . . . We therefore command the various district officials to search for men of brilliant and exceptional talents, to be our generals, our ministers, and our envoys to distant states.

Over time, Chinese emperors tried several ways of finding qualified people to administer their government. One method was to rely on the class of wealthy families. Emperors like Han Wu Di, however, preferred to choose officials for their merit, or worth. During the Han dynasty, candidates for government jobs had to prove their knowledge and ability by passing strict tests. As a result, a class of scholar-officials evolved. Under later emperors, this system developed into a rule by officials of proven merit.

In the 13th century C.E., a nomadic people called the Mongols built a great empire in Asia. Toward the end of the century, the Mongols took over China. Under Mongol emperors, government officials in China were foreigners. Some officials were Mongol friends and relatives of the emperor. Others were trusted people from other lands.

How did these approaches to government affect China? Which method won out? In this chapter, you will explore these questions.

Emperors, such as the Hongwu Emperor of the Ming dynasty, ruled the vast country of China for over one thousand years with the help of a thousands of government officials.

◀ The Chinese held exams for hiring scholar-officials to help the emperor rule.

emperor the political leader of a territory containing several countries or groups of people

imperial belonging or related to an emperor

dynasty a line of rulers descended from one family

15.2 The Government of Imperial China

In 221 B.C.E., Prince Zheng (JUNG), the head of the state of Qin (CHIN), became the first Chinese ruler to claim the title of **emperor**. He took the name Qin Shihuangdi (CHIN shee-HWANG-dee), which means "First Emperor of Qin." From that time on, China usually had an **imperial** form of government headed by an emperor or, sometimes, an empress.

China's Imperial Dynasties Chinese emperors named a relative—often a son—to become emperor after their deaths. In this way they established a **dynasty,** or line of rulers from the same family.

From ancient times, Chinese rulers based their right to govern on the Mandate of Heaven. According to this idea, Heaven had chosen a particular dynasty to rule. The Chinese believed that Heaven supported the dynasty for as long as an emperor ruled well. Natural disasters such as floods, famines, plagues, and earthquakes were taken as signs that Heaven was displeased. If an emperor ruled badly and lost the Mandate of Heaven, the people could overthrow him.

The table below lists the imperial dynasties that ruled China between 221 B.C.E. and 1644 C.E. In this unit, you will focus on the dynasties that followed the Han dynasty.

China's Imperial Dynasties

Dynasty	Time Period	Known for
Qin dynasty	221–206 B.C.E.	unification of China under an emperor
Han dynasty	206 B.C.E.–220 C.E.	a golden age for a united China
Six dynasties	220–581 C.E.	a period of chaos and division
Sui dynasty	589–618 C.E.	reunification of China
Tang dynasty	618–907 C.E.	economic development and growth; many inventions and discoveries
Five dynasties in the north Ten Kingdoms in the south	907–960 C.E. 907–970 C.E.	a period of chaos and division
Song dynasty	960–1279 C.E.	economic development and growth; many inventions and discoveries
Yuan dynasty (the Mongols)	1279–1368 C.E.	control of China by foreigners
Ming dynasty	1368–1644 C.E.	opening up of China to foreign influences at the start of the dynasty; closing down of China by the end of the dynasty

China's Breakup and Reunification

The Han dynasty of ancient China held power for more than 400 years. This was a golden age of expansion and prosperity for China. In 220 C.E., however, the Han rulers lost their grip on power. A long period of disunity and conflict followed. This period ended when the Sui and Tang dynasties reunified China.

What happened to bring about the end of Han rule? Like earlier emperors, the Han governed China with the help of a large **bureaucracy** of government officials. As long as the bureaucracy was skilled, honest, and hard working, China prospered. By 220, however, corrupt, or dishonest, relatives and servants of the emperor had seized control of the government.

The result was disastrous. High taxes sent many families into poverty. Workers were forced to labor for long periods of time on public projects. Bandits attacked farmers in the countryside. This led **warlords** to oppose the emperor and fight against one another. The government grew weak and could not protect farmers.

Small farmers also suffered because they had to pay taxes and give half of everything they produced to their landlords. As they fell into debt, they had to give up their own land to large landowners and work for them, instead.

At last, the farmers rebelled. They believed that the Han dynasty had lost the Mandate of Heaven. No new dynasty took over from the Han. Instead, China broke apart into separate kingdoms, just as Europe did after the fall of Rome. Nomadic invaders ruled the north. Several short-lived dynasties ruled the south.

In 589, the northern state of Sui (SWAY) conquered the south and reunified China. The Sui dynasty created a new central government and ruled for 29 years. By 617, however, heavy taxes led to unrest and a struggle for power.

In 618, a general named Li Yuan declared himself emperor and established the Tang dynasty. Tang rulers built on the accomplishments of the Sui dynasty. They strengthened the central government and increased Tang influence over outlying areas.

Under the Tang, a unified China enjoyed a period of wealth and power that lasted nearly 300 years. Let's look now at how Tang rulers approached problems of government.

Warriors on horseback, like these, fought for the Han emperors as they struggled to maintain control of the empire against warlords and invaders.

bureaucracy a highly complex body of workers with many levels of authority

warlord a military leader operating outside the control of the government

15.3 Aristocracy: The Tang Dynasty

Like earlier emperors, Tang rulers relied on a large bureaucracy. Officials collected taxes and oversaw building and **irrigation** projects. They managed the army and enforced the laws. But how could emperors be sure that they chose the best people for these positions?

Earlier emperors answered this question in different ways. Before the Han dynasty, emperors chose members of the **aristocracy** to help them govern. These people were born into noble families of wealthy and powerful landowners. But simply being wealthy did not make a person talented and knowledgeable.

To improve the bureaucracy, Han emperors created **civil service examinations**. Candidates took long tests to qualify for office. The tests had questions on Chinese classics, poetry, and legal and administrative issues. Mainly, they were based on the works of Confucius (kon-FEW-shus), China's great philosopher and teacher. This began the system under which a class of scholar-officials ran the government.

Later, Tang emperors also used civil service exams to fill some government positions. Early in the dynasty, however, emperors chose aristocrats for most high-level jobs. Some officials were hired because their fathers or grandfathers had held high government rank. Some were hired because of personal recommendations. Often, aristocrats gained positions by marrying into the imperial family.

Even the civil service exams favored aristocrats. The tests were supposedly open to all except for certain groups, such as merchants, actors, and beggars. In theory, any man could attend the university where students prepared for the exams. In reality, however, only the wealthy could afford tutors, books, and time to study. As a result, aristocrats held almost all offices in the early part of the Tang dynasty.

Peasant rebellions and battles between generals ended the Tang dynasty in 907. Once again, China split apart. Five military dynasties followed one another to power in the north. The south broke up into independent kingdoms.

Beginning in 960, the Song (SOONG) dynasty rose. Gradually, Song emperors reunified the country. As you will see, they built on the civil service system to reform how government officials were chosen.

15.4 Meritocracy: The Song Dynasty

Under Song emperors, the idea of scholar-officials reached its height. The Song relied on civil service exams and opened them up to far more candidates. In this way, they created a **meritocracy**.

The exams were influenced by a new school of thought known as neo-Confucianism. This new teaching blended the teachings of Confucius with elements of Buddhism and Daoism (two traditional religions in China).

Civil service exams to choose China's government officials were based largely on the teachings of Confucius, a Chinese thinker and teacher who lived from 551 to 479 B.C.E.

A Confucian scholar, Zhu Xi (JU SHEE), commented on classic Chinese writings. In 1190, his work was published as the *Four Books*. This work became the basis of study for all civil service exams.

Confucius taught that people must act properly in five important relationships: ruler and subject, father and son, older **sibling** and younger sibling, husband and wife, and friend and friend. Except for friends, one person in each relationship is above the other. Those above should be kind to those below. Those below should respect and obey those above. In particular, subjects must be loyal to their rulers. Song emperors and scholars believed that officials who had studied Confucius would be **rational,** moral, and able to maintain order.

Under the Song, people from lower classes gained the ability to become scholar-officials. They could attend the new state-supported schools and go on to the university. If they passed a local test, they could take the imperial exam in the capital. On those exams, they wrote essays and poems in a certain style. They answered questions about political and social problems based on Confucian ideas.

The exams were set up to prevent cheating. Candidates were locked in a small room for several days. A second person copied each paper so that the examiners wouldn't know whose work they were reading.

Only a small proportion of candidates passed the difficult exams. Those who failed could take the tests again in the future. Those who passed had to wait a few years before their first appointment. When it came, it was for a job far from their hometown, so that they could not play favorites among family and friends. At the end of three years, officials could move up in rank.

Despite the challenges, people were happy to get such respected jobs. As government officials, they also enjoyed certain privileges, such as being excused from taxes and military service.

During the Song dynasty, scholar-officials performed many tasks. Here scholars organize ancient manuscripts.

15.5 Government by Foreigners: The Period of Mongol Rule

In the 13th century, the Mongols conquered almost all of Asia. In 1276, they captured China's imperial capital. Three years later, the last Song emperor died fleeing from the invaders.

The Mongol leader, Kublai Khan (KOOH-bly KAHN), took the title of emperor of China. He called his dynasty the Yuan dynasty. For nearly 100 years, from 1279 to 1368, China was under Mongol rule.

Under the Mongols, Chinese society was divided into four classes. The Mongols were at the top. Next came foreigners who were their friends. These people included Tibetans, Persians, Turks, and Central Asians. Many of them were Muslims. The third class was made up of the northern Chinese, who were more accustomed to the Mongols than were the southerners. The southern Chinese came last.

Kublai Khan ended the system of civil service exams. He did not believe that Confucian learning was needed for government jobs, and he did not want to rely on Chinese people to run his government. To fill important positions, he chose other Mongols whom he felt he could trust. Some of these people were his relatives.

But there weren't enough Mongols to fill every job. Besides, many were illiterate, or unable to read and write. Kublai and later Mongol emperors needed people who could handle the paperwork of a complex government. They were forced to appoint trusted foreigners to government positions, even some Europeans. Chinese scholars were appointed only as teachers and minor officials. Other Chinese worked as clerks, and some of them rose to important positions.

Without the examination system, however, there was a shortage of capable administrators. In 1315, the Mongols restored the exam system. Even then, they set limits on who could take the exam, favoring Mongol and other non-Chinese candidates.

As time went on, fighting among Mongol leaders weakened the government of China. So did the greed and corruption of officials. The Mongols had also made many enemies among the native Chinese. In the 1350s and 1360s, rebels rose up against them. In 1368, the Mongol dynasty collapsed, and the Chinese reestablished their own government under the Ming dynasty. The Ming ruled China for nearly 300 years.

The Mongols were a dynamic group of nomads who conquered huge areas of Asia, including China.

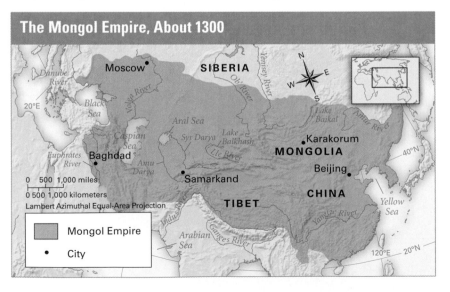

The Mongol Empire, About 1300

Danube River
Moscow
SIBERIA
Yenisey River
20°E
Black Sea
Volga River
Ob' River
Aral Sea
Caspian Sea
Syr Darya
Lake Balkhash
Lake Baikal
Amur River
Euphrates River
Baghdad
Amu Darya
Ili River
Karakorum
MONGOLIA
40°N
Samarkand
Beijing
0 500 1,000 miles
0 500 1,000 kilometers
Lambert Azimuthal Equal-Area Projection
TIBET
CHINA
Yellow Sea
Arabian Sea
Ganges River
Yangzi River
120°E
20°N

☐ Mongol Empire
• City

15.6 The Revival of the Civil Service System

Under Ming emperors, civil service exams were again used to fill government positions. This system lasted into the 20th century.

In many ways, the exam system served China well. It provided a well-organized government. The education of its scholar-officials **emphasized** moral behavior, justice, kindness, loyalty to the emperor, proper conduct, and the importance of family. These values helped to unify Chinese culture.

The civil service system gave poor men who were ambitious and hard working the chance to be government officials. At the same time, it ensured that officials were trained and talented, not merely rich or related to the emperor.

Yet China's civil service system may also have stood in the way of progress. The exams did not test understanding of science, mathematics, or engineering. People with such knowledge were therefore kept out of the government. Confucian scholars also had little respect for merchants, business, and trade. Confucians had often considered merchants to be the lowest class in society because they bought and sold things rather than producing useful items themselves. Under the Ming, this outlook dominated, and trade and business were not encouraged. In addition, the bureaucracy became set in its ways. Its inability to adapt contributed to the fall of the Ming in 1644.

Civil service exams lasted for several days. Candidates were locked in small cells like these during the tests.

Chapter Summary

In this chapter, you have learned how China was governed between 220 and 1644 C.E. Chinese emperors relied on a bureaucracy to help them govern. At different times, they used various methods of choosing government officials.

Imperial Government In 221 B.C.E., a prince of Qin became the first Chinese emperor under the name Qin Shihuangdi. For more than 1,500 years, China was ruled under an imperial government by a series of dynasties.

Aristocracy Early emperors chose officials from the aristocracy. The Han tried to improve government by creating a civil service examination system. Candidates for government jobs had to pass tests based mostly on Confucian learning. Under the Sui and Tang dynasties civil service exams continued, but aristocrats filled most government jobs under the Tang.

Meritocracy Rulers of the Song dynasty used civil service exams to create a meritocracy of scholar-officials.

Government by Foreigners Mongol emperors from outside of China relied on family members, friends, and trusted foreigners to help run the government.

Civil Service System Restored Under the Ming, the Chinese restored their civil service system. Bureaucrats became set in their ways, and innovation was not encouraged.

Chapter 16

China Develops a New Economy

How did the Chinese improve their economy during the Tang and Song dynasties?

16.1 Introduction

In this chapter, you will learn about the growth of China's economy during the Tang and the Song dynasties. This period lasted from about 618 to 1279 C.E.

The Song period was a time of great prosperity in China. Changes in agriculture, especially a boom in the production of rice, fueled the growth of the economy. Trade and business flourished. These developments had started during the Tang dynasty. Under the Song, they would help make China one of the most advanced economies in the world.

Along with prosperity came the growth of cities. During this period, China's huge cities dwarfed the cities of medieval Europe.

An Italian traveler named Marco Polo first saw China toward the end of the Song dynasty. He marveled at China's crowded cities and bustling markets. Polo was especially impressed by the boat traffic on the Grand Canal. This great waterway linked northern China with the Chang Jiang (Yangtze) river valley in the south. Farmers and merchants used the canal to ship their crops and goods. Polo wrote, "It is indeed surprising to observe the multitude [vast number] and the size of the vessels that are continually passing and repassing, laden [loaded] with merchandise of the greatest value."

In this chapter, you will learn how changes in agriculture, trade and commerce, and urbanization made China so prosperous. Let's begin by finding out how changes in agriculture improved China's economy during the Tang and Song dynasties.

The Grand Canal continues to be an important waterway. Barges still transport goods along its length. What similarities and differences can you notice between this photo and the image on the opposite page?

◄ The Grand Canal provided a waterway between northern and southern China.

16.2 Changes in Agriculture

Changes in agriculture were a major reason for the growth of China's **economy** during the Song dynasty. This period saw a huge increase in the production of rice, as well as new and better farming methods. Let's look at how and why these changes happened.

Reasons for Agricultural Changes There were several reasons for the changes in agriculture. The first was the movement of farmers to the fertile basins of the Chang Jiang in southern China.

During the Tang dynasty, northern China was the wealthiest and most populous part of the country. But wars and attacks by tribes from Mongolia drove many landowners to move south. Under the Song, southern China continued to grow. By 1207, about 65 million people lived in the south, compared to 50 million in the north.

The move to the south changed what farmers grew. Northern farmers had cultivated wheat and millet. These crops grew well in the north's cold, dry climate. In contrast, the south's climate was warm and wet. Wetlands covered most of the Chang Jiang valley. These conditions were ideal for cultivating rice plants, which need a lot of water.

Rice farmers, though, did face challenges. Rice crops were frequently destroyed by periods of drought and violent storms, called typhoons. Even if a crop survived, it took five months for the rice to mature from planting to harvest.

During the 11th century, a new variety of rice was brought to China from Southeast Asia. It was resistant to drought, and it matured in two months instead of five. Now farmers could plant at least two crops of rice each year. As a result, rice production in China boomed.

Rice became the most important crop in China in the 13th century. Below left, a farmer uses a harrow pulled by a water buffalo to prepare the rice paddy for planting. Below right, peasants plant rice seedlings in flooded paddies.

Above left, a chain pump provides water for the rice paddy. At right, peasants harvest the rice by hand.

Production increased even more with new and better farming techniques and tools. An improved plow and harrow, a tool used to level plowed ground, made it easier to prepare fields for planting. Farmers also began using fertilizer to produce larger crops. A device called a chain pump, which used containers attached to a loop of chain to move water, helped farmers irrigate land at the edges of lakes, marshes, and rivers. To grow rice on hillsides, farmers created flat areas called terraces. More and more land was devoted to farming, and landowners became wealthier.

Characteristics of the New Agriculture Picture yourself visiting a farming area in southern China during the 13th century. Small farms cover every bit of suitable land. Terraced hillsides spread as far as you can see. Rice grows on the terraces in flooded fields called paddies. **Elaborate** irrigation systems crisscross the paddies, bringing water where it's needed.

Early in the growing season, you see water buffaloes pulling a plow and harrow to level the fields and prepare them for planting. The seeds have been growing in seedbeds for a month. Now, workers will transplant the young plants to the paddy.

Growing rice takes a lot of hard work done by many hands. In the fields, large numbers of workers walk backward as they transplant the rice plants in straight rows. Two months from now, the workers will harvest the rice by hand.

Before and during the growing season, the rice paddy has to be constantly watered and drained. Dams, dikes, gated channels, and chain pumps help to move water into and out of the paddies.

Although rice is the main crop, peasants grow tea, cotton, and sugar. They also grow mulberry trees. The leaves feed silkworms.

In the southern hill area, you see tea plants. The Chinese had once used tea only as medicine. But by the 9th century, tea was the national drink. Tea drinking became a social custom, and teahouses became popular. To meet the demand, farmers grew more tea.

Results of Agricultural Changes The shift to growing rice was an important development for medieval China. First, it increased food production. The new abundance of food helped to support a larger population. For the first time, China's population grew to more than 100 million people.

With ample food, peasants could take time away from farming to weave silk, cotton cloth, and other products to sell or trade. Rice farmers could also market their surplus rice. Landowners became rich enough from growing rice to buy luxury items. All these changes encouraged the growth of trade.

16.3 The Growth of Trade and Commerce

Trade and **commerce** were already underway during the Tang dynasty. Tang emperors eased **restrictions** on merchants, and they actively promoted trade. Products like rice, silk, tea, jade, and porcelain traveled along trade routes to India, Arabia, and Europe. Under the Song, business activity blossomed even more.

Reasons for Growth in Trade and Commerce One reason for the growth of trade and commerce was that wealthy landowners were eager to buy luxuries. The demand for luxuries encouraged an increase in trade, as well as an increase in the number of Chinese artisans, who made silk and other goods.

Commerce was also helped by water transportation. A vast network of rivers and canals connected different parts of China. Farmers in central China could ship their rice north along the Grand Canal. Busy boat owners had plenty of business, because it was cheaper and faster to move goods by water than by road. A long boat with a flat bottom, called a barge, could travel 45 miles a day, compared to 25 miles a day for an oxcart.

Innovations in navigation helped increase foreign and overseas trade. Navigational charts and diagrams, along with the magnetic compass (a Chinese invention), made it easier for sailors to keep to their routes on long voyages.

With so much buying and selling, people needed **currency**. In the 11th century, the government minted huge numbers of copper coins—so many that there was a copper shortage. Therefore, moneylenders began issuing paper money to merchants. The idea caught on, and the government printed paper money in large quantities. The increase in currency further spurred the growth of commerce.

commerce the buying and selling of goods; business

currency the form of money used in a country

Chinese trade goods included objects of high value and beauty, such as this carved jade dragon cup from the Song dynasty.

Characteristics of China's Commercial Growth Let's take a trip on the waterways of China in the 13th century. Our first stop is a market town along a canal. The canal is crowded with barges loaded with rice and other goods. The barges are sailed, rowed, or pushed along with the help of long poles. Oxcarts and pack animals trudge along the roads and over the bridges that cross the canal. Peasants are coming to town to sell their surplus crops and animals, as well as items they have made at home, such as silk and charcoal.

On the streets and bridges, merchants have set up small shops to attract customers who are visiting the city. Street peddlers sell goods from the packs they carry.

You also see "deposit shops" where merchants trade long strings of copper coins for paper money. Paper money is much easier to carry around, but unlike copper, it has no value in itself. If there is too much paper money in **circulation,** it loses its value. For this reason, the government controls the amount of paper money that is available. It also threatens to cut off the heads of counterfeiters who print fake money.

Let's continue our journey to a port city on the eastern coast. In the harbor, men are loading silk, ceramics, sugar, and rice into large sailing vessels called junks. These ships are big enough to hold several hundred men. Their sails are made of bamboo matting. The junks will soon depart for Korea, Japan, Southeast Asia, India, the East Indies, and even Africa. They will return loaded with indigo for making blue dye, spices, silver, ivory, and coral.

Results of the Growth in Trade and Commerce The increase in China's trade and commerce had several effects. First, it resulted in the growth of the merchant class. Second, business brought increased prosperity, giving China the highest living standard in the world at that time. Third, many commercial centers grew into big cities.

Commerce greatly expanded in China under the Song dynasty. This scene shows commercial life in the city of Kaifeng during the 13th century. Kaifeng was an important city, and the capital under both the Tang and the Song dynasties.

China Develops a New Economy **193**

As population increased and commerce grew, huge cities developed, such as Kaifeng. This scene is part of a 15-foot illustrated scroll called *Ch'ing Ming Festival on the River*.

urbanization the growth of cities

16.4 The Growth of Urbanization

Urbanization increased during the Song dynasty as cities sprouted up all over China. Chinese cities became the largest in the world. The city of Hangzhou had perhaps 2 million people within its walls. It's no wonder that Marco Polo was impressed with the cities he visited. European cities of this period had no more than 50,000 residents.

Reasons for Urbanization Why did the growth of cities increase under the Song? One answer is that the growth of commerce encouraged people to move to cities and towns. There, people could make a living as merchants, traders, peddlers, and shopkeepers. In addition, landowners left their farms because they preferred the shops and social life of the cities. More people brought still more opportunities for business and jobs, and cities grew even larger.

Characteristics of Cities China's cities at this time were crowded, exciting places. The crowds in Hangzhou astonished Marco Polo. He wrote, "Anyone seeing such a multitude would believe it impossible that food could be found to feed them all, and yet on every market day all the market squares are filled with people and with merchants who bring food on carts and boats."

Let's stroll through a typical 13th-century city. The streets are filled with rich landowners, merchants, traders, moneylenders, and visiting peasants eager to sell their surplus crops. Signs in the market area identify the goods sold in each shop.

In the entertainment area musicians, jugglers, acrobats, and puppeteers perform outdoors. People are enjoying the theater. They are visiting with friends in restaurants and teahouses. Food vendors carrying trays of food on their heads provide plenty to eat.

You might be surprised to see wealthy young girls whose feet are so tightly bound with cloth that their toes are bent under. These girls will grow up to have tiny feet, which the Chinese consider beautiful. But they will have great difficulty walking.

This custom of foot binding first became common during the Song dynasty. It marked a decline in the status of women. Some followers of Confucianism taught that women were inferior to men. In addition, women of the middle and upper classes in cities did not work. In the countryside, women enjoyed greater status because they did participate in work on farms.

Results of Urbanization The growth of cities changed the way many ordinary Chinese lived. Cities were vibrant centers of activity, from buying and selling, to hobbies and board games. Public-works projects provided employment for many city dwellers. Urbanization also **stimulated** culture, giving artists an audience of wealthy, leisured people. Paintings produced during the Song period are considered some of the finest in the world.

Chapter Summary

In this chapter, you learned about changes in agriculture, trade and commerce, and urbanization during the Tang and the Song dynasties.

Changes in Agriculture During this time, the center of Chinese civilization shifted from the north to the south. The south's climate was ideal for growing rice. Rice became China's most important crop. A new kind of rice seed and improvements in farming methods greatly increased rice production. This helped support a larger population. It also gave landowners money to buy luxuries, which stimulated the growth of commerce.

The Growth of Trade and Commerce Commerce was also helped by a network of rivers and canals. Improvements in navigation made overseas trade easier. Traders and merchants supplied the goods people wanted to buy. As China moved to a money economy, the increase in currency helped business to grow.

The Growth of Urbanization Increased commercial activity contributed to the growth of cities. Merchants, peasants, peddlers, and traders sold all kinds of goods. China enjoyed the highest living standard in the world at that time.

Chapter 17

Chinese Discoveries and Inventions

How have medieval Chinese discoveries and inventions influenced the modern world?

17.1 Introduction

In this chapter, you will explore discoveries and inventions made by the Chinese between about 200 and 1400 C.E. Many of these advances took place during the Tang and Song dynasties, and the influence of these advancements is still seen today.

Over the centuries, Chinese scholars and scientists studied engineering, mathematics, science, and medicine, among other subjects. Their studies led to scientific and technological progress that was often far ahead of advances in the rest of the world.

To understand the importance of one Chinese innovation, suppose that you are a trader in the 10th century. You are far out at sea on a Chinese junk loaded with goods you are bringing to Korea. Without landmarks to guide you, how do you know in which direction you're headed? Normally, you might steer by the sun or the stars. But what if it's cloudy? Can you still figure out which way to travel?

In the past, you might have been lost. But thanks to the **magnetic** compass, you can find your way. Your compass is a magnetized needle that aligns itself with Earth's magnetic poles so that one end points north and the other south. By the Song dynasty, the Chinese were using this type of compass to help them navigate on long voyages. People still use the same kind of device today.

Like the compass, other Chinese inventions and discoveries made it possible for people to do things better than they had before. In this chapter, you will learn about Chinese advances in exploration and travel, industry, military technology, everyday objects, and disease prevention. As you will see, the influence of many Chinese ideas reached far beyond China.

The magnetic compass is a Chinese invention that people still use to help them find their way on long trips on land or at sea.

◀ Scientific advances helped medieval Chinese sailors to make long sea voyages.

17.2 Exploration and Travel

Several Chinese inventions made exploration and travel safer and faster. Some innovations benefited traders and other voyagers who ventured out to sea. Others improved travel on rivers, lakes, canals, and bridges within China.

Paddlewheel boats were easy to maneuver, which made them effective warships, perhaps starting as early as the 6th century.

Improving Travel by Sea The Chinese developed the first compass as early as the 3rd century B.C.E. The first Chinese compasses were pieces of a magnetic mineral called lodestone. Earth itself is like a giant magnet with north and south poles. Because lodestone is magnetic, it is influenced by Earth's magnetic poles. If you put a piece of lodestone on wood and float it in a bowl of water, the lodestone will turn until it points in a north-south direction.

Europeans also developed a compass using lodestone. However, the Chinese eventually replaced the lodestone with a steel needle. They had learned that rubbing a needle with lodestone made the needle act in the same way as the lodestone. However, needle in a compass gave a more accurate reading than a piece of lodestone.

By the time of the Song dynasty, the Chinese were using magnetic compasses for navigation at sea. Compasses made long sea voyages possible because sailors could figure out directions even without a landmark or a point in the sky to steer by. The compass remains an important navigational tool today.

The Chinese also made sea travel safer by improving boat construction. By the 2nd century C.E., they started building ships with separate, watertight compartments. Builders divided the ships into sections and sealed each section with caulk, a sealant that keeps out water. If there were a leak, it would be isolated. The other compartments would not fill with water, keeping the ship afloat. Modern shipbuilders still use this technique.

Improving Travel on Rivers, Lakes, Canals, and Bridges Within China, people often traveled by boat on rivers or across lakes. An innovation of a vessel called a paddlewheel boat made this type of travel much faster.

Have you ever paddled a canoe or other small boat? As you push your paddle through the water, the boat moves forward. In the 5th century, the Chinese adapted this idea by arranging a series of paddles in a wheel. People walked on a treadmill to turn the paddlewheel, which in turn moved through the water, moving the boat forward.

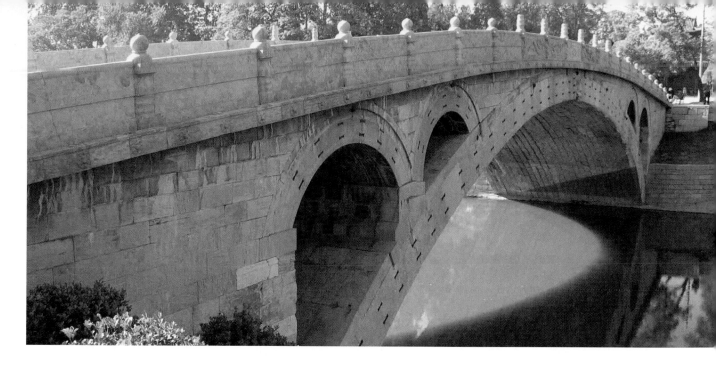

The Romans had also developed a paddlewheel-powered boat, but it was powered by oxen, which are not as easy to direct as people.

The people-powered paddlewheel boats allowed the Chinese to travel much faster on rivers and lakes. These boats were also much easier to maneuver than other types of watercraft. People still use this type of boat for recreational activities.

Another way the Chinese improved transportation was by developing a new type of canal lock, during the Song dynasty. The Chinese used canals extensively to connect the many rivers. As the surrounding land sloped up, parts of canals were at different levels. Before the improved locks were invented, the Chinese had to drag their boats up stone ramps to reach water at a higher level. This was difficult and could damage the boats.

The new canal locks solved this problem. When a boat entered the lock, a gate was lowered to hold in water. The water was then allowed to rise until it reached the level of the water up ahead. Then the boat floated on. To go "downhill," water was released by the lock until it fell to the level of the water down below.

The innovative new type of locks made canal travel much easier. Locks could raise boats more than 100 feet above sea level.

The Chinese also found ways to improve bridges. For example, in 618 C.E., a Chinese engineer completed a new type of arched bridge. In Europe, Roman-designed bridges rested on arches that were half-circles. The new Chinese bridge used arches that were a smaller part, or **segment,** of a circle. This made the bridges broader and flatter than semicircular arches could. Called a segmental arch bridge, the new type of bridge took less material to build and was stronger, as well.

Many cultures developed engineering technologies. However, the segmental arch bridge is one of China's most prized achievements. Bridges of that design stretch over expressways around the world.

The Great Stone Bridge, completed in 618, spans the river Chiao Shui in China. It was the world's first segmental arch bridge. It has a span of 123 feet.

17.3 Industry

Some of the advances made by the Chinese led to new industries. In this section, you will learn about advances and innovations in the way the medieval Chinese made paper, print, tea, porcelain, and steel.

Paper The Chinese invented the art of papermaking by the second century C.E. The earliest Chinese paper was probably made from hemp and then the bark of the mulberry tree. Later, the Chinese used rags.

Papermaking became an important industry in China. For more than 500 years, the Chinese were the only people in the world who knew the secret of making paper. From China, knowledge of papermaking traveled to Japan and across Central Asia. Europeans probably first learned about this art after 1100. Considering how important it is for recording and transmitting information, few inventions touch our daily lives more than paper.

Printing The invention of paper made another key development possible: printing. In about the 7th century, the Chinese invented a technique called woodblock printing. The printer first drew characters (symbols) on paper. He then glued the paper to a wooden block. When the glue was dry, the printer carved out the wood around the characters, leaving the characters raised on the wood.

To print from the block, the printer covered the characters with black ink. Then he spread paper over the block and smoothed the paper with a brush. Some artists still use block printing today to create fine art prints.

By the 8th century, there was an entire woodblock printing industry in China. Printers turned out religious and other works on scrolls. In the 10th century, the Chinese started printing modern-style books with pages.

In the 11th century, during the Song dynasty, the Chinese invented **movable type**. (Europeans developed movable type independently in the 1400s.) Movable type consists of separate blocks for each character. Printers made their type by carving characters out of clay and baking them. To print, they selected the characters they needed and placed them in an iron frame in the order they would appear on the page. When the printing job was done, the type could be removed from the frame and rearranged to use again.

With the invention of movable type, printers no longer had to create a new set of woodblocks for each item they printed. This dramatically lowered the cost and labor of printing. Written materials became more widely available, and advances in printing helped spread learning throughout China. Until the last century, all newspapers, books, and magazines were printed using movable type.

movable type individual characters made of wood or metal that can be arranged to create a printing job and then be used over again

A printer used engraving tools such as these to carve the scene on the woodblock below.

The woodblock was then covered with ink, and paper was pressed onto it to create the print at the bottom.

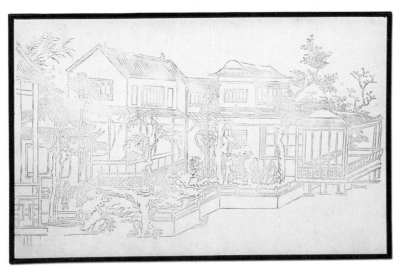

Notice that the printed scene is a mirror image of the carved scene on the woodblock.

Tea We know from written accounts that the Chinese have been drinking tea since at least 2700 B.C. For several thousand years, tea—made by letting tea leaves steep in boiling water—was drunk mostly as medicine. However, by the 8th century C.E., tea had become a hugely popular everyday beverage throughout China. Tea houses had sprung up throughout the country. A famous writer, Lu Yu, wrote a book, *Cha Jing* (*Tea Classic*), describing how to cultivate, prepare, and drink tea. The drink's popularity made tea-plant cultivation a major industry, often involving an entire community.

Basic tea cultivation and processing has not changed much since early times. Tea farmers grow small tea trees or shrubs on high ground—usually above 4,000 feet. When the trees are ready for harvest, only new-growth leaves are picked—by hand. Then the tree is cut back so it will grow new leaves for the next harvest, and the cycle repeats several times a year. Workers then dry the fresh leaves by leaving them out in sunlight for different numbers of days, depending on the variety of tea. The final drying process takes place in a dry wok or in a small oven.

During the Tang Dynasty, the first tea-plant seeds were brought to Japan. Tea cultivation became an industry there by about 1200. Europeans became involved in tea farming and trade by the 18th century. Dutch traders brought seeds from Japan and China to their colonies in Indonesia. Tea plants were found in the British territories of Burma (now Myanmar) and India. The Dutch and British produced and traded tea throughout their empires, spreading the beverage around the world. The two nations competed for the tea trade in the 13 American colonies. During the Boston Tea Party, colonists tossed British tea into Boston Harbor, helping to spark the American Revolution. Today, tea is one of the most popular beverages in the world. And, as in ancient China, people now often drink tea for their health.

The art of making porcelain was invented in China and became a major industry there.

Porcelain Another Chinese invention is a type of fine pottery called porcelain. Some historians think that the Chinese produced the first porcelain as early as the 1st century C.E.

Porcelain is made by combining clay with the minerals quartz and feldspar. The mixture is baked in a kiln, or pottery oven, at very high temperatures. The resulting pottery is white, hard, and waterproof. However, light can pass through it, so that despite its sturdiness it looks quite delicate and beautiful.

By the 10th century, the Chinese were making porcelain of great beauty. Craftspeople learned how to paint pictures on porcelain. They also made colored glazes to decorate their porcelain.

Porcelain making became a major industry in China. Hundreds of thousands of people worked to **mass-produce** dishes, bowls, and vases. Some workers washed the clay. Others applied the glaze or operated the kiln.

Chinese porcelain became a prized item for trade. Europeans did not learn how to make fine porcelain until the 18th century. Many people think that medieval Chinese porcelain is the finest in the world. People today still refer to fine dinnerware as "china."

Works of fine Chinese porcelain, such as this vase from the Ming dynasty, are still prized around the world.

Steel The Chinese first made steel, a very useful metal, before 200 B.C.E. Steel is made from iron, but it is less brittle than iron and easier to bend into different shapes.

The earliest Chinese steel was made from cast iron. The Chinese were the first to learn how to make cast iron by melting and molding iron ore. Later they learned that blowing air into molten, or melted, cast iron causes a chemical reaction that creates steel. Steel is a great deal stronger than iron.

These developments eventually made it possible to produce large amounts of steel cheaply. In the 1800s, the mass production of steel was crucial to the Industrial Revolution in the West. Today, iron and steel making are among China's most important industries.

mass-produce to make quantities of an item by using standardized designs and dividing steps of production among the workers

This model of a 14th-century bees' nest rocket launcher was re-created based on a medieval drawing and written descriptions.

17.4 Military Technology

During the Song and Mongol periods, the Chinese developed powerful weapons. The invention of **gunpowder**—one of the most significant inventions in history—made these weapons possible.

The Development of Gunpowder The Chinese who first made gunpowder were alchemists, people who practiced a blend of science and magic known as alchemy. Alchemists experimented with mixtures of natural ingredients, trying to find a substance that might allow people to live forever. They also searched for a way to make gold out of cheaper metals.

Chinese alchemists experimented with a mineral called saltpeter. They may have believed that saltpeter could extend life. Perhaps by accident, they discovered that it could be used to make an explosive powder. In 850 C.E., during the Tang dynasty, alchemists recorded a formula for gunpowder. They warned others to avoid it because it was extremely dangerous.

By the 10th century, the Chinese had made the first weapon that used gunpowder: the flamethrower. Early flamethrowers contained gunpowder mixed with oil. The Chinese used them to spray enemies with a stream of fire.

Between the 11th and 14th centuries, the Chinese created many other weapons using gunpowder. Artillery shells, for example, exploded after being hurled at enemies by a war machine called a catapult. The sound of the exploding shells confused the enemy and terrified their horses. Small bombs, or grenades, were lit and thrown by hand.

In the 13th century, the Chinese used large bombs that were as explosive as modern bombs. Around the same time, they developed weapons much like today's rifles and cannons.

By the early 1300s, travelers had brought the knowledge of gunpowder to Europe. Gunpowder forever changed the way people waged war. Eventually, weapons like crossbows, swords, and spears gave way to guns and cannons.

Rocket Technology Rocket technology was developed in China during the Song dynasty. Rockets were powered by a black powder made of saltpeter, charcoal, and sulfur. At first, rockets were used only in fireworks. Later, the Chinese used them as weapons. They even developed a two-stage rocket for their armies. The first stage propelled the rocket through the air. The second stage dropped arrows down on the enemy.

By 1300, rockets had spread through much of Asia and into Europe. The rockets that we use to explore space today are based on principles discovered by the Chinese.

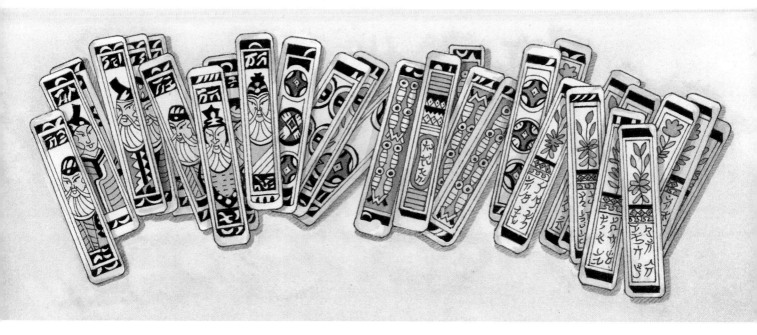

17.5 Everyday Objects

Do you ever play games with a deck of cards? If so, you are using a Chinese invention. The Chinese invented a number of everyday objects people use today, including game cards, paper money, and mechanical clocks. All these inventions were developed during the Tang dynasty.

Game Cards and Paper Money Game cards were invented in China in about the 9th century. Printers used woodblock printing to make the cards from thick paper. Famous artists drew the designs that appeared on the backs of the cards. Europeans were introduced to card games by the late 1300s. Today, card games are played throughout the world.

Paper money was invented by the Chinese in the late 8th or early 9th century. Before that time, coins were the only form of currency. Like game cards, paper money was printed with wood blocks. By 1107, Song printers were using multiple wood blocks to print each bill. A single bill would have many colors. Paper money is the most common form of currency in the world today.

The Development of the Mechanical Clock The Chinese developed the first mechanical clock in about the 8th century. The new clock was more accurate than earlier timekeeping devices, such as sundials and hourglasses. The Chinese devised a wheel that made one complete turn every 24 hours. Dripping water made the wheel turn. Every quarter hour, drums would beat; and every hour, a bell would chime. The sounds let people know what time it was.

Cards were invented in about the 9th century in China. A typical pack had 30 cards and was used to play many different games.

The Chinese improved the mechanical clock in 1092, during the Song dynasty. The new clock worked on the same principles as the earlier one, but it was much more complex and accurate.

Europeans first developed mechanical clocks in the late 1200s. As with Chinese clocks, a bell rang to indicate the hour. Later, dials and hands were added. Modern-day mechanical clocks are based on the same **fundamental** principles as early Chinese clocks.

17.6   Disease Prevention

Chinese knowledge of medicine and disease prevention dates to ancient times. Before the 1st century C.E., the Chinese developed a way of fighting infectious diseases. An infectious disease is one that can spread from person to person. When a person died from an infectious disease, the Chinese burned a chemical that gave off a poisonous smoke. They believed that the smoke would destroy whatever was causing the disease.

Today, we know that many diseases are caused by germs. We prevent the spread of disease by using disinfectants—substances, such as chlorine bleach—that kill germs. The poisonous smoke used by the Chinese was a type of disinfectant.

Doctors and patients in China during the medieval period benefited from new knowledge of medicine and treatment of diseases.

During the Song dynasty, the Chinese discovered another way to prevent the spread of disease. A Chinese monk recommended steaming the clothes of sick people. He believed that the steam would prevent others from becoming ill. The idea was sound, because hot temperatures kill many germs. Today, people boil medical instruments to kill disease-causing germs.

Sometime around the 10th century, the Chinese discovered how to **inoculate** people against smallpox, a dreaded infectious disease. Inoculation is a way of stimulating a person's immune system to fight a particular disease. It works by exposing the person to a disease-carrying substance. To inoculate people against smallpox, Chinese physicians took a small part of a scab from an infected person and made it into a powder. Then they inserted the powder into the nose of the person they wanted to immunize, or protect against the disease.

inoculate to protect against disease by transmitting a disease-causing agent to a person, stimulating the body's defensive reactions

The Chinese knew that they had to take care when exposing people to smallpox. Sometimes the treatment itself caused people to become ill. To be as safe as possible, the Chinese took the infectious material from people who had already been inoculated.

Chinese knowledge about smallpox inoculation eventually led to the development of drugs called vaccines. We now have vaccines for many diseases, including smallpox and the flu.

Chapter Summary

In this chapter, you learned about Chinese inventions and discoveries between about 200 and 1400 C.E. The influence of many of these advances spread far beyond China. Many Chinese inventions and discoveries continue to affect our lives today.

Exploration and Travel Several Chinese ideas improved travel and exploration. They include the magnetic compass, paddlewheel boats, canal locks, and segmental arch bridges.

Industry Advances in papermaking and printing, including movable type, helped spread learning. Chinese porcelain became famous for its quality and beauty. The Chinese also discovered ways to make steel.

Military Technology The Chinese revolutionized military technology. They discovered how to use gunpowder to make powerful weapons. They also developed the first rockets.

Everyday Objects A number of Chinese inventions enriched people's everyday lives. Among them are game cards, paper money, and mechanical clocks.

Disease Prevention The Chinese also made great strides in medicine and disease prevention. They discovered how to stop the spread of disease by using disinfectants and steam. Inoculations were used to protect individuals from catching smallpox.

Chapter 18

China's Contacts with the Outside World

How did the foreign-contact policies of three medieval Chinese dynasties affect China?

18.1 Introduction

In this chapter, you will learn about medieval China's foreign contacts. You will focus on three important dynasties: the Tang dynasty (618–907), the Mongol, or Yuan (YOO-an), dynasty (1279–1368), and the Ming dynasty (1368–1644).

At times, the Chinese welcomed foreign contacts. Great cultural exchange resulted as new ideas and products flowed into and out of China. Buddhism, which originally came from India, reached its height of influence during the Tang dynasty. A Chinese monk, Xuan Zang (zhwoo-AN ZANG), traveled to India at this time. He brought back thousands of Buddhist scriptures. The Chinese honored him for making Buddhism more widely known. Although it was foreign in origin, Buddhism became very popular in China.

Many Chinese, however, resented foreign influence. Less than two centuries after Xuan Zang's trip to India, one scholar-official harshly criticized Buddhism. "Buddha," he said, "was a man of the barbarians who did not speak the language of China and wore clothes of a different fashion. His sayings did not concern the ways of our ancient kings, nor did his manner of dress conform to their laws." More than once, such feelings led rulers to try to limit the influence of foreigners.

In this chapter, you will learn how the Chinese both welcomed and rejected foreign contacts. You will find out how cultural exchange affected China. You will also discover how Ming emperors tried to close China's doors to foreign influence entirely.

Work began on this stone Buddha statue during the Tang dynasty. At that time, the influence of the Indian religion of Buddhism was at its height in China.

◀ The gates of the imperial Forbidden City were open to foreigners at times.

18.2 Foreign Contacts Under the Tang Dynasty

During the Tang dynasty (618–907), China welcomed contact with foreigners. Traders and visitors brought new ideas, goods, fashions, and religions into the country.

The Influence of Traders and Visitors Beginning in the Han dynasty, traders and visitors came to China by a network of trade routes across Central Asia. From Chang'an, China's capital, camel caravans crossed the deserts of Central Asia between oases. The routes followed by the caravans are known collectively as the Silk Road, though many goods besides silk were traded.

For a time, travel along the Silk Road became unsafe because of fighting in Central Asia. The Tang made travel safe again by taking control of much of Central Asia. As a result, trade flourished with Central Asian kingdoms, Persia (modern-day Iran), and the Byzantine Empire. Traders also traveled by sea between China and Korea, Japan, Indonesia, and India.

Merchants, missionaries, and other visitors also came to China. Thousands of Arabs, Turks, Persians, Tibetans, Indians, Jews, Koreans, Japanese, and other foreigners lived in seaports and in Chang'an.

All these foreign contacts brought about much cultural exchange. The Chinese sent their silk, porcelain, paper, iron, and jade along the trade routes. In return, they **imported** ivory, cotton, perfumes, spices, and horses. From India the Chinese learned to make sugar from sugarcane and wine from grapes. New medicines also came from India.

The rulers of the Tang dynasty were open to foreign contact, and their control over much of Central Asia made the Silk Road an important trade route again, as it had been in earlier times.

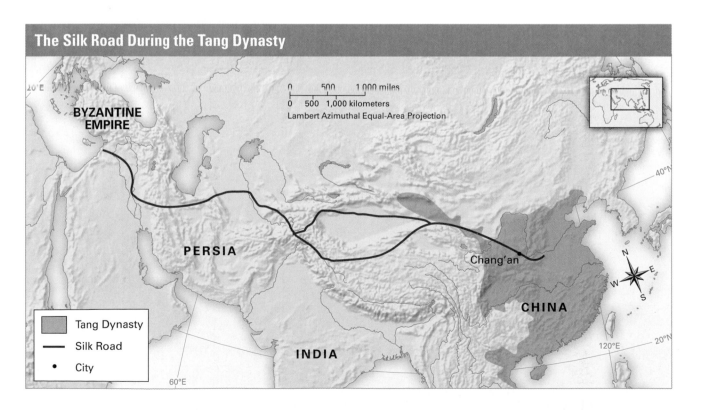

The Silk Road During the Tang Dynasty

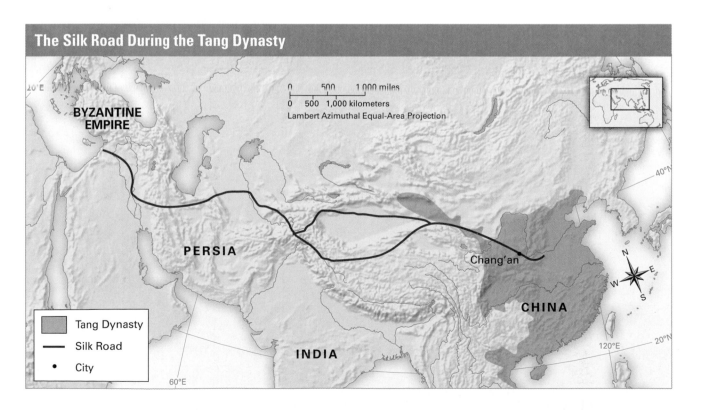

BYZANTINE EMPIRE

PERSIA

Chang'an

CHINA

INDIA

Tang Dynasty
Silk Road
City

0   500   1,000 miles
0 500 1,000 kilometers
Lambert Azimuthal Equal-Area Projection

The Tang Chinese, especially the upper classes, welcomed new products and ideas from foreign cultures. They wore rubies, pearls, and other jewels. They drank from goblets made of glass, a material that had been unknown in China. They ate new foods, such as spinach, garlic, mustard, and peas. They used cloves, a type of spice, to treat toothaches. Sitting in chairs from Central Asia instead of on floor cushions became a **status** symbol. The game of polo, a Persian sport played on horseback, became the rage among the upper-class.

Chinese music was greatly influenced by melodies and musical instruments from India, Persia, and Central Asia. Artists and artisans also imitated new foreign styles. Silversmiths, for example, began using Persian designs.

New religions also came to China, which the Tang tolerated. Jews, Christians, and Muslims built houses of worship in Chang'an. They could even preach, although they converted few Chinese.

The Indian religion of Buddhism had come to China hundreds of years earlier. Under the Tang, it became a major part of Chinese life. Many Chinese became Buddhists. Buddhist monks came from India to teach in China, and Chinese pilgrims went to study in India. Buddhist monks and nuns paid no taxes. They ran schools, public baths, hospitals, and lodgings for travelers. Monasteries **accumulated** great wealth. Buddhism influenced Chinese art by providing new subjects for painting and sculpture. Buddhist festivals became popular.

Foreign visitors, such as those from the west and Korea, were always welcome at the courts of the Tang emperors.

Changing Attitudes Toward the end of the Tang dynasty, foreigners and their beliefs became less welcome in China. The government placed restrictions on foreigners when a people called the Uighurs (WEE-gourz) began attacking China from across the border. In cities, violence broke out against foreign merchants. Many Chinese resented their prosperity.

The wealth of Buddhist monasteries also brought resentment. Some people, it was said, became monks just to avoid paying taxes. In addition, influential Chinese began attacking Buddhism as a foreign religion. In 843, the Tang government, which needed money, began seizing Buddhist property. Thousands of Buddhist monks and nuns were forced to give up their way of life. Monasteries, shrines, and temples were destroyed. Precious metals from statues were melted down and turned over to the treasury. The persecution of Buddhists lasted only a few years, but it greatly weakened the power of the monasteries.

Despite this distrust of foreigners, the Chinese continued to trade with other lands. By the end of the Tang dynasty, trade was shifting from the Silk Road. A flourishing sea trade developed between China, India, and the coastal cities of Southeast Asia. Thanks to the compass and improved shipbuilding techniques, overseas trade continued to thrive during the Song dynasty (960–1279).

China's Contacts with the Outside World   **211**

Mongols foreign rulers of China from Mongolia who established the Yuan dynasty

maritime relating to the sea

18.3 Foreign Contacts Under the Yuan Dynasty

As you learned in Chapter 15, the Song dynasty came to an end when the **Mongols** conquered China. Recall that the Mongol leader Kublai Khan became emperor of China in 1279. He called his dynasty the Yuan dynasty. Under the Mongols, foreigners ruled China for nearly 100 years.

The vast Mongol empire stretched clear across Asia. Travel along the Silk Road became very safe, since the entire region was now under the control of one government. The Mongols also developed a far-reaching **maritime** trade. Travel and trade expanded as never before, and more and more foreigners came to China.

National Palace Museum, Taipei, Taiwan, Republic of China/The Granger Collection, New York

The powerful ruler Kublai Khan (top, center) founded the Yuan dynasty, which ruled China for almost 100 years.

Thriving Trade and Cultural Exchange

By welcoming traders and other foreigners, the Yuan leaders encouraged cultural exchange. They respected merchants and actively promoted trade. They set up stations along the Silk Road every 20 miles, where traders could find food and a place to sleep. Muslim merchant associations managed the Silk Road trade. They traded Chinese silk and porcelain for medicines, perfumes, and ivory.

Some of the foreign visitors who traveled the Silk Road from Europe to China were Christian missionaries. They wanted to convert the Chinese to Christianity. They also wanted Kublai Khan to form an alliance with Europeans against the Muslims. Both goals failed. Still, Christian missionaries did make some converts, and they helped bring new ideas to China.

Sea trade also flourished under the Yuan emperors. Ships from India brought diamonds and pearls. Ginger, cotton, and muslin came from Ceylon (now Sri Lanka). From Java came black pepper, white walnuts, and cloves.

Many foreigners who came to China brought special skills. Muslim architects, for example, built the Yuan capital of Dadu, today's Beijing. Persians brought their advanced knowledge of **astronomy,** mathematics, medicine, and water management. Jamal al-Din, a Persian astronomer, introduced new and better astronomical instruments. He also helped to develop a new calendar and set up an observatory, a special building for the study of astronomy. Muslim and Persian doctors established new hospitals.

Foreign contacts also allowed skills and information to flow from China and spread to other parts of the world. Europeans, for example, learned about the Chinese inventions of gunpowder and printing.

The Role of Foreigners in China Foreigners enjoyed high status under the Yuan rulers. Foreign merchants were given special privileges. Unlike Chinese merchants, they could travel freely and didn't have to pay taxes. They also spoke other languages, which the Chinese were forbidden to learn.

Kublai Khan appointed many visiting foreigners to official positions in his government. The most famous was Marco Polo, a young Italian merchant and adventurer who traveled throughout China.

Polo first traveled to China as a teenager with his father and uncle, who were merchants from Venice in Italy. Their route took them across Persia and along the southern branch of the Silk Road. Throughout the long journey, Marco Polo paid attention to the interesting new things he saw.

After three and a half years and over 5,000 miles, the Polos reached the court of Kublai Khan. The khan liked Marco and enjoyed his accounts of his travels. He sent Marco to represent him on inspection tours around China.

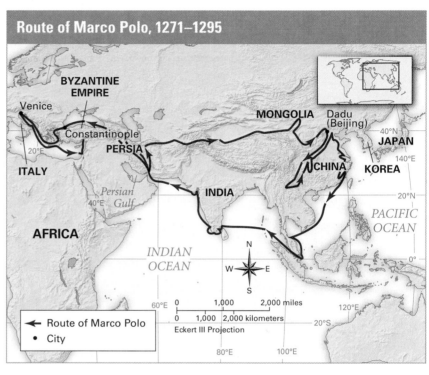

Marco Polo followed a land route to reach China. He returned home by sea.

Although Marco Polo did not read or write Chinese, he observed carefully. He traveled around China for about 17 years before beginning his journey home. When he returned to Italy, he dictated an account of his experiences to an author who wrote a book about him. The tale of Polo's travels gave Europeans firsthand knowledge of China and further stimulated interest in trade.

Under Kublai Khan, life was more pleasant for Mongols and foreigners, such as Marco Polo, than it was for the native Chinese. The Chinese were at the bottom of the social order. They resented the restrictions placed on them. They also disliked being ruled by foreigners, especially since a few foreign government officials were harsh and dishonest. The Chinese hated a Muslim finance minister named Ahmed so much that they assassinated him. The resentment that built up under Yuan rule helped make the Chinese suspicious of further contact with foreigners.

18.4 Foreign Contacts Under the Ming Dynasty

The Chinese eventually rebelled against the Yuan. From 1368 to 1644, the **Ming** dynasty ruled China. Although foreign contacts continued, later Ming rulers tried to isolate China from foreign influences.

Tributaries and Maritime Expeditions The Ming saw China as the oldest, largest, most civilized, and most important country in the world. Other nations, they felt, should acknowledge China's superiority by paying tribute.

Under the Ming, many other countries were China's **tributaries**. The Chinese emperors acknowledged their rulers, provided military help, and allowed them to trade with China. When ambassadors from the tributaries visited China, they had to kowtow before the emperor. This meant they had to kneel and touch their heads to the floor three times.

In return for bringing tribute, the ambassadors were given valuable gifts. They were also allowed to buy and sell goods at official markets. These exchanges benefited the foreigners as well as the Chinese.

Emperor Chengzu (sheng-ZOO), who came into power in 1402, wanted more tributaries. He gave a trusted adviser, Zheng He (JENG HAY), the title "Admiral of the Western Seas" and told him to sail to "the countries beyond the horizon . . . all the way to the end of the earth." Zheng He was to display China's power, to give gifts, and to collect tribute.

In 1405, Zheng He set off with a fleet of more than 300 ships. The fleet was the largest in the world at that time. It carried more than 27,000 men. They included sailors, soldiers, translators, merchants, and doctors. To feed this enormous force, ships carried huge loads of rice and other food. They had tubs of soil for growing vegetables and fruit onboard. Large watertight compartments were converted into aquariums that held fresh fish for the crew.

The largest ships had four decks, nine masts with twelve sails, and twelve watertight compartments. Cabins were provided so that merchants on long trading voyages could bring their wives.

Zheng He made seven expeditions between 1405 and 1433. At first, he traveled only as far as India.

One of the great explorers of history, Zheng He made several long voyages. He even reached the east coast of Africa.

Naval Voyages of Zheng He, 1405–1433

— Route of Zheng He
• City

Later, he reached the Persian Gulf and even sailed to ports along the east coast of Africa. Thirty or more of the places he visited became tributaries of China.

Zheng He's ships returned laden with precious cargo. From India they brought sashes made of gold thread, decorated with pearls and gems. They also carried medicinal herbs, dyes, spices, gems, pearls, and ivory. There were even exotic animals such as zebras, ostriches, lions, leopards, and giraffes aboard.

Turning Inward When Zheng He died, in about 1434, a new emperor ruled China. The government needed money to fight off attempts of the Mongols to retake control. Scholar-officials persuaded the emperor to stop the expensive expeditions.

From that time on, the dynasty turned inward. Ming rulers wanted to protect their people from foreign influences, so they forbade travel outside China. All contact between Chinese people and foreigners had to be approved by the government.

The Ming dynasty and its scholar-officials wanted a strongly unified state based on a single ruler and traditional values. The huge and complex government bureaucracy was staffed by scholar-officials chosen by examinations. The conservative outlook of these officials dominated Chinese thought and government into the 20th century.

The Ming desire for uniformity made it difficult for the government to change in response to new conditions. In the end, it became too rigid to adapt. Peasant rebellions helped to bring down the government in 1644, ending the Ming dynasty.

The Chinese had never seen a giraffe before explorer Zheng He brought one back with him.

Chapter Summary

In this chapter, you learned that medieval Chinese rulers welcomed or rejected foreign contacts at various times, depending on the policies of the particular dynasty.

Foreign Contacts Under the Tang During the Tang dynasty, ideas and goods from other places flowed into China. Buddhism, imported from India, became very popular. Eventually, however, many Chinese came to resent foreigners and foreign influences.

Foreign Contacts Under the Yuan Coming from outside China themselves, the Mongols of the Yuan dynasty promoted trade and gave foreigners important positions in the government. Cultural exchange flourished. At the same time, the Chinese began to resent their non-Chinese rulers. This attitude lasted long after the Yuan dynasty was overthrown.

Foreign Contacts Under the Ming Under the early Ming rulers, China collected tribute from other lands and undertook great maritime expeditions, such as those led by Zheng He. Later Ming emperors, however, tried to close China off from foreign influence, even forbidding Chinese people to travel abroad.

Chinese admiral Zheng He was one of the world's great early explorers.

The Explorations of Admiral Zheng He

Six hundred years ago, Admiral Zheng He led Chinese sailors on seven extraordinary expeditions to India, Arabia, and Africa. At the time, Chinese ships, called junks, were far more advanced than European vessels. Sailing those magnificent ships, Zheng He traded with countries on two continents. But suddenly, in the 1430s, the Chinese stopped trading and exploring. What happened?

The year was 1405. Admiral Zheng He stood on the deck of his ship. At almost seven feet in height, Zheng He towered over everyone around him. People who knew him said, "His eyebrows were like swords and his forehead wide, like a tiger's." When he gave an order, his sailors obeyed immediately.

From his deck, Zheng saw his ships spread behind him as far as he could see. He looked with pride at the vessels that followed his out of the harbor of Luijia, near Nanjing, China's capital. They carried about 28,000 people. The fleet was heading for the cities of India.

"Treat Distant People with Kindness"

Zheng He was known as the "Admiral of the Western Seas." He led the greatest fleet of merchant vessels up to that time. The man who sent out the fleet was Emperor Chengzu, a bold and ambitious leader. Chengzu wanted his people to explore the world and expand trade. In 1403, he ordered his royal carpenters to build a huge fleet. For the next three years, they tackled this vast job.

The emperor selected Zheng He to be the admiral of this powerful new fleet. The two had been friends since boyhood. Zheng came from a Muslim family in western China. When the Chinese defeated the Mongols in the region in 1382, they took Zheng prisoner and brought him to Chengzu's court. The two boys hunted and rode horses together, and soon became good friends.

Later, Zheng He served in the Chinese army. He showed a talent for strategy, and commanded the respect and obedience of others. He also won Chengzu's complete trust.

The emperor directed Zheng He to sail west to faraway lands, "confer presents," and "treat distant people with kindness." We know the emperor's exact words because Zheng He carved reports about the expeditions into stone tablets that still exist. Chengzu ordered merchants across China to supply trade goods for the expedition. These goods included silk, cotton, wine, tea, silk robes, and porcelain.

The Greatest Fleet in the World

Zheng He's ships were far more technologically advanced than were European ships of that time. The largest vessels in his fleet were the treasure ships. They were enormous, measuring about 400 feet long and 160 feet wide. In contrast, the *Santa Maria,* Christopher Columbus's flagship, was about 85 feet long. The treasure ships had 9 masts and 12 sails of red silk. Each vessel had more than 50 luxurious staterooms for officers and merchants.

As the fleet sailed out of Luijia Harbor, Zheng He set a course toward Calicut, a city-state on the west coast of India. The most advanced navigation tools in the world helped them sail across the Indian Ocean. Ninety years later, Columbus wouldn't have equipment as good as Zheng He's.

The key was the magnetic compass. The Chinese invented this essential tool in the 11th century. The compass allowed the Chinese to steer their ships even under cloud cover.

Chinese sailors could also figure their latitude, or the distance north of the equator. Each evening they took readings to find the North Star's position above the horizon. The closer the star's position to the horizon, the farther south they were. The farther the star's position from the horizon, the farther north they were.

Equipped with advanced navigation tools, Zheng He was able to steer his huge fleet across the Indian Ocean on his great expedition.

During the first expedition, Zheng He's fleet traded for spices, such as these, with Indian merchants at the port of Calicut.

The expeditions of Zheng He were the earliest and largest of the medieval period.

Success in India

Zheng He and his fleet reached Calicut in late 1406. Calicut was wealthy, and its merchants had fabulous goods to trade, such as spices. Eagerly, the Indian merchants boarded Zheng He's ships and drove hard bargains. But the bargaining was always honest. One observer wrote that they "have all joined hands and sealed our agreement with a handclasp."

Zheng He returned in triumph from India in 1407. Along with trade goods, he brought ambassadors from Calicut and other Asian countries. All of them paid tribute to Emperor Chengzu and gave him gifts. Zheng He had expanded China's influence all the way to India. The Chinese celebrated him as a great hero.

Sailing to Arabia and Africa

Zheng He made a total of seven voyages of discovery. His second and third expeditions, which took place between 1407 and 1411, built on the success of the first. On the third voyage, Zheng He sailed to the South Asian kingdoms of Malacca and Ceylon (now Sri Lanka).

In 1412, the emperor began to plan the fourth expedition, which included 62 ships. In 1414, after two years of preparation, Zheng He launched his fleet. This time he sailed beyond India to Hormuz, a wealthy Arabian city. Chinese merchants on this expedition traded for pearls, rubies, sapphires, and beautiful carpets.

In addition, Zheng He wrote, "Hormuz presented lions, leopards with gold spots, and large western horses." On their way back home to China, one of Zheng He's officers received another gift for the emperor—a giraffe. The Chinese marveled at the creature's long neck and believed that it was a *quilin*, or mythical creature.

When Zheng He returned to China, the emperor and the people again welcomed him as a hero. In 1416, he left on his fifth voyage, again to Arabia. But this time the fleet continued to eastern Africa.

Voyages of Discovery, 1405–1521

Explorer	Number of Ships	Number of Crew
Zheng He (1405–1433)	48–317	28,000
Christopher Columbus (1492)	3	90
Vasco da Gama (1498)	4	170
Ferdinand Magellan (1521)	5	265

When Zheng He reached the city of Mogadishu in Somalia, the city's leaders refused to welcome him. Angered, he launched explosives over the walls of the city. Finally Mogadishu's doors opened to him. According to Zheng He, "Mogadishu presented . . . zebras as well as lions."

Zheng He made his sixth voyage in 1421. Partway through the expedition, however, he returned to China to help Emperor Chengzu celebrate the opening of Beijing, China's new capital. In 1424, Emperor Chengzu died, ending the men's nearly fifty-year friendship

Disagreements over Expeditions

The new emperor did not share Chengzu's adventurous spirit, and put a stop to Zheng He's voyages. When that emperor died in 1426, however, his successor allowed Zheng He to resume exploring. The admiral, now over sixty, made his seventh and final voyage in 1431 to the southern coast of Arabia. He and his crew were also received by the sultan of Egypt. But the years had caught up with Zheng He. He died on the way home, and was buried at sea.

By 1435, another new emperor was on the throne, and China began to turn inward. The new leadership was very traditional. They claimed that China already had the best of everything and had no need to trade. The royal government even destroyed Zheng He's records of his voyages because they feared that they might inspire others. In 1525, the emperor ordered all ships capable of ocean voyages to be destroyed.

China was increasingly isolated from the rest of the world and began a long decline. Only in the last decades has China, once again, begun to reach beyond its own borders. Now, it is a major trading partner with the United States and other nations. Today, the spirit of Zheng He is alive and well.

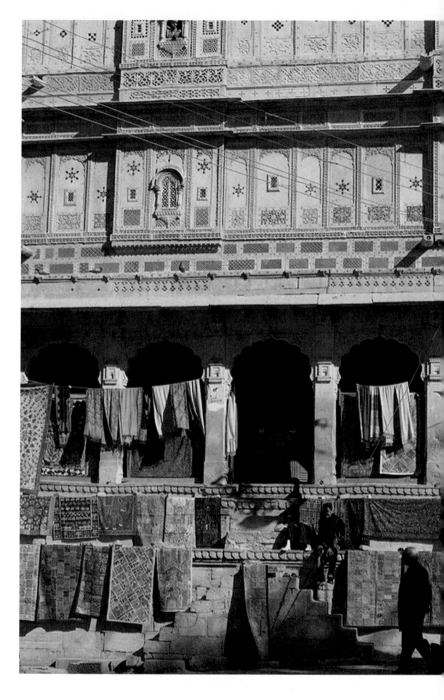

At the Arabian port of Hormuz, Zheng He acquired gems, as well as beautiful carpets, such as these.

Imperial China

About 960 C.E.
Merit-Based Exams Begin
During the Song dynasty, people of all classes become scholar-officials through a merit-based civil service exam based on the works of Confucius.

206 B.C.E.–220 C.E.
Han Dynasty
The Han dynasty rules over a golden age of expansion and prosperity for China.

About 850 C.E.
Gunpowder Invented
A formula for gunpowder is recorded in China, and allows for the later development of weapons such as grenades, flamethrowers, artillery shells, and bombs.

| 300 B.C.E. | 100 B.C.E. | 100 C.E. | 300 C.E. | 500 C.E. | 700 C.E. |

618–907 C.E.
Tang Dynasty
During the Tang dynasty, Buddhism spreads from India to China and gains many Chinese followers.

960–1279 C.E.
Song Dynasty
During the Song dynasty, agricultural improvements increase food production, allowing for growth in areas other than farming, such as trade and commerce.

About 1050 C.E.
Movable Type Invented
Movable type is invented in China, which lowers the cost of printing and makes written materials more widely available.

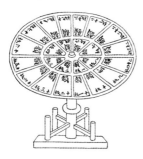

1279–1368 C.E.
Yuan Dynasty
After conquering most of Asia, the Mongols establish the Yuan dynasty in China and greatly favor foreigners to fill important government positions.

1405–1433 C.E.
Voyages of Zheng He
Zheng He's seven maritime voyages display China's power and gain new tributary states for China during the Ming dynasty.

700 C.E.   900 C.E.   1100 C.E.   1300 C.E.   1500 C.E.   1700 C.E.

1100s C.E.
Papermaking Spreads to Europe
Nearly 1,000 years after it was developed in China, the art of papermaking spreads to Europe. Paper becomes crucial for recording and transmitting information.

Late 1200s C.E.
Marco Polo Visits China
Marco Polo travels through China as a guest of the Mongol emperor Kublai Khan; a book about his travels becomes a European best-seller.

1368–1644 C.E.
Ming Dynasty
Mongol rule of China ends in 1368. The Chinese establish their own government under the Ming dynasty. The Ming build the Forbidden City.

Japan During Medieval Times

This gate on Itsukushima Island forms the entrance to one of Japan's most famous Shinto shrines. Shinto is a traditional religion that shows respect for nature. The island is also called Miyajima, which means "shrine island" in Japanese.

RUSSIA

CHINA

ASIA

Hokkaido

HIDAKA RANGE

Sea of Japan
(East Sea)

KOREA

KOREAN
PENINSULA

Honshu

JAPANESE ALPS

PACIFIC
OCEAN

KANTO
PLAIN

Mount Fuji ▲
(12,388 ft., 3,776 m)

Strait

CHUGOKU RANGE

Korea

Shikoku

Kyushu

East
China
Sea

Philippine
Sea

N
W   E
S

Elevation

Feet	Meters
Over 10,000	Over 3,050
5,001–10,000	1,526–3,050
2,001–5,000	611–1,525
1,001–2,000	306–610
0–1,000	0–305
Below sea level	Below sea level

▲   Mountain peak

〰   Present-day
boundary

0   100   200 miles

0   100   200 kilometers

Lambert Conformal Conic Projection

[handwritten top margin: how was it different from the mainland? What was Japan like during medival times?]

Japan During Medieval Times

In this unit, you will explore the civilization of Japan from about 500 to 1700 C.E. Japan is *[handwritten: number of islands]* located off the coast of East Asia. The country consists of four large islands and about 3,900 smaller ones. On a map, these islands form the shape of a crescent.

[handwritten: main islands]

Together, the Japanese islands make up an area about the size of Montana. Japan's four large islands are Hokkaido, Honshu, Shikoku, and Kyushu. Of these, you can see that Honshu is the largest and most centrally located. To the west, the Sea of Japan (East Sea) separates Japan from Korea and China. To the east of Japan lies the Pacific Ocean.

[handwritten: postives to living on an island]

In medieval times, being surrounded on all sides by water served Japan well, because no enemy could approach without being seen. In addition, the oceans were highways to other countries and provided an unending supply of food.

[handwritten: Japan's mountains]

About three-quarters of Japan is made up of mountains. This made farming difficult in ancient and medieval times. The highest mountain in Japan is Mount Fuji on the Pacific coast in central Honshu. Mount Fuji soars more than 12,000 feet and is always covered with snow. It looms above cities, lakes, and farms. On a clear day, Mount Fuji can even be seen from Tokyo, 60 miles away.

[handwritten: natural disasters]

Volcanoes are common in Japan. Many of Japan's mountains are actually volcanoes, and occasionally one of them erupts. Mount Fuji is a volcanic mountain, but it has not had a major eruption since 1707.

[handwritten: earthquakes]

Earthquakes are also quite common in Japan. They are usually minor, but at times severe destruction and loss of life have resulted from a major earthquake.

[handwritten: Japans climate]

Japan is a land of beauty. Because of its mild temperatures and abundant rainfall, Japan has lush forests. Throughout the islands, rugged, tree-covered mountains meet cascading rivers and sparkling streams. In wintertime, snow-frosted trees surround crystalline lakes. Barren, rock-strewn shores rise above the blue waves of the sea. In medieval times, artists and poets found inspiration in the breathtaking scenery of their nation.

[handwritten: climate & crops]

Japan's mild temperatures and heavy rainfall provide perfect conditions for growing crops such as rice and tea. The Japanese people learned to cut into the mountains to make level areas, or terraces, on which to grow food. They also grew crops in the low valleys between the mountains. The soil was enriched by nutrients that washed down into the valleys from the highlands.

[handwritten: cultural influence]

Japan's location off the coast of Asia has been a key to its history. At first, Japan developed in isolation because it was surrounded by water. Later, however, cultural ideas traveled to Japan from China and India by way of the Korean Peninsula. This peninsula lies about one hundred miles from the coast of Kyushu.

Medieval Japan

[handwritten on map: → boat travel must be common → more peacefull than mainland? → what does Japan export?]

RUSSIA

ASIA

CHINA

Hokkaido

135°E

130°E
40°N

Sea of Japan (East Sea)

KOREA

Nagaoka

Honshu

Edo (Tokyo)

PACIFIC OCEAN

Heian-kyo (Kyoto)

Kamakura

Korea Strait

Yodo River

35°N

Nara

Shikoku

East China Sea

Kyushu

30°N

Philippine Sea

0   200   400 miles
0   200   400 kilometers
Lambert Conformal Conic Projection

Chapter 19

The Influence of Neighboring Cultures on Japan

[handwritten: What Agriculture was brought over?]
[handwritten: How did the arts change? (because of new materials)]
[handwritten: How did shintoism change because of cultural influences?]

In what ways did neighboring cultures influence Japan?

19.1 Introduction *[handwritten: Overveiw]*

The island country of Japan lies just off the eastern coast of the Asian mainland. Japan's culture was enriched by borrowing from other places in Asia. In this chapter, you will explore how Japan's neighbors influenced Japanese culture from the 6th to the 9th centuries C.E. *[handwritten: 500–800 C.E.]*

Many ideas traveled to Japan by way of the Korean Peninsula. Some of these ideas originally came from China and India. For example, in the mid-500s, Buddhist priests from Korea visited Japan. In this way, the Japanese were introduced to Buddhism, which had begun in India about one thousand years earlier. *[handwritten: Religion spreading]*

[handwritten sideways: Cultural Influence]

In 593, a female ruler, Empress Suiko, came to power in Japan. Her nephew Prince Shotoku admired Chinese and Korean culture, and he encouraged contact with these mainland countries. In 607, he sent an official representative to the Chinese court. Upper-class Japanese began traveling to China and Korea, where they learned about Chinese literature, art, philosophy, and government. Groups of Koreans also came to Japan, bringing with them their extensive knowledge of Chinese culture. *[handwritten: Important! Will study more]*

Over the next 300 years, Japan absorbed elements of culture—objects, ideas, and customs—from the Asian mainland. As you may remember, the spread of cultural elements is called *cultural diffusion*. In this chapter, you will learn how cultural diffusion helped to shape medieval Japanese culture. You will also discover how the Japanese blended ideas from other cultures into their own unique civilization. *[handwritten: Japanese Culture (like american culture) has many influences.]*

[handwritten: How does Chinesse Government influence Japan?]

This pagoda in Nara, Japan, was based on an architectural style originally used in China.

◀ This scroll illustrates the exchange of products and ideas between China and Japan.

Prince Shotoku a Japanese ruler who encouraged cultural diffusion from countries on the Asian mainland

19.2 Cultural Influences on Japan

By the time Empress Suiko and **Prince Shotoku** came to power in 593, cultural influences from the Asian mainland had been reaching Japan for hundreds of years. For example, craftspeople from the Korean Peninsula had brought knowledge of bronze casting and advanced ironworking to Japan. Immigrants and visitors from Korea had also introduced Japan to Confucianism and Buddhism. But as Suiko, Shotoku, and later rulers sought out contact with the mainland, the pace of cultural diffusion quickened.

Japan in Empress Suiko's and Prince Shotoku's day was a **rural,** agricultural society. People grew rice and other crops. The upper classes owned slaves and lived in houses with wooden floors and roofs of wood or thatch. The common people lived in huts with dirt floors and thatched roofs. Family life centered on the mother, who raised the children. Fathers often lived apart from their families. Compared to later eras, women enjoyed relatively high status.

Japan at this time was far from being a unified country. Power was divided among chiefs of a number of clans called *uji* (OOH-jee). But one ruling family in the region of Yamato, on the island of Honshu, had grown powerful enough to loosely control much of Japan. Empress Suiko and Prince Shotoku, who ruled as regent under the empress, came from this line of rulers.

Under Suiko, Shotoku, and later rulers, the government of Japan took an active interest in Korean and Chinese culture. Sometimes, knowledge of mainland culture came from Japanese who traveled to China. Sometimes, it came in the form of gifts, such as books and art objects, sent from the mainland to Japan. Sometimes, it came from Korean workers who settled in Japan, bringing their knowledge and skills with them.

During the next three centuries, Japan sent officials, students, translators, and monks on ships across the sea to China. These people often remained in China for years. When they returned home, they brought with them what they had learned. They also brought many examples of mainland culture, including paintings, religious statues, and musical instruments. As a result of these contacts, the Japanese **acquired** new ideas in government, the arts, architecture, and writing.

The Japanese didn't just change their old ways for new ways, however. Instead, they blended new ideas with their own traditions to create a unique culture. Let's look at several areas in which this happened, beginning with government.

The cultures of China, India, and Korea were major influences on the culture of medieval Japan.

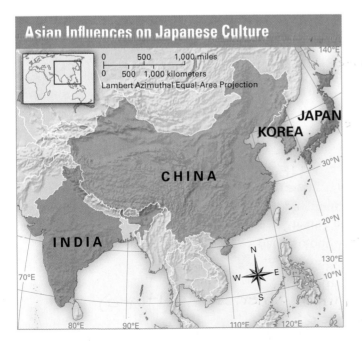

Asian Influences on Japanese Culture

19.3 Government: Imitating the Chinese System

Starting with Prince Shotoku, Japanese rulers adopted new ideas about government from China. China's form of government was both like and unlike Japan's. For example, the emperors in China and Japan had quite different powers. The emperor in China was the sole ruler. In Japan, the emperor had only loose control over the semi-independent uji. Each uji controlled its own land. The uji leaders struggled among themselves for the right to select the emperor and influence his decisions.

While Japanese emperors depended on local leaders, the Chinese emperor ruled with the help of a bureaucracy of government officials. At least in theory, appointments to government jobs were based on merit. Any man who did well on an examination could become an official.

During the 7th and 8th centuries, Japanese rulers adopted a Chinese style of government. Japanese tradition credits Prince Shotoku with starting this development. Borrowing Confucian ideas, the prince created ranks for government officials. In 604, he issued a set of guidelines called the Seventeen Article Constitution. The guidelines stated that the emperor was the supreme ruler: "In a country there are not two lords; the people have not two masters. The sovereign is the master of the people of the whole country."

Later rulers went much further in bringing Chinese-style changes to Japan. In the late 7th century, Emperor Tenmu and his wife and successor Empress Jitō reformed and strengthened the central government. Control of the land was taken away from clan leaders and given to the emperor. The emperor then redistributed the land to all free men and women. In return, people paid heavy taxes to support the imperial government.

By the 700s, Japan's imperial government looked much as China's did. It was strongly centralized and supported by a large bureaucracy. Over time, however, one key difference emerged. Prince Shotoku had called for government officials to be chosen on the basis of their ability, as in China. But during the 9th century, a powerful aristocracy developed in Japan. As a result, members of noble families held all the high positions in the government.

Prince Shotoku was the first Japanese ruler to borrow ideas about government from China. Shotoku is shown here between his two sons.

Shinto a Japanese religion that expresses love and respect for nature

meditation a spiritual discipline that involves deep relaxation and clearing the mind of distracting thoughts

19.4 City Design: Adapting Chinese Ideas for a Magnificent City

With a stronger central government and a large bureaucracy, Japan needed a new capital city. In 710, the imperial government built a Chinese-style capital on the site of the modern city of Nara.

The new city was a smaller version of Chang'an, China's capital. Chang'an had an area of 35 square miles and a population of 2 million people. Nara, with about 8 square miles, had no more than 200,000 people. As in Chang'an, Nara's streets were laid out in an orderly checkerboard pattern. A wide boulevard ran down the center. In the northern section, Buddhist temples and monasteries clustered near the imperial palace.

There was one major difference between the two capitals. Chang'an was surrounded by a wall as protection against enemies. Nara did not have a wall.

19.5 Religion: Buddhism Comes to Japan

Nara's Buddhist temples were another result of cultural diffusion. Buddhism began in India in the 500s B.C.E. About one thousand years later, it came to Japan from China by way of Korea.

Japan's original religion was **Shinto**. This religion expresses the love and respect of the Japanese for nature. Its followers worship spirits called *kami*. Kami are impressive natural objects, such as wind, lightning, rivers, mountains, waterfalls, large trees, and unusual stones. So are the emperor and other special people.

Instead of emphasizing a code of morality, Shinto stresses purifying whatever is unclean, such as dirt, wounds, and disease. Touching the dead also makes one unclean. Most of all, however, Shintoists celebrate life and the beauty of nature.

In contrast, Buddhists see life as full of pain and suffering. The founder of Buddhism, Siddhartha Gautama, taught that life is an endless cycle of birth, death, and rebirth. To escape this cycle, one must follow a moral code called the Eightfold Path. Buddhism's moral code emphasizes showing respect for others, acting rightly, and achieving wisdom through **meditation**. Following the path leads to **enlightenment,** or seeing the world as it really is. Those who achieve enlightenment can enter *nirvana,* a state of perfect peace. They will never be born again into a life of suffering.

The buildings at Nara, Japan, with their upturned roofs, reflect the influence of Chinese architecture and the religious influence of Indian Buddhism.

By finding the path to enlightenment, Siddhartha became the *Buddha,* or "enlightened one." As Buddhism spread throughout India, a new form arose, called Mahayana, or "Greater Vehicle." This name symbolizes a core teaching of Mahayana: that all people can reach nirvana. Its followers believe in *bodhisattvas,* Buddhists who can enter nirvana but choose instead to help others reach enlightenment. These godlike spirits live in different paradises. Worshippers pray to them in hopes of being reborn into one of these paradises. It is this form of Buddhism that spread along trade routes to China. The influence of Chinese culture brought Buddhism to Korea.

Mahayana Buddhism arrived in Japan in 552 when a Korean king sent the Japanese emperor a statue of the Buddha and a recommendation for the new religion. The statue arrived at the emperor's court surrounded by chanting monks, books of prayer, gongs, and banners. The emperor was not quite sure what to make of it. "The countenance [expression] of this Buddha," he said, "is of a severe dignity such as we have never at all seen before. Ought it to be worshipped or not?" The members of an uji clan called the Soga, who were originally from Korea, were the main supporters of the new religion.

After a fierce controversy, the emperor and his court adopted the new religion. They admired its wisdom and rituals, and they considered the Buddha a protector of families and the nation. Later rulers, such as Prince Shotoku, learned more about Buddhism through Korean monks and teachers.

Buddhism did not replace Shinto. Instead, both religions thrived and even blended. Buddhists built shrines to kami, and Shintoists enshrined bodhisattvas. Even today, ceremonies to celebrate birth and marriage often come from Shinto, the joyful religion. Funeral ceremonies are Buddhist, the religion that acknowledges suffering and pain.

In this painted scroll from Nara, people sit in meditation or prayer at a Buddhist temple.

The kana system of writing, shown here, was used by many women writers in medieval Japan.

19.6 Writing: Applying Chinese Characters to the Japanese Language

Ancient Japanese was only a spoken language. The Japanese had no writing system of their own. Written documents were in Chinese, a language the Japanese had learned from Korean scholars. Over time, however, the Japanese adapted Chinese characters, or written symbols, to write their own language.

First, Japanese scholars began using *kanji,* or "Chinese writing," to write Japanese words. Kanji allowed the Japanese to keep records, record legends, and develop their own literature. But using Chinese characters to read and write Japanese was difficult. The two languages have different grammar, sounds, and pronunciations.

By 900, the Japanese invented *kana.* In Japanese, *kana* means "borrowed letters." In kana, simplified Chinese characters represent Japanese syllables. Kana allowed the Japanese to spell out the sounds of their own language. As a result, they were able to write freely in Japanese. Both kanji and kana are still part of written Japanese.

19.7 Literature: Adapting Chinese Poetic Form

The earliest literary works in Japan are poems that date from the 7th and 8th centuries. Using Chinese characters, Japanese poets developed a form of poetry called *tanka.* This form developed out of songs from Japan's oral tradition.

Tanka is based on the number of syllables in each line. Each short poem has 31 syllables, divided into five lines of 5, 7, 5, 7, and 7 syllables. The poems are often devoted to love and to the beauty of nature.

Try to count the syllables in this Japanese tanka. On the right is an English translation. Has the translator kept to the tanka form?

Haru tateba	*When spring comes*
Kiyuru koori no	*The melting ice*
Nokori naku	*Leaves no trace;*
Kimi ga kokoro mo	*Would that your heart too*
Ware ni tokenan	*Melted thus toward me.*

19.8 Sculpture: Carving Techniques Travel to Japan

Like Buddhism, new techniques and subjects of sculpture came to Japan from Korea and China. Like Buddhism, these sculptural ideas began their journey in India and Central Asia, and spread through Korea and China to Japan.

Archeologists have found examples of early Japanese sculpture around burial mounds that date to the 4th and 5th centuries. The sculptures are clay figures of armored warriors, saddled horses, robed ladies, and objects such as houses and boats. They were probably meant to accompany or protect the dead.

Meanwhile, Buddhism was inspiring new subjects for sculpture on the Asian mainland. As these ideas moved east, sculptors' techniques and materials gradually changed. You can see this in the work of three different artists—one Chinese, one Korean, and one Japanese—shown at the right.

At the top, from China, is a stone image of the Buddha. The Chinese began carving images like these on cave walls near the end of the 5th century. Notice the faint smile, the way the hand touches the face, and the positions of the arms and legs. The figure's position and gestures identify him as the Buddha of the future, whose arrival will begin a golden age.

The second statue was fashioned by a Korean artist. This time, the Buddha has been cast in bronze and covered in gold leaf. How is this Buddha statue similar to the stone carving from China? In what ways is it different?

The third Buddha statue is located near the Horyuji Temple in Nara. It was carved by a Japanese artist in the 7th century. Artistic styles change as artists travel from place to place, as do materials, depending on what is locally available. This sculpture is made of wood. Using wood allowed the artist to make the figure look more natural, especially in the upper body and the folds of the clothing.

From the middle of the 6th century to the middle of the 7th century, Chinese and Korean immigrants created most of Japan's religious art. Japanese artists learned new techniques from them.

These Buddhas were created by a Chinese artist (top), a Korean artist (center), and a Japanese artist (bottom). How are they alike? How are they different?

The Influence of Neighboring Cultures on Japan **233**

The Heian-Jingu Shrine in Kyoto, Japan, is a fine example of the pagoda, an architectural form imported from China.

19.9 Architecture: Adapting Temple Designs

New forms of temple design came to Japan from India by way of China. Like sculpture, temple architecture evolved as it moved east. In India, Buddhist monasteries featured shrines called *stupas* with roofs shaped like bells or inverted bowls. The Chinese replaced the bell shape with a series of stories and curved roofs, creating structures called **pagodas**. These towerlike buildings always had three, five, seven, or nine roofs.

When Buddhism arrived in Japan, the Japanese adopted the pagoda design. For Buddhist worship, Prince Shotoku founded the Horyuji, a magnificent temple in Nara. Its wooden buildings included a hall for worship and a pagoda. Lofty pagodas soon appeared all around the capital city. They were intended to contain relics of the Buddha and of bodhisattvas, as well.

Buddhist pagodas may have inspired Shinto priests to build their own permanent shrines. Shinto shrines reflected Japan's agricultural society and the Japanese love of nature. Based on the idea of the raised storehouse, a symbol of plenty, these shrines had raised floors and thatched roofs. Unpainted and undecorated, they blended in with their natural surroundings.

pagoda a tower-shaped structure with several stories and upturned, tiled roofs

19.10 Music: Adopting New Music and Instruments

Japan's native music consisted of chanted poems, war songs, folk songs, and Shinto prayers. All were recited, using just a few notes. Sculpted clay figures from early Japan show musicians playing the cither (a stringed instrument), flutes, and percussion instruments.

As contacts with the Asian mainland increased, the Japanese imported music from the region, especially from China. *Gagaku* (gah-GAH-koo), a form of Chinese court music, arrived in Japan in the 6th century. Gagaku is still sometimes played in Japan, much as it was in China 1,500 years ago.

New kinds of music required new musical instruments. One of the most interesting was a wind instrument the Chinese called a *sheng*. The Japanese pronounce the name *sho*. The sho is a type of mouth organ. It was designed to look like a phoenix, a **mythical** bird. Its sound was said to imitate the call of the phoenix.

This quartet, in traditional costume, is playing gagaku music with medieval instruments, including a sho (far left).

Chapter Summary

In this chapter, you learned how, from the 6th to the 9th centuries, the Japanese acquired and adapted elements of other Asian cultures, creating a unique civilization.

Cultural Influences on Japan Objects, ideas, skills, and customs flowed to Japan from India, China, and Korea, encouraged by Prince Shotoku and other early Japanese rulers.

Government and Cities From China, the Japanese borrowed the idea of a strong central government supported by a bureaucracy. To house the imperial government, they built a new capital modeled after China's capital city.

Religion Buddhism, which began in India, came to Japan from China by way of Korea. Buddhism strongly influenced Japanese religion, art, and architecture.

Writing and Literature Koreans introduced Chinese writing to Japan. The Japanese invented kanji and kana to write Japanese words and sounds with Chinese characters. Poets used Chinese characters to write tanka, a type of poetry based on Chinese models.

Sculpture, Architecture, and Music Like Buddhism, ideas about sculpture traveled from India to Korea and China, and then to Japan. Similarly, India's stupas inspired Chinese pagodas. Japan then adapted this architectural style. New kinds of music, such as gagaku, and instruments came to Japan from China.

Chapter 20

Heian-kyo: The Heart of Japan's Golden Age

What was life like for aristocrats during the Heian period?

[handwritten: What was government like? What inventions were created? How did religion change?]

20.1 Introduction

The culture of medieval Japan was rich and varied due to exchanges with other Asian peoples. In this chapter, you will see how a unique Japanese culture flowered from the 9th to the 12th centuries. [handwritten: intro]

As you may know, Japan is close enough to the mainland of Asia to be affected by cultural ideas from that region. At the same time, the waterways separating Japan from mainland Asia helped protect the Japanese from conquest by other Asian peoples. As a result, Japan remained politically independent and had the chance to develop its own civilization. [handwritten: cultural diffution & independence]

For most of the 8th century, the city of Nara was the imperial capital of Japan. During this time, contacts with China brought many new cultural ideas to Japan. Then, in 794, the emperor Kammu moved the capital to Heian-kyo (hay-AHN-keeyo). This event marks the start of the Heian period, which lasted until 1185. [handwritten: capital]

The Heian period is often called Japan's golden age. During this time, **aristocrats** led a great flourishing of Japanese culture. The aristocrats prized beauty, elegance, and correct manners. Over time, they developed new forms of literature and art. Poets wrote delicately about feelings and the fragile beauties of nature. Court women composed diaries and other types of nonfiction, as well as fiction. Painters and sculptors invented new styles of art. Performers entertained the court with new kinds of music, dance, and drama. [handwritten: art] [handwritten: overview]

The brilliant culture of the Heian period still influences Japanese art and life. In this chapter, you will learn more about Japan's golden age. You will look at how Heian aristocrats lived and how they created new kinds of Japanese art and literature.

In 794, the emperor Kammu moved the Japanese capital from Nara to Heian-kyo. This began the Heian period, a time of rich cultural development.

Japan, 794

◀ This scene from the *Tale of Genji* illustrates the luxurious lifestyle of the aristocrats during the Heian period.

The Phoenix Hall was one of the most beautiful structures built in the new capital city of Heian-kyo.

20.2 A New Capital

During the 8th century, the Buddhist priests of Nara gained a great deal of influence over the Japanese court. In 784, the emperor Kammu decided to move his capital away from Nara, in part because he thought the priests' power was damaging to the government. The emperor also wanted a larger, grander city for his capital.

The first site Kammu chose was Nagaoka, about 30 miles from Nara. But the move was troubled from early on. As money poured in to build the new city, rumors of corruption, or dishonesty, flew. People said the land had been acquired through a deal with a rich Chinese family. The site also seemed to be unlucky, because the emperor's family suffered illnesses at this time. In 794, the emperor stopped work on the city. Once again, he ordered that the capital be moved.

This time, Kammu chose a village on the Yodo River. The site was both lovelier than Nagaoka and easier to defend. There, Kammu began building a new city he called Heian-kyo. *Kyo* means "city" in Japanese. *Heian-kyo* means, "The Capital of Peace and Tranquility." This event marks the beginning of the **Heian period**.

Heian-kyo became the first truly Japanese city. Today, it is the city of Kyoto. As with Nara, Heian-kyo was laid out in a checkerboard pattern like the Chinese city of Chang'an. Built on a grand scale, the walled city was lovely and elegant. It was set in forested hills, amid streams, waterfalls, and lakes. It had wide, tree-lined streets. Shrines and temples blended with the area's natural beauty.

Heian-kyo's crisscrossing streets were modeled after those of Chang'an, but the city's architecture was Japanese. In the center of the city were palaces and government offices. Wealthy Heian families lived in mansions surrounded by beautiful gardens with artificial lakes. The grounds of each home covered three to four acres and were enclosed by white stone walls.

Heian period the cultural flowering in Japan that took place between the late 8th and the late 12th centuries

Inside the mansions, large rooms were divided by screens or *[furnture]* curtains and connected with open-air covered hallways. Simplicity was considered beautiful, so there were few objects on the wood floors other than straw mats and cushions. The Japanese did not use chairs.

Daily life was very formal, and correct manners were extremely *[Formal lives]* important. For example, a Heian lady sat behind a portable screen. The screen hid her from view while she talked and took part in life around the house. An unmarried lady would permit her suitor to see past the screen only after a romance had become serious.

20.3 The Rise of the Fujiwara Family

During much of the Heian period, which was a **golden age,** aristocrats were the political and cultural leaders of Japan. By the mid-9th century, the real power in the imperial court shifted from the emperor to aristocratic families. The most important of these noble families were the Fujiwara, who controlled Japan for nearly 300 years.

The Fujiwara were never actually rulers. The Japanese believed that the emperor's family was descended from Japan's sun goddess. This gave the royal family a special right to govern. But the Fujiwara had other ways of exercising power. *[real rulers of Japan]*

First, beginning in 858, the Fujiwara married many of their daughters into the royal family. They also made sure that sons of Fujiwara royal wives were chosen to be emperors. Second, the Fujiwara acted as advisers to the emperor. In reality, they had more power than the rulers they guided. They often coaxed older emperors to retire so that a child or youth could take the throne. Then the Fujiwara ruled as regents in the young emperor's name.

> **golden age** a period in a nation's past during which its culture and society attained the height of achievement and power

[Power in Japan]

Fujiwara Michinaga, one of the most powerful leaders during Japan's golden age, was very wealthy. In this page from the diary of Lady Murasaki, Michinaga is entertained by watching boats on a lake at his home.

The most successful Fujiwara leader was Fujiwara Michinaga, who led Japan from 995 to 1028. He never had an official position in the government. However, this smart, ambitious man had the respect of all around him. He was the father-in-law of four emperors and the grandfather of three more. He lived a life of great wealth and luxury. Michinaga rightly said, "This world, I think, is indeed my world."

Michinaga is one of the best-known figures in Japan's history. During his time in power, the Fujiwara family became even richer. They built palaces, mansions, and temples. After Michinaga's death, his son built a famous temple that came to be called Phoenix Hall. It likely earned this name because it was shaped like a bird in flight. Part of the temple still stands as a gracious reminder of Japan's golden age.

The Fujiwara family used their power to better their own lives. However, they also kept peace in Japan for nearly three centuries. This peace helped Japanese culture blossom during the Heian period.

20.4 Social Position in the Heian Court

Rank was very important during this period. It was determined almost completely by a person's birth family's rank. Birth into a high-ranking family mattered more than personal qualities or skills.

There were nine main ranks in the Heian court hierarchy. High court nobles filled the top three ranks. These nobles were appointed by the emperor. Less important officials filled the fourth and fifth ranks. Nobles in all these ranks received profits from rice farms throughout the country. They also received money from taxes paid by peasant farmers. The sixth through the ninth ranks were filled by minor officials, clerks, and experts in such fields as law and medicine.

Noble women in higher ranks had servants to help them with their personal needs from morning to night.

The nine main ranks were divided into classes, such as senior and junior, upper and lower. In all, there were some 30 sub-ranks. Each rank brought with it specific privileges and detailed rules of **conduct.** Members of different ranks had different types of houses and carriages. Rank determined the number of servants people had, and even the number of folds in the fans they carried. Men of the first, second, and third ranks carried fans with 25 folds. Men of the fourth and fifth ranks used fans with 23 folds. The fans of those in lower ranks had only 12 folds.

This precise ranking system also determined such matters as what color clothing a noble could wear and the height of the gatepost in front of his family's home. In addition, if a person were found guilty of a crime, rank determined how harsh the sentence would be.

courtier a male member of a ruler's court

20.5 Beauty and Fashion During the Heian Period

Heian society prized beauty, elegance, and fashion. To be described as *yoki* (good), people had to come from an important family. They also had to look nice and be sensitive to beauty in nature, poetry, and art. Individuals were judged on whether or not they had good taste. The ability to recognize beauty was valued over qualities like generosity and honesty.

Both men and women groomed themselves with great care. Small, pointed beards were considered attractive on male **courtiers.** For women, long hair was an important beauty feature. Ideally, a woman's hair would grow longer than she was tall.

The Japanese of this time considered white teeth unattractive, so both men and women carefully blackened their teeth. They used a dye made from iron and other ingredients soaked in tea or vinegar. Personal scent was also very **significant,** so both men and women wore perfume. Perfume competitions were frequent and popular. People guarded their perfume recipes carefully.

For women, makeup was also important. Women used white face powder to make themselves look very pale. Over the chalky powder, a Heian woman put touches of red on her cheeks. Then she painted on a small red mouth. She also plucked out her eyebrows and painted on a set in just the right spot on her forehead.

A woman's clothing needed to be ornate and beautiful. An aristocratic woman might wear as many as 12 silk underrobes at one time. When she rode in a carriage, she might dangle a wrist so that people in the street would notice the lovely layers of colored silk.

The love of beauty also showed in Heian architecture, calligraphy, poetry, and artwork. Concern with form and beauty was so great that courtiers sometimes had to perform stylized dances as part of their official duties.

Long hair, eyebrows painted high on the forehead, and bright red lips were signs of beauty during the Heian period.

Heian-kyo: The Heart of Japan's Golden Age **241**

Noblemen, dressed in silk robes and court hats, enjoy a game of *kemari*. The object of the game was to keep the ball in the air as long as possible.

20.6 Entertainment at the Heian Court

Heian-kyo's aristocrats had plenty of leisure time for sporting events, games, and contests. Men enjoyed watching horse races, archery contests, and sumo wrestling. In sumo wrestling, which is still very popular in Japan, men of great weight try to throw each other to the ground or out of the ring. When the weather was warm, men and women alike enjoyed watching boat races along the river that ran through the city.

Groups of courtiers played a game called *kemari,* in which they kicked a leather ball back and forth, keeping it in the air for as long as possible. They played in the same elegant robes they wore at court. Women used the stone pieces of the popular board game Go to play a game called *rango.* The object was to balance as many stones as possible on one finger.

Each of the many festivals and celebrations on the Heian calendar had its own customs. Many involved contests that tested athletic, poetic, or artistic skill. For example, in the Festival of the Snake, cups were floated in a stream. Guests took a cup and drank from it. Then they had to compose and recite a poem. Other special days featured contests that judged the best-decorated fans, the most fragrant perfumes, the loveliest artwork, or the most graceful dancing.

Dancing was an important skill for Heian-kyo's nobles, since dance was part of nearly every festival. *Bugaku* (boo-GAH-koo) performances were a popular form of entertainment. Bugaku combined dance with music and drama. Bugaku dancers wore masks and acted out a simple story using memorized movements.

20.7 Sculpture and Painting During the Heian Period

During the Heian period, many artists continued to be influenced by Chinese art. Gradually, however, sculptors and painters created their own Japanese styles.

Early Heian sculptors commonly made an entire work from a single piece of wood. Later in this period, sculptors made statues by carving separate pieces from carefully selected wood and then joining them. With the help of assistants, sculptors could make the separate parts in large quantities. As a result, they could create a group of similar statues quickly and precisely. Jocho, an artist who worked for Fujiwara Michinaga, probably developed this technique.

Jocho made perhaps the greatest masterpiece of Heian sculpture, the Amida Buddha. This Buddha, "The Lord of Boundless Light," was the subject of much popular worship in Japan. Jocho's beautifully carved statue expresses a sense of deep peace and strength.

In painting, Heian artists consciously developed a Japanese style. To distinguish it from Chinese styles, they called it *yamato-e,* or "Japanese painting." Painters drew their scenes with thin lines and then filled them in with bright colors. Lines were made quickly to suggest movement. In a restful scene, lines were drawn more deliberately.

At first, artists used the new style to paint Buddhist subjects. But over time they focused on nonreligious scenes. There were four main types of yamato-e: landscapes showing the four seasons, places of natural beauty, people doing seasonal tasks, and scenes from literature (called "story paintings").

The new style of painting was used to decorate walls, screens, and the sliding doors of houses and temples. Some of the most famous examples of yamato-e, however, are scroll paintings. A scroll painting shows a series of scenes from right to left, so that viewers see events chronologically as they unroll the scroll. Scroll painting had been invented in China, but Heian painters added their own distinctive touches. For example, they often showed scenes inside buildings from above, as if the viewer were peering down though an invisible roof.

The sculptor Jocho developed the technique called *yosegi-zukuri,* in which blocks of wood were hollowed out, carved, and then assembled. This Amida Buddha by Jocho is one of the great works of Heian sculpture.

20.8 Writing and Literature During the Heian Period

Writing was the most valued form of expression in Heian Japan. Everyone was expected to show skill in using words well. Early Heian writers composed artful poems in Chinese. As time passed, distinctly Japanese ways of writing developed, both in daily life and in the creation of works of literature.

Writing in Daily Life Poetry was part of daily life in Heian-kyo. People were expected to compose poetry in public. If they could not think up a few clever lines to fit an occasion, others noticed the failure. Men and women carefully created poems to charm each other. When someone received a poem from a friend, family member, or acquaintance, he or she was expected to write one in response. The responding poem was supposed to be written in the same style and mood, and have the same imagery, as the original.

In earlier times, the Japanese had used *kana* to write the syllables of their language. It was based on simplified Chinese characters. In Heian times, there were two ways of writing, much like we have cursive and print letters in English. One, *katakana,* was more formal. Men used katakana when they wrote anything important. The second form of writing was *hiragana*. Characters in hiragana are formed with simple strokes that make writing and reading easier and faster. Hiragana was mostly seen as "women's writing." Court women favored hiragana for personal writing, such as diaries, and some of them used it to create lasting works of literature. Over time, hiragana took its place alongside katakana as part of Japan's written language.

Heian writers took care to present their work in a beautiful manner. Calligraphy skills were as important as the ability to create poetry. People believed that handwriting revealed their character and goodness better than the words they used. Calligraphy was often displayed on colorful, handmade paper. Sometimes the paper was even perfumed.

Murasaki Shikibu, shown here at her desk, was a leading writer during the Heian period. She wrote the *Tale of Genji,* considered by many to be the world's first novel.

Women Become Japan's Leading Writers The female companions to the courtiers of Heian-kyo were usually selected for their intelligence. They often took a great interest in literature. As a result, women led in the flowering of Japanese literature in the golden age of the 10th and 11th centuries.

The best-known Heian writer was Murasaki Shikibu, often referred to as Lady Murasaki. Born into the Fujiwara family, she served as a lady-in-waiting to one of the daughters of Fujiwara Michinaga. Her novel, the *Tale of Genji* (GEN-jee), is a Heian masterpiece. Today, it is known as one of the great works of world literature.

The *Tale of Genji* is often called the world's first novel. The book follows the life of Genji, a fictional prince. It paints a vivid picture of life in the Heian court. Much of the book focuses on the thoughts and feelings of the characters, particularly the women. For this reason, the *Tale of Genji* has served as a model for the modern romance novel.

Murasaki also kept a diary about her life in the court. Like her novel, her diary offers a close look at court life in the period.

The other leading writer of the time was Sei Shonagon. Like the *Tale of Genji*, Shonagon's *Pillow Book* presents a detailed picture of life in Heian-kyo. *Pillow Book* is a collection of clever stories, character sketches, conversations, descriptions of art and nature, and various lists. Here is Shonagon's list of "Things That Should Be Short":

> *a piece of thread when one wants to sew something in a hurry*
> *a lamp stand*
> *the hair of a woman of the lower classes*
> *the speech of a young girl*

Like Sei Shonagon, many Heian women wrote their thoughts and experiences in diaries. A book called *The Gossamer Years* is the earliest existing example. This diary by an unknown noblewoman describes her unhappy life as companion to a Fujiwara leader. Writers often included artwork, poems, and letters in their diary entries.

The *Tale of Genji* describes the life of Japanese nobles during the Heian period. This detail of a painting on a six-panel screen is an illustration of a scene from the novel.

Tale of Genji a Japanese novel and Heian masterpiece written by Murasaki Shikibu; considered one of the great works of world literature

The wealthy nobles of the Heian period ignored the problems of poor people, such as these, in Japan's rural areas.

20.9 The End of the Heian Period

The Heian period is known as Japan's golden age of peace. But despite the glittering imperial court, problems were brewing that would bring an end to this flourishing cultural era.

Aristocrats in Heian-kyo lived very well, but in Japan's rural areas most people were quite poor. The peasants' farming and other work supported Heian-kyo's rich. Even so, the wealthy looked down on the poor and ignored their problems.

While the rich focused on culture in Heian-kyo, events in the countryside began to weaken the Heian court. The practice of giving large estates to top nobles slowly **eroded** the emperors' power. Those who owned these estates paid no taxes. After a time, tax-free land was quite common. The government could no longer collect enough taxes to support the emperor.

Japan's rulers began to lose control. Bandits roamed the countryside. People of different religions began to band together to attack and rob one another. The government was now too weak to provide law enforcement. Estate owners created their own police forces and armies to protect their lands. The profits from landowners' estates went to paying the warriors instead of supporting the emperor.

By the 12th century, the power of some local lords rivaled that of the weakened imperial government. Fighting broke out over control of the land. Meanwhile, various clans struggled for power in the capital. By 1180, there was civil war in Japan.

In 1185, Minamoto Yoritomo (meen-ah-MOE-toe yor-ee-TOE-moe), the head of a military family, seized power. A new era began in which military leaders controlled Japan.

20.10 The Effect of the Heian Period on Japan Today

As you have learned, the Heian period witnessed the birth of a unique Japanese culture. The effects of this cultural flowering are still felt today. In fact, much of Japan's culture has remained quite constant since the Heian period. This can be seen most clearly in Japan's literature and drama.

Heian authors influenced many later Japanese writers. The *Tale of Genji* by Murasaki Shikibu and *Pillow Book* by Sei Shonagon are classics. They are as basic to Japanese culture as Shakespeare's works are to the English-speaking world.

The success of these writers had a major effect on Japan's written language. Today, Japanese people write with the same characters used in the *Tale of Genji*.

Heian influence is also seen in modern poetry. The short poems called tanka were very popular in Heian times. Tanka poetry is still a vibrant part of Japanese literature.

Modern Japanese drama also shows Heian influences. As you may recall, the bugaku performances of Heian times blended dance and drama. Bugaku led to Japan's unique Noh theater. In Noh dramas, a chorus sings a heroic story as performers dance and act it out. Noh theater is centuries old, but it is still a popular form of entertainment in Japan.

Chapter Summary

In this chapter, you learned about the golden age of Japanese culture, called the Heian period.

A New Capital and the Fujiwara Family In 794, the emperor Kammu built a new Japanese capital, Heian-kyo. This began the Heian period. Aristocrats—especially the Fujiwara family—dominated the new imperial court. They created a uniquely Japanese culture.

Social Position, Beauty and Fashion, and Entertainment Born into a particular social rank, the aristocrats of Heian-kyo lived in great luxury. They prized beauty, elegance, and correct manners.

Sculpture, Painting, Writing, and Literature Heian artists created new Japanese forms of sculpture and painting. Court women, such as Lady Murasaki, wrote classic works of Japanese literature.

The End of the Heian Period and Its Effects The Heian period ended in civil war and the rise of new military leaders. However, the effects of this golden age are still felt in Japan today. Japan's culture has remained fairly constant since the Heian period, especially in literature and drama.

Chapter 21

The Rise of the Warrior Class in Japan

What was the role of the samurai in the military society of medieval Japan?

21.1 Introduction

During the Heian period, Japan experienced a golden age. That period was followed by civil war. In this chapter, you will learn how a powerful warrior class arose out of the strife of that time—the *samurai*.

Minamoto Yoritomo came to power in Japan in 1185. In 1192, he took the title of *shogun,* or commander-in-chief. Yoritomo did not take the place of the emperor. Instead, he set up a military government with its own capital in the city of Kamakura. While the imperial court remained in Heian-kyo, emperors played an increasingly less important role in the government of Japan.

The start of the Kamakura government marked the beginning of a new era in Japanese history. Eventually, professional warriors—the samurai—became Japan's ruling class. The era of the samurai lasted for 700 years, until the emperor was restored to power in 1868.

Over time, an elaborate culture and code of conduct grew up around the samurai. A samurai was expected to be honest, brave, and intensely loyal to his lord. In fact, the word *samurai* means "those who serve." The samurai code was very strict. Samurai sometimes killed themselves with their own swords rather than "lose face," or personal honor.

The samurai were more than fearless fighters. They were educated in art, writing, and literature. Many were devout Buddhists. Their religious faith helped them prepare for their duties and face death bravely.

In this chapter, you will meet Japan's samurai. You will learn about their code of conduct and the role they played in the military society of medieval Japan.

Minamoto Yoritomo was Japan's first shogun. Here he watches wild cranes on the beach near his castle.

◀ Fierce samurai fought individual battles with samurai of equal rank.

21.2 The Rise of the Samurai

The military government established by Minamoto Yoritomo was led
by a **shogun,** or commander-in-chief. Although emperors continued
to rule in name, the real power shifted to the shoguns.

Samurai Under the Shoguns Shoguns, such as Yoritomo and
his **successors,** rewarded warriors, or **samurai,** with appointments
to office and land grants. In return, the samurai pledged to serve and
protect the shogun.

The rise of the samurai brought a new emphasis on military values
in Japanese culture. All samurai trained in the arts of war, especially
archery. During this period, women, as well as men, could be samurai.
Girls and boys alike were trained to harden their feelings and to use
weapons. One samurai wrote,

> Of what use is it to allow the mind to concentrate on the
> moon and flowers, compose poems, and learn how to play
> musical instruments? . . . Members of my household, including
> women, must learn to ride wild horses, and shoot powerful
> bows and arrows.

Shifting Loyalties By the 14th century, Japan's warrior society
resembled the lord-vassal system of medieval Europe. The shogun now
ruled with the help of warrior-lords called **daimyos** (DIE-mee-os). In
turn, the daimyos were supported by large numbers of samurai. The
daimyos expected to be rewarded for their obedience and loyalty with
land, money, or administrative office. The samurai expected the same
from the daimyos they served.

Over time, the position of the shogun weakened as daimyos
became increasingly powerful. Daimyos began to view their lands
as independent kingdoms. Samurai now allied themselves with their
daimyo lords.

In the late 15th century, Japan fell into chaos. Daimyos warred
with one another for land and power. Samurai fought fierce battles on
behalf of their lords.

After a century of bloody warfare, a series of skilled generals
defeated rival daimyos and reestablished a strong military government.
In 1603, the last of these leaders, Tokugawa Ieyasu (TAW-koo-GAH-
wah EE-yeh-YAH-soo), became shogun. Tokugawa established a new
capital in Edo, present-day Tokyo.

For the next 250 years, Japan was at peace. Samurai served under
shoguns and **administered** the government. It was during this time
that the samurai ideal came to full flower. Let's look now at the samurai way of life.

21.3 The Samurai's Armor and Weapons

A samurai was first and foremost a warrior. Let's look at what a samurai wore in battle and the weapons he used.

Armor A samurai went into battle dressed in heavy armor. Under the armor, he wore a colorful robe called a *kimono* and baggy trousers. Shin guards made of leather or cloth protected his legs.

Samurai armor was unique. It was made of rows of small metal plates coated with lacquer and laced together with colorful silk cords. This type of armor was strong, yet flexible enough for the samurai to move freely.

Boxlike panels of armor covered the samurai's chest and back. Metal sleeves covered his arms. Broad shoulder guards and panels that hung over his hips provided additional protection. Some samurai wore thigh guards as well.

After dressing in his body armor, the samurai put on a ferocious-looking iron mask that was meant to frighten his opponents as well as to protect his face. Last came his helmet. Before putting on the helmet, he burned incense in it. In that way, his head would smell sweet if it were cut off in battle.

The clothing and armor of a samurai was extremely complex and took several stages to complete.

Samurai wore elaborate armor with many layers. The layers protected the samurai while allowing free movement.

Weapons Samurai fought with bows and arrows, spears, and swords. A samurai's wooden bow could be up to eight feet long. Such long bows required great strength to use. In battle, samurai on horseback rode toward each other, pulling arrows from the quivers on their backs and firing them at the enemy.

In hand-to-hand combat, some foot soldiers used spears to knock riders off their horses and to kill an enemy on foot with a powerful thrust.

The samurai's most prized weapon, however, was his sword. Japanese sword makers were excellent craftsmen. Samurai swords were the finest in the world. They were flexible enough not to break, but hard enough to be razor sharp. Samurai carried two types of swords. To fight, they used a long sword with a curved blade.

Wearing a sword was the privilege and right of the samurai. Swords were passed down through generations of warrior families and given as prizes to loyal warriors. Even after peace was established in the 17th century, samurai proudly wore their swords as a sign of their rank.

21.4 Military Training and Fighting

The way the first samurai warriors trained and fought was called "The Way of the Horse and the Bow." Later, the art of swordsmanship became more important than archery.

Military Training Learning the skills of a samurai required extensive training. Young samurai were apprenticed to archery masters who taught them mental and physical techniques. Samurai practiced until they could shoot accurately without thinking. They also learned to breathe properly and to shoot at their enemies while riding on the back of a galloping horse.

The art of fencing, or swordsmanship, was just as demanding. A samurai had to learn how to force an enemy to make the first move, how to stay out of range of an enemy sword, and how to fight in tight spaces or against more than one opponent. He practiced continually until he could fence well without thinking about it.

Sometimes in battle a samurai might lose or break his sword. Samurai learned to continue the fight by using other objects as weapons, such as metal fans or wooden staffs. They also learned how to fight without weapons by using **martial arts**. This type of fighting often involves using an opponent's strength against him.

martial arts styles of fighting or self-defense, such as modern-day judo and karate, that began mostly in Asia

Battle According to early texts, the samurai had a unique style of battle. First, messengers from opposing sides met to decide the time and place of combat. Then the two armies faced each other a few hundred yards apart. Samurai on both sides shouted out their names, ancestors, heroic deeds, and reason for fighting. Only then did the armies charge, with mounted samurai firing arrows as they urged their horses forward.

As the two armies clashed, samurai fought each other in hand-to-hand combat. Enemies fought a series of one-on-one duels. Each samurai found an opponent who matched him in rank. He would try to knock his opponent off his horse, wrestle him to the ground, and kill him.

21.5 Mental Training

A samurai's education in the art of war included mental training. Samurai had to learn self-control so that they could overcome emotions that might interfere with fighting, especially the fear of death. They also learned to be always alert and prepared to fight.

Training in Self-Control To learn how to endure pain and suffering, young samurai went for days without eating, marched barefoot in snow on long journeys, and held stiff postures for hours without complaining. To overcome the fear of death, they were told to think of themselves as already dead.

Samurai classes in swordsmanship, or fencing, taught samurai essential skills for battle.

Training in Preparedness A samurai could never relax. An attack could come when least expected, even while a samurai was playing music or dancing. For this reason, samurai had to develop a "sixth sense" about danger. This came from long and grueling training.

The experience of one young samurai illustrates this kind of training. The young man's fencing master used to whack him with a wooden sword throughout the day whenever he least expected it. These painful blows eventually taught the young student to always stay alert.

Teachers also told stories about being prepared. One story was about a samurai who was peacefully writing when a swordsman tried to attack him. Using his sixth sense, the samurai felt the attack coming. He flicked ink into his attacker's eyes and escaped. In another story, a samurai woman who was suddenly attacked thrust a piece of rolled-up paper into her attacker's eyes and gave a war shout. Her attacker ran away.

Samurai learned to control their emotions and to always be prepared.

21.6 Training in Writing and Literature

By the more peaceful 17th century, samurai had to be students of culture, as well as fierce warriors. They were expected to be educated in both writing and literature.

Samurai practiced calligraphy, the art of beautiful writing. A calligrapher's main tools were a brush, a block of ink, and paper or silk. The calligrapher moistened the ink block and rubbed it on an ink stone until the ink reached the right consistency. Then he carefully drew each character with his brush.

Samurai also wrote poetry. One famous samurai poet was Matsuo Basho. He invented a new form of short poetry that was later called *haiku* (high-KOO). A haiku has three lines of 5, 7, and 5 syllables, making 17 syllables in all. A haiku poet uses imagery to suggest an idea or create a mood. Basho added to the beauty of haiku by choosing simple words. Here is his most famous haiku:

Furu ike ya	*An ancient pond*
Kawazu tobikumu	*A frog jumps in*
Mizu no oto	*The splash of water*

Samurai were trained in the art of writing, or calligraphy.

The Rise of the Warrior Class in Japan   **255**

21.7 Training for the Tea Ceremony

Another aspect of culture that samurai studied was the tea ceremony. The tea ceremony fostered a spirit of harmony, reverence, and calm among these warriors. It also served as an important way to form political alliances.

Each step of the ceremony had to be performed in a certain way. A tea master invited guests into a small room. They entered through a doorway so low that they had to crawl.

The tearoom was very simple. The only decorations were a scroll painting or an artistic flower arrangement. The guests sat silently, watching the master make and serve the tea. They then engaged in **sophisticated** discussions as they admired the utensils and the beautiful way the tea master had combined them.

To make the tea, the master heated water in an iron urn over a charcoal fire. Then he scooped powdered green tea from a container called a tea caddy into a small bowl. He ladled hot water into the bowl with a wooden dipper and then whipped the water and tea with a bamboo whisk. Each guest in turn took the bowl, bowed to the others, took three sips, and cleaned the rim with a tissue. Then he passed the bowl back to the master to prepare tea for the next guest.

21.8 Training in Spiritual Strength

Most samurai were Buddhists. Two forms of Buddhism that became popular in Japan were Amida and Zen. Samurai were drawn to both kinds of Buddhism, but especially to Zen.

Many samurai worshipped the Amida Buddha, shown in this statue.

Amida Buddhism In the 12th century, a monk named Honen founded a popular form of Buddhism, **Amida Buddhism**. These Buddhists believed that all people could reach paradise. Honen taught that believers could do this by relying on the mercy of the Amida Buddha.

Amida had been an Indian prince. When he became a Buddha, it was said, he set up a western paradise called the Pure Land. Honen said that believers could enter the Pure Land by prayerfully repeating Amida's name over and over—up to 70,000 times a day. Then, when a believer died, Amida Buddha and a group of bodhisattvas would be waiting to escort the believer into the Pure Land.

Honen's disciple Shinran made this "Pure Land Buddhism" even more popular. He taught that believers could reach the western paradise by sincerely saying Amida's name only once.

Zen Buddhism The form of Buddhism called Zen appealed to many samurai because of its emphasis on effort and discipline. Zen stresses self-reliance and achieving enlightenment through meditation.

To reach enlightenment, Zen Buddhists meditate for hours. They must sit erect and cross-legged without moving.

According to the beliefs of **Zen Buddhism,** becoming enlightened requires giving up everyday, logical thinking. To jolt the mind into enlightenment, masters pose puzzling questions called *koans* (KOH-ahnz). Probably the most well-known koan is, "What is the sound of one hand clapping?"

Zen masters created gardens to aid in meditation. These artfully arranged gardens were often simple and stark. They symbolized nature instead of imitating it. Rocks in sand, for example, might represent islands in the sea.

Zen Buddhism was a good match for the samurai way of life. Zen helped samurai learn discipline, focus their minds, and overcome their fear of death.

Samurai who believed in Zen Buddhism might have sat in simple gardens like this one while they meditated.

Zen Buddhism a form of Buddhism that stresses self-reliance and enlightenment through meditation

Bushido a samurai code that called on warriors to be honest, fair, and fearless

21.9 The Code of Bushido and Samurai Values

The samurai code developed over several centuries. By the 17th century, it took final form in **Bushido,** "The Way of the Warrior."

The code of Bushido, like the code of chivalry in medieval Europe, governed a samurai's life. It called on samurai to be honest, fair, and fearless in the face of death. Samurai were expected to value loyalty and personal honor even more than their lives.

Samurai were fair, honest, and loyal to their lords, above all else. They would fight deadly duels to avenge an insult or their lord's death.

Loyalty and Personal Honor A samurai's **supreme** duty was to be so loyal to his lord that he would gladly die for him. If his lord was murdered, a samurai might avenge his death. A samurai poem says,

> *Though a time come*
> *when mountains crack*
> *and seas go dry,*
> *never to my lord*
> *will I be found double-hearted!*

Samurai were also expected to guard their personal honor. The least insult on the street could lead to a duel. One samurai, for example, accidentally knocked his umbrella against another samurai's umbrella. This quickly turned into a quarrel and then a sword fight, resulting in the first samurai's death.

Ritual Suicide The price for failing to live up to the code of Bushido was *seppuku,* or ritual suicide. There were many reasons for seppuku, including preserving personal honor and avoiding capture in battle. Samurai might also perform seppuku to pay for a crime, a shameful deed, or an insult to a person of higher rank. Some samurai even killed themselves when their lord died or as a form of protest against an injustice.

21.10 Women in Samurai Society

The position of women in samurai society declined over time. In the 12th century, the women of the warrior class enjoyed honor and respect. By the 17th century, however, samurai women were treated as **inferior** to their husbands.

Samurai Women in the 12th Century In the 12th century, samurai women enjoyed considerable status. A samurai's wife helped manage the household and promote the family's interests. When her husband died, she could inherit his property and perform the duties of a vassal. Though women rarely fought, they were expected to be as loyal and brave as men.

Some women, like Tomoe Gozen (TOH-moh-eh GO-zen), did take part in battles alongside men. Fighting one-on-one, she killed several enemies in a battle. Then she fenced with the enemy leader, who tried to drag her from her horse. When he tore off her sleeve, she spun her horse around and killed him.

A woman named Koman is another famous warrior. During a battle on a lake, she saved her clan's banner by swimming to shore under a shower of arrows with the banner clenched in her teeth.

In the 12th century, women, as well as men, were taught the military skills needed to become samurai.

Samurai Women in the 17th Century As the warrior culture developed, women's position weakened. By the 17th century, samurai men were the unquestioned lords of their households. According to one saying, when young, women should obey their fathers; when grown, their husbands; and when old, their sons.

Girls did not choose their own husbands. Instead, families arranged marriages for their daughters to increase their position and wealth. Wives were expected to bear sons, manage the home, and look after their husbands.

A popular book of the time told women how to behave. They were to get up early and go to bed late. During the day they must weave, sew, spin, and take care of their households. They must stick to simple food and clothes and stay away from plays, singing, and other entertainment.

Not all Japanese women were treated the same way. Peasant women had some respect and independence because they worked alongside their husbands. But in samurai families, women were completely under men's control.

21.11 Comparing Japan and Europe in the Middle Ages

The Japan of the samurai period was both like and unlike Europe
during the Middle Ages. In both societies, ties of loyalty and obligation bound lords and vassals. Both had rulers who rose to power as
military chiefs. But in Europe, a military leader like William the
Conqueror ruled as king. In Japan, the shogun ruled in the name of
the emperor.

The daimyos of Japan were like the landholding lords of medieval
Europe. Both types of lords built castles and held estates that were
worked by peasants.

Both the samurai of Japan and the knights of Europe were warriors who wore armor, rode horses, and owned land. Just as European
knights had a code of chivalry, the samurai had the code of Bushido.
The samurai code, however, was much more strict, since it demanded
that a samurai kill himself to maintain his honor.

21.12 The Influence of Samurai Values and Traditions in Modern Times

Japan's warrior society lasted until 1868, when political upheavals led
to the **restoration** of the emperor to ruling power. Modern Japan still
feels the influence of the long era of the samurai.

In the 1940s, the Japanese who fought in World War II stayed true
to the samurai warrior code. Many soldiers killed themselves rather
than surrender. Suicide pilots crashed planes loaded with explosives
into enemy battleships. These pilots were called *kamikazes* ("divine
winds") after the storms that helped destroy an invading Chinese fleet
in the 13th century.

Samurai fought individual battles with
other samurai of equal rank. Like the
medieval European knights, the samurai
also fought on horseback.

Today, instructors teach samurai fighting techniques to students wearing traditional padded armor. These students are practicing the ancient martial art of kendo.

Japanese and other peoples around the world study martial arts. Sports such as judo and fighting with bamboo swords reflect samurai discipline and skill.

Other elements of samurai culture persist today. People in Japan continue to write haiku and practice calligraphy. Zen gardens and the tea ceremony remain popular. And the samurai ideals of loyalty to family and respect for rank are still alive in modern Japan.

Chapter Summary

In this chapter, you learned how a class of warriors, called samurai, rose to prominence in medieval Japan. They dominated Japan for nearly 700 years, serving shoguns and daimyos. Over time, an elaborate samurai culture developed.

Armor, Weapons, and Military, Mental, and Spiritual Training Samurai wore flexible armor, rode horses, and fought with bows, spears, and swords. They were trained as fearless fighters. The discipline of Zen Buddhism especially appealed to them.

Training in Writing, Literature, and the Tea Ceremony Samurai also studied literature, the arts, and the complex tea ceremony. They were expected to be able poets and to be skilled at calligraphy.

Bushido and Samurai Values Samurai were expected to live by a strict code called Bushido. This code prized honor, loyalty, and fearlessness.

Women Samurai Women enjoyed high status in early samurai society, and some women fought as warriors. Over time, however, the status of samurai women declined.

Japan and Europe in the Middle Ages Japan's samurai society resembled feudalism in medieval Europe. In both places, a lord-vassal system developed. Samurai and European knights both had a code of behavior, fought on horseback, and pledged loyalty to their lords.

The Samurai Influence Today Samurai values and traditions continue to influence Japan. For example, people practice samurai martial arts, write haiku, and create Zen gardens.

Female samurai Tomoe Gozen is a legendary hero to the Japanese.

Tomoe Gozen: History or Legend?

Japanese history tells stories about women warriors of the samurai period. Strong and skillful fighters, they were willing to die with honor rather than face defeat and disgrace. Tomoe Gozen is one of the most well known of these fierce Japanese women samurai. The tales say that she was an important figure in the wars of the late Heian period. But was she a real woman or a fictional character?

Tomoe Gozen is first mentioned in *The Tale of the Heike* (HAY-keh). The most famous epic from medieval Japan, the tale is actually a series of stories about the Genpei War, which took place in the 1180s, during the late Heian period. The war was a struggle between two powerful rival clans for control of Japan.

The Tale of the Heike had many authors. Storytellers repeated the narrative over several generations before it was written down. Experts say the most definitive version of the Heike tale probably was first recorded in the 1300s. Many other versions and translations have appeared since then.

A Woman Warrior

Tomoe appears only briefly in *The Tale of the Heike*, fighting for a general named Yoshinaka. However, she makes a strong impression:

> *Tomoe was especially beautiful. . . . She was also a remarkably strong archer, and as a swordswoman, she was a warrior worth a thousand, ready to confront a demon or a god, mounted or on foot. She handled unbroken horses with superb skill; she rode unscathed [unhurt] down perilous descents. Whenever a battle was imminent [about to begin], Yoshinaka sent her out as his first captain, equipped with strong armor, an oversized sword, and a mighty bow; and she performed more deeds of valor than any of his other warriors.*

Some versions of the story say that Tomoe was General Yoshinaka's wife, while others state she was not. In either case, she was a strong woman warrior. In the final battle of the Genpei War, as described in the Heike tale, Tomoe fights bravely, but General Yoshinaka is mortally wounded. She wants to stay and die with him, but he orders her to leave the battlefield. Tomoe obeys, but is very frustrated. She thinks, "Ah! If only I could find a worthy foe! I would fight a last battle for His Lordship to watch."

Suddenly, a powerful and strong enemy leader appears nearby. Tomoe rides toward him, drags him from his horse, pulls him down against her saddle, cuts off his head, and throws it aside. When she is done, she removes her armor and helmet and rides off toward the eastern provinces.

Was Tomoe a Real Person?

This brief but powerful appearance of Tomoe in *The Tale of the Heike* is all we know about her. Was she a real person? To decide, historians looked at the evidence. Since *The Tale of the Heike* is one of the main sources for historical knowledge of the Genpei War, historians had to read all the versions of it written over the centuries.

Historians have good evidence that Tomoe was, in fact, a real person. First, much samurai history says that there actually were female warriors, like Tomoe, who fought just as skillfully and fiercely as men. Second, *The Tale of the Heike* says that General Yoshinaka "had brought . . . two female attendants, Tomoe and Yamabuki" with him to the wars. Since other figures and events in the book are real, historians conclude that Tomoe was most likely real, too.

Not only was Tomoe Gozen a brave and talented warrior, she was also an excellent horsewoman. Here, she rides ahead into battle.

Actors, such as the one in the center of this image, took on the role of Tomoe Gozen. Stories and plays about her allowed her legend to grow.

The Legend Begins

How does a legend start? Generally, it starts with a historical figure. Over the years, people retell the person's story. New details are added from one generation to the next. These details tend to make the story more exciting, but less realistic. The historical figure becomes super-human, extremely wise, strong, or magical. He or she may also become a symbol, standing for positive or negative characteristics that capture people's imagination.

Robin Hood is a good example of a legendary figure in Western culture. Some historians think he might have been real. As his story was retold, however, he turned from a historical figure into a legend, fighting for the poor against the rich. Countless ballads, plays, poems, movies, and TV series have told about his adventures.

Similarly, over the centuries, Tomoe became a legend in Asian culture. Her story was retold over centuries in Japan. Details were added to explain what happened to her after she went off to the eastern provinces. Various versions have her running away, dying with Yoshinaka, getting married, or becoming a Buddhist nun.

One thing is certain: over time, Tomoe came to symbolize loyalty, strength, and bravery, and became a role model of a strong and powerful woman. Her unknown fate would be the seed of her growing legend. As it grew, Tomoe the Heian warrior became Tomoe Gozen. *Gozen* is a title of respect, similar to the English title "Lady."

The Legend Grows

From the 14th to the 17th centuries, Tomoe and her story were a favorite theme for dramatists. *Tomoe* is the title of a haunting Japanese drama written in the 14th century. The story takes place at a shrine built where General Yoshinaka died. There, a figure appears—the spirit of Tomoe. She cries as she tells the story of Yoshinaka and Tomoe. She says that Yoshinaka ordered her to leave him dying on the battlefield so that someone would live to tell his story. A monk comforts her ghost. The audience is left with the idea that Tomoe will someday reappear. "For where I suffered . . . I shall rise," the ghost says.

Traveling entertainers also helped keep her story alive. Many became the character of Tomoe. These "Tomoes" earned a living by traveling to famous battle sites. Audiences watched in awe as the actor "Tomoe" related the sad story of Yoshinaka's death as if he or she had been an eyewitness. In this way, her story spread.

New and largely made-up details were added to Tomoe's story by these wandering entertainers. One expert thinks that it was they who created most of the later explanations of Tomoe's fate. At this point, she was becoming one of the most important cultural icons in the history of Japan.

Between the 17th and 19th centuries, Tomoe Gozen's image and story became even more popular. She appeared as a character in Kabuki theater. Kabuki is a type of Japanese drama with song and dance and very elaborate costumes. Artists also created both painted scrolls and woodblock prints showing some of the best-known incidents in her life. In fact, there are many more print portraits of Tomoe Gozen than of her more famous commander, Yoshinaka.

Tomoe Gozen Today

Today, Tomoe Gozen has inspired many types of artistic expression. Artists and writers have given Tomoe Gozen new life in novels, comic books, graphic novels, TV series, anime films, and video games. Some, like the wandering entertainers of the past, add details to her story to explain her life after Yoshinaka's death. Others reinvent her into a modern woman warrior.

In the Japanese comic book *Samurai Deeper Kyo,* Tomoe comes back to life as the character Saisei (SIGH-say). In the Japanese samurai comic *Usagi Yojimbo,* Tomoe Ame (AH-meh) is a woman warrior partly based on the historic Tomoe. In the 21st century, Tomoe Gozen has become almost a superhero, like Superman or Batman.

Tomoe Gozen's name and image have survived for more than 800 years. Whether she lived or not, may not be important; her loyalty, bravery, and strength make her an important role model.

Tomoe Gozen has inspired modern anime artists to create fictional female warriors, like Tomoe Ame.

Tomoe Ame from Usagi Yojimbo™ © Stan Sakai. All rights reserved. Used with permission.

Japan During Medieval Times

552
Buddhism Reaches Japan
Buddhism spreads to Japan when a Korean king sends a statue of the Buddha to Japan along with a recommendation for a new religion.

710
New Capital for Japan
Japan's government builds a new capital city called Nara. It is modeled after China's capital, Chang'an.

By 900
New Style of Writing
The Japanese invent *kana,* a style of writing that uses simplified Chinese characters to stand for syllables.

500   700   900   1100

593
Prince Shotoku's Rule Begins
By encouraging an interest in Korean and Chinese cultures, Prince Shotoku helps create a unique Japanese culture of blended ideas.

794–1185
Heian Period
The Heian period, also called Japan's golden age, ushers in a great flourishing of culture led by Japan's aristocrats.

995–1028
Fujiwara Michinaga Rules
Fujiwara Michinaga, the most successful of the Fujiwara rulers, leads Japan peacefully, despite never having an official government role.

About 1010
Tale of Genji
Completed
Murasaki Shikibu finishes writing the *Tale of Genji,* considered to be the world's first novel.

1185
Minamoto Yoritomo Comes to Power
Minamoto Yoritomo, head of a military family, seizes control and sets up a military government in Japan.

1300   1500   1700   1900

1192–1867
Feudalism in Japan
A lord-vassal system of shoguns, daimyos, and samurai dominates Japan. A warrior code known as *Bushido* develops.

1180
Civil War in Japan
As the power of local feudal lords grows and the imperial government weakens, civil war erupts, clans struggle for power, and local rulers fight to control land.

1603–1867
Samurai Culture
Samurai culture flourishes under the Tokugawa shogunate, which begins with the reign of Tokugawa Ieyasu.

Unit 6

Civilizations of the Americas

The Mayas built great stone pyramids in what is now present-day Mexico. Shown here is a step pyramid at Chichén Itza on the Yucatán Peninsula. Stairways on four sides lead to the top.

NORTH AMERICA

ATLANTIC OCEAN

Gulf of Mexico

BAJA CALIFORNIA

Gulf of California

SIERRA MADRE OCCIDENTAL

MEXICAN PLATEAU

SIERRA MADRE ORIENTAL

Tropic of Cancer

Cabo San Lucas

Pico de Orizaba
(18,855 ft.
5,747 m)

YUCATÁN PENINSULA

Cuba

BAHAMAS

WEST INDIES

Jamaica

Hispaniola

Caribbean Sea

Lake Managua
Lake Nicaragua

ISTHMUS OF PANAMA

Lake Maracaibo

Orinoco River

Angel Falls

LLANOS

GUIANA HIGHLANDS

Gulf of Panama

Marajó Island

Gulf of Guayaquil

Negro River

AMAZON

SELVAS

BASIN

Amazon River

Madeira River

Xingú River

Tocatins River

São Francisco River

MATO GROSSO PLATEAU

BRAZILIAN HIGHLANDS

Equator

GALÁPAGOS ISLANDS

Equator

PACIFIC OCEAN

ANDES MOUNTAINS

Lake Titicaca

ATACAMA DESERT

Mt. Aconcagua
(22,831 ft.
6,959 m)

ANDES MOUNTAINS

GRAN CHACO

Iguazú Falls

Paraná River

Uruguay River

Tropic of Capricorn

PAMPAS

Rio de la Plata

ATLANTIC OCEAN

PATAGONIA

CHONOS ARCHIPELAGO

Gulf of San Jorge

Laguna del Carbón
(-344 ft. -105 m)

FALKLAND ISLANDS

Strait of Magellan

Tierra del Fuego

Cape Horn

Elevation

Feet	Meters
Over 10,000	Over 3,050
5,001–10,000	1,526–3,050
2,001–5,000	611–1,525
1,001–2,000	306–610
0–1,000	0–305
Below sea level	Below sea level

▲ Mountain peak

Present-day boundary

0   500   1,000 miles
0   500   1,000 kilometers
Lambert Azimuthal Equal-Area Projection

40°N

20°N

120°W

100°W

80°W

60°W

40°W

20°W

40°S

20°S

0°

Civilizations of the Americas

In this unit, you will learn about the civilizations that developed in Mexico, Central America, and South America. This region is also known as Latin America.

Suppose you could fly over this entire region in just a few hours. What would you see? Beginning in Mexico and Central America, and flying south, you would see mostly rugged mountains. In the middle of the country, these highlands include volcanoes and vast farmlands that spread out for miles. In the southernmost part of this region, the land becomes very narrow, only 30 miles wide.

This thin land bridge leads into South America. From your plane, you would see a dramatic mountain range called the Andes. The Andes extend along nearly the entire western coast of South America. East of the Andes, in the central part of the continent are rainforests, deserts, and grasslands. You would glimpse rivers flowing through the rainforests. One river, the Amazon, is the longest in South America. As you finish your flight, you would cross over the pointy tip of South America, a flat area that rises from the Atlantic to the Andes.

Mexico, Central and South America were home to several advanced early civilizations. In the Andes, a group known as the Incas built the largest empire in the Americas. To link their huge mountain empire, they built roads and bridges across deep ravines and raging rivers.

Two groups of people lived in Mexico and Central America: the Mayas and the Aztecs. The Mayas survived by learning to grow food in the hills, swamps, and forests they inhabited. The Aztecs, too, used their natural resources. They constructed a complex system of canals by which they traded with people far away. You will begin your exploration of these early civilizations with the Mayas.

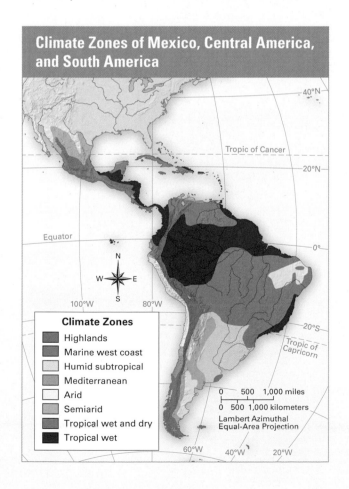

Climate Zones of Mexico, Central America, and South America

Climate Zones
- Highlands
- Marine west coast
- Humid subtropical
- Mediterranean
- Arid
- Semiarid
- Tropical wet and dry
- Tropical wet

Lambert Azimuthal Equal-Area Projection

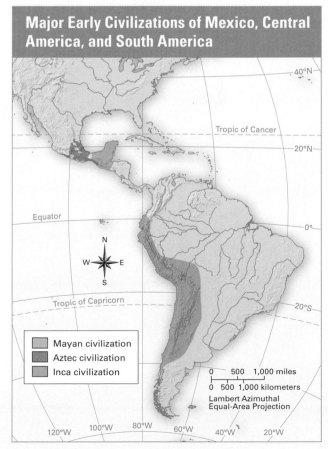

Major Early Civilizations of Mexico, Central America, and South America

- Mayan civilization
- Aztec civilization
- Inca civilization

Lambert Azimuthal Equal-Area Projection

Chapter 22

The Mayas

What led to the rise, flourishing, and fall of the Mayan civilization?

22.1 Introduction

In this chapter, you will learn about some of the most important achievements of the Mayan civilization. This civilization lasted 3,500 years, from about 2000 B.C.E. to 1500 C.E. At its peak, it included present-day southern Mexico and large portions of Central America. Visitors can still see the ruins of some amazing stone cities built by the Mayas (MY-uhz). The ruins of the ancient city of Tikal (tee-KAHL), shown on the opposite page and at right, lie deep in the jungles of present-day Guatemala.

Picture yourself standing at the heart of this city in the year 750 C.E. You are in a large, open plaza surrounded by eight soaring temple-pyramids. On the ground, as far as you can see, are structures on raised platforms. The structures are painted in bright colors. Nearby, in the center of the city, you see large palaces made of limestone blocks. These palaces are the homes of the ruler, priests, and nobles. Farther out are the stone houses of the merchants and artisans. At the very edge of the city are thousands of small, thatched-roof house-mounds where the peasants live.

Tikal was only one of more than forty Mayan cities. How did the Mayas create such great cities and such an advanced civilization? In this chapter, you will trace the development of Mayan civilization. Then you will take a closer look at several aspects of Mayan culture, including class structure, family life, religious beliefs and practices, and agricultural techniques.

This photograph shows the ruins of the Temple of the Jaguar at the Mayan city of Tikal.

◀ The Mayas built great stone pyramids such as this one at Tikal.

One of the great achievements of the Olmecs was the creation of monumental stone heads, believed to be portraits of their leaders. More than thirty of them have been found. They stand over eight feet high and weigh about ten tons. The massive heads were sculpted without metal tools.

22.2 The Development of Mayan Civilization

The **Mayas** were creating an advanced civilization in the Americas around the same time the Roman Empire was declining in western Europe. Mayan civilization reached its height between 300 and 900 C.E. During this time, Mayan culture spread over a great deal of **Mesoamerica,** including part of present-day southern Mexico, Belize, most of Guatemala, and parts of Honduras and El Salvador.

The landscape in which the Mayas lived varied greatly. In the south, pine forests covered the mountain highlands. In the northern and central regions were rainforests, grasslands, and swamps. These regions are known as the lowlands. Thick jungle covered the southern part of the lowlands. Today, this area is called the Petén (pay-TAYN) region of Guatemala. It is the area in which Mayan civilization reached its highest development.

The Origins of Mayan Civilization The Mayas built their civilization, in part, on ideas they inherited from a people called the Olmecs. The Olmecs lived in the jungle areas on the east coast of Mexico. Their civilization reached its peak between 1200 and 500 B.C.E.

Like early civilizations in other parts of the world, the Olmec civilization was based on agriculture. By 2000 B.C.E., people in parts of Mexico had turned from hunting and gathering to farming as their main source of food. A particularly important crop at the time was maize, or corn.

Farming allowed the Olmecs to create permanent settlements. The Olmecs established farming villages throughout the region. They also created trade routes that stretched for hundreds of miles.

By 1400 B.C.E., the Olmecs had a capital city that boasted palaces, temples, and monuments. They were the first Mesoamericans to develop large religious and ceremonial centers. They were also the first to use a solar calendar, or a calendar based on the cycles of the sun. The Mayas would build on all these achievements.

Three Periods of Mayan Civilization Mayan civilization began to develop in eastern and southern Mexico around 2000 B.C.E. Historians divide the history of Mayan civilization into three main periods: Pre-Classic, Classic, and Post-Classic.

The long Pre-Classic period lasted from about 2000 B.C.E. to 300 C.E. During this time, the Mayas farmed the land and lived in simple houses and compounds, or groups of buildings.

Gradually, Mayan culture became more complex. As the Mayan population grew, settlements became larger. The Mayas began constructing public buildings for governmental and religious purposes.

Possibly as early as 300 B.C.E., they began to adapt the writing system of the Olmecs and to develop their own system of **hieroglyphic** writing. Mayan civilization reached its peak during the Classic period, from around 300 to 900 C.E. The achievements you will study in this chapter date from this time.

hieroglyphic writing that uses pictures as symbols

During the Classic period, the Mayas adapted and developed other ideas they had learned from the Olmecs. For example, they improved on Olmec building techniques. Even though the Mayas lacked metal tools and had not discovered the wheel, they built enormous stone cities with elaborate and highly decorated temple-pyramids and palaces. The Mayas also built observatories for studying the sky. They charted the movements of the moon, stars, and planets. They used their knowledge of astronomy and mathematics to create complex and highly accurate calendars.

Mayan society during the Classic period consisted of many independent states. Each state included farming communities and one or more cities. At its height, the Mayan Empire included more than forty cities, including Tikal, Copan (kaw-PAHN), Chichén Itzá, and Palenque (pah-LENG-kay).

Around 900 C.E., the Classic civilization collapsed. The Mayas **abandoned** their cities in the southern lowland area, and the once thriving communities fell into ruin in the jungle. No one knows for certain why this happened. At the end of this chapter, we will look at some theories that may explain the mystery.

To the north, on the Yucatán (you-kuh-TAN) Peninsula, Mayan cities continued to prosper during the Post-Classic period. This period lasted from about 900 C.E. to 1500 C.E. During this time, the Mayas continued their warfare and empire building, but they had fewer great artistic and cultural achievements.

Even at the height of their empire, the Mayas were not one unified nation. Instead, they lived in many city-states with their own governments. What united them as Mayas was their common culture: their social system, languages, calendar, religion, and way of life.

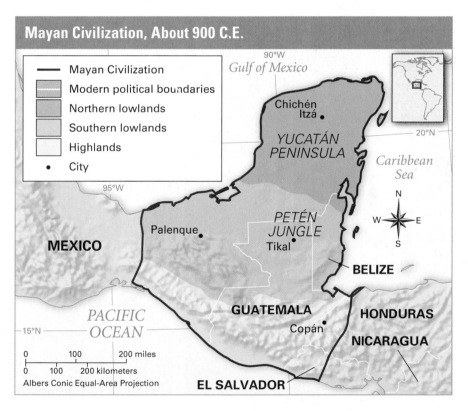

Mayan Civilization, About 900 C.E.

- Mayan Civilization
- Modern political boundaries
- Northern lowlands
- Southern lowlands
- Highlands
- City

90°W
Gulf of Mexico
Chichén Itzá
YUCATÁN PENINSULA
20°N
Caribbean Sea
95°W
Palenque
MEXICO
PETÉN JUNGLE
Tikal
BELIZE
PACIFIC OCEAN
15°N
GUATEMALA
Copán
HONDURAS
NICARAGUA
0   100   200 miles
0   100   200 kilometers
Albers Conic Equal-Area Projection
EL SALVADOR

At the height of their civilization, the Mayas occupied large parts of modern Central America.

22.3 Class Structure

Within each Mayan city-state, society was structured like a pyramid. The ruler of each city-state was at the top of this **social pyramid**. The rest of the members of Mayan society were organized into a series of ranks below the ruler.

The Ruler The highest authority in the state was the *halach uinic* (hah-lach WEE-nik), a Mayan phrase that means "true man." He ruled the state with the help of his advisers. He decided when and with whom to go to war.

The Mayan ruler was considered a god-king. During religious ceremonies, he wore a headdress that was as tall as a person. When he died, a son or another close male relative succeeded him. Mayan rulers were almost always men, but scholars believe that some women had **considerable** influence, probably through family relationships.

Nobles and Priests The next layer in the social pyramid was made up of nobles and priests. They, along with the ruler, were the only members of Mayan society who knew how to read and write.

The nobles served as scribes and officials, and oversaw the administration of the states. They gathered taxes, supplies, and labor for projects, such as the construction of temples. Nobles led peasant armies in times of war. During battles, they wore elaborate costumes, including gold jewelry and animal robes made from the skins of jaguars.

The social pyramid of the Mayan civilization shows the ruler of each city-state at the top, with the rest of Mayan society below him. Each layer of the pyramid represents the people at different levels of importance. Notice that there are many more people at the bottom of the pyramid than at the top.

Priests were important because it was their job to maintain favor with the gods. Like nobles, priests inherited their position from their fathers. Priests led **rituals**, offered **sacrifices**, and foretold the future. They were consulted to determine the best days for going to battle. In addition to their religious duties, priests were often mathematicians, astronomers, and healers.

ritual a set of actions that is always performed the same way as part of a religious ceremony

sacrifice a gift of an animal for slaughter to honor the gods

Merchants and Artisans Although the Mayan economy was based mostly on farming, trade and crafts were also important. These functions were carried out by merchants and artisans.

The Mayas were accomplished traders. They traveled by sea, river, and well-constructed roads to trade with other city-states. Merchants in the lowlands imported valuable products from the highlands. These products included stones such as obsidian and jade; copal, a tree sap that the Maya used as incense during religious ceremonies; and quetzals, birds whose shiny green feathers were used in headdresses.

Mayan artisans made a wide variety of objects, many of them designed to pay tribute to the gods. They painted books on paper made from the bark of fig trees. Artists painted murals of Mayan life, important battles, and other major events. They created sculptures for temples and decorative designs on palace walls. The Mayas were also skilled weavers and potters.

Mayan artists created many objects, such as this terra cotta figure, to honor their gods.

Peasants The peasants were the backbone of Mayan society. They worked hard on the land, growing maize, squash, beans, and other crops to feed the population. During the growing season, men spent most of the day in the fields, farming with wooden hoes. Women usually stayed closer to home, preparing food, weaving, and sewing.

When they were not farming, peasants had to spend time building pyramids and temples. In exchange for their work, they sometimes attended royal weddings and religious events. Peasants also served as soldiers during wars.

Slaves At the bottom of the social pyramid were the slaves. Slaves performed manual labor for their owners. Some were born into slavery, but free people sometimes became slaves. Some children became slaves when their parents sold them to feed the rest of the family. War prisoners of humble origin were enslaved. (Those of higher rank were sacrificed to the gods.) And some people were enslaved as a punishment for serious crimes.

In general, the Mayas did not mistreat slaves. Sometimes, slaves actually had easier lives than peasants, depending on what jobs they did and their owners' social rank. But slaves were not free to come and go as they pleased. Often, they were sacrificed when their owners died.

Mayan families had many daily tasks, including weaving, cooking, washing clothes, fishing, and working the land.

22.4 Family Life

In city-states like Copan, located in present-day Honduras, Mayan peasants lived in one-room huts built of interwoven poles and covered with dried mud. Several family houses were often grouped around a shared courtyard. A separate kitchen building might be directly behind the main house. Peasant families worked hard, but ceremonies and rituals provided a break from work and a chance to celebrate important events.

Duties of Family Members Life for Mayan peasant families was not easy. Mayan women rose before dawn to get the fire burning in the fireplace. With the help of her daughters, a Mayan woman cleaned the corn that had been boiled and left to soak and soften overnight. Then she set to work at the grinding stone, pounding corn into meal. She patted the meal into *tortillas* (tawr-tee-uhs), a Spanish word meaning "little breads," or *tamales* (tuh-MAH-leez) and cooked them over the fire. These might serve as the morning meal or they might be saved for dinner. On special days, the family might also have hot chocolate, a drink the Mayas made from cacao (kuh-KAY-oh) beans.

During the day, women and older girls cared for small children and for the family's few animals, like ducks and turkeys. They swept their homes, and they gathered, spun, and wove cotton into cloth.

Mayan fathers and sons ate their morning meal quickly before leaving to work in the fields. When they weren't busy with the crops, men and boys hunted and trapped animals.

Special Occasions Mayan families took time to celebrate the important events in their lives. The birth of a child was a time for rejoicing. As soon as possible after the birth, the family called in a priest to perform a ceremony much like baptism. The priest forecast the baby's future and gave advice to help guide the parents in raising the child.

At three months of age, girls went through another ceremony. The number three was special to Mayan women because it represented the three stones of the home hearth, or fireplace. In the three-month ceremony, the baby girl was introduced to the tools she would use throughout her life. Small items were placed in the baby's hands, such as tools for spinning and weaving, carrying water and cooking, and soaking and grinding maize.

A similar ceremony was held for boys at four months of age. The number four was special to Mayan men. It represented the four sides of the plot of land where a boy would spend his life. The baby boy was given farmer's tools, such as axes and planting sticks, and the spears, knives, and traps of a hunter.

Another important event in every Mayan child's life was the coming-of-age ceremony. Girls went through this ceremony at age 12, boys at 14. The long ceremony involved confessing, cleansing with water, and reciting the rules of behavior. Finally, the priest cut a white bead from the boys' hair and removed a string of red shells from around the girls' waists. Boys and girls had worn these symbols of innocence since they were quite young.

Marriage Customs The next big moment in the life of a Mayan youth was marriage. Men usually married around age 20. Women married when they were as young as 14.

The bride and groom did not choose each other. Instead, marriages were negotiated by the village *atanzahab,* or matchmaker. Families had to agree on how much food and clothing would be given to the bride's family. They also had to agree on the number of years a young man would work for his new wife's family.

Once the details of a marriage were worked out, the villagers built a hut for the couple behind the home of the bride's parents. When the home was ready, the bride and groom put on clothing woven for the occasion. After a priest blessed the marriage, the villagers celebrated.

The marriage ceremony was an important event in the life of a young Mayan.

22.5 Religious Beliefs and Practices

Religion was very important to the Mayas. They built their cities around religious and ceremonial centers. Their magnificent temple-pyramids rose high above the jungle canopy, like mountains reaching into the sky. Temple plazas provided gathering places for people to attend rituals and ceremonies.

Scholars have learned about the Mayan religion from studying present-day Mayan practices, ancient artifacts, and documents written during the Post-Classic period. Here are some things they discovered.

Beliefs and Rituals The Mayan religion was polytheistic, which means it included many gods. The Mayas believed in more than 160 gods. The primary Mayan gods were forces or objects in nature that affected people's daily lives, such as rain, corn, and death. Many gods had animal characteristics. The jaguar was especially important to the Mayas.

The Mayas believed that the gods had created the world and could influence or even destroy it. The same god that sent life-giving rain could also ruin the crops with hailstones. So, it was extremely important to honor the gods.

According to Mayan beliefs, only priests could explain **divine** signs and lead people through rituals aimed at pleasing the gods. Priests performed sacrifices and conducted ceremonies. They consulted sacred books, read omens, interpreted signs, and predicted the future. No decision was made without seeking the gods' advice. No action was taken without first honoring the gods.

The Mayas honored their gods with offerings such as plants, food, flowers, feathers, jade, and shells. The Mayas believed that blood gave the gods strength, so they also made blood offerings by sacrificing animals and, sometimes, humans. The people who were sacrificed were usually orphans, slaves, or nobles captured during war.

In this reproduction of a Mayan painting, a richly dressed priest is being served by slaves during a Mayan religious ceremony.

This is the ball court at the ancient Mayan city of Chichén Itzá. Notice the height of the stone rings embedded in the walls and how small the holes are.

Human sacrifice also played a role in an ancient Mayan game called *pok-a-tok*. Every Mayan city had at least one ball court where the game took place. Scholars believe that there were two teams of nobles. Players tried to hit a solid rubber ball through a stone ring by using their leather-padded elbows, wrists, and hips. People from all levels of Mayan society attended the popular games. However, the outcome often had serious results. Surviving art from the ball courts shows members of the losing team being sacrificed and the captain of the defeated team being beheaded.

The Sacred Calendar The Mayas used their knowledge of mathematics and astronomy to develop a complex calendar system. They used two main calendars for religious and other purposes. The first was a daily calendar, based on the solar (sun) year. It divided the year into 18 months of 20 days each, plus 5 "unlucky" days. This totaled 365 days, as our calendar does.

The second calendar was the sacred, or ritual, calendar. It was called the *tzolkin* (TSAWL-keen), or Sacred Round. The Sacred Round was based on 13 months of 20 days each, making 260 days in all. It had two cycles that worked together to identify a particular day. One cycle was made up of the numbers 1 to 13. The other cycle was a set of 20 day names. Each of the day names represented a particular god. Every 260 days, a given combination of numbers and day names, such as *1 Ik,* would occur.

Only priests could "read" the hidden meaning of the Sacred Round. Priests used the sacred calendar to determine the best days to plant, hunt, cure, do battle, and perform religious ceremonies. To this day, there are calendar priests in southern Mexico who still use the 260-day calendar in this way.

Like Mayan art and architecture, the calendar system reflects a highly advanced civilization. This high level of civilization was possible due to the ability of the Mayas to create a stable food supply.

Cutting and burning plants and trees is an easy way to clear land for farming, and the ashes help to fertilize crops. However, this slash-and-burn technique uses up the soil quickly and can be dangerous, as fires sometimes get out of control.

slash-and-burn agriculture
a farming technique in which vegetation is cut away and burned to clear land for growing crops

22.6 Agricultural Techniques

The Mayas were creative, skillful farmers. They used their knowledge of calendars and seasonal change to help them become even better at growing food. But Mayan farmers faced many challenges. In the end, crop failure may have played a key role in the collapse of the Classic Mayan civilization.

Challenges Facing Mayan Farmers The primary Mayan food was maize, or corn. Other typical Mayan crops were beans, squash, and chili peppers. Fortunately, beans and squash, when eaten with corn, supply people with a naturally healthful and balanced diet.

One of the most difficult challenges the Mayas faced was how to grow enough food to feed their growing population. Farming was not easy in the regions where they lived. Their land included dense forests, little surface water (such as lakes or streams), and poor soil.

The Mayas responded to this challenge by developing different agricultural techniques for the various environments in which they lived. In the mountainous highlands, they built terraces, or flat earthen steps, into the hills to make more land available for planting. In the swampy lowlands, the Mayas constructed raised-earth platforms surrounded by canals that drained off extra rainwater. This technique helped them to grow more food without having to conquer or clear more land.

A different technique was used in the densely forested lowland areas. In city-states like Palenque (in present-day Mexico), the Mayas used **slash-and-burn agriculture**. First, they cleared the land by cutting and burning plants and trees. Then they planted their crops. Unfortunately, this type of farming wears out the soil. Lowland soil was not very rich to begin with, so land that was planted for two to four years had to be left to rest for two to ten years. Slash-and-burn farmers had to have a lot of land, since each year some areas were planted while others were recovering.

The Mayan agricultural system worked as long as settlements were spread out and not too large. As populations increased, the Mayas had trouble raising enough food to feed everyone. In the constant quest for land, they drained swamps and cleared hillsides. They also used household gardens in the cities to help supplement the food supply.

The End of the Classic Period Creative agricultural techniques were not enough to save Classic Mayan civilization. For about six hundred years, the great cities of the southern lowlands thrived. Then, in the space of fifty to one hundred years, the civilization that supported these centers fell apart. By 900 C.E., the Mayas had abandoned their large cities to the jungle.

The collapse of Classic Mayan civilization is one of the great mysteries of Mesoamerican history. Many theories have been offered to explain what happened. Some historians believe that the populations of the cities grew faster than the Mayan farming systems could **sustain** them. Scholars have also proposed that long periods of drought caused massive crop failure.

Another possible cause of the Mayas' downfall was uncontrolled warfare. In the centuries after 300 C.E., the skirmishes that were common among city-states grew into full-fledged wars. A final possibility is that invaders from central Mexico helped to destroy the Mayan city-states.

Perhaps a combination of factors ended the Classic period. What we do know is that the great cities disappeared. The Mayas migrated away from the old Mayan heartland and returned to village life. Stone by stone, the jungle reclaimed the great pyramids and plazas.

Although the great Mayan cities are ruins today, Mayan culture lives on. About two million Mayas still live in the southern Mexican state of Chiapas. Millions more are spread throughout the Yucatán Peninsula and the cities and the rural farm communities of Belize, Guatemala, Honduras, and El Salvador.

The walls of Mayan tombs were painted with scenes of important events and daily life. This tomb painting shows warriors in battle.

Chapter Summary

In this chapter, you read about the Mayan civilization, which existed in what is now Mexico and Central America between about 2000 B.C.E and 1500 C.E.

The Development of Mayan Civilization The Mayas' greatest achievements came in the Classic period, between 300 and 900 C.E. With a writing system and building techniques adapted from the earlier Olmecs, the Mayas built complex, stone cities. At its height, their empire consisted of more than forty city-states and covered much of Central America.

Class Structure and Family Life Mayan society was a social pyramid, with the ruler at the top. Most Mayas were peasants. Women and girls cared for small children, kept house, and cooked the meals. Men and boys worked in the fields or hunted. Mayan girls celebrated reaching adulthood at 12; boys at age 14. Marriages were arranged by a matchmaker.

Religious Beliefs and Practices Mayan religion was polytheistic. The gods were forces of nature who could influence or destroy the world. Only priests could understand divine signs and read the sacred calendar, and no decisions were made without first consulting the gods.

Agricultural Techniques Farming techniques, such as terraces, slash-and-burn agriculture, and raised-earth platforms, allowed the Mayas to create a stable food supply.

Chapter 23

The Aztecs

How did the Aztecs rise to power?

23.1 Introduction

In this chapter, you will learn about the Aztecs, a Mesoamerican people who built a vast empire in what is today central Mexico. The Aztec Empire flourished from 1428 C.E. until 1519 C.E., when it was destroyed by invaders from Spain.

The Aztecs told a legend about the beginnings of their empire. Originally a wandering group of hunter-gatherers, the Aztecs believed that one day they would receive a sign from the gods. They would see an eagle perched on a great cactus with "his wings stretched out toward the rays of the sun." In its beak, the eagle would hold a long snake. When they saw this eagle, the Aztecs would know they had found the place where they would settle and build a great city.

In the mid-1200s C.E., the Aztecs entered the Valley of Mexico, a fertile basin in present-day central Mexico. Several times, other groups in the valley pushed the Aztecs away from their lands in the valley.

In 1325, the Aztecs took refuge on an island in Lake Texcoco. There, Aztec priests saw the eagle on the cactus, just as the gods had promised. The Aztecs set about building a city on the site, which they called Tenochtitlán (tay-nawh-tee-TLAHN). Its name means "the place of the fruit of the prickly pear cactus." In time, the island city became the center of the Aztec Empire.

In this chapter, you will learn where the Aztecs came from and how they built their magnificent capital city. You will also discover how the Aztecs rose to power.

The symbol on the Mexican flag—an eagle on a cactus grasping a snake—celebrates the the legendary founding of the Aztec empire.

◄ These drawings were created in Mexico around 1540, and show details of Aztec life.

Teotihuacán, the "City of the Gods," was a large city of plazas, pyramids, and avenues. The Pyramid of the Moon, shown above, was constructed of volcanic rock and limestone.

Aztecs a Mesoamerican people who built an empire in central Mexico that flourished from 1428 to 1519 C.E.

23.2 The Aztecs in the Valley of Mexico

The Aztec Empire arose in the Valley of Mexico, a fertile area nearly eight thousand feet above sea level. By the time the **Aztecs** arrived, in the mid-1200s C.E., the valley had been a center of civilization for more than a thousand years. Two earlier groups, in particular, had built civilizations there that strongly influenced the Aztecs.

Civilization in the Valley of Mexico From about 100 to 650 C.E., the Valley of Mexico was dominated by the Teotihuacáns (TEH-aw-tee-wah-KAHNZ). These people built an **enormous** capital city, Teotihuacán. One of the city's buildings, the Pyramid of the Sun, was more than two hundred feet high.

After Teotihuacán's collapse around the 700s, a group from the north, the Toltecs (TOHL-teks), migrated into the valley. Toltec civilization reached its height in the 10th and 11th centuries. The Toltecs built a number of cities. Their capital, Tollán (toh-LAHN), boasted large pyramids topped with temples.

During the 1100s, new groups invaded the valley. They took over Toltec cities and established new city-states. But the influence of the Teotihuacáns and the Toltecs continued to be felt in the new culture that was developing in the valley.

The Arrival of the Aztecs Sometime around 1250 C.E., a new group of people arrived in the Valley of Mexico. This nomadic band of hunter-gatherers called themselves the *Mexica* (meh-HEE-kah). We know them today as the Aztecs.

The name *Aztec* comes from Aztlán (az-TLAN), the Mexicans' legendary homeland. According to Aztec tradition, Aztlán was an island in a lake northwest of the Valley of Mexico. The Aztecs left the island around 1100 C.E. They wandered through the deserts of northern Mexico for many years before coming to the Valley of Mexico.

When the Aztecs came to the heart of the valley, they found lakes dotted with marshy islands. Thriving city-states controlled the land around the lakes.

The Aztecs had a difficult time establishing themselves in the valley. The people living in the city-states thought the Aztecs were crude barbarians. But the Aztecs were fierce warriors, and the city-states were willing to employ them as **mercenaries**.

After they settled in the valley, the legacy of the Teotihuacáns and the Toltecs began to influence the Aztecs. They made pilgrimages to the ancient ruins of Teotihuacán. They adopted Quetzalcoatl (ket-sahl-koh-AHT-l), the Teotihuacáns' feathered serpent god, as one of their own gods.

The Aztecs thought even more highly of the Toltecs, as rulers of a golden age. Aztec rulers married into the surviving Toltec royal line. The Aztecs even began to claim the Toltecs as their own ancestors.

In 1319, stronger groups forced the Aztecs to move away from Chapultepec (chuh-PUHL-teh-pek), a rocky hill where they had made their home. The Aztecs fled to the south, where they became mercenaries for the city-state of Culhuacán. But trouble came again when the Aztecs sacrificed the daughter of the Culhua chief. This led to a war with the Culhuas, who drove the Aztecs onto an island in the shallow waters of Lake Texcoco.

It was here, the Aztecs said, that they spotted an eagle perched atop a cactus with a long snake in its beak. The Aztecs took this as a sign that they should stay in this place, and set to work building the city they called **Tenochtitlán**.

The island turned out to be a good site for the Aztecs' city. The lake provided fish and water birds for food, and the island was easy to defend. Over time, the Aztecs' new home would grow into one of the great cities of the world.

From Mercenaries to Empire Builders The Aztecs started building Tenochtitlán in 1325 C.E. For the next 100 years, they again served as mercenaries for a powerful group called the Tepanecs. Through this **alliance** the Aztecs gained land, trading connections, and wealth.

Eventually, however, the Aztecs rebelled against the heavy-handed rule of the Tepanecs. Under the Aztec leader Itzcoatl (itz-koh-AHT-l), Tenochtitlán joined with two other city-states in what was called the Triple Alliance. In 1428, the alliance fought and defeated the Tepanecs. Together, the allies began a series of conquests that laid the foundation for the Aztec Empire.

As Tenochtitlán became a great power, Itzcoatl set out to reshape Aztec history. He burned records that referred to his people's humble origins. Instead, he connected the Aztecs to the distinguished Toltecs.

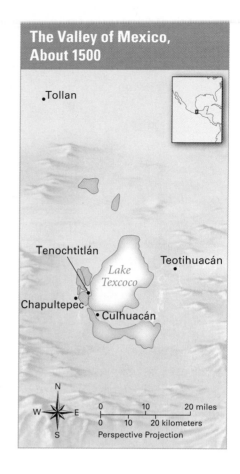

The Valley of Mexico, About 1500

The Aztecs settled in the Valley of Mexico around 1250. By 1500 they controlled most of the region.

mercenary a professional soldier who is paid to fight for another country or group

Tenochtitlán the capital city of the Aztec Empire

alliance a group of countries, city-states, or other entities who agree to work together, usually for common defense or trade

23.3 Tenochtitlán: A City of Wonders

As the Aztecs' power grew, their capital city of Tenochtitlán developed into one of the largest cities in the world. When Spanish explorers first arrived at Tenochtitlán in 1519, they were amazed to see a majestic city crisscrossed by canals and boasting **impressive** temples and palaces. With a huge population for the time, of between 200,000 and 300,000 people, Tenochtitlán was larger than London, Paris, or Venice.

How did the Aztecs turn an island into such a great city? First, they reclaimed land from the lake by sinking timbers into the water to serve as walls. Then, they filled in the area between the timbers with mud, boulders, and reeds. In this way, they created small islands called *chinampas,* or "floating gardens." Eventually, the Aztecs expanded the city's land surface until it covered over five square miles. They even merged Tlatelolco (tlah-TEH-lohl-koh), originally a separate island, with Tenochtitlán.

Gradually, Tenochtitlán grew into the magnificent city that later amazed the Spanish. At the center of the city lay a large ceremonial **plaza**. Here, the Aztecs gathered for religious rituals, feasts, and festivals. A wall about eight feet high enclosed this area. It was studded with sculptures of serpents. The palaces and homes of nobles lined the outside of the wall.

Inside the plaza, a stone pyramid called the Great Temple loomed 150 feet into the sky. People could see the pyramid, which was decorated with bright sculptures and murals, from several miles away.

plaza a public square or open area in a city where people gather

The Aztecs of Tenochtitlán built the city and farmed on chinampas, small artificial islands they constructed from timbers, mud, and plants.

It had two steep stairways leading to double shrines. One shrine was dedicated to the chief god, Huitzilopochtli (wee-tsee-loh-POHCH-tlee). The other was dedicated to Tlaloc (tlah-LOHK), the rain god. In front of the shrines stood the stone where priests performed human sacrifices. An altar, called the *tzompantli*, ("skull rack") displayed the skulls of thousands of sacrificial victims. Other structures in the plaza included more shrines and temples, the ritual ball court, military storehouses, and guest rooms for important visitors.

Just outside the plaza stood the royal palace. The two-story palace seemed like a small town. The palace was the home of the Aztec ruler, but it also had government offices, shrines, courts, storerooms, gardens, and courtyards. At the royal aviary, trained staff plucked the valuable feathers from parrots and quetzals. Wild animals captured throughout the empire, such as pumas and jaguars, prowled cages in the royal zoo.

The city's main marketplace was located in the northern section, in Tlatelolco. Each day, as many as sixty thousand people came from all corners of the Aztec Empire to sell their wares. Goods ranged from luxury items, such as jade and feathers, to necessities, such as food and rope sandals. Merchants also sold gold, silver, turquoise, animal skins, clothing, pottery, chocolate, vanilla, tools, and slaves.

Although Tenochtitlán spread over five square miles, people had an easy time getting around. Four wide avenues met at the foot of the Great Temple. A thousand workers swept and washed down the streets each day, keeping them cleaner than streets in European cities. At night, pine torches lit the way. People also traveled on foot on smaller walkways or by canoe on the canals that crossed the city. Many of the canals were lined with stone and had bridges.

Three **causeways** linked the island to the mainland. The longest of them stretched five miles. The causeways were 25 to 30 feet wide. They all had wooden bridges that could be raised to let boats through or to protect the city in an enemy attack.

The city boasted other technological marvels, like the aqueducts that carried fresh water for irrigation. Twin pipes ran from the Chapultepec springs, three miles away. While one pipe was being cleaned or repaired, the other could transport water. A dam ten miles long ran along the east side of the city to hold back floodwaters.

Temples dedicated to various gods rose along the streets and canals of the city of Tenochtitlán.

causeway a solid earthen roadway built across water or low ground

23.4 The Aztec Empire

Tenochtitlán began as simply the Aztecs' home city. After the Aztecs and their allies defeated the Tepanecs in 1428 C.E., the city became the capital of a growing empire. Under Moctezuma I in the mid 1400s, the Aztecs extended the area under their control.

By the early 1500s, the Aztec Empire stretched from the Gulf of Mexico to the Pacific Ocean, as you can see on the map on this page. It covered much of Central Mexico, and reached as far south as Mexico's current border with Guatemala. At its height, the empire ruled more than five million people.

conformity uniform behavior according to a set of social or cultural rules or beliefs

An Empire Based on Tribute Unlike other empire builders, the Aztecs did not start colonies. Nor did they force **conformity** on their subjects. Instead, the Aztec Empire was a loose union of hundreds of city-states that had to pay tribute to the Aztecs.

Collecting tribute was the empire's most **vital** business. The Aztecs relied on tribute to support Tenochtitlán's huge population. Tribute took the form of whatever valuable items a city could provide. Cities might pay in food, cacao, gems, cotton, cloth, animals, animal skins, shells, building materials, or even soldiers. Tax collectors stationed around the empire made sure that cities paid regularly.

Each year, huge amounts of goods flowed into Tenochtitlán. An average year brought 7,000 tons of maize; 4,000 tons each of beans, seed, and grain; and at least 2 million cotton cloaks. Warriors, priests, officials, servants, and other workers and craftspeople all received payment in tribute goods.

By the 1500s, the Aztecs had established a huge and powerful empire in the Valley of Mexico.

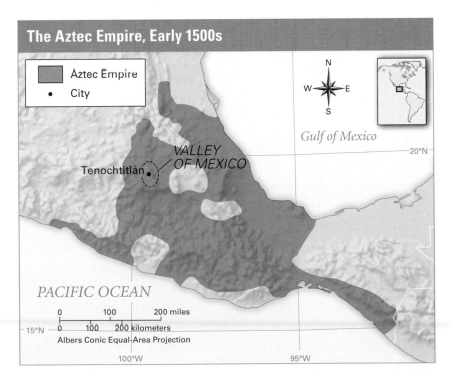

The Aztec Empire, Early 1500s

Aztec Empire
• City

Gulf of Mexico

VALLEY OF MEXICO

Tenochtitlán

20°N

PACIFIC OCEAN

0   100   200 miles
0   100   200 kilometers
Albers Conic Equal-Area Projection

15°N

100°W   95°W

Warfare Warfare was the center of Aztec life. Successful battles allowed the Aztecs to increase their sources of tribute. They also gained additional territory, laborers, and sacrificial victims.

Every male Aztec was trained to be a soldier. In battle, the Aztecs used bows and arrows, spears, clubs, and swords with sharp stone blades. Warrior knights carried shields decorated with figures of animals, such as the jaguar and eagle. The figures represented different strengths that the Aztecs believed they received from these animals.

An Aztec declaration of war followed a ritual pattern. First, the Aztecs asked a city to join the empire as an ally. The city had 60 days to agree. If the city's ruler refused, the Aztecs declared war.

Most wars ended after one battle, usually with an Aztec victory. Afterward, the Aztecs brought the soldiers they had **captured** to Tenochtitlán. Some became slaves, but most ended up as sacrifices.

The Aztecs made only a few demands on the defeated city. The people had to pay tribute, honor the god Huitzilopochtli, and promise obedience to the Aztec ruler. In most other ways, conquered cities remained independent. They kept their religion, customs, and language. They usually even kept their leaders.

These conditions made it easy for the Aztecs to rule. But most of the conquered people never thought of themselves as true Aztecs. They wanted their freedom and resented paying tribute. These feelings led to a lack of unity in the Aztec Empire. Eventually, the Spanish would take advantage of that weakness by making allies of the Aztecs' enemies when they invaded Mexico in 1519.

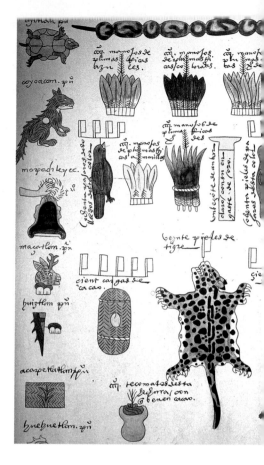

These drawings show some of the many forms of tribute paid to the Aztecs, such as feathers, jade, and jaguar skins.

Chapter Summary

In this chapter, you learned about the rise of the Aztecs from a band of nomads to the masters of a great empire.

The Aztecs in the Valley of Mexico The Aztecs arrived in the Valley of Mexico in the mid-1200s C.E. For a long time, they served as mercenaries for, and adapted the gods and culture of, more powerful groups, such as the Teotihuacáns, Toltecs, and Tepanecs.

Tenochtitlán In 1325, the Aztecs began building their great capital, Tenochtitlán, in Lake Texcoco. They chose the location based on a sign from the gods—an eagle perched on a cactus, with a snake in its beak. At its height, the impressive city boasted huge stone temples, canals, and a population greater than any European city of the time.

The Aztec Empire The Aztec Empire began in 1428, when the Aztecs and their allies won a victory against the Tepanecs. The Aztecs went on to conquer most of the Valley of Mexico. Over the next nearly 100 years, the Aztecs expanded their empire through warfare and alliances. Eventually the empire included hundreds of cities and millions of people, who supported the Aztecs through vast amounts of tribute goods.

Chapter 24

Daily Life in Tenochtitlán

What was daily life like for Aztecs in Tenochtitlán?

24.1 Introduction

The Aztecs built their large empire in central Mexico. In this chapter, you will explore what life was like in the Aztecs' capital city of Tenochtitlán.

Suppose you are an Aztec child living outside Tenochtitlán in the 1400s C.E. One morning your father, a chili pepper farmer, takes you to the Great Market at Tenochtitlán. Your father finds the vegetable section, where he spreads out a mat and displays the peppers on it. Then he begins to shout out prices. He gladly trades with a noblewoman, exchanging peppers for precious cacao beans. Later he trades his remaining peppers for a hand-made clay cooking pot for your mother.

After all the peppers are gone, your father takes you on a walk around the city. You see the Great Temple, where priests perform sacrifices, and the ball court where nobles play a game called *tlachtli*. You gaze in wonder at the beautiful houses of the noble families and the splendid palace of the Aztec ruler. When you return home, you eat a simple mush made of maize before going to sleep.

This imaginary trip to Tenochtitlán shows aspects of daily life experienced by many Aztecs in the 1400s. In this chapter, you will learn more about how the people of Tenochtitlán lived. You will explore Aztec class structure, marriage, family life, food, markets, religious practices, and recreation.

The Aztec capital of Tenochtitlán was a huge community of several hundred thousand people, featuring massive public spaces and temples.

◀ The Great Market in the city of Tenochtitlán was a center of daily life for the Aztecs.

Daily Life in Tenochtitlán **293**

24.2 Class Structure

Aztec society was divided into five main social classes. At the top of the class structure were the ruler and his family. Next, came a noble class of government officials, priests, and high-ranking warriors. The third and largest class was made up of commoners, citizens who were not of noble rank. Below the commoners were the peasants, who were neither slaves nor citizens. At the bottom of the class structure were the slaves.

Each class had its own privileges and responsibilities. However, an Aztec's status was not fixed. Commoners could move up in social class by performing brave deeds in war or by studying to be priests. A noble could fall in rank if he failed to live up to his responsibilities.

semidivine half-human and half-god

hereditary passed on from parent to child; inherited

This artwork shows people from various classes of Aztec society. Use the information from the text and visual clues in the image to identify which group in the Aztec class structure each figure represents.

The Ruler The Aztec ruler, or emperor, was considered **semidivine**. Called *tlatoani,* or "he who speaks," the emperor maintained the empire and decided when to wage war.

The position of ruler was not **hereditary,** as it was in many other societies. When an emperor died, his son did not automatically become ruler. Instead, a group of advisers chose the new ruler from the emperor's family. Each new ruler was expected to acquire new wealth of his own. This was an important motive for constant warfare.

Government Officials, Priests, and Military Leaders The emperor was supported by a noble class of government officials, priests, and military leaders. Officials in Tenochtitlán counseled the emperor, worked as judges, and governed the city's four districts. Other nobles throughout the large empire ruled cities, collected tribute, or managed the construction of public buildings and roads.

The emperor appointed government officials for life. Although noble status was not hereditary, most sons of nobles earned high offices themselves.

Priests conducted all religious rites and served individual gods. Some priests ran the schools that trained boys for government jobs and the priesthood. Other priests studied the skies and made predictions about the future. Generally, only nobles became priests, but sometimes an Aztec from lower classes was **elevated** to this position. Girls could become priestesses.

Commoners could also rise to become military leaders. All Aztec men were trained to be soldiers. A common soldier could become a leader by capturing enemies in battle. Military leaders commanded groups of soldiers and took part in war councils.

Commoners The broad class of commoners included several smaller classes. The highest-ranking commoners were professional traders called *pochteca*. The pochteca led caravans to distant lands to acquire exotic goods. Some also served as spies for the emperor, reporting what type of tribute a city could provide.

The pochteca worshipped their own god and lived in a separate section of Tenochtitlán. They paid taxes with rare goods. They enjoyed many privileges. For example, they could own land and send their children to the nobles' schools. Unlike the nobles, membership in this class was hereditary.

Aztec painters created beautiful murals for emperors and other high-ranking Aztec officials.

Below the pochteca came craftspeople and artisans, such as potters, jewelers, and painters. Some worked in their homes and traded their goods at the market. Others worked in the royal palace and made items especially for the emperor.

Most commoners worked as farmers, fishers, laborers, and servants. Instead of owning land, they were loaned plots of land for homes and farms by their *calpulli,* or **ward**. All commoners paid tribute to the nobility in the form of crops, labor, or manufactured goods.

> **ward** a political unit within a city, often a neighborhood

Peasants About thirty percent of the Aztec people were peasants. Unlike slaves, people in this class were free, but were considered inferior to commoners. Peasants did not belong to a calpulli and were not loaned land to farm. Instead, they hired out their services to nobles.

Slaves At the bottom of Aztec society were the slaves. Prisoners of war, lawbreakers, or debtors might be forced into slavery. Unlike slaves in many societies, Aztec slaves had a number of rights. They could own property, goods, and even other slaves. In addition, slaves did not pass their status on to their children, who were born free. In fact, the mother of the emperor Itzcoatl was a slave. Many slaves could be **emancipated** after working off a debt, upon completing their term of punishment for a crime, or when their masters died.

24.3 Marriage

Marriage and family life were important to Aztecs of all social classes. Marriage marked an Aztec child's entry into adulthood. Most men married around age twenty, while young women tended to marry around sixteen.

Marriages were arranged by the families of the bride and groom. The young man's family chose the bride. They then engaged the services of a matchmaker, an older woman who approached the bride's family. It was customary for the bride's family to refuse at first. The matchmaker then returned a few days later. This time the bride's family usually accepted the union and set the dowry, or the money or goods a woman brought to her husband upon marriage.

Even among commoners, an Aztec wedding was as elaborate as the families could afford. The festivities began at the bride's house. Relatives, friends, the groom's teachers, and the important people of the calpulli enjoyed a banquet with the bride and gave her presents.

That evening, the guests marched to the groom's home for the wedding ceremony. An old woman, usually the matchmaker, carried the bride on her back. To symbolize the bond of marriage, during the ceremony the matchmaker tied the groom's cloak to the bride's blouse.

After the ceremony, the young couple went to the bridal chamber to pray for four days, while their guests celebrated. On the fifth day, the couple emerged and attended another grand banquet. Then they settled down on a piece of land in the groom's calpulli.

This page from the *Codex Mendoza* shows a young couple's marriage festivities. (A *codex* is a kind of early book.) Can you identify the bride, the groom, and the matchmaker?

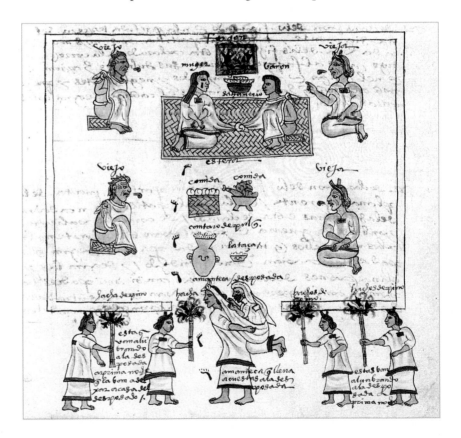

The Aztecs permitted men to practice **polygamy**, or to have multiple wives. An Aztec man could take as many wives as he could afford. However, only one of the wives was considered the primary wife, and only marriage to the primary wife was celebrated with special rites and ceremonies.

When a marriage was unhappy, either spouse could ask for a divorce. A man could divorce his wife if she neglected her duties at home, had a bad temper, or did not bear any children. A woman could divorce her husband if he beat her, deserted her, or failed to support her and her children. However, Aztec society encouraged divorced women to remarry.

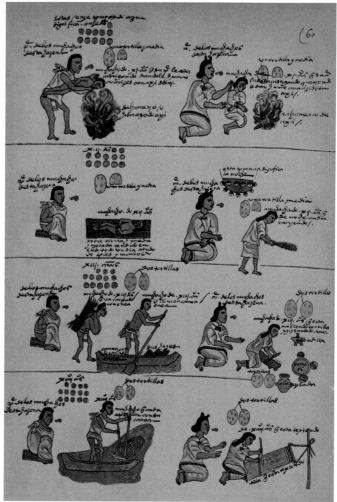

polygamy having more than one spouse at one time

24.4 Family Life

Men had higher status than women in Aztec society, and, within the family, the father was the master of the house. Aztec women, however, had their own rights and responsibilities. Married women could own property and sell goods. Some older women also practiced a profession, such as matchmaking or midwifery.

Among commoners, the skills of both men and women were necessary to care for the household and the family. Men built the house and worked as farmers or at a craft. Women fixed meals, tended the garden, and looked after livestock. Many Aztec women wove beautiful cloth of many colors. Some made cloaks in patterns of sun designs or with images of shells, fish, cacti, snakes, or butterflies. Women traded these cloaks for other goods at the market.

One of a woman's most important jobs was to have and care for children. The Aztecs believed that the purpose of marriage was to bring children into the world, so they honored a woman's role in giving birth as much as they did a man's role in fighting wars.

Aztec parents began training their children at a young age. All children of commoners helped out around the house. Young boys fetched water and wood, while older boys learned how to fish and handle a canoe. Eventually, boys accompanied their fathers to work or to the market. Girls' tasks centered on running a home, and included cleaning house and grinding maize. When they were about seven years old, girls began learning to weave from their mothers.

Aztec family members performed daily tasks such as farming, collecting firewood, cooking, childcare, and weaving.

In addition to working, all boys attended school. Commoners probably started school around the age of six, but they only attended part-time. At the *telpochcalli,* or "house of youth," boys mostly trained to be soldiers. The sons of nobles went to the *calmecac,* instead. There, they learned the skills to become priests, government officials, or military commanders.

24.5 Food

The Aztecs of Tenochtitlán ate both homegrown foods and foods imported from distant places. The mainstay of the Aztec diet, however, was maize. The Aztecs found maize so useful because it could be dried and then stored for a long time. Women boiled and skinned maize kernels and ground them into flour. Then they baked fresh tortillas for each meal on clay griddles. They also made tamales by wrapping maize in its husks and steaming it.

The daily routine of Aztec commoners shows the importance of maize. After working for several hours, commoners ate a simple meal in the late morning. The meal usually consisted of a maize porridge called *atole.* The porridge was often seasoned with peppers or sweetened with honey. At midday, commoners ate their main meal of tortillas, maize cakes, boiled beans, or tamales. Pepper or tomato sauce sometimes spiced up these dishes. Most families had only two meals. But some people ate a thin porridge, usually made of maize, just before going to bed.

Aztec commoners had occasional variety in their meals. To provide meat for special occasions, families might raise a few turkeys. They might also hunt wild game, such as rabbits and pigeons.

Aztec farmers also grew such crops as red peppers, tomatoes, sage, squash, green beans, sweet potatoes, and avocados. In periods when crops were bad, the Aztecs turned to other sources of food. They caught frogs and shrimp and collected insect eggs. They even skimmed algae, a type of plant, off the surface of the lake and formed it into small cakes.

The wealthy ate quite a different diet, both on a daily basis and at the feasts they attended. They prized delicacies, such as winged ants and a lizardlike creature called an *axolotl.* They enjoyed cocoa with their morning meals and pineapples, oysters, and crabs at their banquets.

The preparation of tortillas and other foods was a daily task for Aztec women.

24.6 Markets

Markets were an important part of the Aztec economy. Each city in the empire had its own market, usually located in the plaza in front of the town's temple. Large towns held markets every day, while small villages held them about every five days. Some towns had their own specialties. The people of Tenochtitlán might travel to nearby Texcoco for fine cloth and to faraway Acolman to buy meat.

At Tlatelolco, the bustling market in Tenochtitlán, people bought and sold everything from food and utensils to warrior costumes, quetzal feathers, and slaves. Instead of using money, Aztecs used a barter system, trading one kind of good for another. Some expensive goods had an agreed-upon value. For instance, a warrior's costume and shield were worth about 60 cotton cloaks.

Many individuals brought their wares to market. Farmers brought their surplus crops, while craftspeople brought goods they had made. The pochteca had a special place in the markets, since they imported goods from faraway places. They provided raw materials that were unavailable around Tenochtitlán. For example, they sold metals, such as gold and silver, as well as tortoiseshells for making spoons.

Guards watched over the market to make sure sellers acted honestly. When a **dispute** arose—for example, if a buyer accused a seller of cheating—the guards took the parties to a court located at one end of the market. Three judges sat there, waiting to hear each case and to give their verdict.

The market also had a social purpose. People went there to meet friends, gossip, and hear the news of the day. Some people simply enjoyed strolling up and down the aisles, buying snacks and browsing among all the items the sellers had to offer.

People bartered, or traded, in the marketplace for the things they needed.

This illustration from the 1500s shows Aztecs making a human sacrifice to the sun god.

24.7 Religious Practices

Religion was central to Aztec life and society. The Aztecs believed that humans needed the gods for survival. It was the gods who granted a good harvest or, if they were displeased, sent earthquakes and floods. So it was important to please the gods through elaborate rituals and ceremonies. Priests presented the gods with flowers, ears of maize, clothing, or images made of wood.

The Aztecs adopted some of their gods from other Mesoamerican groups. For example, Tlaloc, the rain god, was an ancient Mesoamerican god. Quetzalcoatl ("feathered serpent") had been worshipped by the Teotihuacans. But the Aztecs' own chief god was Huitzilopochtli, the god of the sun and of war. In fact, the Aztecs called themselves the "people of the sun."

The Aztecs saw the sun as a warrior who fought each night against the forces of darkness. In Aztec belief, the survival of the universe depended upon the sun winning these battles. The way to keep the sun strong was to offer him nourishment in the form of blood.

For this reason, most Aztec rituals included some form of blood sacrifice. Every morning, Aztec priests sacrificed hundreds of birds to Huitzilopochtli. Priests also pierced their skin with cactus spikes to offer their own blood.

The highest form of sacrifice, however, was that of humans. The Aztecs particularly valued the sacrifice of warriors captured in battle, because they believed that the blood of strong warriors was especially nourishing to Huitzilopochtli. Scholars think the Aztecs also used human sacrifice to frighten other groups into accepting their rule.

In Tenochtitlán, up to several thousand people may have gone to sacrificial deaths each year. Four priests pinned the victim to the stone in front of Huitzilopochtli's temple, while another cut out his heart. Some victims may have died willingly in the belief that they would accompany the sun god in his daily battle across the sky.

The Aztecs also made sacrifices to other gods. They threw the sacrificial victims of the fire god into a great blaze. To honor the corn goddess, they cut off women's heads. Overall, the Aztecs practiced human sacrifice on a much larger scale than other Mesoamerican groups.

24.8 Recreation

While work, warfare, and ritual were all important to the Aztecs, they also had some time for recreation. They enjoyed music and dancing, and nobles liked to go on hunts.

One entertainment was *patolli*, a game played on a cross-shaped board divided into 52 squares. The board symbolized the 260-day calendar, which the Aztecs shared with the Mayas and other Mesoamerican peoples. Five times around the board equaled 260 days.

To move around the board, players threw beans marked with holes, similar to dice. The holes told them how many spaces to move the colored stone game pieces. The first person around the board five times won.

All social classes played patolli, but it's likely that only members of the nobility played the ball game tlachtli. Tlachtli was played on a long, narrow court shaped like the letter *I* and with high walls. A small ring projected over the court from each side wall. Two teams faced each other across a line that ran between the rings. The object was to get a rubber ball through the ring on the other team's side. Players could not touch the ball, so they threw themselves on the ground to hit the ball with their elbows, knees, and hips.

Along with its entertainment value, tlachtli had a religious meaning. The Aztecs believed that the tlachtli court represented the world and that the ball represented a heavenly body. Because of this, the Aztecs built the tlachtli courts near the most important temples, like the Great Temple in Tenochtitlán.

Patolli was a popular game among Aztecs and other Mesoamerican peoples. Beans marked with holes were thrown like dice to tell players how many spaces they could move on the cross-shaped board.

Chapter Summary

In this chapter, you learned about daily life in the Aztecs' capital city of Tenochtitlán.

Class Structure Aztec society had five classes. At the top was the ruler and his family, followed by the nobles, priests, and high-ranking warriors. Next came the commoners. Below them were the peasants. Slaves were the lowest class, but their children were born free.

Marriage and Family Life Aztec marriages were arranged; men married at about 20 and women at about 16. Men had higher status, but both spouses worked to run the home, and women were honored for their ability to give birth. Men farmed and hunted. Women raised the children and wove cloth. Children did chores around the house.

Food and Markets Maize was the main food, but the Aztecs enjoyed other local and imported foods, as well as fish and game. Markets were an important part of the Aztec economy. In daily or weekly markets, using a barter system, the Aztecs bought and sold everything from food and armor to clothing and slaves.

Religious Practices Religion was central to the Aztecs. They believed that their chief god, Huitzilopochtli, god of the sun and of war, needed blood for nourishment. Because of this, the Aztecs practiced human sacrifice more than other Mesoamerican groups.

Recreation The Aztecs enjoyed games, including a board game called patolli and a ball game called tlachtli.

Chapter 25

The Incas

How did the Incas manage their large and remote empire?

25.1 Introduction

In this chapter, you will learn about the Inca Empire, a complex society that developed in the Andes Mountains of South America. The Inca Empire arose in present-day Peru in the 1400s C.E. It lasted until 1532, when the Incas were conquered by Spanish explorers.

From north to south along the the South American continent, the Inca Empire stretched for over 2,500 miles. To communicate across this vast distance, the Incas used runners called *chasquis* (CHAHS-kees) to relay messages from one part of their territory to another.

Picture yourself as a young chasqui. From your messenger station along the Royal Road, you see another chasqui racing toward you. You know he carries an important message from the emperor.

You dart out of the messenger station and run alongside the other runner while he hands you a set of strings called a *quipu* (KEE-pooh). Knots tied at different places in the strings stand for numbers. They will help you remember the message. The other chasqui also gives you a verbal message. Once he is certain that you have both parts of the message, he stops running. His work is over. Now it is up to you to get the message to the next station as quickly as possible.

This remarkable relay system helped the Incas manage their far-flung empire. In this chapter, you will explore how the Incas built and maintained their empire. You will also learn about the Incas' class structure, family life, religion, and relations with other peoples.

To maintain their large empire, the Incas developed an extensive network of roads, like this one leading to the Incan city of Machu Picchu.

◀ The city of Machu Picchu may have been a religious center during the Inca Empire.

Incas people of a culture in the Andes Mountains of South America that arose in the 1400s C.E. and lasted until 1532

25.2 The Rise of the Inca Empire

At the height of their power in the early 1500s C.E., the **Incas** ruled over a vast, well-organized empire. From north to south, the Inca Empire stretched almost the length of the Andes mountain range, a distance of about 2,500 miles. It reached from the Pacific Coast in the west to the Amazon River Basin in the east. Today, this territory includes most of Peru and Ecuador, as well as parts of Bolivia, Chile, and Argentina. Perhaps ten million people lived under Incan rule.

How did the Incas build and manage such a huge empire? In part, they adopted ideas and institutions that had been pioneered by earlier cultures. Two peoples who had an especially strong influence on the Incas were the Moches (MOH-chayz) and the Chimus (chee-MOOZ).

The Moches lived along the northern coast of Peru from about 100 B.C.E. to 700 C.E. They built cities, dug irrigation canals, and developed special classes of workers.

The Chimu kingdom in northern Peru flourished during the 1300s and 1400s. Like the Moches, the Chimus built well-planned cities and used elaborate irrigation methods. They preserved the artistic traditions of the Moches and passed them on to the Incas. They also built good roads and created a message system using runners. The Incas **adapted** and improved upon all these advances.

Beginnings of the Empire The center of the Inca Empire was the capital of Cuzco (KOOZ-koh), which was located high in the mountains of southern Peru. The Incas first settled in this area around 1200 C.E. Apart from this fact, their early history is cloaked in legend.

According to one Incan legend, the people were descended from Inti, the sun god. Inti commanded his son, Manco Capac, to rise from the waters of Lake Titicaca. Manco Capac then founded the Inca tribe.

In another legend, Inti appeared before a later Incan ruler. He said the Incas must become a great power and educate the people they met. But for more than two hundred years, the Incas increased their territory by only about a dozen miles around Cuzco.

The Incas began expanding their empire in 1438, when they were attacked by the neighboring Chancas. The Incan emperor and many citizens fled Cuzco. But one of his sons, Yupanqui, stayed behind and led his army against the Chancas. Incan legend says that the stones on the battlefield turned into powerful warriors. Yupanqui's victory made his people the strongest group in the area.

After driving off the Chancas, Yupanqui took the name Pachacuti, which means "earthshaker." He also seized the throne. Pachacuti and his son, Topa Inca, then launched a series of conquests against other nearby tribes. With each victory, the Incan army became larger and more skilled.

The Inca Empire, About 1500

COLOMBIA
ECUADOR
PERU
ANDES
Cuzco
Lake Titicaca
BOLIVIA
ATACAMA DESERT
PACIFIC OCEAN CHILE
MOUNTAINS
ARGENTINA

0   500   1,000 miles
0   500   1,000 kilometers
Sinusoidal Projection

Inca Empire, about 1500 C.E.

Modern political boundaries

• City

The Inca Empire consisted of a huge territory that stretched along most of the west coast of South America.

Soon the Incas controlled almost every major group in the central Andes region. In 1470, they conquered the Chimus. By the 1500s, their empire covered about three hundred and fifty thousand square miles.

Roads and Messengers

To manage the empire, Incan leaders came to rely on a system of roads. The two main routes were the coastal road and the inland road, which was called the Royal Road. Smaller roads connected them.

Some historians have said that the Incas' system of roads was as impressive as that of ancient Rome. About 15,000 miles of road linked all corners of the empire. The roads crossed tropical jungles, high mountains, and raging rivers. Incan officials used the roads to travel throughout the empire. There was a shelter along the roads every 15 to 30 miles to give travelers a place to rest.

The roads allowed the emperor at Cuzco to communicate with officials in distant places. The Incas sent messages by an elaborate relay system. They built messenger stations every couple of miles along the main roads. Chasquis, or messengers, carried the messages from one station to the next. Using this system, messages could travel more than 250 miles a day.

A message consisted of memorized words and sets of strings called quipus. The quipus served as memory aids. Knots tied at various places and on strings of different colors represented numbers.

The Incas had no system of writing, but the quipus proved to be an effective substitute for written language. The Incas used them to keep track of civil and military populations, as well as to record their legends and achievements.

Chasquis counted the knots and strings on quipus to relay messages about various matters, such as the number of people in a military troop or the amount of goods given in tribute to an Incan leader.

Incan legend says that the emperor was descended from Inti, the sun god. He was thus the "son of the sun." Shown here is the last emperor to rule before the Spanish conquered the Inca Empire.

25.3 Class Structure

Incan society was based on a strictly organized class structure. There were three broad classes: the emperor and his immediate family, nobles, and commoners. Throughout Incan society, people who were "Incan by blood"—those whose families were originally from the capital city of Cuzco—had higher status than non-Incas. As the empire grew, its class structure became more complex.

The Emperor At the top of Incan society was the emperor, called the Sapa Inca. The Incas believed that the Sapa Inca was descended from Inti, the sun god. For this reason, the Sapa Inca ruled with complete authority.

Everything in the empire belonged to the Sapa Inca. He lived in great splendor. When the Spanish came to Cuzco in the 1500s, they were dazzled to see fine gardens, golden statues, and jars made of gold and silver studded with emeralds. Servants carried the Sapa Inca everywhere on a golden litter, an elaborate covered chair. His subjects dared not look him directly in the eye.

The Sapa Inca could have many wives and hundreds of children. But he had one primary wife, who was called the Coya.

Nobles Below the Sapa Inca were the nobles. The Incan nobility was made up of leaders who helped to rule and administer the vast empire.

All nobles enjoyed certain privileges. They received gifts of land, servants, llamas, and fine clothing. They did not pay taxes, and the men had the right to marry more than one wife. However, nobles were not all of equal rank. There were three main classes of nobles: Capac Incas, who were considered relatives of the emperor; Hahua Incas, who did not share the royal blood; and *curacas,* who were leaders of people conquered by the Incas.

The highest-ranking nobles were the Capac Incas. Like the emperor himself, they were believed to be descended from Manco Capac, the legendary founder of the Incan dynasty.

Capac Incas controlled the empire's land as well as its valuable resources, such as llamas, coca leaves, and gold. They held the most important posts in the government, the army, and the priesthood. The *apus,* or governors, of the four quarters of the empire belonged to the group of Capac Incas.

As the empire grew, the Incas needed more nobles to staff the government's complex bureaucracy. As a result, some people who were not true Incas also gained entry into the noble class. Called Hahua Incas, they were considered "Incas by privilege." Often non-royal leaders from around Cuzco became Hahua Incas. Sometimes people of common birth gained this status as well.

Additional conquests created a need for the third class of nobles, the curacas. The curacas were local leaders of conquered peoples. Curacas carried out various jobs. Many collected taxes. Others worked as inspectors, making sure everyone followed Incan laws and customs, such as wearing proper clothing and keeping clean homes. Curacas were required to spend time in Cuzco learning these laws and customs. They were allowed to rule their people only if they followed Incan ways.

Commoners Most people in the Inca Empire were commoners who worked as farmers and herders. The Incas did not practice slavery in the usual sense of the word. However, they did require commoners to support the government, both through the products of their labor and by working on government-sponsored projects. Men did jobs like building roads, while women might weave cloth.

Incan farmers grew a variety of crops, including squash, peppers, beans, peanuts, more than 20 types of corn, and more than 200 types of potato. The most important crop was the potato, which could survive heavy frosts at altitudes as high as 15,000 feet above sea level. Corn could be grown nearly as high up. The Incas enjoyed corn fresh, fried, and popped.

Incan farmers were required to give most of their crops to the government. The government placed the crops it collected in storehouses throughout the empire. The food was then distributed to warriors, temple priests, and people in need. For example, the government gave food to people who could no longer work, particularly the aged, the sick, and the disabled.

In this illustration, dating from about 1565, Incan farmers harvest potatoes.

ayllu an Incan clan (group of related families), the basic unit of Incan society

communal shared by a community or group

In this Incan coming-of-age ceremony, a boy receives the weapons of an Incan warrior.

25.4 Family Life

Families in the Inca Empire belonged to larger groups, or clans, called **ayllus**. The ayllu (EYE-yoo) was the foundation of Incan society. Everyone was born into an ayllu, and most people lived their entire lives within the borders of its land. So to understand family life in the Inca Empire, we need to begin with the ayllu.

Life in the Ayllu Groups of families made up the ayllus, which ranged in size from small villages to large towns. Each ayllu had its own farmland and homes, but the ayllu did not own the land. As you have read, everything in the empire belonged to the emperor. The government loaned land to the ayllus for living and for farming. The people of an ayllu then worked this **communal** land cooperatively to grow crops and produce goods.

Everyone had responsibilities to the ayllu and to the government. All members of the ayllu had to work, except for the very young and the very old. The leaders of the ayllu made sure all the work got done. For instance, a leader might assign some men to clear the fields and others to dig irrigation ditches.

The households of the ayllu came under the authority of a series of curacas. One head of household ruled every ten households. Fifty of these heads of household came under the supervision of a higher-level curaca. At still higher levels, curacas managed groupings of 100, 500, 1,000, 5,000, and 10,000 households.

One of the functions of the curacas was to make sure ayllus paid their taxes. The Incas had no currency, so taxes were paid in the forms of goods and labor. The Sapa Inca claimed one-third of everything an ayllu produced. Another third supported the Incan temples. Commoners kept the remaining third for themselves.

In addition, men had to pay the *mit'a*, or public duty tax. Men paid the mit'a by contributing labor to government projects each year. In response to the government's needs, the leaders of an ayllu assigned work to members. For example, men might repair roads, build storehouses, or work in the mines.

Childhood Most Incas were born into ayllus of hardworking commoners. The children of commoners learned about their responsibilities early in life. Young children performed simple tasks around the home. As they grew older, girls took care of the babies, fetched water, cooked, made clothing, and learned to weave. Boys looked after the animals and helped in the fields.

The children of most commoners did not receive any formal education. Instead, they learned the skills they needed, as well as Incan customs, from their elders. Some especially talented boys were trained in crafts or record keeping so they could serve the emperor.

Unlike boys from commoner families, the sons of nobles had special *amautas,* or tutors. Amautas taught religion, geometry, history, military strategy, public speaking, and physical training.

At about age fifteen, all boys received a loincloth, a strip of cloth worn around the waist. The sons of nobles underwent a much more elaborate ritual. These boys had to pass month-long tests of courage, strength, and discipline. After passing these tests, the boys swore loyalty to the Sapa Inca and received the weapons of an Incan warrior.

Marriage Young men and women remained at home until they married. Unlike the emperor and the nobility, male commoners married only one wife. Young men married in their early 20s, while girls could marry at 16.

People usually married within their ayllu. Some marriages were arranged by families or by the young people themselves. In some cases, the local curaca chose a wife for a young man who was not yet married. When a couple agreed they would marry, they held hands and exchanged sandals.

Once married, a couple established their own home. Commoners typically lived in one-room houses made of adobe bricks or stone. Noble families had fancier houses with several rooms. While nobles enjoyed the help of servants, commoners worked hard to produce their own food and clothing and to fulfill their responsibilities to the ayllu.

Incan couples agreed to marry by holding hands and exchanging sandals.

In this Incan festival held in honor of the sun god, Inti, men in traditional dress carry skeletons on platforms.

25.5 Religion

Religion was an important part of Incan life. Like other early groups in the Americas, the Incas believed that the gods influenced their daily lives. As a result, they showed their devotion to the gods through a number of practices.

Religious Beliefs The Incas believed in many gods who controlled various aspects of nature. For example, Illapu was the weather god and rain giver. Paca Mama was the Earth Mother and Mama Cocha was the goddess of the sea. The Incas believed that all these gods had received their power from a supreme god called Viracocha, the creator of the world.

But to the Incas, the most important god was Inti, the sun god. Inti was important for two reasons. First, Incas believed that the emperor's family was descended from Inti. Second, Inti was also the god of agriculture, which was the basis of Incan life.

The Incas also believed that spirits dwelled in certain sacred objects and places, called *huacas.* Huacas (WHAH-kuz) included temples, charms, and places in nature such as springs and rocks. Because the Incas believed in an afterlife, the tombs and bodies of the dead were also considered huacas. People often prayed and made offerings to all these huacas.

Religious Practices The Incan religion was highly formal and required a large number of priests to conduct rituals and ceremonies. Priests worked at temples and shrines devoted to the gods.

The most important temples were those **dedicated** to Inti. The high priest, a close relative of the Sapa Inca, presided over the Sun Temple in Cuzco. Priests who worked in the sun temples in the countryside came from the families of curacas.

Like the Mayas and the Aztecs, the Incas offered sacrifices to the gods. Some sacrifices took place regularly. For example, each day priests threw corn on a fire to encourage the sun to appear. "Eat this, Lord Sun," the priests said, "so that you will know we are your children." In many rituals, the Incas sacrificed live animals, usually llamas or guinea pigs. The Incas also practiced human sacrifice, but only on the most sacred occasions or in times of a natural disaster.

In addition to performing rituals and sacrifices, priests practiced divination, or the art of predicting the future. Divination helped the Incas decide upon a course of action, For example, a priest might ask an **oracle** when the army should attack another tribe.

oracle a person through whom a god or spirit is believed to speak about the future

Chosen Women A unique aspect of Incan religion was the role played by women. Each year, government officials visited all the towns in the empire to search for the most beautiful, graceful, and talented girls between the ages of eight and ten. Selected girls were honored as Chosen Women and taken to live in convents. There they studied Incan religion, learned how to prepare special food and drink for religious ceremonies, and wove garments for the Sapa Inca and the Coya.

Around age fifteen, many Chosen Women left their convents. Some went to work in temples or shrines. Others became convent teachers, called *mamaconas*. Still others went to Cuzco and became wives of nobles or secondary wives of the Sapa Inca himself.

A few Chosen Women were sacrificed at important religious ceremonies. The rest spent almost their entire lives either serving Inti or fulfilling their roles as wives of nobles or the emperor. Only in old age were they sometimes allowed to return to the homes and families they had left so many years earlier.

The Chosen Women in Incan society were honored as servants of Inti.

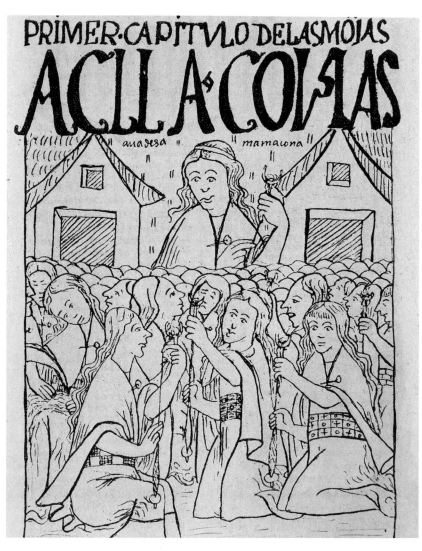

25.6 Relations with Other Peoples

The Incas had several methods of bringing other groups of people into the empire. They did not immediately declare war. Instead, the Sapa Inca generally sent a delegate to meet with a tribe. The delegate explained that the tribe could join the Inca Empire and enjoy peace and prosperity. Everyone understood that the **alternative** was war with the strong Incan army.

As the Incas expanded their empire, foreign tribes could choose to join the empire or face Incan warriors in battle.

When faced with these options, many tribes chose to join the empire. Their leaders were then allowed to retain some local power. In this way, the Incas expanded their empire without always having to fight.

If a tribe resisted, however, the two sides met in battle. The Incas used a variety of weapons, including spears, axes, and clubs. They were especially skilled at hurling stones with a sling. The fighting often cost the enemy tribe many of its men. Usually, the Incas won. Sometimes, the Incas moved a defeated tribe to other parts of the empire, so that its people lost their native lands as well.

Becoming part of the empire meant adopting Incan ways. The leaders of a conquered tribe had to build a sun temple. While the tribe could go on worshipping its own gods, it had to accept the Incan gods as the most powerful. Local leaders and their sons were brought to Cuzco to study Incan laws, as well as Quechua, the official language. Then they returned to their people as curacas.

As the new territory accepted Incan ways, teachers arrived to create Incan-style villages. When necessary, they organized ayllus and taught the people how to build storehouses, irrigation systems, and terraced fields for farming.

Meanwhile, the Incas took an important religious object belonging to the tribe and kept it in Cuzco. The Incas claimed they acted out of respect for the local religion. In reality, the object was held "hostage." If the tribe rebelled, the government could destroy the sacred object.

Despite these efforts, sometimes the Incas failed to bring a tribe fully into their empire. In such cases they might remove—and usually kill—the local leader. Some **rebellious** tribes were forced to move far away. The government then settled loyal members of the empire in their place. In this way, the Incas reduced the chance of resistance to their rule.

Incan soldiers often led captive people away from their homelands to be resettled elsewhere in the empire.

Many historians have wondered what drove the Incas to conquer such a huge empire. Part of the answer may lie in a unique Incan belief. The Incas thought that even after death the Sapa Inca continued to rule the lands he had conquered. In order for the new emperor to establish his own source of power and wealth, he had to take new lands. Only then would he have land that belonged to him alone.

Chapter Summary

In this chapter, you learned about life in the Inca Empire, which arose in the west of South America in the 1400s C.E.

The Rise of the Inca Empire In the 1400s, the Incas began rapidly expanding their power from their capital city, Cuzco. Eventually, they created a huge empire that extended almost the length of the Andes. An impressive system of roads and messengers helped the emperor manage his vast territory.

Class Structure, Family Life, and Religion Incan class structure had three main levels: the emperor and his family, the nobility, and the commoners. All Incas belonged to ayllus, which provided the empire with crops, goods, and labor. Like other early peoples in the Americas, the Incas engaged in many religious practices to maintain proper relationships with their gods, especially their chief god, Inti, god of the sun.

Relations with Other Peoples The Incas used a variety of means to bring others under their control. Conquered peoples had to build a sun temple, study Incan laws, and learn Quechua. The Incas also took a sacred object as a hostage. Rebellious tribes were forced to relocate.

Chapter 26

Achievements of the Mayas, Aztecs, and Incas

What were the significant achievements of the Mayas, Aztecs, and Incas?

26.1 Introduction

There were three great peoples of the early Americas: the Mayas, the Aztecs, and the Incas. In this chapter, you will study the cultures of these peoples and explore their unique achievements.

The history of these civilizations stretches from very ancient times to just a few centuries ago. Mayan civilization dates back to 2000 B.C.E. It reached its height in what is called the Classic period, from about 300 to 900 C.E. The Aztecs and the Incas built their empires in the two centuries before the Spanish arrived in the 1500s.

Scholars have learned about these cultures in various ways. They have studied artifacts found at the sites of old settlements. They have read accounts left by Spanish soldiers and priests. And they have observed traditions that can still be found among the descendants of the Mayas, Aztecs, and Incas.

The more we learn about these cultures, the more we can appreciate what was special about each of them. The Mayas, for example, made striking advances in writing, astronomy, and architecture. Both the Mayas and the Aztecs created highly accurate calendars. The Aztecs adapted earlier pyramid designs to build massive stone temples. The Incas showed great skill in engineering and in managing their huge empire.

In this chapter, you will study these and other achievements of the Mayas, the Aztecs, and the Incas. You will focus on three main areas of culture: science and technology, arts and architecture, and language and writing.

Civilizations of the Americas, 300–1500 C.E.

ATLANTIC OCEAN

Gulf of Mexico

MEXICO

Gulf of California

BELIZE

HONDURAS

Caribbean Sea

GUATEMALA

EL SALVADOR

NICARAGUA

COSTA RICA

PANAMA

GUYANA

SURINAME

FRENCH GUIANA

VENEZUELA

COLOMBIA

ECUADOR

PERU

BRAZIL

PACIFIC OCEAN

BOLIVIA

CHILE

PARAGUAY

ARGENTINA

URUGUAY

N W E S

0   1,000   2,000 miles
0   1,000   2,000 kilometers
Robinson Projection

Mayan Civilization (around 900 C.E.)

Aztec Empire (early 1500s C.E.)

Inca Empire (around 1500 C.E.)

Between 300 and 1500 C.E., three major powers arose: the Mayas and Aztecs in Mexico and Central America and the Incas in South America.

◀ The cultures of Mexico, Central, and South America produced great art work, such as this Aztec container.

26.2 Achievements of the Mayas

Many of the greatest achievements of the Mayas date from the Classic period (about 300 to 900 C.E.). Hundreds of years later, their ideas and practices continued to influence other Mesoamerican groups, including the Aztecs.

solar year the time it takes Earth to travel once around the sun

Science and Technology The Mayas made important breakthroughs in astronomy and mathematics. Throughout Mayan lands, priests studied the sky from observatories. They were able to track the movements of stars and planets with great accuracy. The Mayas used their observations to calculate the **solar year**. The Mayan figure for their year of 365.2420 days is amazingly precise.

These calculations allowed the Mayas to create their solar calendar of 365 days. They also had a sacred 260-day calendar. Every 52 years, the first date in both calendars fell on the same day. This gave the Mayas a longer unit of time that they called a Calendar Round. For the ancient Mayas, this 52-year period was something like what a century is to us.

Mayan astronomy and calendar-making depended on a deep understanding of mathematics. In some ways, the Mayan number system was like ours. The Mayas used place values for numbers, just as we do. However, instead of being based on the number 10, their system was based on 20. So instead of place values for 1s, 10s, and 100s, the Mayas had place values for 1s, 20s, 400s (20 times 20), and so on.

Mayan priests still use the sacred calendars. This priest is at a ceremony to celebrate the end of the Mayan solar year of 5115. He prays for peace and prosperity in the coming year.

The Mayas also recognized the need for zero—a discovery made by few other early civilizations. In the Mayan system for writing numbers, a dot stood for one, a bar for five, and a shell symbol for zero. To add and subtract, people lined up two numbers and then combined or took away dots and bars.

Arts and Architecture The Mayas were equally gifted in the arts. They painted, using colors mixed from minerals and plants. We can see the artistry of Mayan painters in the Bonampak murals, which were found in Chiapas, Mexico. The murals show nobles and priests, as well as battle scenes, ceremonies, and sacrifice rituals.

The Mayas also constructed upright stone slabs called **steles** (STEE-leez), which they often placed in front of temples. Most steles stood between 5 and 12 feet tall, although some rose as high as 30 feet. Steles usually had three-dimensional carvings of gods and rulers. Sometimes, the Mayas inscribed them with dates and hieroglyphics in honor of significant events.

Another important art was weaving. We know from steles and paintings that the Mayas wove colorful fabric in complex patterns. Women made embroidered tunics called *huipiles* and fashioned lengths of cloth for trade. Mayan women still use similar techniques today. They still make their huipiles in traditional designs. People from different towns can be distinguished by the colors and patterns of their garments.

In architecture, the Mayas built temple-pyramids from hand-cut limestone bricks. An unusual feature of Mayan buildings was a type of arch called a corbel vault. Builders stacked stones so that they gradually angled in toward each other to form a triangular archway. At the top of the arch, where the stones almost touched, one stone joined the two sides. The archway always had nine stone layers, representing the nine layers of the underworld (the place where souls were thought to go after death).

Language and Writing The Mayas developed the most complex system of writing in the ancient Americas. They used hieroglyphics, or picture symbols, to represent sounds, words, and ideas. Hieroglyphic inscriptions have been found on stoneware and other artifacts dating from possibly as early as 300 B.C.E.

Over time, the Mayas created hundreds of **glyphs**. Eventually, scribes could write down anything in the spoken language. They often wrote about rulers, history, myths and gods, and astronomy.

Not all Mayan groups shared the same language. Instead, they spoke related **dialects**. Today, about four million Mesoamericans still speak one of thirty or so Mayan dialects.

stele a vertical stone slab or pillar with carvings or inscriptions

glyph a symbol for a word, idea, or sound in a hieroglyphic system of writing

dialect a regional variety of a language

Weaving is a traditional Mayan art passed down through generations of women.

26.3 Achievements of the Aztecs

The Aztecs adapted many ideas from earlier groups, including their calendars and temple-pyramids. But the Aztecs improved on these ideas and made them their own.

Science and Technology One of the Aztecs' most remarkable technological achievements was the construction of their island city, Tenochtitlán. The Aztecs enlarged the area of the city by creating artificial islands called *chinampas*. Today, flower farmers in Xochimilco, near Mexico City, still use chinampas. Tourists enjoy taking boat trips to see these "floating gardens."

Just as impressive as the chinampas were the three causeways that connected Tenochtitlán to the mainland. The causeways were often crowded with people traveling in and out of the capital. During the rainy season, when the waters of the lake rose, the causeways also served as dikes.

To manage time, the Aztecs adapted the Mayan solar and sacred calendars. The 365-day solar calendar was especially useful for farming, since it tracked the seasons. Priests used the sacred 260-day calendar to predict events and to determine "lucky" days for such things as planting crops and going to war.

Adapted from the Mayan calendar, the Sun Stone calendar shows the face of the Aztec sun god. It includes a 365-day agricultural calendar and a 260-day sacred calendar.

One of the most famous Aztec artifacts is a calendar called the Sun Stone. Dedicated to the god of the sun, this beautifully carved stone is nearly twelve feet wide and weighs almost twenty-five tons. The center shows the face of the sun god. Today, the Sun Stone is a well-known symbol of Mexico.

Arts and Architecture The Aztecs practiced a number of arts, including poetry, music, dance, and sculpture. Poets wrote verses to sing the praises of the gods, to tell stories, and to celebrate the natural world. Poetry was highly valued. Aztec poets sung their poems or recited them to music. Sometimes, actors performed them, creating a dramatic show with dialogue and costumes.

Music and dance were important features of Aztec ceremonies and holidays. People dressed up for these special occasions. Women wore beautiful blouses over their skirts. Men painted their faces, greased their hair, and wore feathered headdresses. The dancers formed large circles and moved to the beat of drums and the sound of rattle bells. The dances had religious meaning, and the dancers had to perform every step correctly. Sometimes, thousands of people danced at one time. Even the emperor occasionally joined in.

The Aztecs were also gifted painters and sculptors. Painters used brilliant colors to create scenes showing gods and religious ceremonies. Sculptors fashioned stone statues and relief sculptures on temple walls. They also carved small, lifelike figures of people and animals from rock and semiprecious stones, such as jade. In technical craft and beauty, their work surpassed that of earlier Mesoamerican cultures.

In architecture, the Aztecs are best remembered today for their massive stone temples. The Aztecs were unique in building double stairways, like those of the Great Temple in Tenochtitlán. The staircases led to two temples, one for the sun god and one for the god of rain. Smaller pyramids nearby had their own temples, where sacrificial fires burned before huge statues of the gods.

Language and Writing Spoken language was raised to an art in Aztec society. Almost any occasion called for dramatic and often flowery speeches. The rich **vocabulary** of the Aztec language, Nahuatl, allowed speakers to create new words and describe **abstract** concepts.

The Aztec system of writing used both glyphs and **pictographs**. A pictograph is a drawing that depicts a word, phrase, or name, rather than symbolizes it. For example, the Aztec pictograph for war was a symbol of a shield and a club. The Aztecs did not have enough pictographs and glyphs to express everything that could be spoken in their language. Instead, scribes used writing to list data or to outline events. Priests used these writings to spark their memories when relating stories from the past.

This woman performs a traditional dance in Mexico City, where Aztec dancers celebrated over 600 years ago.

pictograph a drawing that stands for a word, phrase, or name

26.4 Achievements of the Incas

Like the Aztecs, the Incas often borrowed and improved upon ideas from other cultures. But the Incas faced a unique challenge in managing the largest empire in the Americas. Maintaining tight control over such a huge area was one of their most impressive accomplishments.

Science and Technology The Incas' greatest technological skill was engineering. The best example is their amazing system of roads.

The Incas built roads across the length and width of their empire. To create routes through steep mountain ranges, they carved staircases and gouged tunnels out of rock. They also built **suspension bridges** over rivers. Thick rope cables were anchored at stone towers on either side of the river. Two cables served as rails, while three others held a walkway.

In agriculture, the Incas showed their technological skill by vastly enlarging the system of terraces already in use by earlier Andean farmers. The Incas anchored their step-like terraces with stones and improved the drainage systems in the fields. On some terraces, they planted different crops at elevations where the plants would grow best.

To irrigate the crops, the Incas built canals that brought water to the top of a hillside of terraces. From there, the water ran down, level by level. People in South America still grow crops on Incan terraces.

The Incas also made remarkable advances in medicine. Incan priests, who were in charge of healing, practiced a type of surgery called **trephination**. Usually, the patient was an injured warrior. Priests cut into the patient's skull to remove bone fragments that were pressing against the brain. As **drastic** as this sounds, many people survived the operation and recovered full health.

Arts and Architecture Making textiles for clothing was one of the most important Incan arts. The quality and design of a person's clothes were a sign of status. The delicate cloth worn by Incan nobles often featured bright colors and bold geometric patterns. Incan women also made feather tunics, or long shirts, weaving feathers from jungle birds right into the cloth.

Fashioning objects out of gold was another important art. The Incas prized gold, which they called the "sweat of the sun." Gold covered almost every inch inside the Temple of the Sun in the Incan capital city of Cuzco. Incan goldsmiths also fashioned masks, sculptures, knives, and jewelry.

Music was a major part of Incan life. The Incas played flutes, seashell horns, rattles, drums, and panpipes. Scholars believe that the modern music of the Andes region preserves elements of Incan music.

suspension bridge a bridge held up by cables anchored at each end

trephination a type of surgery in which a hole is made in the skull

Terraces anchored with stones can still be seen in the ruins of the Incan city of Machu Picchu.

Peruvian musicians today use instruments similar to some of those used by the Incas, such as these panpipes and drums.

In architecture, the Incas are known for their huge, durable stone buildings. The massive stones of Incan structures fit together so tightly that a knife blade could not be slipped between them. Incan buildings were sturdy, too—many remain standing today.

Language and Writing The Incas made their language, Quechua (KECH-wah), the official language of the empire. As a result, Quechua spread far and wide. About ten million people in South America still speak it.

The Incas did not have a written language. Instead, they developed an **ingenious** substitute: the knotted sets of strings called *quipus*. The Incas used quipus as memory aids when sending messages and recording information.

Chapter Summary

In this chapter, you explored the cultural achievements of the Mayas, Aztecs, and Incas. All three peoples accomplished advances in science and technology, arts and architecture, and language and writing.

Achievements of the Mayas The Mayas are admired for their writing system, calendar, knowledge of astronomy, and architecture. They were able to calculate the length of a solar year and also developed the concept of zero. Mayan steles and other structures stand today.

Achievements of the Aztecs The Aztecs are noted for their calendar and their massive temples, as well as their great capital city. People still travel to Mexico to visit the remains of Tenochtitlán and view the chinampas, the floating islands invented by the Aztecs.

Achievements of the Incas The Incas showed great skill in managing their huge empire and in engineering. They built an extensive road system of about 15,000 miles. Quipus allowed them to record and transport important information. They also made remarkable advances in medicine, such as a type of surgery called trephination.

Talented engineers, the Incas developed a way to create safe bridges out of grass rope. The technology is still used today.

Walking Across Space:
Incan Rope Bridges

You're standing at the edge of a canyon high in the Andes Mountains, looking down at a raging river far below. You look across to the other side. The only way to get there is to walk across a narrow rope bridge. You grit your teeth and step out into space. The bridge sinks beneath your weight. Will the bridge hold? Will it flip you over into the gorge below? Don't worry—this bridge was built by people who really know what they're doing!

The Incas lived in a land of high mountains separated by rivers and deep valleys. They built a vast system of roads to help them travel and communicate. They also built amazing bridges that crossed the vast chasms between cliffs and canyons. These bridges were made of thick rope cables woven from grass. That's right—grass.

For centuries, these rope bridges played a critical role in transportation throughout the Andes Mountains. Massachusetts Institute of Technology (MIT) professor John Ochsendorf is a structural engineer who has spent years studying Incan rope bridges. He thinks that the bridges were just as important as the Incan road system. They allowed the Incas to cross natural barriers, such as canyons and rivers. Without out the amazing engineering that created these rope bridges, the Incas could not have connected the roads into the effective communication system that helped them create and control their large empire.

Bridges Made from Grass

In the Quechua language, a grass rope bridge is called a *Keshwachaka*. According to Ochsendorf, there were two types of rope bridges: large and small. Each type was carefully planned and maintained. There is evidence that the Incan emperor himself drew plans for large bridges and made sure that they were repaired and protected.

Large bridges had a *Chaka Camayoc,* which means "bridgekeeper" in the Quechua language. Living at the bridge, the Chaka Camayoc was responsible for guarding and repairing it. Large bridges were usually located on the Royal Road, built between the present-day cities of Cuzco, Peru, and Quito, Ecuador.

Smaller bridges connected rural communities to one another and to the Royal Road. The local people were responsible for building and maintaining them as part of their annual service to the empire. Working together, they repaired or rebuilt these bridges every year.

Building a Rope Bridge

The last remaining Incan rope bridge is believed to be located in the remote village of Huinchiri, Peru. It hangs about two hundred feet over the Apurimac River and spans a distance of over one hundred feet. People in the area use a modern metal bridge for everyday transportation across the river. But each year, Quechua villagers hold a three-day festival during which they cut down the old rope bridge and build a new one. Using weaving and construction techniques that have passed from generation to generation, they honor their culture and ancestors. Tourists come from around the world to watch the villagers rebuild the bridge.

During the festival, villagers organize the work in the same way it has been done for centuries. Each household is responsible for a certain job. There are four key tasks in constructing a bridge: making rope; braiding it into cables; repairing or rebuilding the stone anchors on either side of the river; and making the ties, the handrails, and a floor system.

The basic material that makes up the huge cables needed to hold up the bridge is a thin, two-ply rope. Hundreds of families work before the festival begins to make this rope. They start by gathering dry stalks of grass. Then they twist pieces of grass together. As they add grass, the rope becomes longer and longer. The villagers make the rope in lengths of about fifty yards. Approximately ten miles of rope are needed to build the bridge.

During a three-day festival, Quechua villagers rebuild a rope bridge over the Apurimac River in Peru, using the methods of their Incan ancestors.

To form the bridge, thick rope cables are first strung across the river using guide ropes and then anchored to each bank.

On the first day of the festival, construction begins. Families bring their handmade thin ropes to the bridge site. The chief bridge builder and the priest make offerings to *Paca Mama*, or Mother Earth. They ask that she bless their work. They also ask that the bridge stay safe and strong until they rebuild it next year.

Next, the men make large cables. They braid the thin ropes together, three at a time, to make thicker cables. Then they braid these cables together to make even thicker ones. Each cable measures 6 inches in diameter, weighs about 150 pounds, and is 150 feet long. Six of these big cables are needed to make the bridge. Four cables form the bridge floor to carry the weight of people and animals, and the remaining two cables serve as handrails.

On the second day, the villagers cut down the old bridge and let it fall into the river. Then the men put up new cables. A guide rope is attached to each cable. Using the guide rope, the men pull each cable across the river. They lift each one to the top of the cliff on the other side of the canyon. Then, they pull on the cables to make sure they are very tight. Finally, they connect the cables to strong timbers and stone anchor blocks located on each side of the river.

On the festival's final day, people gather at the bridge in colorful party clothes. They watch the current bridgekeeper connect rope ties from the floor cables to the handrail cables. Other men lay down cross-ties, or sticks that will help keep the floor cables in place. Finally, they lay reed floor mats over the cross-ties and floor cables to complete the bridge.

Walking Across the Rope Bridge

Once the bridge is finished, a celebration begins. The villagers may offer guests or tourists a traditional Quechua meal. Then anyone who wants to is invited to walk across the bridge. Would you walk across it?

When Spanish soldiers first saw these bridges, they were terrified. Some soldiers crawled across them on their hands and knees. The bridges were strong and safe, however. The Spanish even crossed them with their horses and cannons.

Ephraim George Squier, an American visitor to Peru in the 1870s, gave good advice about crossing the rope bridge over the Apurimac. He wrote, "It is usual for the traveler to time his day's journey so as to reach the bridge in the morning, before the strong wind sets in; for, during the greater part of the day, it sweeps up the canyon of the Apurimac with great force, and then the bridge sways like a gigantic hammock, and crossing is next to impossible."

An American scientist who crossed the newly rebuilt bridge described her walk with words that echoed those of Ephraim Squier from the 1870s. As she crossed slowly to keep the bridge from swaying too much or flipping over, she said, "I want to look down, but I'm afraid to look down, so I'm looking at everybody across. I know I can do this. I think I'm going to be sick. No, I'm not."

Many tourists accept the invitation to walk across the newly finished bridge. After watching its construction, they feel sure that it is sturdy and safe. Laboratory tests done by Professor John Ochsendorf show that the bridge is quite strong. It can hold 56 people spread out in a row across the bridge at one time, or 4,200 pounds of weight.

What the Incas accomplished centuries ago makes their Quechua descendants very proud. They know that their ancestors were gifted engineers. The Incas solved the problem of connecting roads by using the resources at hand. They also know that these bridges function well, since they were rebuilt again and again for more than 400 years, until metal bridges started to replace them in the 19th century. Anyone watching the Incas' Quechua descendents build a bridge in just three days will see that they are living examples of a way of life that has endured for centuries.

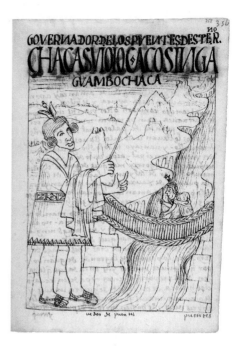

The Incan method of bridge building has been in use for over 400 years.

The Incan bridge is extremely strong. It can hold more than two tons of weight at a time.

Civilizations of the Americas

About 2000 B.C.E.–1500 C.E.
Mayan Civilization
The Mayan civilization consists of independent states that contain elaborate stone cities and extensive farming communities.

About 300 C.E.–900 C.E.
Classic Period of
Mayan Civilization
Great cultural achievements, including the construction of observatories and the development of an accurate 365-day solar calendar, occur during the Classic period of Mayan civilization.

2000 B.C.E.	1500 B.C.E.	1000 B.C.E.	500 B.C.E.	1 C.E.

About 300 B.C.E.
Mayan Hieroglyphics
Developed
The Mayas develop hieroglyphics, which can be found on stoneware and other artifacts from the Pre-Classic period.

About 1200 C.E.
Incas Settle in Cuzco
The Incas settle in Cuzco, high in the Andes Mountains of southern Peru, where they live for more than 200 years before beginning to expand their empire.

About 1325 C.E.
Aztecs Build Tenochtitlán
The Aztecs build their capital of Tenochtitlán in Lake Texcoco by creating artificial islands called *chinampas*.

1300s–1400s C.E.
Aztec Religious Practices
Aztec religious practices include human sacrifice.

1438 C.E.–1532 C.E.
Inca Empire
The Inca Empire expands rapidly by forcing defeated tribes to adopt the ways of the Incas, including Incan-style villages with communal land.

1519–1532 C.E.
Aztec and Incan Civilizations Conquered
The Spanish defeat the Aztec Empire in 1519 and the Inca Empire in 1532.

1 C.E.	500 C.E.	1000 C.E.	1500 C.E.	2000 C.E.

1428 C.E.–1519 C.E.
Aztec Empire
The Aztec Empire expands to include most of central Mexico. The Aztecs make many enemies through warfare and an empire system based on tribute.

1479 C.E.
Aztec Calendar
The Aztecs adapt the Mayan 365-day solar calendar, which is especially useful for farming since it tracks the seasons. This Aztec calendar dates to 1479.

1400s–1500s C.E.
Incan Roads and Bridges
The Incas build an extensive system of roads and bridges to help them manage their empire.

Civilizations of the Americas **327**

Europe's Renaissance and Reformation

The cathedral of Santa Maria del Fiore, also called the Duomo, is one of the most important buildings in Florence, Italy. Its construction ended in 1496 during the Renaissance. In this unit, you will find out what feature makes the cathedral so famous.

Physical Features of Europe

80°N

0°   10°E   20°E   30°E   40°E
10°W   50°E   60°E   70°E   80°E

20°W

40°W   30°W   70°N

60°N   ICELAND   Arctic Circle

Norwegian
Sea

50°N   FAROE ISLANDS
(Den.)

SHETLAND ISLANDS
(U.K.)

SCANDINAVIA

ATLANTIC
OCEAN

Ben Nevis
(4,406 ft.; 1,343 m)

North
Sea

Baltic Sea

NORTHERN   EUROPEAN   PLAIN

BRITISH
ISLES

Thames
River

Celtic
Sea

English Channel

Seine River

Rhine River

Elbe River

Bay of
Biscay

Loire River

Danube River

CARPATHIAN MOUNTAINS

Black Sea

A L P S

Mont Blanc
(15,781ft.; 4,810m)

Po River

PYRENEES

ADRIATIC Sea

BALKAN MTS.

Bosporus

IBERIAN
PENINSULA

Corsica

APPENNINES

BALKAN
PENINSULA

40°N   Sardinia

Tiber
River

Aegean Sea

ASIA

BALEARIC
ISLANDS

ITALIAN
PENINSULA

Strait of Gibraltar   Tyrrhenian Sea   Ionian
Sea   PELOPONNESUS

Sicily   Crete

Mediterranean   Sea

Elevation
Feet	Meters
Over 10,000	Over 3,050
5,001–10,000	1,526–3,050
2,001–5,000	611–1,525
1,001–2,000	306–610
0–1,000	0–305
Below sea level	Below sea level

▲   Mountain peak

〰   Present-day
boundary

AFRICA

N
W   E
S

0   250   500 miles
0   250   500 kilometers
Lambert Azimuthal Equal-Area

Europe's Renaissance and Reformation

Understanding the political geography of Europe during the 1300s to the 1600s will give you a foundation on which to build your upcoming study of two crucial periods: the Renaissance and the Reformation.

Much of the power in Europe from the 1300s to the 1600s lay in three major areas: the city-states of Italy, the Papal States, and the Holy Roman Empire.

During these years, Italy was not the unified country it is today. Instead, it was a collection of city-states, or large, self-governing cities and their surrounding communities and farms. From the 1300s to the 1600s, several of these independent city-states prospered. Places such as Florence, Venice, and Milan grew in power and influence, due mostly to an increase in trade and banking.

The city of Rome was also a prosperous and important city. It was part of an area known as the Papal States. These were territories in central Italy controlled by the pope, the spiritual leader of the Roman Catholic Church. Life was changing in Europe in the 1500s, however, and the power of the Church and the Papal States was just beginning to weaken.

To the north of the Papal States and the Italian city-states lay the Holy Roman Empire. Established by King Charlemagne in the 700s, the empire during the period of the Renaissance encompassed a large piece of land that stretched to the North Sea. Its borders changed often, as territories were won and lost. Within the Holy Roman Empire, powerful princes ruled over smaller territories. The influence of the empire as a whole, however, was beginning to weaken, despite repeated attempts by successive emperors to gain an advantage over the pope and the Catholic Church.

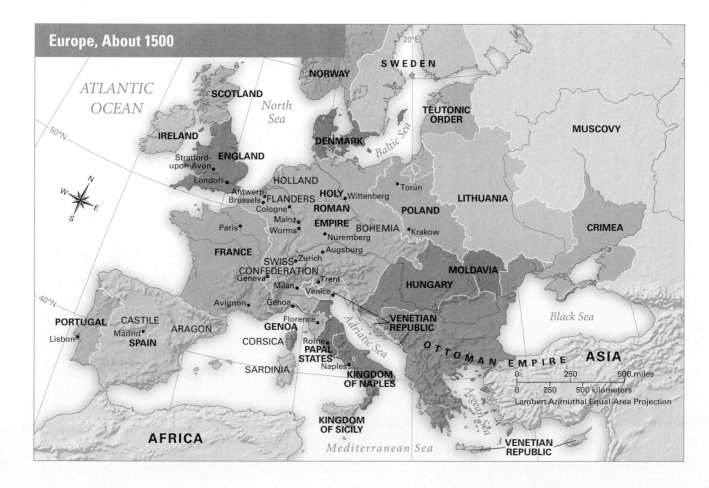

Europe, About 1500

Chapter 27

The Renaissance Begins

What changes in Europe led to the Renaissance?

27.1 Introduction

Toward the end of the Middle Ages, a great flowering of culture called the Renaissance began in Italy. In this chapter, you will learn about the Renaissance and how it began.

Renaissance is a French word that means "rebirth." Historians use the word to describe the rebirth of widespread interest in classical art and learning that took place in Europe from about 1300 to about 1600 C.E. "Classical" refers to the cultures of ancient Greece and Rome. Although there was no sudden end to the Middle Ages, the Renaissance changed many aspects of people's lives over time.

Medieval European society was based on feudalism. Most people lived on feudal manors. The Roman Catholic Church encouraged people to think more about life after death than about daily life on Earth. Except for the clergy, few people were educated.

By the Late Middle Ages, changes were occurring that paved the way for the Renaissance. Trade and commerce increased. Cities grew larger and wealthier. Newly wealthy merchants and bankers supported the growth of arts and learning. A renewed interest in ancient cultures started a flood of new ideas. Greek and Roman examples inspired new styles of architecture, approaches to the arts, and ways of thinking.

Beginning in Italy, a philosophy called *humanism* developed. Humanists believed in the worth and potential of all individuals. They balanced religious faith with belief in the power of the mind. Humanists took a fresh interest in human society and the natural world. This thinking contributed to the burst of creativity during the Renaissance.

In this chapter, you will explore how the Renaissance differed from the Middle Ages and classical times. Then you will examine some changes in European life that led to the Renaissance.

Ruins left by the ancient Greeks and Romans inspired new interest in classical styles during the Renaissance.

Leonardo da Vinci's *Lady with an Ermine* reflects Renaissance ideas.

27.2 What Was the Renaissance?

The **Renaissance** began in Italy in the 1300s and spread to other parts
of Europe in the 1400s and 1500s. Let's look more closely at this "great
rebirth" of interest in **classical art** and learning. Then we will explore
the link between the Renaissance and the classical world.

Renewed Interest in the Classical World The Renaissance
began with the rediscovery of the classical world of ancient Greece and
Rome. After the fall of Rome in the 5th century C.E., classical culture
was never entirely forgotten. Clergy of the Roman Catholic Church
helped keep knowledge of ancient times alive by copying documents
that survived from the classical period. Still, this knowledge reached
relatively few people during most of the Middle Ages.

In the Late Middle Ages, merchants and Crusaders brought back
goods and ideas from the East, including classical learning that had
been preserved in the Byzantine Empire. Europeans also read classical
works that came to them from Muslim scholars.

This flow of ideas led to a rediscovery of Greek and Roman culture.
Scholars started collecting and reading ancient manuscripts from
monasteries. Artists and architects studied classical statues and buildings. The renewed interest in classical culture led to the great flowering
of art and learning that we call the Renaissance.

Exploring the Rebirth of Classical Ideas Through Art We
can trace the link between the classical world and the Renaissance
by looking at art. Let's explore some of the characteristics of art from
classical, medieval, and Renaissance times.

Classical Art The classical period lasted from about 500 B.C.E. to
500 C.E. The classical artists of Greece and Rome created sculptures,
pottery, murals, and mosaics. The purpose of much of their art was to
show the importance of ordinary people and civic leaders, as well as
gods and goddesses. Here are additional characteristics of classical art:

- Artists valued balance and harmony.
- Figures were lifelike but often idealized, or more perfect than
  in real life.
- Figures were nude or draped in togas, or robes.
- Bodies looked active and motion was believable.
- Faces were calm and without emotion.
- Scenes showed either heroic figures or real people doing tasks from
  daily life.
- In paintings, there was little background or sense of perspective.
  Perspective is a visual technique used to make people and objects
  look closer or farther away and to give realistic depth to a scene.

This Roman copy of a Greek statue was
created in 450 B.C.E. A discus thrower,
it celebrates the classical ideals of
athleticism, balance, and power.

Medieval Art The medieval period lasted from about 500 to about 1300 C.E. Medieval artists created stained glass windows, sculptures, illuminated manuscripts, paintings, and tapestries. The purpose of much medieval art was to teach religion to people who could not read or write. Here are additional characteristics of medieval art:

- Most art was religious, showing Jesus, saints, and people from the Bible.
- Important figures in paintings were shown larger than others around them.
- Figures looked stiff, with little sense of movement.
- Figures were fully dressed in stiff-looking clothing.
- Faces were serious and showed little expression.
- Painted figures looked two-dimensional, or flat.
- Paint colors were bright.
- Backgrounds were mostly one color, often blue or gold.

This example of medieval art was created for a church in France in 1120 C.E. It shows Jesus sending his apostles out to preach.

This example of Renaissance art is titled *The School of Athens*. It was painted by the artist Raphael around 1510. Ancient Greek philosophers, such as Plato and Aristotle, are shown here, surrounded by some of the Renaissance artists they later inspired.

Renaissance Art The Renaissance lasted from the 1300s to the early 1600s. Artists created sculptures, murals, drawings, and paintings. The aim of much Renaissance art was to show the importance of people and nature, not just religious ideas. Artists also began using new techniques. Here are additional characteristics of Renaissance art:

- Artists showed religious and nonreligious scenes.
- Art reflected a great interest in nature.
- Figures looked lifelike and three-dimensional, reflecting an increasing knowledge of anatomy.
- Figures were shown in action.
- Figures were either nude or clothed.
- Scenes showed real people doing everyday tasks.
- Faces expressed what people were feeling.
- Colors were shown responding to light.
- Paintings were often symmetrical, or balanced, with the right and left sides having identical elements.
- Full backgrounds showed perspective, adding depth.

If you compare these three styles, you can see that Renaissance artists were inspired more by classical art than medieval art. Like classical artists, Renaissance painters and sculptors depicted subjects that were not always religious. They tried to show people as lifelike and engaged in everyday activities. They also tried to capture the way things look in the real world.

Renaissance art reflects a rebirth of interest in the classical world. What changes brought about this revival of classical culture?

27.3 The Growth of Trade and Commerce

One reason for the flowering of culture during the Renaissance was the growth of trade and commerce. Trade brought new ideas as well as goods into Europe. A bustling economy created prosperous cities and new classes of people who had the wealth to support art and learning.

Increased Contact Between East and West Starting in the 11th century, the Crusades strengthened contacts between western Europe and Byzantine and Muslim cultures. Merchants brought goods and ideas from the East that helped to reawaken interest in classical culture. In the 13th century, the Mongol conquests in Asia made it safer for traders to travel along the Silk Road to China. The tales of the Italian traveler Marco Polo sparked even greater interest in the East. Food, art, and luxury goods, such as silk and spices, moved along the trade routes linking Europe to Africa and Asia.

Cities, such as Venice and Genoa in Italy, were centrally located on the trade routes that linked the rest of western Europe with the East. They became bustling, prosperous trading centers that attracted merchants and customers, as did cities in northern Europe, such as Bruges and Brussels. Trade ships carried goods to England, Scandinavia, and present-day Russia by way of the English Channel and the Baltic and North seas. Towns along the routes connecting southern and northern Europe, such as Cologne and Mainz in Germany, provided inns and other services for traveling merchants.

This 15th-century French illustration shows people exchanging goods for money in a shop in a Renaissance town.

city-state an independent state consisting of a city and its surrounding territory

A New Economy The increase in trade led to a new kind of economy. During the Middle Ages, people bartered, or traded, goods. By the Renaissance, people were using coins to buy merchandise, creating a money economy. Coins came from many places, so money changers were needed to convert one type of **currency** into another.

As a result of all this activity, craftspeople, merchants, and bankers became more important in society. Craftspeople produced goods that merchants traded across Europe. Bankers exchanged currency, loaned money to merchants and rulers, and financed their own businesses.

Some merchants and bankers grew very rich. With their abundant wealth, they could afford to make their cities more beautiful. Wealthy patrons commissioned (ordered and paid for) new buildings and art. They also helped to found universities. Prosperous Renaissance cities grew into flourishing educational and cultural centers.

27.4 The Influence of Italian City-States

The Renaissance began in northern and central Italy. One reason why it began there was the prosperity of Italian **city-states**.

In the Late Middle Ages, most of western Europe was made up of fiefs ruled by nobles. Above the nobles were monarchs. In Italy, however, growing towns developed into independent city-states. Each city-state consisted of a powerful city and the surrounding **territory**, which might include other towns.

This is a late-15th-century map of Florence, one of Italy's most powerful city-states.

FIORENZA

Major Italian City-States During the Renaissance

Venice
Milan • Mantua • Padua
Turin •
Parma • Ferrara
Genoa • Bologna •
Florence • Ravenna
Siena • Urbino

Adriatic Sea

Rome •

Tyrrhenian Sea

Naples •

Naples
Papal States
Siena
Florence
Milan
Genoa
Venice
Sicily
Minor city-states

0   100   200 miles
0   100   200 kilometers
Lambert Azimuthal Equal-Area Projection

N
W—E
S

Mediterranean Sea

At the time of the Renaissance, Italy was not a unified nation. It was divided into many different city-states, some of which were extremely powerful.

The Italian city-states conducted their own trade, collected their own taxes, and made their own laws. Some, such as Florence, were **republics** that were governed by elected councils.

In theory, the power in republics belonged to the people. In fact, it often lay in the hands of rich merchants. During the Middle Ages, guilds of craftspeople and merchants became very powerful. During the Renaissance, groups of guild members, called boards, often ruled Italian city-states. Boards were supposed to change members frequently. However, wealthy families often gained long-term control. As a result, some city-states were ruled by a single rich family, such as the Medici (MED-uh-chee) family in Florence.

Trade made the Italian city-states dazzlingly wealthy. Italy's central Mediterranean location in the middle of the trade routes connected distant places with the rest of western Europe. People from all over Europe came to northern Italy to buy, sell, and do their banking.

Some Italian city-states developed specializations. Florence became a center for cloth making and banking. Milan produced metal goods and armor. The port city of Genoa was a trade center for ivory and gold from northern Africa. Venice, the most powerful city-state, had hundreds of ships that controlled the trade routes in the Mediterranean Sea. Silk, spices, and perfume from Asia flowed into Venice.

republic a form of government in which citizens elect representatives to rule for them

The city-states' wealth encouraged a boom in art and learning. Rich families paid for the creation of statues, paintings, beautiful buildings, and elegant avenues. They built new centers of learning, such as universities and hospitals. From the city-states of Italy, Renaissance ideas spread to the rest of Europe.

27.5 The Growth of Humanism

The interest in learning during the Renaissance was spurred on by **humanism**. This way of thinking sought to balance religious faith with an **emphasis** on individual dignity and an interest in nature and human society.

Humanism first arose in Italy as a result of the renewed interest in classical culture. Many early humanists eagerly hunted for ancient Greek and Roman books, coins, and other artifacts that could help them learn about the classical world.

One of the first humanists was an Italian poet named Francesco Petrarch. Petrarch especially loved old books. He searched for them all over Europe and encouraged his friends to bring him any they found. Eventually, he created a large collection of ancient Latin and Greek texts, which he made available to other scholars.

Scholars from all over Europe traveled to Italy to learn about the new humanist ideas inspired by classical culture. They studied such subjects as art, architecture, government, and language. They read classical history and poetry. They began to ask probing questions. What did classical artists find most beautiful about the human body? How did the Romans construct their buildings?

In their studies of classical culture, humanists discovered a new way of looking at life. They began to create a philosophy based on the importance and dignity of each individual. Humanists believed that all people have the ability to control their own lives and achieve greatness. In education, they stressed study of the **humanities**—a group of subjects that focus on human life and culture. These subjects include grammar, rhetoric (the study of persuasive language), history, poetry, and ethics (the study of moral values and behavior).

Humanists tried to put ancient ideas into practice. Architects, for example, studied Greek and Roman ruins. They designed buildings with pillars, arches, and courtyards like those of classical buildings.

The humanists did not simply imitate classical achievements. They tried to improve on the work of the ancient Greeks and Romans. In universities, scholars began to teach methods of observation and experimentation. Renaissance scientists proposed new ideas about the stars and planets. Artists and students of medicine closely studied human anatomy. Poets wrote about both religious subjects and everyday experiences. Writers produced works of history and studies of politics.

Francesco Petrarch is considered to be the founder of Italian Renaissance humanism. A well-known poet, he wears a laurel wreath in this portrait to symbolize his crowning as poet laureate in Rome in 1341.

humanism a philosophy that tries to balance religious faith with an emphasis on individual dignity and an interest in nature and human society

humanities collectively, areas of study that focus on human life and culture, such as history, literature, and ethics

The influence of classical ideals changed ideas about government. Humanists separated the state and its right to rule from the Church. In doing so, they helped lay the foundation for modern thinking about politics and government.

Humanist ideals also changed people's thinking about social standing. In feudal times, people were born into a certain status in society. If someone was born a peasant, he or she would always have less status than a noble. In general, Renaissance thinkers prized individual achievement more than a person's class or family. This emphasis on **individualism** was an enormous shift from medieval thinking.

The humanists' new ideas sometimes brought them into conflict with the Catholic Church. The Church taught that laws were made by God and that those who broke them were sinful. It encouraged people to follow its teachings without question to save their souls. For the Church, life after death was more important than life on Earth. In **contrast,** humanists believed that people should use their minds to question everything. Most tried to balance religious faith and its emphasis on the afterlife with an active interest in daily life. Some directly challenged teachings that were important to the Church. An Italian humanist, Giordano Bruno, paid for his ideas by being burned at the stake.

individualism the belief in the importance of an individual's achievements and dignity

Humanist scholars in the Renaissance spent time reading, studying, and writing about classical culture.

Chapter Summary

In this chapter, you explored the beginnings of the period in Europe that followed the Middle Ages, called the Renaissance.

What Was the Renaissance? The Renaissance was a flowering of art and learning that was inspired by a rediscovery of the classical cultures of Greece and Rome. It began in Italy around 1300 and spread throughout Europe, lasting to the early 1600s.

The Growth of Trade and Commerce Italy's location made it a perfect crossroads for trade between Europe and Asia, which began to increase at this time. This growth of trade and commerce created prosperous cities and classes of people with enough wealth to support education and the arts.

The Influence of Italian City-States The developing wealth and power of the individual Italian city-states helped to promote and spread Renaissance ideas. Civic leaders and wealthy private individuals paid for new works of art and built new centers of learning.

The Growth of Humanism The new philosophy of humanism spurred interest in learning and fresh ways of thinking. Humanists, such as Francesco Petrarch, sought to balance religious faith with an emphasis on individualism, the workings of the natural world, and human society. They sought to separate the workings of government from the Church.

Chapter 28

Florence: The Cradle of the Renaissance

What advances were made during the Renaissance?

28.1 Introduction

The Renaissance began in 14th-century Italy. In this chapter, you will visit the Italian city-state of Florence to learn about a number of advances made there during the Renaissance.

Florence is located on the Arno River, just north of central Italy. The city is often called the "cradle of the Renaissance." Between 1300 and 1600, it was home to some of the greatest artists and thinkers of the Renaissance.

During the Renaissance, Florence was—as it still is—a beautiful city. One of its most notable buildings is the cathedral of Santa Maria del Fiore with its towering *duomo* (DWOH-moh), or dome. The cathedral was the center of the city's religious life. Nearby is the Palazzo Vecchio (VEK-ee-oh), or Old Palace. This building was the headquarters of the city government. The grand Palazzo Medici was the home of Florence's ruling family, the Medici. A more humble house was the Casa di Dante (kah-sah dee DAHN-tay), or Dante's House. Dante is one of Italy's most celebrated poets.

During the Renaissance, Florence was the banking center of Europe. People came to the Mercato Nuovo to trade their coins for florins, the gold coins of Florence. Another busy spot was the Ponte Vecchio. This beautiful bridge spanned the Arno River and, even today, is lined with the shops of fine jewelers and goldsmiths.

Florence's wealth helped to make it a leading cultural center of the Renaissance. In this chapter, you will explore Renaissance Florence's architecture and engineering, painting, sculpture, literature, science, and mathematics. You will also find out about Florentine politics, commerce, and trade.

This map shows some of the main features of Renaissance Florence, including the Duomo of the Santa Maria del Fiore cathedral, the Palazzo Medici, and the Arno River.

◄ The city of Florence, Italy, was the center of Europe's Renaissance.

During the Renaissance, the Palazzo Vecchio housed the government of Florence. Today, city offices are still in the building, but parts are also a museum.

28.2 The City of Florence

Florence was Italy's leading cultural center during the Renaissance. The city was the birthplace of the great poet Dante Alighieri (ahl-ee-GARE-ee). The famed painter and sculptor Michelangelo grew up there. So did the brilliant thinker and artist Leonardo da Vinci. Other Florentines, such as the sculptor Donatello, also achieved great works of art, wealth, and fame during the Renaissance.

What factors helped Florence to become such a wealthy city? One answer is its location. Renaissance Italy was divided into city-states. Florence was one of them. The city's location on the Arno River made it an important center for trade and commerce. Florence became the hub of woolen-cloth trading for all of Europe. In the early 14th century, Florence also became Europe's banking center. About one hundred thousand people lived inside the city walls.

Renaissance Florence was dominated by a single family known as the Medici. The Medici acquired their wealth through banking. They helped Florence become the banking center of Europe.

Banking, along with the wool trade, created wealth that supported **intense** cultural activity in Florence. The city and its rich residents could afford to be patrons of talented artists and thinkers. The Medici family, for example, spent lavish sums on art. Their home was a gathering place for artists, such as Michelangelo, philosophers, and poets.

Over time, Florentines inspired still more creative activity. People learned from one another, and they sometimes competed to produce even greater works of art. Florentines were also influenced by ideas from other places. The city drew travelers from many parts of the world. Some came to do business. Some came to study art with Florence's master artists. Others came to learn at the city's schools and libraries. These visitors brought new ideas, goods, and technologies to the city.

Florentines were also inspired by the freedom of ideas that was at the core of humanism. Humanists prized the individual and tried to look with fresh eyes at nature and human society. You will see the influence of humanism throughout this chapter as you study examples of Renaissance advances.

28.3 Advances in Architecture and Engineering

Humanist scholars of the Renaissance were influenced by classical ideas. So, too, were architects and engineers. Renaissance architects studied Greek and Roman ruins. They modeled their own buildings on what they learned. They were particularly attracted to rounded arches, straight columns, and domed roofs.

Renaissance Architecture and Engineering

Renaissance architects also added their own ideas to classical building styles. During the Renaissance, wealthy families built private townhouses known as *palazzi* (pahl-AH-tzee), which is Italian for "palaces." Many had shops on the ground floor and homes above. Most *palazzi* were built around a private courtyard, which might contain statues or other works of art.

Public spaces were often influenced by humanist ideals. For example, humanists valued good citizenship. Architects designed public buildings with outdoor plazas where citizens could gather in settings that were grand, yet welcoming.

Innovations in engineering made new kinds of architecture possible. One of the most impressive architectural feats of the Renaissance is Santa Maria del Fiore, the great cathedral in Florence. Florentines started building this eight-sided cathedral in 1296, but they had to leave an opening for the dome. At the time, they didn't know how to build a sufficiently large dome that would not collapse. It took a Renaissance architect, Filippo Brunelleschi (feel-EE-poh broon-el-ES-key), to solve the problem.

The dome of Santa Maria del Fiore in Florence rises from the octagonal (eight-sided) cathedral. The dome's design is one of the great engineering achievements of the Renaissance.

Building Florence's Dome Brunelleschi had studied ancient ruins in Rome. He had also learned about the mathematics involved in constructing buildings. The dome he designed for the cathedral took true engineering genius. It used no internal support beams or columns. Instead, eight huge stone arches met at the top of the dome and leaned against each other. Hoops of iron, wood, and brick wrapped around the arches, keeping them in place.

The magnificent dome was finished in 1436. It rose more than three hundred feet above the city. Santa Maria del Fiore, also known as the Duomo, still stands today, more than five hundred years later. From its top you can see most of the city of Florence.

28.4 Advances in Painting

Wealthy patrons made Renaissance Florence a thriving center of art. The Medici family spent huge sums of money on fine palaces, paintings, and statues. The Palazzo Medici was filled with works of art commissioned, or ordered, by the family. Patrons such as the Medici family created opportunities for talented painters, who made a number of advances in style and technique.

Renaissance painters were influenced by the renewed interest in classical culture and the spread of humanism. They wanted to depict real people who were posed in lifelike ways and whose faces expressed emotions. They also wanted to include realistic settings. The result was a new style of painting.

Renaissance painters were the first to use techniques of perspective. This is Botticelli's *Adoration of the Magi.* Notice the sense of distance, or depth, in the painting.

The Use of Perspective One key advance made by Renaissance painters was the use of perspective. Painters use perspective to create the appearance of depth on a flat surface. Renaissance artists used several techniques to achieve depth. One was the size of objects. The smaller a painted object, the farther away it appears to be. The larger an object, the closer it appears to be. Painters also learned that a feeling of depth could be created by lines that came closer together as they receded into the distance. They discovered that careful shading could give figures and objects depth to make them look three-dimensional. *Adoration of the Magi,* a famous painting by Sandro Botticelli, shows some of these techniques.

The Influence of Science and Mathematics Science and mathematics also helped artists make other advances. The Florentine artist Masaccio used geometry to figure out how to divide the space in a painting to make scenes appear more lifelike. Some artists studied anatomy. They observed bodies and how they moved. Their studies helped them to portray the human body more realistically.

Renaissance science gave painters new materials, such as oil-based paints. Oil paint was made by mixing powdered pigments with linseed oil. This type of paint was thicker and dried more slowly than the older, egg-based paint, so artists did not have to work so quickly. Oil paint also allowed artists to paint over previous work and to show details and **texture** in new ways.

28.5 Advances in Sculpture

Like painters, Renaissance sculptors were influenced by the humanist interest in realism. They were also inspired by ancient Roman statues dug up from ruins. Sculptors began carving figures that looked like real people.

For the first time since the days of ancient Greece and Rome, sculptors made freestanding statues that could be viewed on all sides. This was very different from the sculptures of medieval times. The new statues caused a sensation. They seemed to symbolize the humanist ideals of nature, realism, and the importance of the individual.

The Work of Donatello A Florentine artist named **Donatello** was one of the first sculptors to use the new, more lifelike style. His work expressed personality and mood. A good example is his life-sized statue of David, the young warrior in the Bible story of David and Goliath. In the 1500s, Giorgio Vasari, an architect and painter, wrote that Donatello's *David* is "so natural . . . it is almost impossible . . . to believe it was not molded on the living form." This statue is thought to be the first freestanding statue since ancient times.

Donatello a Florentine sculptor who was one of the first to use a realistic, lifelike style

Michelangelo's *David* (left) and *La Pietà* (right), are two of the world's most-admired sculptures. The term *pietà* refers to any image of Mary holding the body of her son Jesus after his crucifixion.

Michelangelo a Renaissance artist, renowned for his painting and sculpture

The Work of Michelangelo Donatello's sculpture influenced **Michelangelo,** another great artist of the Renaissance. Michelangelo is known for both for his painting and his sculpture. He was also a talented poet and architect. Of all these arts, he preferred sculpture because it seemed to bring his subjects to life.

Michelangelo created his own majestic statue of David. It may be the world's most widely admired sculpture. Carved in white marble, Michelangelo's *David* stands about seventeen feet tall. The statue's expression shows the concentration and tension of a real youth on the verge of battle.

Michelangelo's *David* was installed in the Piazza della Signoria, the plaza in front of the Palazzo Vecchio. It became the prized expression of Renaissance genius in Florence, and Michelangelo had an enormous influence on other artists.

28.6 Advances in Literature

During the Renaissance, literature also was changed by the rebirth of interest in classical ideas and the rise of humanism. The topics that people wrote about changed. So did their style of writing and the language in which they wrote.

New Topics and Styles of Writing In medieval times, literature usually dealt with religious topics. Most writers used a formal, impersonal style, and wrote in Latin. Their work could be read only by a few highly educated people.

In contrast, Renaissance writers were interested in individual experience in the real world. Writing about **secular,** or nonreligious, topics became more common. Writers used a more individual style, and expressed thoughts and feelings about life. Most importantly, by the end of the Renaissance, most writers were writing in their own languages, instead of in Latin. As a result, far more people could read their work.

Dante and *The Divine Comedy* The first well-known writer to create in a native language was **Dante Alighieri** (DAHN-tay ahl-ee-GAIR-ee) of Florence. He wrote his best-known work, *The Divine Comedy,* in Italian in the early 1300s. This long poem describes Dante's imaginary journey through the afterlife. With the spirit of the ancient Roman poet Virgil as his guide, Dante witnesses the torments of souls condemned to the *Inferno,* which according to Christian belief is the place of punishment after death for one's sins. Virgil also takes Dante to *Purgatorio,* which according to Catholic tradition is a place where souls await entry into heaven. Then a beautiful woman named Beatrice shows Dante *Paradiso,* or heaven, which according to Christianity is a place of eternal life.

The Divine Comedy is a social commentary. It contains characters who were real people. The inhabitants of the *Inferno* include people of whom Dante disapproved. People he admired appear in *Paradiso.*

Dante's work became a model for other Renaissance writers, such as Petrarch and Boccaccio. They described people's lives with a new intensity of feeling. Like Dante, they wrote using the vernacular, or native language, so their words reached many more people.

secular relating to earthly life rather than to religious or spiritual matters

Dante Alighieri a great Italian author of the Renaissance who wrote *The Divine Comedy*

Dante Alighieri, a Renaissance author in Florence, wrote a long narrative poem called *The Divine Comedy.* This plaque in Florence shows Dante with scenes described in his poem. The city of Florence is shown on the right.

Leonardo da Vinci a famous
Renaissance artist, scientist,
and inventor

28.7 Advances in Science and Mathematics

The Renaissance was not just a time of progress in the arts. Scholars and others also made great advances in science and mathematics.

Before the Renaissance, most of what people believed about the natural world was based on ideas in ancient Greek and Roman texts. As the humanist spirit took hold, people started questioning old ideas. They began carefully observing the world around them. Instead of relying on old books and theories, scientists began to perform experiments. They **analyzed** the results using mathematics and logic. This approach to research changed the study of science.

Leonardo da Vinci One of the most creative Renaissance thinkers was **Leonardo da Vinci**. Leonardo was an artist, a scientist, an engineer, and an inventor. He studied under artists in Florence and did his early work there.

Leonardo da Vinci studied many topics, including human anatomy. These sketches of the muscles of the arm are from his notebooks.

Leonardo was endlessly curious about all aspects of the world around him. He did not accept anything as true until he had proved it himself. In his notebooks, he made sketches and wrote about an amazing variety of topics. He wrote about geometry, engineering, sound, motion, and architecture. He studied anatomy, including the circulation of blood and the workings of the eye. He learned about the effects of the moon on Earth's tides. He was the first person to draw maps from an aerial, or above-ground, view. He designed bridges, weapons, and many other machines. Among his many farsighted ideas were an underwater diving suit and a helicopter.

Paving the Way for Modern Science and Mathematics

Other Italian scientists and mathematicians made breakthroughs, as well. Girolamo Cardano solved complex equations in algebra. Cardano did pioneering work in probability, the science of chance. Galileo Galilei conducted important experiments about gravity. He proved that a heavier object and a lighter object fall at the same rate. If the two objects are dropped from the same height, they reach the ground at the same time. Galileo also built the first telescope used to look into space. With his telescope, he was able to discover sunspots and the moons of the planet Jupiter. By emphasizing observation and experimentation, Galileo and other Renaissance scholars paved the way for modern science and mathematics.

28.8 Florentine Politics

The local government of Florence was housed in the Palazzo Vecchio, or Old Palace. Like other Italian city-states, Florence was ruled under a series of governing boards. These boards were often controlled by rich families. The powerful Medici family controlled Florence for nearly three centuries.

The Medici Family The Medici maintained their power in a number of ways. With their vast wealth, they built palaces and were able to maintain a strong army. They were involved in or controlled all aspects of life in the city. They were great sponsors of artists, writers, and musicians, whose works beautified Florence and made the city famous. The Medici also were constantly watchful for enemies who plotted against the family.

One of the most powerful members of the Medici family was Lorenzo the Magnificent. A leading patron of art and scholarship, Lorenzo ruled Florence for more than twenty years, from 1469 until his death in 1492. Two years later, a revolution forced the Medici into temporary exile. In 1512, the family regained power.

The Procession of the Magi is a fresco in one of the Medici palaces. It includes images of three generations of the powerful Renaissance family.

Niccolò Machiavelli a Renaissance statesman and historian who wrote *The Prince*

A Book About Politics A Florentine statesman and historian, **Niccolò Machiavelli** (mahk-ee-uh-VEL-ee), watched these struggles for power. During the Medici's exile, he reorganized the city's defenses. He also served as a diplomat and spent time observing the actions of other Italian rulers.

Machiavelli used his experiences to write a book called *The Prince*. The book is his account of how politics and government really work. Machiavelli advises rulers to make their states strong by doing what works best, rather than by doing what is good or moral. He said that they should even lie if it helps them to rule. In his view, the end, or purpose, justifies the means—the actions taken to achieve that purpose. Rulers, he wrote, should be feared rather than loved.

The Prince seems to contradict humanist ideals about people's goodness. Its cold realism shocked many readers of the time. Yet in other ways, the book shows the influence of humanist ideas. It is the product of one individual's careful observation and thinking. It is concerned with how things really work in the world. It also separates ideas about government from ideas about religion. In this respect, *The Prince* is a very modern work.

28.9 Florentine Commerce and Trade

One reason why Florence became a cultural center was the wealth that trade and commerce brought to the city. A thriving banking industry developed. Over time, Florence became Europe's banking hub, and richer than the largest kingdoms in Europe. Popes and kings alike borrowed money from its 80 banks.

There were two market centers in Renaissance Florence. At the Mercato Vecchio, or Old Market, people bought everyday items, such as food. The Mercato Vecchio was crowded and noisy. People from all over Europe came there to buy and sell goods.

The Mercato Nuovo, or New Market, was built in the mid-1500s as a center for the city's cloth and banking industries. City officials banned food and weapons there. They wanted it to be clean and orderly to show that commerce was highly valued in Florence.

The Mercato Nuovo became one of the largest financial marketplaces in Europe. People traveled from far and wide to get loans or to convert their money into florins, which could be exchanged for goods anywhere in Europe.

During the Renaissance, florins, the coins of Florence, were the most valuable coins in all of Europe. This one features a portrait of Lorenzo de Medici, known as "the Magnificent."

Chapter Summary

In this chapter, you visited Renaissance Florence to learn about advances that were made there in a number of fields.

The City of Florence Florence was the leading culture center of the Renaissance. Many Renaissance figures were born or grew up there. Located on the Arno River, the city also became a business center. Florentines used their wealth to support the arts and education.

Advances in Architecture and Engineering Renaissance architects and engineers studied Greek and Roman structures. They created new works based on classical styles, but were influenced by humanism and their own ideas. Brunelleschi's cathedral dome is a lasting symbol of Renaissance achievements in architecture and engineering.

Advances in Painting, Sculpture, and Literature Renaissance humanism also influenced artists, such as Donatello and Michelangelo, and writers, such as Dante. They created works based on experience in the real world. Dante was the first major writer to use the vernacular.

Advances in Science and Mathematics Renaissance thinkers began to experiment and use mathematics and logic to analyze the world. Figures such as Leonardo da Vinci and Galileo emphasized direct observation, paving the way for modern scientific methods.

Florentine Politics, Commerce, and Trade The powerful Medici family controlled Florence for nearly three centuries, and were involved in all aspects of the city's life. Niccolò Machiavelli used his experience and observations of Florentine politics to write *The Prince*. Under the Medici, the city became Europe's banking hub. The Mercato Vecchio and the Mercato Nuovo became two major centers of European trade and commerce.

Chapter 29

Leading Figures of the Renaissance

In what ways have various leading figures of the Renaissance affected modern society?

29.1 Introduction

The period in Europe known as the Renaissance began in Italy around 1300. In this chapter you will learn how Renaissance ideas spread from Italy across Europe. You will study the lives and work of ten leading figures of this rich cultural period.

From the 14th through the 16th centuries, Europe crackled with energy. Trade and commerce boomed. Cities grew. Artists and writers experimented with their crafts and created wonderful works of art and literature. New ways of thinking led to inventions and scientific discoveries. Rulers and wealthy patrons supported the work of artists, scientists, and explorers.

Why was there so much creative energy during the Renaissance? One reason was the Renaissance idea that people should be educated in many areas. People who studied art or music, for example, were also interested in science. To this day we still use the term "Renaissance person" to describe someone who is skilled and knowledgeable in many fields.

Leonardo da Vinci is often considered to be the ideal Renaissance person. Leonardo trained mainly as a painter, but he was also a scientist, engineer, musician, and architect. He designed fortifications, waterways, and machines. He studied and drew plants, animals, and people. In his notebooks, he sketched ideas for inventions that were far ahead of his time.

Leonardo is one of the ten Renaissance people you will study in this chapter. You will learn how contributions made by these leading figures affect society today. You will also learn how the Renaissance spread from its birthplace in Italy throughout Europe.

Leonardo da Vinci, shown in this self-portrait, was a major figure of the Renaissance. Because of his work in so many areas he became known as the ideal "Renaissance person."

◄ Renaissance artist Albrecht Dürer painted this self-portrait at age 26.

Johannes Gutenberg a German inventor who, in about 1450, developed the first printing press with movable type in Europe

After Gutenberg invented movable type, print shops, such as this one, created books and pamphlets more quickly and easily.

29.2 The Renaissance Spreads Through Europe

As you have read, the Renaissance began in Italy. From there it spread to France, Germany, Flanders (modern-day Belgium), Holland, England, and Spain.

The diffusion of Renaissance ideas occurred through trade, travel, and education. Italy was the gateway to Europe for much of the trade from Asia, Africa, and the Greek-speaking cities of the east. Traders moved through Italy to the rest of Europe, bringing a rich flow of new ideas along with their goods.

Visitors to Italy also helped spread Renaissance ideas. People from all over Europe traveled to Italy to learn, as well as to trade. Scholars went to study humanism and medicine. Artists studied Italian painting and sculpture to learn new styles and techniques.

When these travelers returned home, many of them founded art schools and universities. Artists taught others what they had learned in Italy. Scholars began to teach the new ideas of experimentation, observation, and logic.

The spread of ideas was made even easier by the invention of the printing press. This machine pressed inked type or plates onto paper to create many copies of a work. You may recall that the Chinese had learned to make paper and to print using wooden blocks. The Koreans had invented a kind of movable type. Gradually, knowledge of papermaking and examples of Asian printing reached Europe.

In about 1450, a German named **Johannes Gutenberg** dramatically improved on existing printing methods. He invented a printing press that used movable type—characters that could be rearranged and used over again. Unlike the Chinese, who used wooden blocks, Gutenberg cast his type in metal, which was much more durable.

Before Gutenberg's invention, most books were written and copied by hand. It could take four or five months to copy a 200-page book. The new press could produce 300 pages in a single day. As a result, books and short works, called pamphlets, could be made much more quickly and cheaply.

The number of printers in Europe increased rapidly. People used printed matter to communicate new ideas, discoveries, and inventions. And, since printed material was more widely **available,** more people learned to read.

29.3 Michelangelo, Italian Sculptor and Painter

Michelangelo (1475–1564) was one of the leading artists of the Renaissance. He was born in a small village near Florence and grew up to be one of the greatest painters and sculptors in history.

In this famous scene from the Sistine Chapel ceiling by Michelangelo, God reaches out to give life to Adam. According to the Bible story of creation, Adam was the first human on Earth.

Personality and Training Historians say that Michelangelo had a difficult childhood. His mother died when he was six years old. His father was stern and demanding. Perhaps this troubled early life contributed to Michelangelo's famously bad temper. Although he was very religious, he was known to use fierce words when he was angry. He was also intensely ambitious.

When Michelangelo was 13, he became an apprentice to a painter in Florence. At 15, he began studying with a sculptor who worked for the powerful Medici family. Michelangelo lived for a time in the Medici household. There he met many leading thinkers, artists, and writers.

Talents and Achievements Michelangelo was gifted in both sculpture and painting. His art combines Renaissance ideals of beauty with **emotional** expressiveness.

Michelangelo's sculptures show his amazing talent for carving lifelike figures from blocks of marble. When he was just 24, he carved his famous *La Pietà*. A *pietà* is a depiction of Mary, the mother of Jesus, mourning over her dead son. Michelangelo's *Pietà* shows Mary tenderly holding the body of Jesus across her lap.

Two other magnificent sculptures by Michelangelo are his *David* and *Moses*. Michelangelo's *David* is 17 feet tall. The statue combines great beauty with the intense look of a youth who is about to go into battle. Michelangelo's *Moses* is a strong, powerful figure. The statue shows Moses holding the Ten Commandments, which the Bible tells he received from God.

Michelangelo is perhaps best known for painting the ceiling of the Sistine Chapel, the pope's chapel in Rome. Michelangelo labored for almost four years on a high platform to complete this work. He covered the curved ceiling with brilliantly colored scenes from the Bible. The scenes contain over three hundred figures and continue to awe visitors to Rome today.

29.4 Titian, Italian Painter

Titian (TISH-uhn), who lived from about 1488 to 1576, was born in the Italian Alps. Early in life, his talent took him to the wealthy city-state of Venice. He became the city's greatest Renaissance painter.

This is one of many portraits of Holy Roman emperor Charles V that Titian painted during his years as court painter of Italy.

Personality and Training As a boy, Titian was sent to Venice to train with famous painters. He worked with an artist named Giorgione, who was a master of fresco painting. A *fresco* is a painting made on the wet plaster of a wall or ceiling. Titian also studied examples of art from Rome and Florence. In time, he outgrew the influence of his teachers and created his own style.

Titian was a persuasive man. According to legend, long after he was rich and famous, he persuaded patrons to support his art by claiming to be poor. But he was also quite generous with his friends.

Talents and Achievements Titian's early work was precise and detailed. Later he developed a freer style. He used blobs of paint to create vivid forms, colors, and textures. He was known for his inspired use of color and for loose, lively brushwork that made his pictures appear lifelike. His art also had a flair for expressing human personality.

Titian painted many scenes of classical myths and Bible stories. As a court painter, he created portraits of the rich and powerful. In 1516, he was named the official painter of Venice. Later, Holy Roman emperor Charles V made him court painter of Italy. Titian made many portraits of Charles V and other royalty.

Charles V greatly admired Titian's work. There is a story that the emperor once picked up a paintbrush that had fallen to the floor. Titian protested, "I am not worthy of such a servant." The emperor replied, "Titian is worthy to be served by Caesar," referring to the emperor of ancient Rome. Charles even made Titian a knight—a first-time honor for a painter.

29.5 Albrecht Dürer, German Artist

Albrecht Dürer (AHL-brekht DOOR-er), who lived from 1471 to 1528, was from the German city of Nuremberg. He earned fame for his paintings, drawings, prints, and essays about art.

Personality and Training As a boy, Dürer received a diverse education. The son of a goldsmith, he learned his father's trade. At 15, he began training with a well-known painter and printmaker. A printmaker uses printing to make copies of works of art. Dürer also studied math, Latin, and classical literature.

As a young man, Dürer traveled through Germany, Italy, and the Netherlands. He became friends with many humanist artists, writers, and thinkers. He studied classical sculpture for years to learn ideal human **proportions.** He wanted to be able to show the parts of the human body correctly sized in relation to each other.

Dürer's self-portraits show him to be a fashionable, confident man. He had an intellectual approach to life and art. He asked himself, "What is beauty?" His art was an attempt to answer that question.

Talents and Achievements In his painting, Dürer blended the detailed style of Germany with the perspective and idealized beauty he learned from Italian painting. He encouraged all artists to study mathematics as the key to understanding Renaissance and classical art.

Dürer was especially skilled at making engravings and woodcuts. These are prints made from an original that is specially prepared for printing. The original may be etched, or engraved, in metal or it may be cut into a block of wood. Then it is inked and re-inked to make copies. In Renaissance times, printers used engravings and woodcuts to illustrate books.

Much of Dürer's art shows religious figures. He also painted subjects from myths. Like other artists of his time, he made many portraits of royalty and wealthy patrons. He worked for years as a court artist for the Holy Roman emperor Maximilian I.

Dürer's work is widely admired, particularly his beautiful engravings and woodcuts. They set a new standard in print-making because of their clarity, expressiveness, and fine detail.

Dürer's woodcut *The Four Horsemen of the Apocalypse* illustrates a vision of the end of the world described in the Christian Bible.

29.6 Nicolaus Copernicus, Polish Scientist

Nicolaus Copernicus (1473–1543) was born in Torun, Poland. He is often called the "father of modern astronomy."

Personality and Training When Copernicus was ten years old, his father died. His uncle, a Catholic bishop, became his guardian. He made sure that Copernicus received a good education.

As a young man, Copernicus attended the University of Krakow in Poland. Then he went to Italy to study medicine and Church law. In Italy, he rented rooms from an astronomy teacher. Soon he became fascinated by astronomy.

Copernicus's scientific work would show that he was highly creative. He was also a free thinker, unafraid to question accepted beliefs.

Talents and Achievements Copernicus was skilled in mathematics and observation. He based his thinking on what he truly saw, rather than on what he thought he should see.

Like other people of his time, Copernicus had been taught that Earth was at the center of the universe. According to this idea, the sun, stars, and planets travel around Earth.

As Copernicus studied the motion of the planets, he became dissatisfied with this explanation. He proposed a revolutionary idea. In reality, Earth and the other planets **orbit** the sun. Earth rotates, or turns, on its axis. This turning is what makes the sun and other objects in the heavens seem to move across the sky around Earth.

In 1514, Copernicus printed a booklet that outlined his theory. Then he began years of work on a full-length book. He titled it *On the Revolutions of the Celestial Spheres.* (*Celestial* means "heavenly.")

Copernicus dedicated his book to the pope. However, the idea of Earth traveling around the sun went against the Roman Catholic Church's belief that God had placed humans at the center of the universe. In 1616, the Church forbade people to read Copernicus's book.

Despite the Church's disapproval, Copernicus's theory had a major influence on a few key scientists. Eventually, it was proved to be correct. Today, the Copernican theory is part of the basis of modern astronomy.

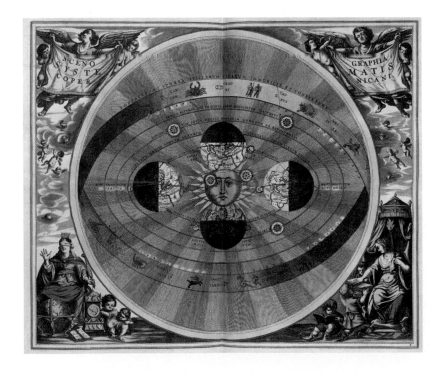

Since ancient times, most people believed that Earth was at the center of the universe. This engraving illustrates Copernicus's theory that Earth and the other planets travel around the sun.

29.7 Andreas Vesalius, Belgian Scientist

Andreas Vesalius (1514–1564) was born in Brussels, in what is now Belgium. He became an outstanding scientist. His work changed medicine and the study of anatomy.

Personality and Training Vesalius came from a family of doctors and pharmacists. Pharmacists are people who prepare medicines. He was always interested in living things and, especially, in anatomy.

Vesalius attended universities in Flanders, France, and Italy. In 1537, he earned his medical degree, specializing in anatomy. Later, he became a personal doctor to Italian and Spanish royalty.

Vesalius was hardworking, curious, and confident. He was also said to be gloomy and distant at times.

Talents and Achievements Vesalius was a talented observer and an independent thinker. He also had the artistic skill necessary to make detailed drawings of his scientific observations.

In Vesalius's time, physicians' understanding of human anatomy was based on the works of the ancient Greek physician Galen. Vesalius studied Galen, but he soon broke with this tradition. Like Copernicus, he was determined to observe things for himself.

Vesalius began dissecting, or cutting apart to study, dead human bodies. His research showed that Galen's work had relied on studies of animals. As a result, it had many errors when applied to human anatomy and medicine.

Vesalius made many discoveries about the human body. For example, he showed that the human heart has four hollow areas, called chambers. His discoveries led him to write his own seven-volume textbook of anatomy.

Vesalius called his book *On the Structure of the Human Body*. It explains how the body functions. The book contains prints by artists that were based on Vesalius's drawings of the body.

Vesalius's book was a major breakthrough. It changed what people knew about human anatomy and how they studied it. It also changed physicians' understanding of medicine. His book is considered to be the world's first modern medical textbook.

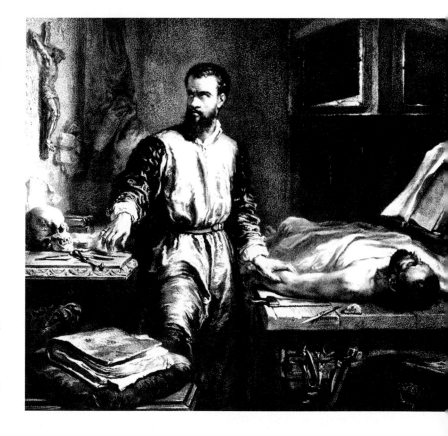

Vesalius dissected dead bodies to study human anatomy. He insisted on performing dissections himself, rather than relying on untrained assistants.

Queen Isabella I helped sponsor Christopher Columbus's attempt to find a route across the Atlantic Ocean to Asia. Instead of Asia, Columbus found the Americas.

29.8 Isabella I, Queen of Spain

Queen Isabella I (1451–1504) was born in the Spanish kingdom of Castile. She is best known for creating a unified Spain and for sponsoring the voyages of Christopher Columbus.

Personality and Training Isabella was the daughter of the king of Castile. She was highly intelligent, strong-willed, and a devoted Catholic. Girls at that time received little education, so Isabella's schooling was limited. In adulthood, she educated herself by learning Latin. As queen, she supported scholarship and art, collected fine paintings, and built schools.

Talents and Achievements Isabella was a forceful and brave ruler. In 1469, she married Prince Ferdinand of Aragon, the other major kingdom in Spain at that time. In 1474, Isabella became queen of Castile. When Ferdinand inherited the throne of Aragon in 1479, the two monarchs ruled jointly over much of Spain. They fought several battles to unify the rest of the nation.

Isabella and Ferdinand actively encouraged exploration. Isabella gave her support to Christopher Columbus, an Italian who proposed finding a new sea route to Asia. In 1492, Columbus sailed across the Atlantic and stumbled upon the Americas. His discovery of this so-called **New World** would lead to a Spanish empire and create great wealth for Spain.

New World the name given by Europeans to the Americas, which were unknown to most Europeans before the voyages of Christopher Columbus

Isabella and Ferdinand also sought to strengthen Spain as a unified Catholic country. Jews who refused to convert to Catholicism were forced to leave. This harsh action cost Spain many of its most talented and productive citizens. For Spanish Jews, it was a tragedy.

29.9 Elizabeth I, Queen of England

Queen Elizabeth I (1533–1603) was one of England's most popular and successful monarchs. Born in London, she was the daughter of King Henry VIII and his queen at the time, Anne Boleyn.

Personality and Training When Elizabeth was two years old, King Henry lost interest in Queen Anne. Claiming that Anne had been unfaithful to him, he ordered her beheading.

Elizabeth was raised in a separate household, largely away from the royal court. An English scholar became her teacher and educated her as a possible future monarch. Elizabeth was a gifted student. She became highly educated and learned to speak Greek, Latin, French, and Italian.

Elizabeth was a strong-minded ruler, but she was not stubborn. As monarch, she was willing to listen to good advice and always kept in mind what was best for the people of England.

Talents and Achievements Elizabeth became queen at age 25 and reigned for 45 years, until her death. She never married, because she feared that a husband would take her power. She said she was married to the people of England.

One of the great monarchs of England, Elizabeth I created peace and stability during her long rule.

Elizabeth was a hard-working and able ruler. She was independent, but she was also flexible. She was willing to change unpopular policies. She showed political skill in balancing the interests of different people in her court. She inspired great love and loyalty from her subjects, who called her "Good Queen Bess."

Elizabeth's long reign is often called England's Golden Age. Culture thrived under her rule. She supported theater, fashion, literature, dance, and education. Poets and playwrights during her rule composed some of the greatest works in the English language.

Elizabeth worked to strengthen England's economy, and she encouraged trade and commerce. She **authorized** English trading companies in Africa, Asia, and the Americas. Her funding of sea exploration helped England gain territory in North America. In 1588, the English navy defeated the Spanish Armada, a mighty fleet that tried to attack England. This victory sparked a national celebration and further strengthened England's sea power. By the time Elizabeth died, England was one of the strongest and richest countries in the world.

29.10 William Shakespeare, English Poet and Playwright

William Shakespeare (1564–1616) was born in the English town of Stratford-on-Avon. He was a major figure of the English Renaissance. He is widely considered to be the world's greatest playwright and one of its finest poets.

Personality and Training As a boy, Shakespeare studied Latin and classical literature in grammar school. He never went to a university. His plays, however, show a broad knowledge of many subjects, from history and politics to music and art.

In his early twenties, Shakespeare became an actor with a theater company in London. He learned about drama by performing and writing plays. Many of his plays were first presented at London's Globe Theatre. Queen Elizabeth, among many others, enjoyed his work.

Shakespeare had a reputation for being quiet and a bit mysterious. His writings show that he was curious and keenly observant. He thought deeply about life and its sufferings. Yet he also had a sense of humor and found much to laugh at in life.

Talents and Achievements Shakespeare was a skilled actor, but he was an even greater poet and playwright. He had an enormous talent for expressing thoughts and feelings in memorable words. His plays show that he had a deep understanding of human behavior and emotions. Above all, he had the skill to present his understanding through vivid characters and exciting drama.

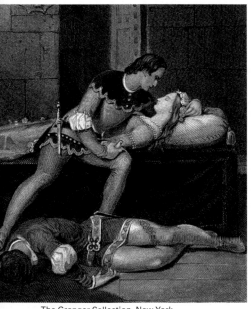

The Granger Collection, New York

Shakespeare wrote about life with both humor and drama. This tragic scene is from his play *Romeo and Juliet.*

Shakespeare's poetry is widely admired, especially the 14-line poems called sonnets. He is best known, however, for his 38 plays. He wrote both comedies and tragedies. Many of his plays are still performed around the world, and several have been made into television series or movies. Among the most popular are *Romeo and Juliet, Hamlet, Macbeth, Julius Caesar, All's Well That Ends Well,* and *The Merchant of Venice.*

Shakespeare's plays cover a broad range of subjects. He wrote about history, romance, politics, prejudice, murder, and war. His plays remain popular in part because he wrote about timeless, universal themes such as love, jealousy, power, ambition, hatred, and fear.

Shakespeare has had a deep influence on later writers. He also left a lasting mark on the English language. Many common sayings come from Shakespeare, such as "Much ado about nothing." People often quote his witty, wise lines, sometimes without knowing that they owe their clever or graceful words to Shakespeare.

Miguel Cervantes the Spanish Renaissance author of the masterpiece *Don Quixote*

29.11 Miguel Cervantes, Spanish Writer

Miguel Cervantes (mi-GEL ser-VAN-tayz) was born near Madrid, Spain. He lived from 1547 to 1616. He is best known for his comic novel *Don Quixote* (DON kee-HOH-tay).

Personality and Training Little is known about Cervantes' education. He may have studied with priests influenced by humanism. It is certain that he loved to read.

Much of Cervantes' education came through experience. At 23, he became a soldier. In a battle at sea, he was shot twice in the chest. He also injured his left hand so badly that the hand became useless. Several years later, he was taken prisoner at sea by pirates. He spent five years as a slave in North Africa until his family bought his freedom.

Cervantes' early life shows that he was adventurous and courageous. His sense of humor could be biting, but he also turned it on himself. He once bragged that the public liked his plays enough not to boo them off the stage or throw vegetables at the actors.

Talents and Achievements A gifted writer, Cervantes wrote many plays, poems, and novels. He had a particular talent for satire. His masterpiece, *Don Quixote,* pokes fun at romantic stories of heroic knights, as well as at Spanish society. The novel's title character, Don Quixote, is an elderly man who has read too many tales of glorious knights. Although the age of knights is past, he dresses up in rusty armor and sets out to do noble deeds. With him is short, stout Sancho Panza. Sancho is an ordinary farmer who rides a mule, but Don Quixote sees him as his faithful squire, or armor bearer.

Don Quixote is the hero of Cervantes' comic novel of the same name. This sculpture in Spain shows Don Quixote dressed as a knight. At his side is Sancho, a farmer whom Don Quixote named as his squire.

Together the two men have a series of comic adventures. In Don Quixote's imagination, country inns turn into castles and windmills become fearsome giants. While his adventures are very funny, there is something noble about the way he bravely fights evil, even if his deeds are only in his mind.

Don Quixote was very popular in Spain. King Philip III supposedly saw a man reading and laughing so hard that he was crying. The king said, "That man is either crazy or he is reading *Don Quixote*." Today, *Don Quixote* is considered one of the masterpieces of world literature.

29.12   Leonardo da Vinci, Renaissance Person

Leonardo da Vinci (1452–1519) was born in a village near Florence in Italy. His wide range of interests and accomplishments made him a true Renaissance person.

The *Mona Lisa* is one of Leonardo da Vinci's best-known paintings. This surprisingly small painting—only about 20 by 30 inches—has had a huge and lasting influence on other artists.

Personality and Training   Leonardo trained in Florence under a master sculptor and painter. All his life he studied many subjects, including painting, sculpture, music, math, anatomy, botany, architecture, and engineering.

Leonardo spent much of his life in Florence and Milan. He worked as an artist, engineer, and architect for kings, popes, and wealthy commoners. He had a special love for animals. Sometimes he bought caged animals at the market and set them free. He also was a vegetarian, which was quite unusual at the time.

Talents and Achievements   Leonardo was gifted in many fields. He was an accomplished painter, sculptor, architect, and engineer.

Leonardo's notebooks show him to be one of the greatest creative minds of all time. Like Albrecht Dürer, he closely studied proportions. He made precise drawings of people, animals, and plants. He also sketched out ideas about geometry and mechanics, the science of motion and force. He designed weapons, buildings, and a variety of machines. Many of the inventions he imagined, such as a helicopter and a submarine, were centuries ahead of their time.

Leonardo's paintings are among the world's greatest works of art. One of his masterpieces is the *Mona Lisa,* a painting of a woman with a mysterious smile. It is among the most famous paintings in the world. Like his other works, it displays a remarkable use of perspective, balance, and detail. The rich effects of shade and color reveal Leonardo's close study of light. Students of his art also detect how principles of geometry helped him organize the space in his paintings.

Leonardo's work inspired other great artists, such as Michelangelo. With his many interests and talents, Leonardo is a perfect example of the spirit of the Renaissance.

In this chapter, you learned how the Renaissance spread from Italy across Europe. Then you studied the lives and accomplishments of ten major Renaissance figures.

The Renaissance Spreads Through Europe Renaissance ideas spread through trade, travel, and education. People from across Europe went to Italy to learn and to trade. When they returned home, they passed on the new ideas. Many founded schools and universities. The spread of the Renaissance was made even easier by Gutenberg's new printing press.

Michelangelo, Titian, and Dürer Renaissance artists like Michelangelo, Titian, and Dürer created many kinds of art. They studied human anatomy and mathematics that helped them to create works of art based on humanist ideals of realism and beauty.

Copernicus and Vesalius Through observation and fresh thinking, scientists Copernicus and Vesalius dramatically increased human knowledge. Copernicus discovered that Earth and other planets in our solar system revolve around the sun, not Earth. Vesalius' studies of anatomy and his detailed drawings changed how people understood the human body.

Isabella I and Elizabeth I Queen Isabella and Queen Elizabeth were strong leaders who supported the arts and encouraged exploration. Both monarchs improved their nations and financed important explorations that increased Europeans' knowledge of the world.

Shakespeare and Cervantes Shakespeare and Cervantes created masterpieces of world literature. Both writers created lyrical and expressive works that explored humanist ideas and enriched their native languages.

Leonardo da Vinci Leonardo da Vinci was a creative genius who embodied the spirit of the Renaissance. His studies in topics such as art, architecture, and engineering led him to invent many devices that were far ahead of his time, as well as timeless works of art.

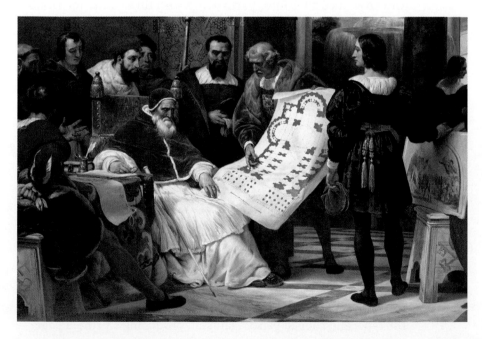

The Renaissance popes were important art patrons. Here, Pope Julius II (seated) reviews plans for St. Peter's Basilica with architect Donato Bramante (center), Michelangelo (left of Bramante), and the artist Raphael (right of Bramante).

Johannes Gutenberg's invention of movable metal type revolutionized the transfer of information in Europe.

From Gutenberg to the Internet

Around 1450, Johannes Gutenberg invented a printing press that used movable metal type. Before Gutenberg's press, books and other printed materials were made by hand. Printed material was costly to make and to buy. Gutenberg's invention changed Europe by making books more affordable and by spreading information faster and to more people. Today, Gutenberg is known as the inventor of printing in Europe. But his achievements were hard won—and his invention was almost taken away from him.

The year is 1455, and Johannes Gutenberg sits in a courtroom. Across from him is Johann Fust, who has sued Gutenberg. The two men are bitter enemies. Gutenberg shifts nervously, waiting for the judges' decision. If the judges rule against him, he will lose everything—including the printing press that he has worked for 20 years to perfect.

Gutenberg was born in Mainz, Germany, sometime between 1394 and 1400. He found, at a young age, that he loved to work with metal. He worked with craftsmen in the city and slowly learned their secrets. He showed an extraordinary talent, mastering the technology of turning metal into beautiful objects. He was also fired with the ambition to do something special that people would remember.

In 1428, Gutenberg moved from Mainz to Strasbourg. He started a business cutting gemstones to make jewelry. The company thrived, and he formed a business partnership with three other men. Soon they were making mirrors and other quality products.

Early Printing and Movable Type

During the 1430s, Gutenberg saw the chance to do something even greater—to develop a printing press that lowered the cost of books. Printing was first developed in China and Japan in the 8th century. Craftspeople in those countries spent hours carving an image into a block of wood. They rolled ink onto the raised parts and pressed the image against paper.

Korean craftspeople were the first to develop metal movable type, in which the characters could be rearranged to form different words. During the 13th century, they formed type by heating bronze to a temperature high enough to make it liquid. They poured the bronze into molds formed in sand, and the bronze hardened and formed type. They then used the type to form all the words on a page, applied ink to the type, and rubbed paper against it, producing a printed page.

In 1377, the Koreans printed a text for Buddhists. It is the oldest known book in the world printed with movable metal type.

Europeans did not develop movable type for another 200 years. Until then, monks and nuns in monasteries painstakingly copied books by hand. Many of the books were unique works of art. They had huge, colorful capital letters, complex illustrations, and the edge of each page was lined with gold. But these books were incredibly expensive. A person had to work an average of 300 days to make just one book. Historians estimate that the typical book might cost between $200 and $250 in today's dollars. Only the very wealthy could afford such items.

Inventing Type, a Press, and Ink

Gutenberg turned his creative genius to developing a way to print books that would cost far less money. He faced three challenges—developing type, creating a printing press, and mixing the right ink. To create type, he had to decide what metal to use. It couldn't be too hard because then it wouldn't melt. It couldn't be too soft because then the type wouldn't last. Finally, he hit on a brilliant idea. Instead of one metal, he would blend different metals. He created an alloy—or combination of metals—which included 80 percent lead, 5 percent tin, and 15 percent of a metal called antimony.

To make the letter *a,* for example, he heated the metal until it melted, poured it into a mold, let it cool, and then removed the metal from the mold. Now he had the type for the letter *a,* which he could use over and over again. He did the same for all the other letters and for punctuation.

With movable type, the printer selects individual letters to form words. The letters can be used repeatedly in different combinations. Although movable type has been mostly replaced by new technology, huge printing presses produce vast amounts of printed information every day.

Although much of the work of type setting and printing books was still done by hand on Gutenberg presses like this one, it was vastly quicker than writing out each copy.

Next, Gutenberg needed to find the right ink. It couldn't be too thin, because then it would leave smudges on the paper. It couldn't be too thick, or it would clog the type. Gutenberg experimented for a long time and finally used linseed oil. To make it black, he added soot, which he got from lamps.

Finally, Gutenberg had to build a press. Historians believe that he probably adapted a press that papermakers used to dry stacks of paper. In his press, Gutenberg set the type and rolled ink onto the type. Then he turned a giant screw that lowered the type onto paper. In a few seconds, he could print a page that would have taken a monk hours to copy. More importantly, he could make many copies of the same page very quickly.

Printing Success and Business Setbacks

Gutenberg made great progress on the printing press, but he faced some serious business problems. First, one of his partners died. Then the man's relatives sued Gutenberg to get control of the business. Gutenberg was relieved when the court ruled in his favor. But even though he won, the lawsuit kept him from finishing his printing press.

Gutenberg's problems got worse. He ignored the jewelry business, and his income sank. Yet he was spending money to buy metals, a press, and inks. He went into debt, but he kept working on the printing press. Finally, in 1446, he had his first major triumph, when he printed a short poem. Soon after, he printed a grammar book. It became a bestseller throughout Europe.

These early books were plain, and Gutenberg wanted to print something wonderfully beautiful. Money was still a big problem. So Gutenberg formed a partnership with Johann Fust, a wealthy businessman in Mainz. Fust loaned him 1,600 guldens, which at that time was a fortune. Historians have estimated that just 100 guldens could buy a small farm. The two men planned to print a book that would sell extremely well and give them a good return on their investment. But what kind of a book should it be?

Printing a Bible

Finally they came up with a brilliant idea—they would print a Bible that was extraordinary in every way. Around 1455, Gutenberg started preparations. The Bible would have two volumes: the Old Testament and the New Testament. It would have 42 lines per page, and the two volumes together would contain 1,282 pages. Every page would have 2,000 letters. For this monumental task, Gutenberg had to create 290 pieces of type, including capital letters, lower case letters, and punctuation. He planned to print 210 copies.

While Gutenberg was aiming for perfection, Fust was growing impatient. He had invested 1,600 guldens in the printing press, but in five years, the investment had not earned him one penny. He filed a lawsuit against Gutenberg, demanding that his money be returned. Gutenberg simply didn't have the money. He desperately needed the judges to find in his favor.

But the judges ruled against Gutenberg. They said that Fust had waited long enough to earn a profit on the money that he had invested. Gutenberg had to repay Fust. Since Gutenberg didn't have the funds, the court allowed Fust to take over the business, including the typefaces and the printing press. Fust even hired away Gutenberg's most skilled assistant. Together, they finished work on the Bible that Gutenberg had started and began to sell it. This remarkable book became an instant bestseller. Fust made a good deal of money from the sweat, tears, and genius that Gutenberg had poured into the project.

Yet Gutenberg was an amazingly stubborn man. Fust had taken away his business, but he couldn't take away Gutenberg's knowledge and skills. He found another financial backer, Dr. Konrad Humery, who helped him set up a printing shop in Mainz. Gutenberg printed philosophical writings, a dictionary, and other works, all with the extraordinary quality that was his trademark. He also trained printers, who spread his printing technology throughout Europe.

Books: The Internet of the Time

Gutenberg's amazing invention made books the Internet of the time. The printing press made it possible to produce books much more quickly and cheaply than ever before. By 1463, printed Bibles cost one-tenth of hand-copied Bibles. The demand for books exploded. By 1500, Europe had more than 1,000 printers and 7,000 books in print.

Like the Internet, books spread new ideas quickly and sped up the process of change. For example, as a young sailor in Genoa, Christopher Columbus read Marco Polo's famous *Travels,* in which he described his journeys to China. Columbus was thrilled by Polo's descriptions. Books also planted the seeds of democracy and human rights in the next generation of thinkers. Newspapers and pamphlets generated information and ideas even faster.

In 1465, the Archbishop of Mainz gave Gutenberg a pension for the "agreeable and willing service" that he had provided to the city and to Germany. Gutenberg died in 1468, and Dr. Humery inherited everything. Yet the Archbishop refused to let the doctor move Gutenberg's printing press. The city was honored to be the birthplace of printing in Europe. Gutenberg would always be known as the father of an invention that truly changed the world.

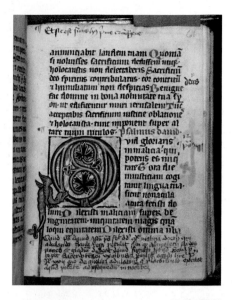

One advantage of the new, printed books, like the Gutenberg Bible (bottom), over the earlier, hand-copied versions (top) was that each printed copy was neat and exactly the same.

Chapter 30

The Reformation Begins

What factors led to the weakening of the Catholic Church and the beginning of the Reformation?

30.1 Introduction

At the height of the Renaissance, western Europe was still Roman Catholic. In this chapter, you will learn about the beginnings of the Reformation. This movement led to the start of many new Christian churches that broke away from the Catholic Church.

The Reformation began in the early 1500s and lasted into the 1600s. Until then, all Christians in western Europe were Catholics. But even before the Reformation, the Church's religious and moral authority was starting to weaken.

One reason for the weakening of the Church was the humanism of the Renaissance. Humanists often were secular, or nonreligious, in their thinking. They believed in free thought and questioned many accepted beliefs.

Problems within the Church added to this spirit of questioning. Many Catholics were dismayed by worldliness and corruption (immoral and dishonest behavior) in the Church. Sometimes, bishops and clergy used questionable practices to raise money. Some popes seemed more concerned with power and wealth than with spiritual matters.

These problems led a number of Catholics to call for reform. They questioned the authority of Church leaders and some of the Church's teachings. Some broke away from the Church entirely. They became known as "Protestants" because of their protests against the Catholic Church. The establishment of Protestant churches divided Christians into many separate groups.

In this chapter, you will learn more about the factors that weakened the Roman Catholic Church. You will learn how a German priest, Martin Luther, ignited a movement that ended the religious unity of Europe. You will also learn about other early reformers and leaders of the Reformation.

German priest Martin Luther called for reforms in the Catholic Church that brought about the Reformation.

◀ Corruption in the Church led to questions about the morals of Church officials.

indulgence a grant by the Catholic Church that released a person from punishment for sins

simony the selling and buying of positions in the Catholic Church

30.2 The Weakening of the Catholic Church

By the Late Middle Ages, two major problems were weakening the Roman Catholic Church. The first was worldliness and corruption within the Church. The second was political conflict between the pope and European monarchs.

Worldliness and Corruption Within the Church During the Middle Ages, the Catholic Church united the Christians of western Europe in a single faith. But the Church was a political and economic institution as well as a religious one. By the 1300s, many Catholics felt that the Church had become far too worldly and corrupt.

Too often, Church officials failed to live up to their role as spiritual leaders. For example, priests, monks, and nuns made vows, or solemn promises, not to marry or have children. Yet many broke these vows. Others seemed to ignore Christian values. Church leaders often behaved like royalty instead of God's servants. For example, the popes, and many cardinals and bishops, were extremely wealthy and powerful.

People were also troubled by the way many Church officials raised money to support the church. One method was the practice of selling **indulgences**. An indulgence is a release from punishment for sins.

The practice of selling indulgences suggested that people could buy forgiveness for their sins. This and other moneymaking practices led people to distrust the Church.

During the Middle Ages, the Church granted indulgences in return for gifts to the Church and good works. People who received indulgences did not have to perform good deeds to make up for their sins. Over time, popes and bishops began selling indulgences as a way of raising money. This practice made it seem that people could buy forgiveness for their sins. Many Catholics were deeply disturbed by the abuse of indulgences.

The Church also sold offices, or leadership positions. This practice is called **simony**. Instead of being chosen based on their merit and accomplishments, buyers simply paid for their jobs. Buying an office was worthwhile because it could be a source of income. Often, people acquired multiple offices in different places without actually going there to perform their duties.

People questioned other practices as well. Some clergy charged pilgrims to see holy objects, such as the relics of **saints.**

The Granger Collection, New York

In addition, all Catholics paid taxes to the Church. Many people resented having to pay taxes to Rome as well as to their own governments.

Political Conflicts with European Rulers In the Middle Ages, the pope became a powerful political figure, as well as a religious leader. The Church also accumulated vast wealth. Its political and economic power presented a problem for monarchs, because the Church claimed that its clergy were independent of political rulers' control.

As monarchs tried to increase their own power, they often came into conflict with the pope. They quarreled with the pope over Church property and the right to make appointments to Church offices. Popes also became involved in other political conflicts. These disputes added to the questioning of the pope's authority. At times, the conflicts damaged the Church's reputation.

When Pope Clement V moved his headquarters from Italy to France in 1309, the quarrel between King Philip IV and the pope ended.

One dramatic crisis unfolded in France in 1301. When King Philip IV tried to tax the French clergy, the pope threatened to force him out of the Church. In response, soldiers hired by the king kidnapped the pope. The pope was soon released, but he died a few weeks later.

The quarrel with the king ended under Pope Clement V. In 1309, Clement moved his headquarters from Rome to the French city of Avignon. He appointed 24 new cardinals during his reign, 22 of whom were French. The next six popes also lived in Avignon and named still more French cardinals. Many Europeans believed that France's kings now controlled the papacy, or the office of the pope. As a result, they lost respect for the pope as the supreme head of the Church.

An even worse crisis developed after Pope Gregory XI moved the papacy back to Rome in 1377. In 1378, Gregory died, and an Italian was elected pope. The new pope refused to move back to Avignon. A group of cardinals, most of them French, left Rome and elected a rival pope. The Church now had two popes, one in Rome and one in Avignon. Later, a Church council elected a third pope. Each pope claimed to be the real head of the Church.

This division in the Church is called the Great Schism. For nearly 40 years, the various lines of popes denounced each other as impostors. Catholics were divided and confused. The Great Schism lessened people's respect for the papacy and sparked calls for reform.

Priest Jan Hus was an early reformer who agreed with Wycliffe's ideas and spoke against the pope. For this, he was burned at the stake as a heretic.

30.3 Early Calls for Reform

By the 1300s, the Church was beginning to lose some of its moral and religious standing. Many Catholics, including clergy, criticized the corruption and abuses in the Church. They challenged the authority of the pope. Some began to question Church teachings and to develop new forms of Christian faith.

Reformers wanted to purify the Church, not destroy it. By challenging the Church's practices and teachings, however, they helped pave the way for the dramatic changes of the **Reformation**.

Reformation a religious reform movement from the early 1500s to the 1600s that led to the formation of new Christian groups

John Wycliffe (About 1330–1384) John Wycliffe (WIH-cliff) was a scholar from England. Wycliffe challenged the Church's right to money that it demanded from England. When the Great Schism began, he publicly questioned the pope's authority. He also criticized indulgences and immoral behavior on the part of the clergy.

During the Middle Ages, Church officials tried to control how the Bible was interpreted. Wycliffe believed that the Bible, not the Church, was the supreme source of religious authority. Against Church tradition, he had the Bible translated from Latin into English so that common people could read it.

The pope accused Wycliffe of heresy, or opinions that contradict official **doctrine**. Wycliffe's followers were persecuted, and some of them were burned to death as heretics, or people who behave against official teachings. After his death, the Church had Wycliffe's writings burned, too. Despite the Church's opposition, however, Wycliffe's ideas had wide influence.

Jan Hus (About 1370–1415) Jan Hus (huhs) was a priest in Bohemia, which today is in the Czech Republic. He read Wycliffe's writings and agreed with many of his ideas. Hus criticized the vast wealth of the Church and spoke out against the pope's authority. The true head of the Church, he said, was Jesus Christ.

Hus wanted to purify the Church and return it to the people. He called for an end to corruption among the clergy. He wanted both the Bible and the mass to be offered in the common language of the people instead of in Latin. In 1414, Hus was arrested and charged with heresy. In July 1415, he was burned at the stake.

Like Wycliffe, Hus had a major influence on future reformers. Martin Luther would later say that he and his supporters were "all Hussites without knowing it."

Catherine of Siena (1347–1380) Catherine of Siena was a mystic—a person deeply devoted to religion and who has spiritual experiences. Born in the Italian city of Siena, she began having visions of Jesus when she was a child.

Catherine spent many long hours in prayer and wrote many letters about spiritual life. She also involved herself in Church affairs. Her pleas helped to convince Pope Gregory XI to move the papacy back to Rome from Avignon. Later, she traveled to Rome to attempt to end the Great Schism.

In 1461, the Church declared Catherine a saint. Her example showed that people could lead spiritual lives that went beyond the usual customs of the Church. She and other mystics emphasized personal experience of God more than formal observance of Church practices. This approach to faith helped prepare people for the ideas of the Reformation.

Desiderius Erasmus (1466–1536) Desiderius Erasmus was a humanist from Holland. A priest and devoted Catholic, he was one of the most outspoken figures in the call for reform.

In 1509, Erasmus published a book called *The Praise of Folly*. (*Folly* means "foolishness.") The book was a sharply worded satire of society, including abuses by clergy and Church leaders. Erasmus argued for a return to simple Christian goodness.

Erasmus wanted to reform the Church from within. He angrily denied that he was a **Protestant** who wanted to break away from the Catholic Church. Yet perhaps more than any other individual, he helped to prepare Europe for the Reformation. His attacks on corruption in the Church contributed to many people's desire to leave Catholicism. For this reason, it is often said that "Erasmus laid the egg, and Luther hatched it."

Protestant a Christian who separated from the Roman Catholic Church during the Reformation; today, any member of a Christian church founded on the principles of the Reformation

Catholic priest Erasmus of Holland was perhaps the most influential person in spreading the ideas of reform before the Reformation.

30.4 Martin Luther Breaks Away from the Church

In the early 1500s in Germany, then part of the Holy Roman Empire, a priest named **Martin Luther** became involved in a serious dispute with Church authorities. Condemned by the Catholic Church, Luther began the first Protestant church, which started the Reformation.

Martin Luther a German priest who broke away from the Catholic Church to start his own religion, Lutheranism. His posting of the Ninety-Five Theses started the Reformation.

Luther's Early Life Luther was born in Germany in 1483 and was raised as a devout Catholic. Luther's father wanted him to become a lawyer. As a young man, however, Luther was badly frightened when he was caught in a violent thunderstorm. As lightning flashed around him, he vowed that if he survived he would become a monk.

Luther kept his promise and joined an order of monks. Later, he became a priest. He studied the Bible thoroughly and earned a reputation as a scholar and teacher.

Luther nailed his list of 95 arguments, called the Ninety-Five Theses, to a church door in Wittenberg, Germany. Church leaders condemned the ideas in this document.

Luther Pushes for Change in the Catholic Church The Church stressed that keeping the sacraments and living a good life were the keys to salvation. Luther's studies of the Bible led him to a different answer. No one, he believed, could earn salvation. Instead, salvation was a gift from God that people received in faith. People, he said, were saved by their faith, not by doing good works.

Luther's views brought him into conflict with the Church over indulgences. In 1517, Pope Leo X needed money to finish building St. Peter's Basilica, the grand cathedral in Rome. He sent preachers around Europe to sell indulgences. Buyers were promised pardons of all of their sins and those of friends and family. Luther was outraged. He felt that the Church was selling false salvation to uneducated people.

Luther posted a list of arguments, called **theses,** against indulgences and Church abuses on a church door in the town of Wittenberg. He also sent the list, called the Ninety-Five Theses, to Church leaders.

Luther's theses caused considerable controversy. Many people were excited by his ideas, while the Church condemned them. Gradually, he was drawn into more serious disagreements with Church authorities.

In response to critics, Luther published pamphlets that explained his thinking. He argued that the Bible—not the pope or Church leaders—was the ultimate source of religious authority. The only true sacraments, he said, were baptism and the Eucharist. The Church's other five sacraments had no basis in the Bible. Moreover, Luther said that all Christians were priests, and, therefore, all should study the Bible for themselves.

In the eyes of Church leaders, Luther was attacking fundamental truths of the Catholic religion. In January 1521, Pope Leo X excommunicated him. To be excommunicated means to no longer be allowed membership in a church.

In April 1521, Luther was brought before the Diet, an assembly of state leaders, in the German city of Worms. At the risk of his life, he refused to take back his teachings. The Holy Roman emperor, Charles V, declared Luther a heretic and forbid the printing or selling of his writings. For a time Luther went into hiding. But the movement he had started continued to spread.

Luther Starts His Own Church Many Germans saw Luther as a hero. As his popularity grew, he continued to develop his ideas. Soon he was openly organizing a new Christian **denomination** known as Lutheranism. The new church emphasized study of the Bible. Luther translated the Bible into German. He also wrote a baptism service, a mass, and new hymns (sacred songs) in German.

Having rejected the Church's hierarchy, Luther looked to German princes to support his church. When a peasants' revolt broke out in 1524, the rebels expected Luther to support their demands for social and economic change. Instead, Luther denounced the peasants and sided with the rulers. He needed the help of Germany's rulers to keep his new church growing. By the time the uprising was crushed, tens of thousands of peasants had been brutally killed. Many peasants, therefore, rejected Lutheranism.

Several princes, however, supported Luther, and Lutheranism continued to grow. Over the next 30 years, Lutherans and Catholics were often at war in Germany. These religious wars ended in 1555 with the Peace of Augsburg. According to this **treaty,** each prince within the Holy Roman Empire could determine the religion of his subjects.

The Peace of Augsburg was a major victory for Protestantism. Christian unity was at an end, and not only in Germany. As you will learn next, by this time a number of other Protestant churches had sprung up in northern Europe.

denomination a particular religious group within a larger faith; for example, Lutheranism is one denomination within Christianity.

At the Diet of Worms, the Holy Roman emperor, Charles V, declared Luther a heretic and forbade the printing of his writings.

The printing press and booksellers, such as this man, helped to spread the ideas of the Reformation.

30.5 Other Leaders of the Reformation

The movement begun by Martin Luther swept across much of Europe. Many people who were dismayed by abuses in the Church remained loyal Catholics. Others, however, were attracted to new forms of the Christian faith. The printing press helped spread new ideas, as well as translations of the Bible, faster than ever before. In addition, government leaders had learned from Luther's experience that they could win religious independence from the Church. The Reformation succeeded most where rulers embraced Protestant faiths.

Many reformers contributed to the spread of Protestantism. Let's take a look at four leaders of the Reformation.

Huldrych Zwingli (1484–1530) Huldrych Zwingli (HUL-drick ZVING-lee) was a Catholic priest in Zurich, Switzerland. Zwingli was influenced by both Erasmus and Luther. After reading Luther's work, he persuaded the local government to ban any form of worship that was not based on the Bible. In 1523, Zurich declared its independence from the authority of the local Catholic bishop.

Zwingli wanted Christians to focus solely on the Bible. He attacked the worship of relics, saints, and images. In the Protestant churches he founded, there were no religious statues or paintings. Services were very simple, without music or singing.

Zwingli carried his ideas to other Swiss cities. In 1530, war broke out between his followers and Swiss Catholics. Zwingli died during the fighting.

John Calvin (1509–1564) In the late 1530s, John Calvin, a French humanist, started another Protestant group in Geneva, Switzerland. His book, *Institutes of the Christian Religion,* became one of the most influential works of the Reformation.

Calvin emphasized that salvation came only from God's grace. He said that the "saved" whom God elected, or chose, lived according to strict standards. He believed firmly in hard work and thrift, or the careful use of money. Success in business, he taught, was a sign of God's grace. Calvin tried to establish a Christian state in Geneva that would be ruled by God through the Calvinist Church.

Calvin influenced many other reformers. One of them was John Knox, a Scotsman who lived in Geneva for a time. Knox led the Protestant reform that established the Presbyterian Church in Scotland.

King Henry VIII (1491–1547) England's Protestant Reformation was led by King Henry VIII. In 1534, Henry formed the Church of England, also called the Anglican Church. Henry named himself as its supreme head.

Unlike Luther and Calvin, King Henry did not have major disagreements with Catholic teachings. His reasons for breaking with the Church were personal and political. On a personal level, he wanted to end his first marriage, but the pope had denied him a divorce. On a political level, he no longer wanted to share power and wealth with the Church. In 1536, Henry closed down Catholic monasteries in England and took their riches.

William Tyndale (About 1491–1536) William Tyndale was an English priest, scholar, and writer. Tyndale traveled to Germany and met Martin Luther. His views became more and more Protestant. He attacked corruption in the Catholic Church and defended the English Reformation. After being arrested by Catholic authorities in the city of Antwerp, in present-day Belgium, he spent over a year in prison. In 1536, he was burned at the stake.

Tyndale is especially important to the Reformation because of his translations of the Bible. To spread knowledge of the Bible, he translated the New Testament and parts of the Old Testament into English. In the early 1600s, his work was used in the preparation of the King James, or Authorized, Version of the Bible. Famed for its beautiful language, the King James Bible had an enormous influence on English worship, language, and literature.

Writer and scholar William Tyndale was burned at the stake for his Protestant beliefs.

Chapter Summary

In this chapter, you learned about the Reformation, which began in the early 1500s. This movement led to the founding of many new Christian denominations in Europe.

The Weakening of the Catholic Church By the Late Middle Ages, the Catholic Church was weakened by corruption, political struggles, and humanist ideas. Many Catholics were dismayed by worldliness and immorality in the Church, including the sale of indulgences and the practice of simony.

Early Calls for Reform A number of Catholics began to call for reform, including John Wycliffe, Jan Hus, Catherine of Siena, and Erasmus. They questioned the practices of Church leaders and some of the Church's teachings.

Martin Luther Breaks Away From the Church In the early 1500s, German priest Martin Luther became involved in a major dispute with the Church over indulgences and other practices. Excommunicated, Luther began the first Protestant church, which started the Reformation.

Other Leaders of the Reformation Other Protestant reformers began to separate from the Catholic Church. The printing press helped to spread their ideas. Zwingli and Calvin began churches in Switzerland. William Tyndale translated the Bible into English. Henry VIII became the supreme head of the new Church of England.

Chapter 31

The Spread and Impact of the Reformation

What were the effects of the Reformation?

31.1 Introduction

In this chapter, you will learn more about the movement called the Reformation and the Protestant churches that emerged in the 1500s. You will also explore the impact of the Reformation on the Catholic Church and on the history of Europe.

As Protestantism spread, it branched out in several directions. By the start of the 1600s, there were already many different Christian churches in Europe.

Each Protestant denomination had its own beliefs and practices. But all Protestants had much in common. They shared a belief in the authority of the Bible, individual conscience, and the importance of faith. They were also united in their desire to **reform** Christianity.

The growth of Protestantism helped to encourage reform within the Catholic Church, as well. This Catholic reform movement is called the Counter-Reformation. Church leaders worked to correct abuses. They clarified and defended Catholic teachings. They condemned what they saw as Protestant **errors.** They also tried to win back areas of Europe that had been lost to the Catholic Church.

The many divisions among Christians led to a series of wars and persecutions. People suffered because of their beliefs. Catholics fought Protestants, and Protestants fought one another. These struggles involved political, economic, and cultural differences, as well as deep religious beliefs.

The Reformation brought much conflict to Europe, but it also created many new forms of the Christian faith. Three new branches of Christianity that developed early in the period were Lutheranism, Calvinism, and Anglicanism.

Ignatius of Loyola founded the Society of Jesus. Known as the Jesuits, this Catholic order was important during the Counter-Reformation.

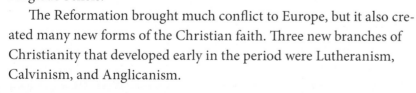

◀ Catholic leaders worked to strengthen the Church in response to the Reformation.

Lutheranism a Protestant denomination of Christian faith founded by Martin Luther

31.2 Lutheranism

The first major Protestant sect was **Lutheranism**. Lutheranism began in Germany after Martin Luther was excommunicated by the Catholic Church in 1521.

Luther was a Catholic priest and scholar. He taught scripture and theology (the study of religion) at the University of Wittenberg. As he studied the Bible, Luther became troubled. He could not find a basis in the Bible for many Church teachings and practices. He was also upset about corruption in the Church, especially the sale of indulgences.

Luther tried to work out his differences with the Church. But after his views were condemned, he started the separate movement that became Lutheranism.

Beliefs About Sin and Salvation Luther and his followers disagreed with the Catholic Church about sin and salvation. Catholics believed that people earned salvation by following the teachings and practices of the Church. Taking part in the sacraments was essential. For example, the sacrament of baptism wiped away original sin. In Christian belief, this was the sinful condition passed on to all people by Adam, the first man created by God. Once they were baptized, people needed to pray, take the sacraments, follow rules laid down by the Church, and perform good works.

Lutherans did not believe that people could do anything to earn their salvation. Salvation, they said, was God's gift, which people received in faith. People would be "justified," or saved, if they sincerely believed in Jesus Christ, were sorry for their sins, and accepted the words of the Bible as truth. Luther called this "justification by faith." Those who have faith perform good works and avoid sin because God commands them to, not in order to earn salvation.

The Augsburg Confession, or statement of faith, was prepared by German reformer Melanchthon in 1530, with Luther's approval. In its modern form, it is the basis of Lutheranism for millions of people around the world.

This painting of a Reformation church shows Lutheran clergy ministering the sacraments of baptism (far left) and Communion (center and right). Luther preaches from the altar at the far right.

Ultimate Source of Authority Lutherans rejected traditional sources of religious authority, such as Church councils and the pope. They believed that the Bible was the only true source of religious guidance. Reading the Bible was the only way to learn how to lead a good life and gain faith in God. Lutherans published the Bible in several languages so that people could read it for themselves.

Rituals and Worship Lutheran services combined Catholic practices with new Lutheran ones. Lutherans met in church buildings that had originally been Catholic. Like Catholics, they used an altar, candles, and a crucifix, which represented the crucifixion of Jesus.

Lutheran services resembled the Catholic mass in several ways. The services included Holy Communion, the Christian ritual of sharing bread and wine to commemorate the last meal Jesus shared with his disciples before his death. Lutheran services also included Bible readings and a sermon, in which clergy explained the day's lesson from the Bible. Like Catholics, Lutherans sang hymns. Luther wrote hymns for his followers. He used German words and often set hymns to popular tunes so everyone could learn them more easily.

Other parts of Lutheran worship were different from Catholic practice. Prayers were written and spoken in German, not in Latin, so that everyone could take part. Instead of having seven sacraments, Lutherans had just two: baptism and Communion. Luther believed that they were the only sacraments clearly named in the Bible.

Calvinism a Protestant denomination of Christian faith founded by John Calvin

John Calvin led a Reformation church in Geneva, Switzerland. Calvinists lived by strict rules that they felt showed them to be good Christians.

Community Life Luther gave his followers certain rules for how to live. Over time, he preached less about the Bible. He began to place greater importance on discipline and strong families. He said that fathers should teach their children religion by having them pray before meals and before bed. "Unless they [pray]," he said, "they should be given neither food nor drink." He also thought that women should get married and give birth to as many children as possible. He believed that these rules would help to strengthen Lutheran communities.

Unlike Catholic priests, Lutheran ministers, or members of the clergy, were free to marry. Luther himself married a former nun.

31.3 Calvinism

Calvinism was founded by John Calvin, a French humanist who did his most influential work in Geneva, Switzerland. In 1541, Calvin took over the leadership of the reform movement in Geneva.

Beliefs About Sin and Salvation Calvinists agreed with Lutherans that people depended entirely on God to be saved. No one deserved salvation, and no one could "force" God to grant it by doing good works. Instead, God chose certain people, the "elect," to be saved and to enjoy eternal life. Religious faith and salvation were God's gifts to the elect. Everyone else was doomed to spend eternity in hell.

Calvin maintained that God knew from the beginning of time who would be saved and who would be condemned. This idea is called *predestination*. There was nothing people could do to change their destiny. Everything, Calvin said, is under God's control.

Calvinists believed that the elect could be known by their actions. They believed that the world was full of opportunities to sin. But only people who were destined not to be saved would sin. Good behavior showed that a person was an elect destined for heaven. The reason for good behavior was to honor God, not to "buy" one's salvation.

Calvinists had many strict rules defining good behavior. For example, singing, dancing, playing cards, and wearing fancy clothing were all forbidden. Many people followed these rules to show that they were saved.

Ultimate Source of Authority Like Lutherans, Calvinists thought that the Bible was the only true source of religious guidance. Part of the task of church leaders was to interpret the Bible and make laws from it. Calvinists believed that all of life should be lived according to God's law. **Consequently,** in a Calvinist state, religious rules also became laws for the government. Anyone who sinned was also committing a crime. A lawbreaker was punished first by Calvinist clergy and then by the local court system. Sins such as blasphemy (showing disrespect to God) were punished as serious crimes.

Rituals and Worship Calvinist churchgoers attended services up to five times a week. Services included sermons that lasted for hours. The sermons explained how to live according to the Bible.

Calvinist church buildings showed Calvin's belief in simplicity. Churches were paneled in plain wood. People sat on long wooden benches. There were no paintings, statues, or stained glass windows. The minister preached from a pulpit in the middle of the room. Men sat on one side, and women and children sat on the other side. Children had to be ready to answer questions from the minister at a moment's notice. Failure to answer correctly would bring them shame or even punishment.

Like Lutherans, Calvinists used only the two sacraments they found in the Bible: baptism and Communion. Calvinists were not allowed to sing any words except those in the Bible. At services, they sang verses from the Bible set to popular tunes. Some Bible songs had new melodies written for them.

Community Life Calvinists believed that each community should be a **theocracy,** or a state governed by God through religious leaders. Calvinists had a duty to try to establish communities in which church and state were united.

Calvinist communities had strict laws based on the Bible. Parents could name babies only certain names from the Bible. Guests at local inns were not allowed to swear, dance, play cards, or insult anyone at the inn. Innkeepers had to report anyone who broke these rules. The same rules applied to people in their homes. Church leaders could inspect homes yearly to see whether families were living by the strict Calvinist laws. Offenders were punished severely. Some were even banished.

theocracy a government or state in which God is the supreme ruler, and religious officials govern in God's name

Calvinist churches were simple and practical with few decorations.

31.4 Anglicanism

Anglicanism was founded in 1534 by King Henry VIII in England.
Henry was not a religious reformer like Martin Luther or John Calvin.
Instead, he broke away from the Catholic Church for political and
personal reasons.

Politically, Henry did not want to share either his power or his
kingdom's wealth with the Church. Personally, he wanted to get a
divorce so that he could marry another woman, Anne Boleyn. He
wanted a male heir, and he and his first wife, Katherine of Aragon,
failed to have a male child.

When the pope refused to grant permission for a divorce, Henry
took matters into his own hands. He compelled Parliament, England's
lawmaking body, to declare him the head of the English church. So
began the Church of England, or Anglican Church, with the monarch
at its head.

Under Henry, the Church of England still greatly resembled the
Catholic Church. Over time, however, it blended elements of Catholicism and Protestantism.

Beliefs About Sin and Salvation Anglican beliefs had much
in common with the beliefs of the Catholic Church. Like Catholics,
Anglicans believed that baptism washed away original sin. Anglicans,
however, were also influenced by Protestant ideas. Unlike Catholics,
they accepted Luther's idea of justification by faith. To go to heaven,
people needed only to believe in God, regret their sins, and receive
God's mercy.

Later, Anglicans believed that people should have privacy in how
they practiced religion. It was up to individuals to figure out how to
live by their religious beliefs.

Despite the pope's refusal to grant
Henry VIII a divorce from his first wife,
Henry (left) secretly married his second
wife, Anne Boleyn (right), in early 1533.
Their marriage signaled Henry's break
with the Catholic Church.

Ultimate Source of Authority Anglicans based their beliefs on the Bible. However, the English monarch, as head of the Church, was the main interpreter of the Bible's meaning. The highest-ranking bishop in England, the Archbishop of Canterbury, helped the monarch with this task. Local clergy and churchgoers could interpret Church teachings in their own ways, as long as they were loyal to the monarch.

Rituals and Worship Anglican services were similar to both Roman Catholic and Lutheran services. Two versions of the Anglican Church service developed. The High Church service was much like the Catholic mass, and very formal. The Low Church service was similar to the Lutheran service.

Anglican services were held in former Catholic Church buildings. Most of the paintings, statues, and other decorations were removed. The inside of each church was painted white, and the Ten Commandments were painted on a plain white wall. Churchgoers sang simple hymns with English words and easy melodies.

Like other Protestant groups, Anglicans used only two sacraments: baptism and Communion. English slowly replaced Latin in Anglican services. Under Henry's son, King Edward VI, an official prayer book, the *Book of Common Prayer,* was published. It provided English-language prayers for services and morning and evening prayers. It also expressed the basic ideas of Anglican doctrine. In the early 1600s, King James I had a committee of scholars prepare a new English translation of the Bible, known as the Authorized Version, or the King James Version.

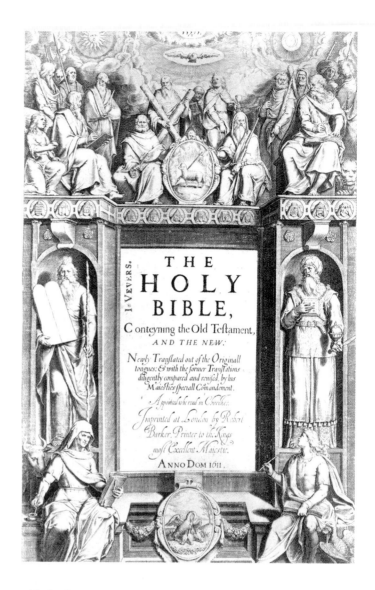

During the Reformation, Protestants published many vernacular versions of the Bible in English, including the King James Version.

Community Life Anglican communities were not all alike. High Church communities, however, were made up mostly of wealthy people. Low Church communities were usually made up of middle-class and working-class people.

Henry VIII's daughter, Queen Elizabeth I, said that no one should be forced to believe or practice a particular kind of Anglicanism. People could choose how to worship as long as they obeyed the laws of England and were loyal to the monarch. Heresy ceased to be a crime. However, citizens had to take care not to attack the monarch or the Anglican Church's place as the official Church of England.

Counter-Reformation a
movement of the Catholic
Church, in reaction to the
Reformation, in which Catholic
leaders worked to correct abuses,
to clarify and defend Catholic
teachings, to condemn what they
saw as Protestant errors, and to
win back members

31.5 The Counter-Reformation

As Protestantism spread, the Catholic Church responded with a program of serious reform. It **clarified** its teachings, corrected abuses, and
tried to win people back to Catholicism. This movement is known as
the **Counter-Reformation**.

The Council of Trent A major feature of the Counter-Reformation
was the Council of Trent. The council was a meeting of Catholic leaders that began in Trent, Italy, in 1545. Pope Paul III summoned the
council to combat corruption in the Church and to fight Protestantism. The council continued its work in more than 20 sessions over the
next 18 years.

In response to Protestant ideas, the council gave a more precise
statement of Catholic teachings. It rejected predestination, declar-
ing that individuals do have a role to play in deciding the fate of their
souls. The council agreed with Protestants that faith was important
and that salvation was God's gift. But it rejected justification by faith
alone. The council insisted that faith, good works, and the sacraments
were all necessary for salvation. It reaffirmed the Catholic belief in
seven sacraments.

This scene from the Council of Trent
shows Roman Catholic leaders as
they meet to reform their own church
and consider ways to fight against the
spread of Protestantism.

The council acknowledged the importance of the Bible. It insisted, however, on the Church's authority to interpret the Bible. It said that the Latin Bible was the only official scripture.

The council also took action to make needed changes in the Church. It required better education and training of its clergy. It called for priests and bishops to spend more time preaching. It corrected many of the abuses involving money and Church offices. It also established rules for services so that they would be more consistent from church to church.

The Council of Trent went a long way toward achieving the goals of Pope Paul III. The council's work brought a higher standard of morality to the Church's clergy and leadership. Its statements of Catholic belief and practices helped to unify the Church. The reformed Church was now better able to compete with Protestantism for the loyalties of Christians.

Catholic Reformers and Missionaries The spirit of reform brought new life to the Catholic Church and its followers. Many individuals and groups helped to reform the Church and spread its message. For example, Teresa of Avila, a nun, started a new religious order in Spain and helped reform the lives of priests and nuns. Her example and writings inspired many Catholics to return to the values taught by Jesus.

Other new orders were formed to preach, to educate people, and to perform such services as feeding the poor. The most important of these orders was the Society of Jesus, also known as the Jesuits.

The Jesuits were founded by Ignatius of Loyola, a Spanish nobleman. As a young soldier, Ignatius had his leg shattered by a cannonball. While he was recovering, he read about the lives of saints. He vowed to become a "soldier for Jesus."

After years of study, Ignatius started the order that became the Society of Jesus, or the Jesuits. The Jesuits were dedicated teachers and missionaries. They founded schools and colleges, and they brought many Europeans back to the Church. They worked to spread Catholicism in Africa, Asia, and the Americas. They became the largest order in the Church and actively supported the pope.

Fighting the Spread of Protestantism The Catholic Church also fought the spread of Protestantism by condemning beliefs that it considered to be errors and by dealing harshly with those it labeled as heretics. It looked to Catholic rulers to support its efforts and to win back lands lost to Protestantism.

The Jesuits became the main religious order of the Counter-Reformation. Known as the "Soldiers of Christ," they played a major role in the Inquisition. Here, Jesuit founder Ignatius of Loyola kneels before Pope Paul III, who officially recognized the order in 1540.

To deal with heresies during the Middle Ages, the Church had established the Inquisition. This body was made up of clergy called inquisitors who sought out and tried heretics. Inquisitors could order various punishments, including fines and imprisonment. Sometimes, they turned to civil rulers to put heretics to death.

King Ferdinand and Queen Isabella used the Spanish Inquisition to persecute Jews. With the start of the Reformation, the Spanish Inquisition also fought the spread of Protestantism. In Rome, the pope established a new Inquisition. The Roman Inquisition also sought out and condemned people whose views were considered dangerous.

31.6 Effects of the Reformation

The Reformation brought lasting change to Europe. Through the influence of Europeans, it also affected other parts of the world.

Religious Wars and Persecution The religious divisions of the Reformation led to a series of wars and persecutions during the 16th and 17th centuries. Catholics and Protestants alike persecuted members of other denominations, as well as each other.

Many people died for their beliefs. Others, like the French Protestants who moved to Switzerland, fled to other Protestant countries.

Bloody civil wars erupted in many countries. In France, for example, wars between Catholics and Protestants between 1562 and 1598 left over a million dead.

The wars in France were not just about religion. They were also about the power of the Catholic monarchy. Similarly, the last major war of the Reformation was both political and religious. Called the Thirty Years' War (1618–1648), it was fought mainly in Germany. The war pitted Catholics against Protestants, and Protestants against each other. But it was also a struggle for power that involved most of the nations of Europe. Nations fought for their own interests, as well as for religious reasons. Catholic France, for example, sided with Protestants to combat the power of the Holy Roman Empire.

The Thirty Years' War ended with the signing of the Peace of Westphalia in 1648. This treaty called for peace between Protestants and Catholics. By deciding the control of territory, it set boundaries between Catholic and Protestant lands. Most of northern Europe, including much of Germany, was Protestant. Spain, Portugal, Italy, and France remained Catholic. So did Bohemia, Austria, and Hungary. This religious division survived into modern times.

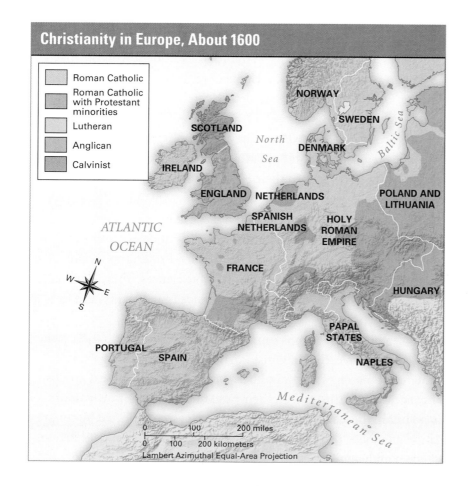

Christianity in Europe, About 1600

Legend:
- Roman Catholic
- Roman Catholic with Protestant minorities
- Lutheran
- Anglican
- Calvinist

By 1600, Protestantism had spread across much of northern Europe, especially in the Holy Roman Empire, Scandinavia, and the British Isles. Small groups were also in the largely Catholic nations of France, Poland, and Hungary.

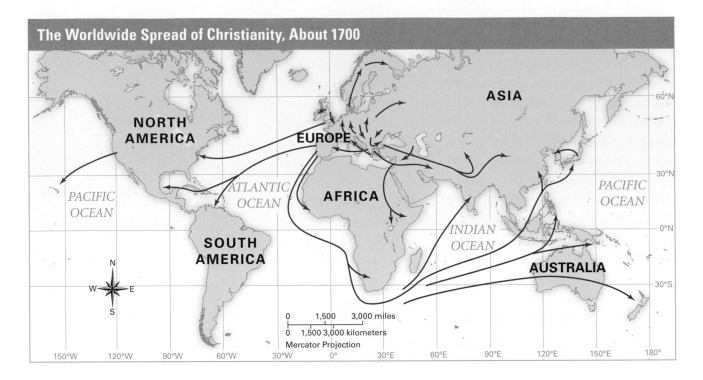

The Worldwide Spread of Christianity, About 1700

As Europeans began to explore beyond their contintent, they brought their religious beliefs with them. By the 18th century, Christianity had been carried around the world.

nationalism the identification with, and devotion to, the interests of one's nation

absolute monarchy a monarchy in which the ruler's power is unlimited

Puritans English Protestants who wanted to "purify" the Anglican Church of Catholic elements

The Rise of Nationalism and Democratic Practices The spread of Protestantism went hand in hand with a growing feeling called **nationalism**. More and more, people identified with their nation, rather than with their local area or lord. Throughout Europe, official state religions strengthened national unity.

Along with nationalism, monarchies were also growing stronger. Protestant rulers claimed authority over religious, as well as secular, matters. Even Roman Catholic rulers became increasingly independent of the pope.

These changes led to what is often called "The Age of Monarchs." Monarchs revived the old idea of the divine right of kings. According to this idea, rulers received their authority directly from God. This way of thinking reached its height in the late 17th and early 18th centuries when some rulers established **absolute monarchies**.

Yet the Reformation also planted the seeds of democratic ideas and practices. Beginning with Martin Luther, Protestants emphasized being true to the Bible and to their own consciences. This belief made people more willing to fight for their own ideas and rights, and to resist authority.

Some persecuted groups sought freedom to worship in their own ways. For example, the Calvinist **Puritans** fled England for North America in search of religious liberty. Many Protestant local groups, or congregations, insisted on their right to control their own affairs. In addition, the leaders of Protestant churches were elected by congregation members, not just by the powerful. Such beliefs about religious freedom and church government helped pave the way for democracy.

The Spread of Christianity By the time of the Reformation, Europeans had embarked upon a great age of exploration. As they voyaged around the world, both Catholics and Protestants worked to spread their faith. By the 1700s, there were missionary societies in several European countries. Jesuit missionaries were particularly active in spreading Roman Catholicism. Jesuits traveled to India, China, Japan, and Southeast Asia. Protestant missionaries worked in Ceylon (now Sri Lanka), India, and Indonesia.

The religious divisions in Europe were repeated in areas controlled by Europeans around the world. This was especially true in the Americas. Most people in English colonies in North America were Protestant. Missionaries and settlers from France brought Catholicism to parts of Canada and the Mississippi Valley. The Spanish and Portuguese brought Catholicism to the American southwest, Mexico, and South America. These patterns of religious faith are evident today.

Chapter Summary

In this chapter, you read about three branches of Protestantism—Lutheranism, Calvinism, and Anglicanism. You also learned about the Catholic response to the Reformation and some of the Reformation's lasting effects.

Lutheranism, Calvinism, and Anglicanism Begun by Martin Luther in 1521, Lutheranism was the first Protestant sect. Calvinism was started by John Calvin in Switzerland in 1541. The Anglican Church was founded when English king Henry VIII separated from the Catholic Church in 1534. All three sects believed that the Bible was the only religious authority and rejected all sacraments except for baptism and Communion. Services were held in the vernacular, not Latin. Clergy could marry. Unlike Lutherans and Anglicans, Calvinists believed in predestination—that salvation of "the elect" was pre-determined by God. They also believed that the Bible should form the basis for secular, as well as religious, law.

The Counter-Reformation The Catholic Church responded to Protestantism with the Counter-Reformation, a period of serious reform. At the Council of Trent, Catholic leaders created a more precise statement of Catholic belief and worked to end corruption. Reformers, such as the Jesuits, actively fought the spread of Protestantism through missionary work and the Inquisition.

Effects of the Reformation By the end of the wars that followed the Reformation, medieval Europe was largely a thing of the past. The Peace of Westphalia in 1648 set boundaries between Catholic and Protestant lands. This religious division survived into modern times and spread to wherever Europeans controlled territory around the world. In the period following the Reformation, Europe experienced a rise in nationalism and a strengthening of the monarchies. Yet, Protestantism also led to the beginnings of modern democracy.

Europe's Renaissance and Reformation

1296
Work Begins on Florence's Cathedral
The cathedral is completed in 1436 with a dome designed by architect Filippo Brunelleschi.

About 1300–1600
Renaissance in Europe
The Renaissance is a rebirth in classical art, learning, and culture, including the development of a new philosophy known as humanism.

1501–1504
Michelangelo Creates *David*
Michelangelo sculpts *David,* now one of the most admired statues in the world.

1200 **1300** **1400**

1309–1377
Pope's Headquarters in France
The office of the pope is located in Avignon, France, causing many Europeans to believe that the French monarchy controls the papacy.

1450
Invention of the Printing Press
Johannes Gutenberg invents a printing press that uses movable type.

1509
The Praise of Folly
Desiderius Erasmus publishes a book that criticizes abuses by church leaders and calls for a reformation of the Catholic Church.

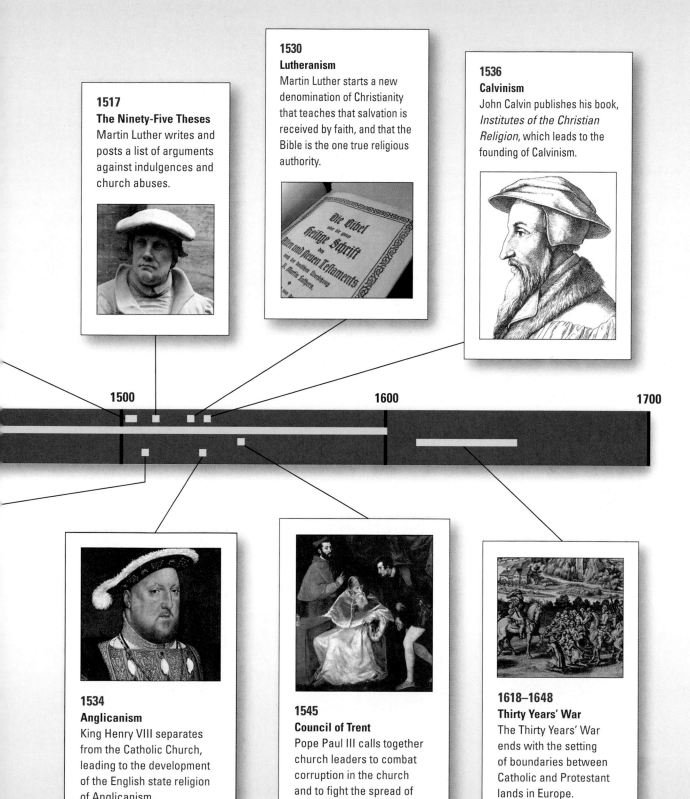

1517

The Ninety-Five Theses
Martin Luther writes and posts a list of arguments against indulgences and church abuses.

1530

Lutheranism
Martin Luther starts a new denomination of Christianity that teaches that salvation is received by faith, and that the Bible is the one true religious authority.

1536

Calvinism
John Calvin publishes his book, *Institutes of the Christian Religion*, which leads to the founding of Calvinism.

1500   1600   1700

1534

Anglicanism
King Henry VIII separates from the Catholic Church, leading to the development of the English state religion of Anglicanism.

1545

Council of Trent
Pope Paul III calls together church leaders to combat corruption in the church and to fight the spread of Protestantism.

1618–1648

Thirty Years' War
The Thirty Years' War ends with the setting of boundaries between Catholic and Protestant lands in Europe.

Europe Enters the Modern Age

Full-sized replicas of the Niña, the Pinta, and the Santa Maria sailed from Spain to the United States to mark the 500th anniversary of Columbus's first voyage to the Americas. The largest ship was the Santa Maria. The smallest was the Niña.

Europe Enters the Modern Age

In this unit, you will learn about Europe during the early modern age. This period lasted from the 1400s to the 1700s. At the same time when Europe was swept up in the Renaissance and the Reformation, other major changes were taking place in the world. These changes originated in Europe, but soon involved other continents. The changes began with a series of voyages during the 1400s, 1500s, and early 1600s when European explorers ventured into the Atlantic and Pacific oceans. Historians call this period the Age of Exploration.

With today's global positioning satellites, Internet maps, cell phones, and superfast travel, it is hard to imagine exactly how it might have

European Exploration and Land Claims, 1488–1610

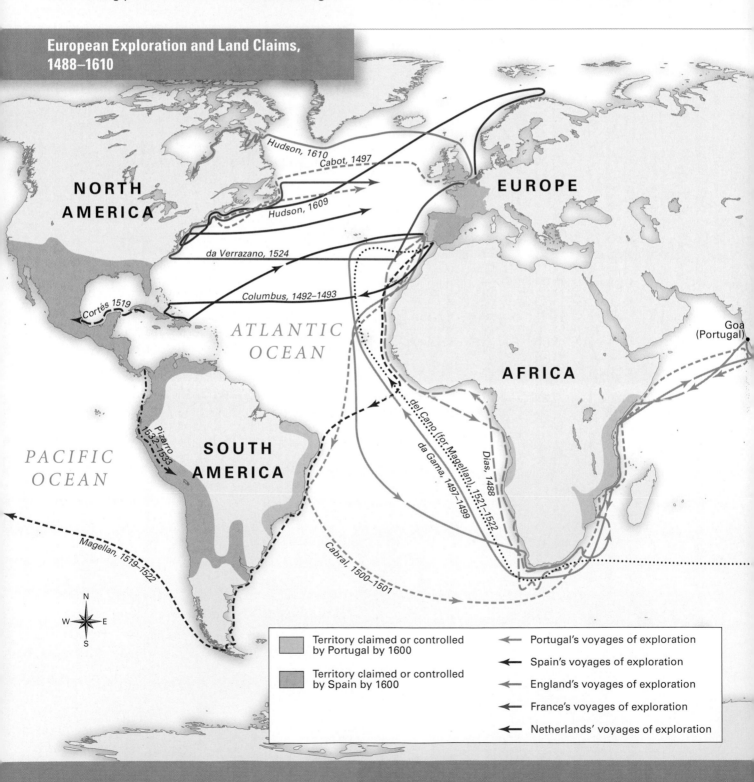

Territory claimed or controlled by Portugal by 1600	Portugal's voyages of exploration
Territory claimed or controlled by Spain by 1600	Spain's voyages of exploration
	England's voyages of exploration
	France's voyages of exploration
	Netherlands' voyages of exploration

felt to embark on a voyage across an unknown ocean. What lay across the ocean? In the early 1400s in Europe, few people knew. How long would it take to get there? That depended on the wind, the weather, and the distance. Days would have run together, with no sounds but the voices of the captain and the crew, the creaking of the sails, the blowing wind, and the splash of waves against the ship's hull.

Would you be willing to undertake such a voyage? Only those most adventurous, most daring, and most confident in their abilities to sail in any weather, manage any crew, and meet any circumstance dared do so. They sailed west from England, Spain, and Portugal to North America. They sailed south from Portugal and Spain to South America, to lands where the Incas lived. They traveled to Africa, past the kingdoms of Ghana, Mali, and Songhai. The crew of one Portuguese expedition even sailed completely around the world.

European explorers changed the world in many dramatic ways. Because of them, cultures divided by 3,000 miles or more of water began interacting. European countries claimed large parts of the world. As nations competed for territory, Europe had an enormous impact on people living in distant lands.

The Americas, in turn, made important contributions to Europe and the rest of the world. For example, from the Americas came crops such as corn and potatoes, which grew well in Europe. By increasing Europe's food supply, these crops helped create population growth.

Another great change during the early modern age was the Scientific Revolution. Between 1500 and 1700, scientists used observation and experiments to make dramatic discoveries. For example, Isaac Newton formulated the laws of gravity. The Scientific Revolution also led to the invention of new tools, such as the microscope and the thermometer.

Advances in science helped pave the way for a period called the Enlightenment. The Enlightenment began in the late 1600s. Enlightenment thinkers used observation and reason to try to solve problems in society. Their work led to new ideas about government, human nature, and human rights.

The Age of Exploration, the Scientific Revolution, and the Enlightenment helped to shape the world we live in today. In this unit, you will begin exploring the early modern age with the Age of Exploration.

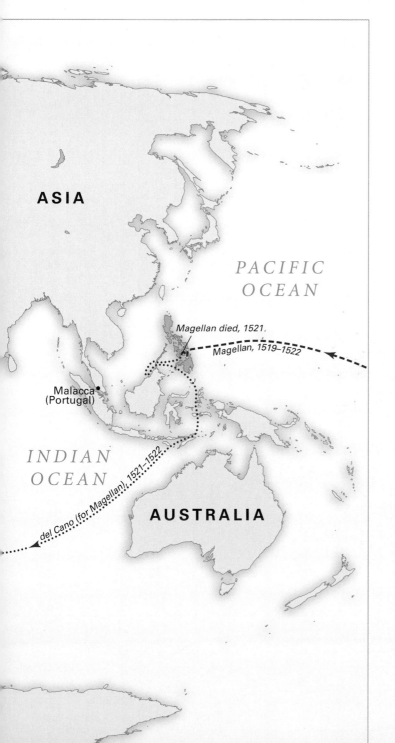

ASIA

PACIFIC OCEAN

Magellan died, 1521.

Magellan, 1519–1522

Malacca (Portugal)

INDIAN OCEAN

del Cano (for Magellan), 1521–1522

AUSTRALIA

Noua Hispania.

Messico.

MARIS ATL

SIVE MAR D.

Florida.

Cuba

Spagnola

Mar Ver-
mejo

Cali-
fornia

S. Ioan

IVCATAN

Iamaica

Nombre de Dios

Cartagena

Cari

Quito.

AM
ME
LIO

Circulus Aequinoctialis.

Isola de la
plata

Peru.

Charc

Isolas de lobos

Chi

Y. de Galopagos

S. Petri

C. de Fortuna

DEL

Prima ego velivolis ambivi cursibus Orbem,
Magellane novo te duce ducta freto.
Ambivi, meritoq; vocor VICTORIA: sunt mi
Vela, alæ; precium, gloria, pugna, mare.

ZVR.

Archipe-
lagus in
sularum

Fretum Magella
nicu

Cum privilegijs Imp. & Reg. Maiestatum,
nec non Cancellariæ Brabantiæ, ad decennium

Chapter 32

The Age of Exploration

How did the Age of Exploration change the way Europeans viewed the world?

32.1 Introduction

In this chapter, you will learn about the Age of Exploration. This period of discovery lasted from about 1418 to 1620. During this time, European explorers made many daring voyages that changed the world.

A major reason for these voyages was the desire to find ocean routes to East Asia, which Europeans called the Indies. When Christopher Columbus sailed west across the Atlantic Ocean, he was looking for such a route. Instead, he reached the Americas. Columbus thought he had reached the Indies. In time, Europeans would realize that Columbus had found what they called the "New World." The Indies in the Atlantic became the West Indies. European nations soon rushed to claim lands in the Americas and elsewhere.

Early explorers often suffered terrible hardships. In 1520, Ferdinand Magellan set out with three ships to cross the Pacific Ocean from South America. He had guessed, correctly, that Asia lay west of South America. But Magellan had no idea how vast the Pacific Ocean was. He thought his crew would sail for a few weeks at most. Instead, the crossing took three months. While the ships were still at sea, the crew ran out of food, nearly **starving** to death. One sailor wrote about the terrible time. "We ate biscuit . . . swarming with worms. . . . We drank yellow water that had been putrid [rotten] for days . . . and often we ate sawdust from boards."

Why did explorers brave such dangers? In this chapter, you will discover some of the reasons for the Age of Exploration. You will learn about the voyages of explorers from Portugal, Spain, and other European countries. You will also learn how the Age of Exploration changed the way people viewed the world.

In 1492, Christopher Columbus came ashore in the Americas while on a voyage to discover a new sea route to Asia from Europe.

◀ In the Age of Exploration, European nations competed to claim new lands.

Age of Exploration a period
of European exploration and
discovery that lasted from about
1418 to 1620

32.2 The Causes of European Exploration

Why did European exploration begin to flourish in the 1400s? Two main reasons stand out. First, Europeans of this time had several **motives** for exploring the world. Second, advances in knowledge and technology helped to make the **Age of Exploration** possible.

Motives for Exploration For early explorers, one of the main motives for exploration was the desire to find new trade routes to Asia. By the 1400s, merchants and Crusaders had brought many goods to Europe from Africa, the Middle East, and Asia. Demand for these goods increased the desire for trade.

Europeans were especially interested in spices from Asia. They had learned to use spices to help preserve food during winter and to cover up the taste of food that was no longer fresh.

Trade with the East, however, was difficult and very expensive. Muslims and Italians controlled the flow of goods. Muslim traders carried goods to the east coast of the Mediterranean Sea. Italian merchants then brought the goods into Europe. Problems arose when Muslim rulers sometimes closed the trade routes from Asia to Europe. Also, the goods went through many hands, and each trading party raised the price.

European monarchs and merchants wanted to break the hold that Muslims and Italians had on trade. One way to do so was to find a sea route to Asia. Portuguese sailors looked for a route that went around Africa. Christopher Columbus tried to reach Asia by sailing west across the Atlantic.

Mapmakers created better, more accurate maps by using navigational tools and information brought back by explorers.

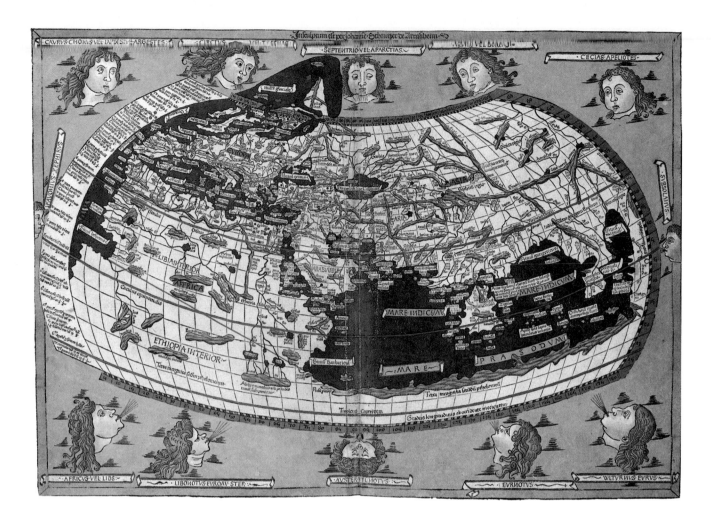

Europe's Age of Exploration produced key advances in cartography. This map dates from the 1400s. How accurate is it compared to a modern map?

Other motives also came into play. Many people were excited by the opportunity for new knowledge. Explorers saw the chance to earn fame and glory, as well as wealth. As new lands were discovered, nations wanted to claim the lands' riches for themselves.

A final motive for exploration was the desire to spread Christianity beyond Europe. Both Protestant and Catholic nations were eager to make new converts. Missionaries of both faiths followed the paths blazed by explorers.

Advances in Knowledge and Technology The Age of Exploration began during the Renaissance. The Renaissance was a time of new learning. A number of advances during that time made it easier for explorers to venture into the unknown.

One key advance was in **cartography,** the art and science of mapmaking. In the early 1400s, an Italian scholar translated an ancient book called *Guide to Geography* from Greek into Latin. The book was written by the thinker Ptolemy (TOL-eh-mee) in the 2nd century C.E. Printed copies of the book inspired new interest in cartography. European mapmakers used Ptolemy's work as a basis for drawing more accurate maps.

cartography the science and art of making maps

Discoveries by explorers gave mapmakers new information with which to work. The result was a dramatic change in Europeans' view of the world. By the 1500s, Europeans made globes, showing Earth as a sphere. In 1507, a German cartographer made the first map that clearly showed North and South America as separate from Asia.

In turn, better maps made navigation easier. The most important Renaissance geographer, Gerardus Mercator (mer-KAY-tur), created maps using improved lines of longitude and latitude. Mercator's mapmaking technique was a great help to navigators.

An improved ship design also helped explorers. By the 1400s, Portuguese and Spanish shipbuilders were making a new type of ship called a caravel. These ships were small, fast, and easy to maneuver. Their special bottoms made it easier for explorers to travel along coastlines where the water was not deep. Caravels also used lateen sails, a triangular style adapted from Muslim ships. These sails could be positioned to take advantage of the wind no matter which way it blew.

Along with better ships, new navigational tools helped sailors travel more safely on the open seas. By the end of the 1400s, the compass was much improved. Sailors used compasses to find their bearing, or direction of travel. The astrolabe helped sailors determine their distance north or south from the equator.

Finally, improved weapons gave Europeans a huge advantage over the people they met in their explorations. Sailors could fire their cannons at targets near the shore without leaving their ships. On land, the weapons of native peoples often were no match for European guns, armor, and horses.

32.3 Portugal Begins the Age of Exploration

The Age of Exploration began in Portugal. This small country is located on the Iberian Peninsula. Its rulers sent explorers first to nearby Africa and then around the world.

Key Portuguese Explorers The major figure in early Portuguese exploration was Prince Henry, the son of King John I of Portugal. Nicknamed "the Navigator," Prince Henry was not an explorer himself. Instead, he encouraged exploration and planned and directed many important expeditions.

Beginning in about 1418, Henry sent explorers to sea almost every year. He also started a school of navigation where sailors and mapmakers could learn their trades. His cartographers made new maps based on the information ship captains brought back.

Henry's early expeditions focused on the west coast of Africa. He wanted to continue the Crusades against the Muslims, find gold, and take part in Asian trade.

Prince Henry the Navigator promoted Portugal's exploration and began a school of navigation.

Gradually, Portuguese explorers made their way farther and farther south. In 1488, Bartolomeu Dias became the first European to sail around the southern tip of Africa.

In July 1497, Vasco da Gama set sail with four ships to chart a sea route to India. Da Gama's ships rounded Africa's southern tip and then sailed up the east coast of the continent. With the help of a sailor who knew the route to India from there, they were able to across the Indian Ocean.

Da Gama arrived in the port of Calicut, India, in May 1498. There he obtained a load of cinnamon and pepper. On the return trip to Portugal, da Gama lost half of his ships. Still, the valuable cargo he brought back paid for the voyage many times over. His trip made the Portuguese even more eager to trade directly with Indian merchants.

In 1500, Pedro Cabral (kah-BRAHL) set sail for India with a fleet of 13 ships. Cabral first sailed southwest to avoid areas where there are no winds to fill sails. But he sailed so far west that he reached the east coast of present-day Brazil. After claiming this land for Portugal, he sailed back to the east and rounded Africa. Arriving in Calicut, he established a trading post and signed trade treaties. He returned to Portugal in June 1501.

The Impact of Portuguese Exploration Portugal's explorers changed Europeans' understanding of the world in several ways. They explored the coasts of Africa and brought back gold and enslaved Africans. They also found a sea route to India. From India, explorers brought back spices, such as cinnamon and pepper, and other goods, such as porcelain, incense, jewels, and silk.

Vasco da Gama

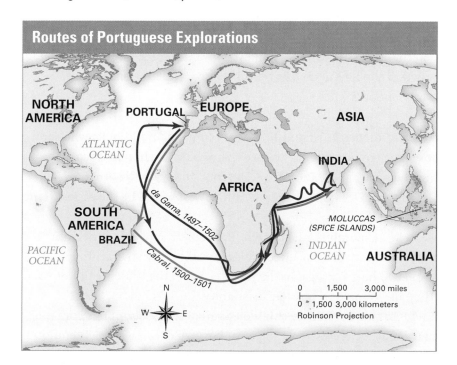

Routes of Portuguese Explorations

Explorers from Portugal were among the earliest Europeans to make long sea voyages of exploration.

Pedro Cabral

colony a territory, often very large, under the political and economic control of another country

After Cabral's voyage, the Portuguese took control of the eastern sea routes to Asia. They seized the seaport of Goa (GOH-uh) in India and built forts there. They attacked towns on the east coast of Africa. They also set their sights on the Moluccas, or Spice Islands, in what is now Indonesia. In 1511, they attacked the main port of the islands and killed the Muslim defenders. The captain of this expedition explained what was at stake. If Portugal could take the spice trade away from Muslim traders, he wrote, then Cairo and Makkah "will be ruined." As for Italian merchants, "Venice will receive no spices unless her merchants go to buy them in Portugal."

Portugal's control of the Indian Ocean broke the hold Muslims and Italians had on Asian trade. With the increased competition, prices of Asian goods— such as spices and fabrics—dropped, and more people in Europe could afford to buy them.

During the 1500s, Portugal also began to establish **colonies** in Brazil. The native people of Brazil suffered greatly as a result. The Portuguese forced them to work on sugar plantations, or large farms. They also tried to get them to give up their religion and convert to Christianity. Missionaries sometimes tried to protect them from abuse, but countless numbers of native peoples died from overwork and from European diseases. Others fled into the interior of Brazil.

The colonization of Brazil also had a negative impact on Africa. As the native population of Brazil decreased, the Portuguese needed more laborers. Starting in the mid-1500s, they turned to Africa. Over the next 300 years, ships brought millions of enslaved West Africans to Brazil.

32.4 Spain's Early Explorations

In the late 1400s, King Ferdinand and Queen Isabella of Spain were determined to make their country a powerful force in Europe. One way they thought to do this was to sponsor explorations to claim new lands for Spain.

Key Explorers for Spain It was Ferdinand and Isabella who sponsored the voyages of Christopher Columbus. The Italian-born Columbus thought that the Indies, or eastern Asia, lay on the other side of the Atlantic Ocean. He believed sailing west would be the easiest route to reach it.

When Columbus failed to win Portuguese support for his idea, Ferdinand and Isabella agreed to pay for the risky voyage. They wanted to beat Portugal in the race to control the trade wealth of Asia. They also wanted to spread Christianity.

In August 1492, three ships left Spain under Columbus's command. For the crew, venturing into the open ocean was frightening.

Christopher Columbus

As the weeks went by, some of the men began to fear they would never see Spain again. Then, on October 12, a lookout sighted land. Columbus went ashore on an island in the Caribbean Sea, and claimed it for Spain.

For three months, Columbus and his men explored nearby islands with the help of native islanders, whom the Spanish called Taino (TY-noh). Thinking they were in the Indies, the Spanish soon called all the local people "Indians."

In March 1493, Columbus arrived back in Spain. He proudly reported that he had reached Asia. Over the next ten years, he made three more voyages to what he called the Indies. He died in Spain in 1506, still insisting that he had sailed to Asia.

Many Europeans, however, believed that Columbus had actually found a land mass that lay between Europe and Asia. One of these was Ferdinand Magellan (muh-JEL-uhn), a Portuguese explorer.

Magellan believed he could sail west to the Indies if he found a strait, or channel, through South America. The strait would connect the Atlantic and Pacific oceans, allowing ships to continue on to Asia.

Magellan won Spain's support for a voyage to find the strait. In August 1519, he set sail with five ships and about two hundred and fifty men.

Magellan looked for the strait all along South America's east coast. He finally found it at the southern tip of the continent. Today, it is called the Strait of Magellan.

Explorer Christopher Columbus convinced King Ferdinand and Queen Isabella of Spain to support his westward voyages.

Ferdinand Magellan

To increase their nation's power, Ferdinand and Isabella of Spain sponsored several expeditions in search of better trade routes and new lands to control.

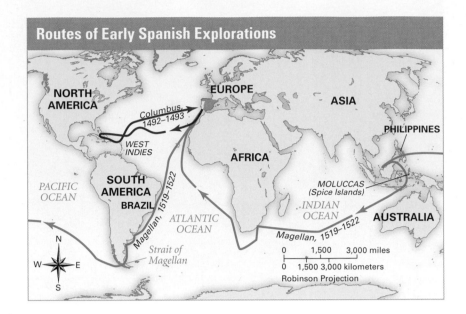

Routes of Early Spanish Explorations

NORTH AMERICA

EUROPE

ASIA

PHILIPPINES

Columbus, 1492–1493

WEST INDIES

AFRICA

PACIFIC OCEAN

SOUTH AMERICA

BRAZIL

Magellan, 1519–1522

ATLANTIC OCEAN

MOLUCCAS (Spice Islands)

INDIAN OCEAN

AUSTRALIA

Magellan, 1519–1522

Strait of Magellan

N W E S

0   1,500   3,000 miles
0   1,500 3,000 kilometers
Robinson Projection

After passing through the strait, Magellan reached the Pacific Ocean in November 1520. It took another three months to cross the Pacific. Continuing west, Magellan visited the Philippines. There he became involved in a conflict between two local chiefs. In April 1521, Magellan was killed in the fighting.

Magellan's crew sailed on to the Spice Islands. Three years after the expedition began, the only ship to survive the expedition returned to Spain. The 18 sailors on board were the first people to travel completely around Earth.

The Impact of Early Spanish Exploration The early Spanish explorations changed Europeans' view of the world a great deal. The voyages of Christopher Columbus revealed the existence of the Americas. Magellan's expedition opened up a westward route to the Indies. It showed that it was possible to sail completely around the world. It also proved that Columbus had indeed found a "New World"—one that Europeans hadn't realized was there.

Columbus's voyages marked the beginning of Spanish settlement in the West Indies. Spain earned great wealth from its settlements. Settlers mined for precious minerals and started sugar plantations. The Spanish also brought new crops, such as sweet potatoes and pineapples, to Europe.

For the native people of the West Indies, however, Spanish settlement was extremely **detrimental.** The Spanish forced native people to work as slaves in the mines and on the plantations. Priests forced many of them to become Christians. When the Spanish arrived, perhaps one or two million Taino lived on the islands. Within fifty years, fewer than five hundred Taino were left. The rest had died of starvation, overwork, or European diseases.

Like Portugal, Spain looked to West Africa for new laborers. From 1518 through the mid-1800s, the Spanish brought millions of enslaved Africans to work in their American colonies.

32.5 Later Spanish Exploration and Conquest

After Columbus's voyages, Spain was eager to claim even more lands in the New World. To explore and conquer "New Spain," the Spanish turned to adventurers called *conquistadors,* or conquerors. The conquistadors were allowed to establish settlements and seize the wealth of natives. In return, the Spanish government claimed some of the treasures they found.

Key Explorers In 1519, Spanish explorer Hernán Cortés (er-NAHN koor-TEZ), with and a band of fellow conquistadors, set out to explore present-day Mexico. Native people in Mexico told Cortés about the Aztecs. The Aztecs had built a large and wealthy empire in Mexico.

With the help of a native woman named Malinche (mah-LIN-chay), Cortés and his men reached the Aztec capital, Tenochtitlán (tay-nawh-tee-TLAHN). The Aztec ruler, Moctezuma II, welcomed the Spanish with great honors. Determined to break the power of the Aztecs, Cortés took Moctezuma hostage.

When Spanish explorer Cortés (right) first entered Mexico, he was welcomed by the Aztec ruler, Moctezuma II (left).

Hernán Cortés

epidemic an outbreak of
a contagious disease that
spreads quickly and over a
wide geographic area

Spanish explorations in the
Americas, especially in Mexico
and Peru, gained much territory
and great wealth for Spain.

Cortés now controlled the Aztec capital. In 1520, he left the city of Tenochtitlán to battle a rival Spanish force. While he was away, a group of conquistadors attacked the Aztecs in the middle of a religious celebration. In response, the Aztecs rose up against the Spanish. The soldiers had to fight their way out of the city. Many of them were killed during the escape.

The following year, Cortés mounted a siege of the city, aided by thousands of native allies who resented Aztec rule. The Aztecs ran out of food and water, yet they fought desperately. After several months, the Spanish captured the Aztec leader, and Aztec resistance collapsed. The city was in ruins. The mighty Aztec Empire was no more.

Four factors contributed to the defeat of the Aztec Empire. First, Aztec legend had predicted the arrival of a white-skinned god. When Cortés appeared, the Aztecs welcomed him because they thought he might be this god, Quetzalcoatl. Second, Cortés was able to make allies of the Aztecs' enemies. Third, their horses, armor, and superior weapons gave the Spanish an advantage in battle. Fourth, the Spanish carried diseases that caused deadly **epidemics** among the Aztecs.

Aztec riches inspired Spanish conquistadors to continue their search for gold. In the 1520s, Francisco Pizarro received permission from Spain to conquer the Inca Empire in South America. The Incas ruled an empire that extended throughout most of the Andes Mountains. By the time Pizarro arrived, however, a civil war had weakened that empire.

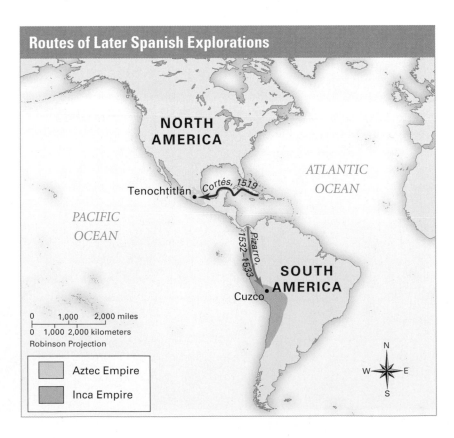

Routes of Later Spanish Explorations

In April 1532, the Incan emperor, Atahualpa (ah-tuh-WAHL-puh), greeted the Spanish as guests. Following Cortés's example, Pizarro launched a surprise attack and kidnapped the emperor. Although the Incas paid a roomful of gold and silver in ransom, the Spanish killed Atahualpa. Without their leader, the Inca Empire quickly fell apart.

The Impact of Later Spanish Exploration and Conquest The explorations and conquests of the conquistadors transformed Spain. The Spanish rapidly expanded foreign trade and overseas colonization. For a time, wealth from the Americas made Spain one of the world's richest and most powerful countries.

Besides gold and silver, ships from the Americas brought corn and potatoes to Spain. These crops grew well in Europe. The increased food supply helped spur a population boom. Conquistadors also introduced Europeans to new luxury items, such as chocolate.

In the long run, however, gold and silver from the Americas hurt Spain's economy. **Inflation,** or an increase in the supply of money, led to a loss of its value. It now cost people a great deal more to buy goods with the devalued money. Additionally, monarchs and the wealthy spent their riches on luxuries, instead of building Spain's industries.

The Spanish conquests had a major impact on the New World. The Spanish introduced new animals to the Americas, such as horses, cattle, sheep, and pigs. But they destroyed two advanced civilizations. The Aztecs and Incas lost much of their culture along with their wealth. Many became laborers for the Spanish. Millions died from disease. In Mexico, for example, there were about twenty-five million native people in 1519. By 1605, this number had dwindled to one million.

Francisco Pizarro

32.6 Other European Explorations

Spain and Portugal dominated the early years of exploration. But rulers in rival nations wanted their own share of trade and new lands in the Americas. Soon England, France, and the Netherlands all sent expeditions to North America.

Key Explorers Explorers often sailed for any country that would pay for their voyages. The Italian sailor John Cabot made England's first voyage of discovery. Cabot believed he could reach the Indies by sailing northwest across the Atlantic. In 1497, he landed in what is now Canada. Believing he had reached the northeast coast of Asia, he claimed the region for England.

Another Italian, Giovanni da Verrazano, sailed under the French flag. In 1524, Verrazano explored the Atlantic coast from present-day North Carolina to Canada. His voyage gave France its first claims in the Americas. Unfortunately, on a later trip to the West Indies, he was killed by native people.

John Cabot

Giovanni da Verrazano

This early 20th-century illustration shows Henry Hudson meeting native people in North America.

Sailing on behalf of the Netherlands, English explorer Henry Hudson journeyed to North America in 1609. Hudson wanted to find a northwest passage through North America to the Pacific Ocean. Such a water route would allow ships to sail from Europe to Asia without entering waters controlled by Spain.

Hudson did not find a northwest passage, but he did explore what is now called the Hudson River in present-day New York State. His explorations were the basis of the Dutch claim to the area. Dutch settlers established the colony of New Amsterdam on Manhattan in 1625.

In 1610, Hudson tried again, this time under the flag of his native England. Searching farther north, he sailed into a large bay in Canada that is now called Hudson Bay. He spent three months looking for an outlet to the Pacific, but there was none.

After a hard winter in the icy bay, some of Hudson's crew rebelled. They set him, his son, and seven loyal followers adrift in a small boat. Hudson and the other castaways were never seen again. Hudson's voyage, however, laid the basis for later English claims in Canada.

The Impact of European Exploration of North America Unlike the conquistadors in the south, northern explorers did not find gold and other treasure. As a result, there was less interest, at first, in starting colonies in that region.

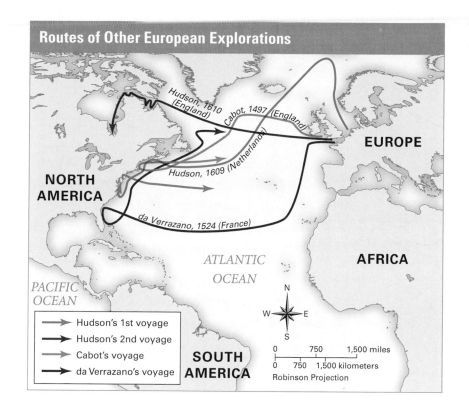

Routes of Other European Explorations

NORTH AMERICA

Hudson, 1610 (England)

Cabot, 1497 (England)

Hudson, 1609 (Netherlands)

da Verrazano, 1524 (France)

EUROPE

AFRICA

ATLANTIC OCEAN

PACIFIC OCEAN

SOUTH AMERICA

N
W — E
S

Legend:
→ Hudson's 1st voyage
→ Hudson's 2nd voyage
→ Cabot's voyage
→ da Verrazano's voyage

0   750   1,500 miles
0   750   1,500 kilometers
Robinson Projection

The English, Dutch, and French also sent out explorers in search of new land claims and new trade goods.

Canada's shores did offer rich resources of cod and other fish. Within a few years of Cabot's trip, fishing boats regularly visited the region. Europeans were also interested in trading with Native Americans for whale oil and otter, beaver, and fox furs. By the early 1600s, Europeans had set up a number of trading posts in North America.

English exploration also contributed to a war between England and Spain. As English ships roamed the seas, some captains, nicknamed "sea dogs," began raiding Spanish ports and ships to take their gold. Between 1577 and 1580, sea dog Francis Drake sailed around the world. He also claimed part of what is now California for England, ignoring Spain's claims to the area.

The English raids added to other tensions between England and Spain. In 1588, King Philip II of Spain sent an armada, or fleet of ships, to invade England. With 130 heavily armed vessels and about thirty thousand men, the Spanish Armada seemed an unbeatable force. But the smaller English fleet was fast and well armed. Their guns had a longer range, so they could attack from a safe distance. After several battles, a number of the armada's ships had been sunk or driven ashore. The rest turned around but faced terrible storms on the way home. Fewer than half of the ships made it back to Spain.

The defeat of the Spanish Armada marked the start of a shift in power in Europe. By 1630, Spain no longer dominated the continent. With Spain's decline, other countries—particularly England and the Netherlands—took a more active role in trade and colonization around the world.

Henry Hudson

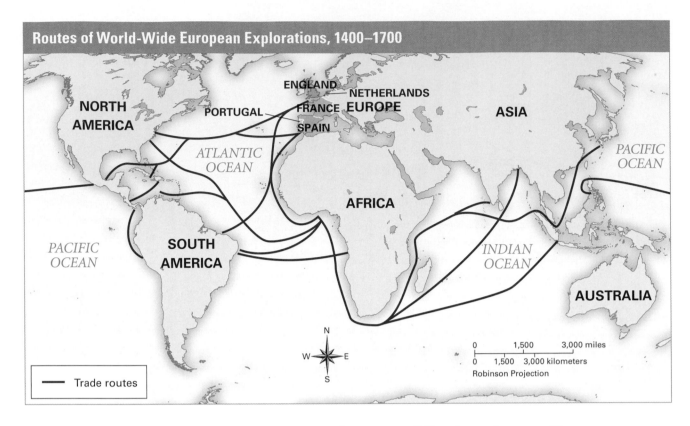

Routes of World-Wide European Explorations, 1400–1700

Trade routes

By the late 1700s, European explorers had voyaged around the world and claimed many lands for their nations.

capitalism an economic system based on investment of money for profit

market economy an economy in which prices are determined by the buying and selling decisions of individuals in the marketplace

cottage industry a small-scale business in which people produce goods at home

mercantilism an economic policy by which nations try to gather wealth by establishing colonies and controlling trade

32.7 The Impact of Exploration on Europe

The voyages of explorers had a dramatic impact on European commerce and economies. As a result of exploration, more goods, raw materials, and precious metals entered Europe. Mapmakers carefully charted trade routes and the locations of newly discovered lands. By the 1700s, European ships traveled trade routes that spanned the globe. New centers of commerce developed in the port cities of the Netherlands and England.

Exploration and trade contributed to the growth of **capitalism**. This economic system is based on investing money for profit. Merchants gained great wealth by trading and selling goods from around the world. Many of them used their profits to finance still more voyages and to start trading companies. Other people began investing money in these companies and shared in the profits. Soon, this type of shared ownership was applied to other kinds of businesses.

Another aspect of the capitalist economy concerned the way people exchanged goods and services. Money became more important as precious metals flowed into Europe. Instead of having a fixed price, items were sold for prices that were set by the open market. This meant that the price of an item depended on how much of the item was available and how many people wanted to buy it. Sellers could charge high prices for scarce items that many people wanted. If the supply of an item was large and few people wanted it, sellers lowered the price. This kind of system, based on supply and demand, is called a **market economy**.

Labor, too, was given a money value. Increasingly, people began working for hire instead of directly providing for their own needs. Merchants hired people to work from their own cottages, turning raw materials from overseas into finished products. This growing **cottage industry** was especially important in the manufacture of textiles. Often, entire families worked at home, spinning wool into thread or weaving thread into cloth. Cottage industry was a step toward the system of factories operated by capitalists in later centuries.

A final result of exploration was a new economic policy called **mercantilism**. European rulers believed that building up wealth was the best way to increase a nation's power. For this reason, they tried to reduce the products they bought from other countries and to increase the items they sold.

Having colonies was a key part of this **policy**. Nations looked to their colonies to supply raw materials for their industries at home. These industries turned the raw materials into finished goods that they could sell back to their colonies, as well as to other countries. To protect this valuable trade with their colonies, rulers often forbade colonists from trading with other nations.

Weaving cloth became a growing cottage industry as families set up looms and workshops in their homes.

Chapter Summary

In this chapter, you learned about the Age of Exploration. Beginning in the 1400s, European explorers went on great voyages of discovery.

The Causes of European Exploration European explorers sought wealth and land for their monarchs and themselves, knowledge, and adventure. They also wanted to spread Christianity. A number of advances in knowledge and technology made their journeys possible.

Portugal Begins the Age of Exploration In the early 1400s, under the leadership of Prince Henry "the Navigator," the Portuguese became the first to purposefully explore the seas beyond Europe. They explored Africa's coasts, charted a sea route to South Asia, and claimed Brazil for Portugal.

Spain's Explorations The voyages of Christopher Columbus led to Spanish colonization in the Americas. Hernán Cortés and Francisco Pizarro conquered vast areas in Mexico and South America. The Aztec and Incan empires were destroyed. West Africans suffered greatly when they were brought to the Americas as slaves.

Other European Explorations England, France, and the Netherlands sent explorers to North America. The expeditions of Henry Hudson were the basis of Dutch land claims in what is now the Hudson River Valley and English land claims in Canada.

The Impact of Exploration on Europe Exploration vastly increased Europeans' knowledge. New foods led to a population explosion. Investments in expeditions and colonies contributed to the growth of capitalism, a market economy, cottage industries, and mercantilism.

Former conquistador Bartolomé de Las Casas became an early defender of the rights of the native peoples conquered by the Spanish.

Las Casas began his experiences in Spanish America on the island of Hispaniola in the Caribbean. There, he managed his family's businesses, which used enslaved Indians as labor.

Bartolomé de Las Casas: From Conquistador to Protector of the Indians

Bartolomé de las Casas experienced a remarkable change of heart during his lifetime. At first, he participated in Spain's conquest and settlement of the Americas. Later in life, he criticized and condemned it. For more than fifty years, he fought for the rights of the defeated and enslaved peoples of Latin America. How did this conquistador become known as "the Protector of the Indians?"

Bartolomé de las Casas (bahr-taw-law-MEY day las KAH-sahs) ran through the streets of Seville, Spain, on March 31, 1493. He was just nine years old and on his way to see Christopher Columbus, who had just returned from his first voyage to the Americas. Bartolomé wanted to see him and the "Indians," as they were called, as they paraded to the church.

Bartolomé's father and uncles were looking forward to seeing Columbus, as well. Like many other people in Europe during the late 1400s, they saw the Americas as a place of opportunity. They signed up to join Columbus on his second voyage. Two years after that, Bartolomé followed in his father's footsteps and voyaged to the Americas himself. He sailed to the island of Hispaniola, the present-day nations of Haiti and the Dominican Republic.

Las Casas as Conquistador and Priest

One historian wrote that when Las Casas first arrived in the Americas, he was "not much better than the rest of the gentlemen-adventurers who rushed to the New World, bent on speedily acquiring fortunes." He supported the Spanish conquest of the Americas and was a loyal servant of Spain's king and queen, Ferdinand and Isabella.

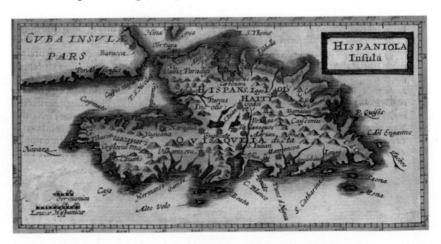

Once in Hispaniola, Las Casas helped to manage his father's farms and businesses. Enslaved Indians worked in the family's fields and mines.

Spanish conquistadors wanted to gain wealth and glory in the Americas. They had another goal, as well—to convert Indians to Christianity. Las Casas shared this goal. So, the young conquistador went back to Europe to become a priest. He returned to Hispaniola sometime in 1509 or 1510. There he began to teach and baptize the Indians. At the same time, he continued to manage Indian slaves.

On a Path to Change

History often seems to be made up of moments when someone has a change of heart. The path that he or she has been traveling takes a dramatic turn. It often appears to others that this change is sudden. In reality, a series of events usually causes a person to make the decision to change. One such event happened to Las Casas in 1511.

Las Casas sailed with Christopher Columbus on his third voyage in 1498. Here the two men are shown arriving on Hispaniola, where Las Casas settled in 1502.

Roman Catholics in Hispaniola witnessed horrible acts of cruelty and injustice against the native peoples of the West Indies at the hands of the Spanish conquistadors. One of the priests there, Father Antonio de Montesinos, spoke out against the harsh treatment of the Indians in a sermon delivered to a Spanish congregation in Hispaniola in 1511. De Montesinos said:

> *You are in mortal sin . . . for the cruelty and tyranny you use in dealing with these innocent people . . . by what right or justice do you keep these Indians in such a cruel and horrible servitude? . . . Why do you keep them so oppressed? . . . Are not these people also human beings?*

One historian called this sermon "the first cry for justice in America" on behalf of the Indians. Las Casas recorded the sermon in one of his books, *History of the Indies*. No one is sure if he was present at the sermon or heard about it later. But one thing seems certain; even though he must have seen some of the same injustices described by de Montesinos, Las Casas continued to support the Spanish conquest and the goals of conquering new lands, earning wealth, and converting Indians to Christianity.

In 1518, Las Casas went before the Holy Roman emperor and ruler of Spain, Charles V, to plead for the rights of the native peoples. Influenced by Las Casas, Charles eventually ended slavery in Spanish America.

However, in 1513, something happened that changed Las Casas's life. He took part in the conquest of Cuba. As a reward, he received more Indian slaves and an *encomienda,* or land grant. But he also witnessed a massacre. The Spanish killed thousands of innocent Indians, including women and children, who had welcomed the Spanish into their town. In his book *The Devastation of the Indies: A Brief Account,* he wrote, "I saw here cruelty on a scale no living being has ever seen or expects to see."

A Turning Point

The Cuban massacre in 1513 and other scenes of violence against Indians Las Casas witnessed finally pushed him to a turning point. He could no longer believe that the Spanish conquest was right. Before, he had thought that only some individuals acted cruelly and inhumanely. Now he saw that the whole Spanish system of conquest brought only death and suffering to the people of the West Indies.

On August 15, 1514, when he was about thirty years old, Las Casas gave a startling sermon. He asked his congregation to free their enslaved Indians. He also said that they had to return or pay for everything they had taken away from the Indians. He refused to forgive the colonists' sins in confession if they used Indians as forced labor. Then he announced that he would give up his ownership of Indians and the business he had inherited from his father.

Protector of the Indians

For the rest of his life, Las Casas fought for the rights of the Indians in the Americas. He traveled back and forth to Europe working on their behalf. He talked with popes and kings, debated enemies, and wrote letters and books on the subject.

Las Casas influenced both a pope and a king. In 1537, Pope Paul III wrote that Indians were free human beings, not slaves, and that anyone who enslaved them could be thrown out of the Catholic Church. In 1542, Holy Roman emperor Charles V, who ruled Spain, issued the New Laws, banning slavery in Spanish America.

In 1550 and 1551, Las Casas also took part in a famous debate against Juan Ginés Sepúlveda in Spain. Sepúlveda tried to prove that Indians were "natural slaves." Many Spanish, especially those hungry for wealth and glory, shared this belief. Las Casas passionately argued against Sepúlveda with the same message he would deliver over and over throughout his life. Las Casas argued that:

- Indians, like all human beings, have rights to life and liberty.
- The Spanish stole Indian land through bloody and unjust wars.
- There is no such thing as a good encomienda.
- Indians have the right to make war against the Spanish.

Las Casas died in 1566. The voices and the deeds of the conquistadors slowly eroded the memory of his words. But in other European countries, people began to read *The Devastation of the Indies: A Brief Account.* As time passed, more of Las Casas's works were published. In the centuries to follow, fighters for justice took up his name as a symbol for their own struggles for human rights.

The Legacy of Las Casas

Today, historians remember Las Casas as the first person to actively oppose the oppression of Indians and to call for an end to Indian slavery. Later, in the 19th century, Las Casas inspired both Father Hidalgo, the father of Mexican independence, and Simón Bolívar, the liberator of South America.

In the 1960s, Mexican American César Chávez learned about injustice at an early age. His family worked as migrants, moving from place to place to pick crops. With barely an eighth-grade education, Chávez organized workers, formed a union, and won better pay and better working and living conditions. Speaking for the powerless, he rallied people to his side with his cry, "Sí, Se Puede!" ("Yes, We Can!") Just as the name "Chávez" will always be connected to the struggles of the farm workers, the name "Las Casas" will forever be connected to any fight for human rights and dignity for the native people of the Americas.

This 19th-century painting, which is part of a series of murals in the U.S. Capitol, symbolizes the role of Las Casas as "Protector of the Indians."

Chapter 33

The Scientific Revolution

How did the Scientific Revolution change the way people understood the world?

33.1 Introduction

In this chapter, you will learn about a major shift in thinking, called the Scientific Revolution. Between 1500 and 1700, modern science emerged as a new way of gaining knowledge about the world. Before this time, Europeans relied on two main sources for their understanding of nature. One was the Bible and religious teachings. The other was the work of classical thinkers, especially the philosopher Aristotle.

During the Scientific Revolution, scientists challenged traditional teachings about nature. They asked fresh questions, and they answered them in new ways. Inventions like the telescope showed them a universe no one had imagined before. Careful observation also revealed errors in accepted ideas about the physical world.

A good example is Aristotle's description of falling objects. Aristotle had said that heavier objects fall to the ground faster than lighter ones. This idea seemed logical, but the Italian scientist Galileo Galilei (gal-uh-LEE-oh gal-uh-LAY) questioned it.

According to his first biographer, Galileo performed a demonstration in the city of Pisa, where he was teaching. He dropped two balls of different weights from the city's Leaning Tower. The results shocked the crowd of students and professors. They expected the heavier ball to land first. Instead, the two balls landed at the same time.

Galileo's demonstration is an application of the scientific method. As you will learn, the scientific method uses both logic and observation to help people understand the natural world.

Thinkers like Galileo gave birth to modern science. In this chapter, you will learn about the roots of the Scientific Revolution. You will meet some of the key scientists of the period and find out about their major discoveries and inventions. You will also learn how the Scientific Revolution changed the way people understood the world.

Galileo tested his ideas about gravity by dropping two balls of different sizes and weights from the top of the Leaning Tower of Pisa.

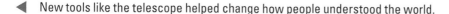

◀ New tools like the telescope helped change how people understood the world.

Humanist ideas and works from the Renaissance influenced later scientific discoveries. Leonardo da Vinci's drawing *Vitruvian Man* (detail) is a famous study of the human body from this period.

33.2 Roots of the Scientific Revolution

Humans have asked questions about nature since ancient times. What was different about the **Scientific Revolution** of the 16th, 17th, and 18th centuries? What factors helped to bring it about?

During the Middle Ages, two major sources guided most Europeans' thinking about the natural world. The first was the Bible. For Christians, the Bible was the word of God. Whatever the Bible seemed to say about nature, then, must be true.

The second source was the teachings of Aristotle. This Greek philosopher had written about logic in the 300s B.C.E. In the late Middle Ages, philosophers like Thomas Aquinas combined Aristotle's thinking with Christian faith. Aquinas argued that reason, or logical thought, could be used to support Christian beliefs. He held that the existence of God, for example, could be proven by reason.

During the Renaissance, many thinkers began to question the conclusions of earlier thinkers. For example, Renaissance scholars rediscovered the cultures of ancient Greece and Rome. Arab, Christian, and Jewish scholars in the Muslim world translated many classical works. They also made advances of their own in such fields as medicine, astronomy, and mathematics.

From the works of these scholars, Europeans learned about a greater variety of ideas. Many European philosophers were influenced by Greek **rationalism**. This was the belief that reason, or logical thought, could be used to discover basic truths about the world. Renaissance thinkers also observed nature directly. The Renaissance physician Vesalius dissected corpses to test ancient ideas about the body. Trust in reason and observation became a key part of modern science.

The Age of Exploration also helped spur the growth of science. For instance, in the 2nd century C.E., Ptolemy had stated that there were only three continents: Europe, Africa, and Asia. Explorers who visited the Americas proved him wrong. Such discoveries encouraged Europeans to question existing knowledge.

Gradually, scientists developed a new method for probing nature's mysteries. Their work led to many dramatic discoveries.

33.3 Copernicus and Kepler: A New View of the Universe

The Scientific Revolution began with the work of the Polish astronomer Nicolaus Copernicus. His work led to a new view of the universe.

For nearly two thousand years, most people believed that Earth was the center of the universe. According to this **geocentric theory**, the sun, stars, and planets—everything believed to be the universe—traveled around a motionless Earth. Aristotle had taught this theory. The Bible seemed to support it, as well. In one Bible story, God stops the sun from moving across the sky. The geocentric theory also seemed to make obvious sense. After all, the sun and stars do look like they travel around Earth.

Aristotle had also taught that all heavenly bodies move in circles. Unfortunately, this belief made it hard to explain the observed movements of planets, such as Mars and Jupiter. In the 2nd century C.E., Ptolemy created a complicated theory to account for this.

Both ancient and medieval writers, including Muslim scientists, pointed out problems with Ptolemy's theory. In the early 1500s, Copernicus tackled these problems. Using observations and mathematics, he proposed a very different idea. According to his **heliocentric theory**, Earth and the other planets travel in orbits around the sun. The sun is at the center of this solar system. Earth also turns on its own axis every 24 hours. This turning explains why heavenly objects seem to move around Earth.

Like Ptolemy, Copernicus had trouble predicting the movement of planets with perfect accuracy. Still, he thought his theory was simpler and more satisfying than Ptolemy's. In 1543, he published a book describing his idea. The book convinced very few people. Some Church officials and scientists attacked it.

Then, in the early 1600s, German scientist Johannes Kepler expanded on Copernicus's theory. After studying detailed observations, Kepler figured out that the orbits of the planets were ovals, not circles. With this insight, he wrote precise mathematical laws describing the planets' movements around the sun.

Kepler's laws agreed beautifully with actual observations. This agreement was evidence that the Copernican theory was correct. Once the theory took hold, people would never again hold the same view of Earth's place in the universe.

geocentric theory a theory that Earth is the center of the solar system or the universe. *Geo* is Greek for "earth."

heliocentric theory a theory that places the sun at the center of the solar system with the planets, including Earth, revolving around it. *Helio* is Greek for "sun."

Copernicus's heliocentric theory put the sun at the center of a solar system. Before his work, most people thought the sun, planets, and universe revolved around Earth.

33.4 Galileo and the Copernican Theory

Galileo Galilei lived at the same time as Johannes Kepler. Galileo explored many questions. He was especially interested in problems of motion. As you have read, he disproved Aristotle's theory that heavy objects fall faster than lighter ones. He made other discoveries about motion, as well. For example, he used mathematics to describe the path of a projectile, or something that is thrown or shot.

Galileo's biggest discoveries came when he turned his curiosity toward the sky. What he learned there made him a champion of the Copernican theory.

Galileo's Discoveries In 1609, Galileo heard about an invention from the Netherlands: the **telescope.** A telescope uses glass **lenses** to make distant objects appear much closer.

Galileo decided to build his own telescope. He figured out how telescopes worked. He learned how to grind glass for lenses. Soon he was building more and more powerful telescopes.

Galileo began studying the sky through a telescope. He saw things no one had seen before. He saw that the moon's surface was rough and uneven. He discovered four of the moons that revolve around the planet Jupiter.

Galileo also observed the planet Venus. To the naked eye, Venus looks like a bright star. Galileo saw something new. You know from looking at the moon that it goes through phases. It takes on what appear to be different shapes, from a thin sliver to the full moon. With his telescope, Galileo could see that Venus also passed through phases. Sometimes it was brightly lit, while at other times it was partially dark.

Galileo's discoveries contradicted the traditional view of the universe. For example, Aristotle had taught that the moon was perfectly smooth. Galileo saw that it wasn't. Aristotle had said that Earth was the only center of motion in the universe. Galileo saw moons moving around Jupiter. Aristotle believed that Venus and other planets traveled around Earth. Galileo realized that the phases of Venus meant that it was traveling around the sun.

Galileo's work with telescopes helped him discover new information about the planets that supported Copernicus's theories.

Conflict with the Church

Galileo's discoveries supported the Copernican heliocentric theory and led him into a bitter conflict with the Catholic Church. Church leaders saw the Copernican theory as wrong and dangerous. To them, the idea that Earth was at the center of the universe was part of their entire system of religious belief.

Church officials feared that attacks on the geocentric theory could lead people to doubt the Church's teachings. In 1616, the Catholic Church warned Galileo not to teach the Copernican theory.

Galileo refused to be silenced. In 1632, he published a book called *Dialogue on the Two Chief World Systems.* The book described an imaginary conversation about the theories of Ptolemy and Copernicus. Galileo did not openly take sides, but the book was really a clever argument for the Copernican theory. The character who upheld the geocentric theory was portrayed as foolish. The one who believed the heliocentric theory was logical and convincing.

Galileo's *Dialogue* caused an uproar. In 1633, the pope called Galileo to Rome to face the Catholic court, known as the Inquisition.

At Galileo's trial, Church leaders accused him of heresy. They demanded that he confess his error. At first Galileo resisted. In the end, the court forced him to swear that the geocentric theory was true. He was forbidden to write again about the Copernican theory.

Galileo's Influence

However, the Church's opposition could not stop the spread of Galileo's ideas. Scientists across Europe read his *Dialogue.* The book helped convert many to the Copernican theory.

Galileo's studies of motion also advanced the Scientific Revolution. Like Kepler, he used observation and mathematics to solve scientific problems. Galileo's theory of motion describes how objects move on Earth. Kepler's laws describe the movements of the planets. The next scientist you will meet united these ideas in a single great theory.

Galileo was tried before the Roman Catholic court known as the Inquisition for heresy, or going against Church teaching. Church leaders demanded that he agree that Earth is at the center of the universe.

gravity the force of attraction between all masses in the universe

mass a measure of the amount of matter in an object

33.5 Isaac Newton and the Law of Gravity

Isaac Newton was born in England in 1642, the same year Galileo died. Newton was a brilliant scientist and mathematician. His greatest discovery was the law of **gravity**.

In later life, Newton told a story about his discovery. He was trying to figure out what kept the moon traveling in its orbit around Earth. Since the moon was in motion, why didn't it fly off into space in a straight line? Then Newton saw an apple fall from a tree and hit the ground. Newton realized that when objects fall, they fall toward the center of Earth. He wondered if the same force that pulled the apple to the ground was tugging on the moon. The difference was that the moon was far away, and Newton reasoned that the force was weaker there. It was just strong enough to bend the moon's motion into an oval orbit around Earth.

This was Newton's great insight. A single force explained a falling apple on Earth, as well as the movements of heavenly bodies. Newton called this force *gravity*.

Newton stated the law of gravity in a simple **formula**. All physical objects, he said, had a force of attraction between them. The strength of the force depended on the masses of the objects and the distance between them. **Mass** is a measure of the amount of matter in an object. For example, the moon and Earth tug on each other. At a certain point in space, these "tugs" cancel each other out. The result is that the moon is trapped in its orbit around Earth. In contrast, an apple has a small mass compared to Earth and is very close to Earth, so gravity pulls it toward Earth's center.

In 1687, Newton published a book known as the *Principia,* or *Principles*. The book presented the law of gravity. It also described three laws of motion. Newton's laws provided an explanation for what earlier scientists had observed. For example, others had shown that the planets moved around the sun. Newton's laws explained why. Just as gravity kept the moon traveling around Earth, it kept the planets traveling around the sun.

Newton's laws dramatically changed people's view of the universe. Many people began to see the universe as a beautifully designed machine. Some compared it to a well-built clock. People needed only to discover how it worked.

Inspiration for new ideas often comes when the ordinary is seen in a new way. Isaac Newton gained insight into the laws of nature after observing an apple fall to the ground.

33.6 The Scientific Method

A key outcome of the Scientific Revolution was the development of the **scientific method**. Two philosophers who influenced this development were Francis Bacon and Rene Descartes (reh-NAY dey-KAHRT).

Francis Bacon was born in England in 1561. Bacon distrusted much of the traditional learning of the Middle Ages. He said that people could gain knowledge only if they rid their minds of false beliefs. He outlined a method of scientific investigation that depended on close observation.

Rene Descartes was born in France in the year 1596. Descartes prized logic and mathematics. To gain knowledge that was certain, he said, people should doubt every statement until logic proved it to be true. Descartes also saw the physical universe as obeying universal mathematical laws.

These ideas helped create a new approach to science. Over time, scientists developed this approach into the scientific method.

The scientific method combines logic, mathematics, and observation. It has five basic steps:

1. The scientist states a question or problem.
2. The scientist forms a **hypothesis,** or assumption, that might explain the problem.
3. The scientist designs and conducts an experiment to test the hypothesis.
4. The scientist measures the data, or information, produced by the experiment and records the results.
5. The scientist analyzes the data to determine whether the hypothesis is correct.

Galileo's demonstration with falling objects shows how this method works. Galileo wondered whether objects of different weights fall at the same speed. He formed a hypothesis that they did. Then he designed and conducted an experiment to test his hypothesis. He dropped a heavy and a light ball together from the same height off a tower and saw that they landed at the same time. This result showed that his hypothesis was correct.

Scientists still use this basic method today. An advantage of the scientific method is that any trained scientist can repeat what another has done. In this way, scientists can test each others' ideas.

In one way, the spread of the scientific method marked a break with the past. Fewer and fewer people looked to traditional authorities for the answers to scientific problems. But that did not mean they discarded all their old beliefs. For example, thinkers such as Descartes and Newton were deeply religious. For many, science was a way to better understand the world God had made.

scientific method a step-by-step method of investigation involving observation and theory to test scientific assumptions

hypothesis an idea or assumption to be tested in an experiment

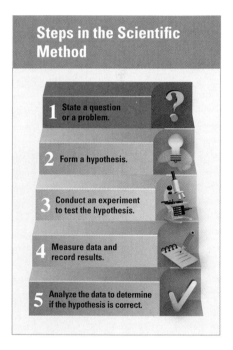

Steps in the Scientific Method

1 State a question or a problem.

2 Form a hypothesis.

3 Conduct an experiment to test the hypothesis.

4 Measure data and record results.

5 Analyze the data to determine if the hypothesis is correct.

33.7 Key Inventions

The Scientific Revolution spurred the invention of new tools for studying the world. These tools, such as the telescope, helped scientists discover new facts and measure data more accurately.

Microscope Scientists use **microscopes** to make small objects appear much larger. The microscope was invented by Dutch lens makers in the late 1500s. In the mid-1600s, Dutchman Antonie van Leeuwenhoek (LAY-ven-hook) designed his own powerful microscopes. He became the first person to see bacteria. Leeuwenhoek was amazed to find a tiny world of living things. He exclaimed, "All the people living in our United Netherlands are not so many as the living animals that I carry in my own mouth this very day!"

Antonie van Leeuwenhoek observed microorganisms through microscopes that he designed (right). A replica of his microscope is shown below. Today's high-powered microscopes are based on the first designs from the 1600s.

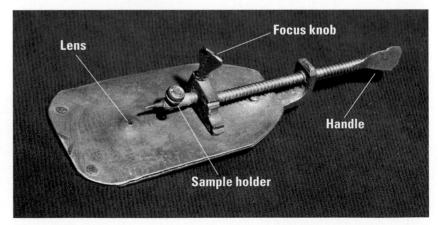

Lens

Focus knob

Handle

Sample holder

Barometer Another important tool developed in this period was the barometer. A barometer measures changes in the pressure of the atmosphere. Evangelista Torricelli (tawr-ih-CHEL-ee) invented the barometer in the 1640s. He filled a glass tube with a liquid metal called mercury. Then he placed the tube upside down in a dish.

Over the next few days, Torricelli watched the tube. He saw that the height of the mercury did not stay the same. The column of mercury moved up and down as the pressure in the atmosphere changed. The barometer soon proved to be a valuable tool in studying and predicting the weather.

Thermometer Galileo likely made the first thermometer. In the early 1700s, however, a German scientist, Daniel Gabriel Fahrenheit, made thermometers more accurate. He put mercury in a glass tube. As the mercury grew warmer, it expanded and rose up the tube. The height of the mercury provided a measure of temperature. Fahrenheit also designed a new temperature scale. In the United States, we still measure temperature using Fahrenheit degrees.

Chapter Summary

In this chapter, you learned about the Scientific Revolution. This movement marked a major shift in the way people thought about the natural world.

The Roots of the Scientific Revolution Several factors contributed to the birth of the Scientific Revolution. Renaissance thinkers questioned traditional learning and observed nature for themselves. Translations of classical texts and some new thinking exposed scholars to new ideas. Discoveries by explorers showed that accepted ideas could be wrong.

Copernicus, Kepler, and Galileo The Scientific Revolution began when Copernicus proposed the daring idea that Earth and the other planets travel around the sun. Kepler built on this heliocentric theory by correctly describing the planets' orbits. Galileo's discoveries about motion and his observations of the planets supported the Copernican theory, although it brought him into conflict with the Catholic Church.

Newton and the Law of Gravity Newton took all this work a giant step forward. His law of gravity explained why planets orbited the sun. Newton also showed that the same laws applied everywhere in the known universe.

The Scientific Method The ideas of Bacon and Descartes helped to shape the scientific method, which proved to be a powerful way of testing ideas about nature.

Key Inventions New tools, such as the microscope, the barometer, and the thermometer, also aided scientific progress. They helped scientists discover new facts and more accurately measure and collect data.

Chapter 34

The Enlightenment

How have the ideas of the Enlightenment influenced modern government?

34.1 Introduction

In this chapter, you will explore the age called the Enlightenment. The *Enlightenment* refers to a period of new thinking among many educated Europeans that began during the late 1600s. This new outlook put great emphasis on reason as the key to human progress. In the 1700s, this way of thinking became widespread in Europe.

Enlightenment thinkers were inspired by the example of scientists, such as Galileo, Bacon, and Newton. Scientists used observation and logic to understand the physical world. Their methods were rapidly overturning old beliefs. Now, thinkers wanted to take a similar approach to problems of human life. These thinkers wanted to forget the teachings of the past because they felt a new age of reason was dawning. In this new age, governments and social institutions would be based on rational understanding, not on errors and superstitions of earlier times.

A Frenchman, Bernard de Fontenelle, expressed this optimistic faith in reason and progress. In 1702, he wrote that the new century "will become more enlightened day by day, so that all previous centuries will be lost in darkness by comparison."

In France, *philosophes* (philosophers) championed these new ideas. These thinkers often gathered in informal meetings, called salons, in private homes. There they exchanged and debated ideas. Many salons were organized by women. Gatherings like these helped to shape and spread the ideas of the Enlightenment.

In this chapter, you will learn about the roots of the Enlightenment. You will meet five philosophers whose ideas greatly influenced the Enlightenment. You will see how their works led to new ideas about government and individual rights. Finally, you will meet several women who played important roles in the Enlightenment.

On the facing page is a scene from a salon in the home of Madame Marie Thérèse Geoffrin (above). She was a leading figure of the Enlightenment.

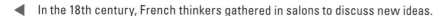

◀ In the 18th century, French thinkers gathered in salons to discuss new ideas.

34.2 The Roots of the Enlightenment

Enlightenment thinkers wanted to examine human life in the light of reason. Rational understanding, they felt, would lead to great progress in government and society.

These thinkers believed they were making a major break with the past. Like everyone, however, they were influenced by what had come before them. In this section, we will first examine the roots of the **Enlightenment**. Then we will consider ways in which the new ideas of the Enlightenment clashed with old beliefs.

Desiderius Erasmus was a humanist scholar of the Renaissance who challenged the authority of the Catholic Church and paved the way for Enlightenment thinkers.

The Scientific Revolution Enlightenment thinking grew out of the Scientific Revolution. In science, observation and reason were revealing natural laws that applied throughout the physical world. The thinkers of the Enlightenment wanted to apply this approach to human life and experience. They asked questions such as: Are there natural laws that tell us how to live? How well do our current institutions follow natural laws? Do natural laws give all people certain rights? What is the best form of government?

Philosophers did not always agree about the answers to these questions. What they all shared was a way of thinking about them. Like scientists, they placed their trust in reason and observation as the best sources of understanding and progress.

The Renaissance and the Reformation The Enlightenment also had roots in the Renaissance and the Reformation. The humanists of the Renaissance questioned accepted beliefs. They celebrated the dignity and worth of the individual. During the Reformation, Protestants rebelled against the Catholic Church. They put individual conscience ahead of religious tradition and authority. Enlightenment thinkers went even further in rejecting authority and upholding the freedom of individuals to think for themselves.

Classical and Christian Influences Like the humanists of the Renaissance, many Enlightenment thinkers were inspired by classical culture. Trust in reason, for example, goes all the way back to the ancient Greeks. So does the idea that people should have a voice in their government. Philosophers who argued for this idea could point to the democracy of ancient Athens or to the republic of ancient Rome.

Christian ideas also influenced Enlightenment thinking. Enlightenment philosophers preferred rational thought to faith based on the Bible. Yet most of them continued to believe in God. They saw the laws of nature as the work of an intelligent Creator. They saw human progress as a sign of God's goodness. Often, their approach to moral problems reflected Christian values, such as respect for others and for a moral law.

New Ideas Versus Old Beliefs The thinkers of the Enlightenment prized reason over authority. They questioned foundations of religion, morality, and government. Everything, they said, must be re-examined in the light of reason. This outlook led to many clashes with accepted beliefs and the ruling powers who upheld them.

Christian faith, for example, was based largely on trust in the Bible as God's word. Enlightenment thinkers believed that humans were perfectly able to discover truth for themselves. Some of them even questioned the existence of God. Others sought a "natural religion" based on reason. To these thinkers, the order in the universe was proof enough of an intelligent Creator. They believed that there was no need to base belief in God on revelations in holy books. Similarly, they maintained that ideas about right and wrong should be based on rational **insight,** not on the teachings of religious authorities.

Enlightenment thinkers also criticized accepted ideas about government. Some questioned the long-held belief that God gave monarchs the right to rule. Many insisted that governments must respect individual rights. Toward the end of the 18th century, these ideas played a major role in revolutions in both America and France.

Ideas from ancient Greek and Rome, such as representative government, inspired Enlightenment philosophers. This painting shows a scene in the Roman senate.

34.3 Thomas Hobbes: Absolute Rule by Kings

Thomas Hobbes was born in England in 1588. He wrote about many subjects, including politics and government. He tried to give a rational basis for absolute, or unlimited, rule by kings.

The son of a clergyman, Hobbes studied at Oxford University. As an adult, he traveled to other European countries, where he met many writers, scientists, and philosophers. He studied mathematics and science, as well as history and government. His studies inspired him to take a scientific approach to problems of human society.

Hobbes's thinking about society was greatly influenced by events in England in the mid-1600s. King Charles I was struggling for power with Parliament, England's lawmaking body. In 1642, civil war broke out between supporters of the monarch and Parliament. Hobbes sided with the king.

In 1649, the king was beheaded. For the next several years, England was ruled by Parliament's House of Commons. But disorder and discontent continued. Finally, in 1660, the monarchy was restored.

The chaos of these years had a powerful impact on Hobbes. What, he asked, is the basis of social order? To answer this question, he tried to reason from his observations of human nature.

In Hobbes's view, human beings were naturally cruel, selfish, and greedy. In 1651, he published a book called *Leviathan*. In this book, he wrote that people are driven by a restless desire for power. Without laws or other social controls, people would always be in conflict. In such a "state of nature," life would be "nasty, brutish and short."

Governments, Hobbes said, were created to protect people from their own selfishness. Because people were selfish by nature, they could not be trusted to make decisions that were good for society as a whole. Only a government that has a ruler with absolute authority could maintain an orderly society.

Later Enlightenment thinkers came to quite different conclusions about human nature and the best form of government. Hobbes was important, however, because he was one of the first thinkers to apply the tools of the Scientific Revolution to problems of politics. During the Enlightenment and the years that followed, many European countries moved away from absolute monarchy.

In his book *Leviathan,* Hobbes argued that people are inherently selfish and that governments are created to make decisions that are best for society as a whole.

04.4 John Locke. Natural Rights

John Locke was born in England in 1632. His thinking about government and people's rights had a major impact on the Enlightenment.

Thomas Hobbes had argued that kings should have absolute power. In contrast, Locke favored **constitutional monarchy**. In this type of government, a basic set of laws limits the ruler's power.

Locke's ideas reflected a long tradition of limitations on the English monarchy. This tradition dates to 1215, when English nobles forced King John to sign Magna Carta, or the "Great Charter." Magna Carta established the idea that even monarchs had to obey English laws and respect certain individual rights.

Over time, Parliament became the main check on the monarch's power. During the civil war of the 1640s, Locke's father fought on the side of Parliament. The young Locke was greatly influenced by his father's beliefs.

In the 1680s, another crisis developed. The new king, James II, was Catholic. His enemies in Protestant England feared that he wanted to put Catholics in power. In 1688, they forced James to flee the country.

In 1698, Parliament gave the crown to James's Protestant daughter Mary and her husband, William. Parliament also passed a **bill of rights**. The English Bill of Rights strengthened the power of Parliament as the representative of the people. For example, it forbade the monarch to keep a standing army in peacetime or to levy taxes without Parliament's consent. It also listed individual rights. Among them were protection in court cases from excessive fines and "cruel and unusual punishment."

constitutional monarchy a form of government in which the monarch's power is limited by a basic set of laws

bill of rights a list of basic human rights that a government must protect

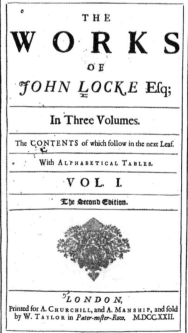

John Locke believed that all people have natural rights, including the rights to life, liberty, and property.

Locke approved of these changes in England. In 1690, he published *Two Treatises of Government.* In this book, he offered a theory of government that justified Parliament's actions.

Locke denied the divine right of monarchs to rule. The true basis of government, he wrote, was a **social contract,** or agreement, among free people. Under this agreement, the purpose of government was to protect people's **natural rights**. These included the right to life, liberty, and property. The people are the sole source of power. They agree to give power to the government to rule on their **behalf**. Therefore, according to Locke's social contract, a government's authority was based on the consent of the governed. If the government failed to respect people's rights, it broke the contract and could be overthrown.

Locke's view of government had a wide influence. In 1776, his ideas would be echoed in the American Declaration of Independence.

34.5 Montesquieu: Separation of Powers

Charles-Louis de Secondat was born in France in 1689. He is better known by his title, the Baron de Montesquieu (MON-tuh-skyoo).

In his youth, Montesquieu attended a Catholic school. Later he became a lawyer. When his uncle died in 1716, Montesquieu inherited the title of baron along with his uncle's fortune. He also became president of the local parliament.

In 1721, Montesquieu achieved fame as a writer with a book called *Persian Letters*. The book described French society as seen by fictional travelers from Persia. It used humor to criticize French institutions, including the king's court and the Catholic Church. It quickly became very popular, and Montesquieu became an admired guest in the salons of Paris.

Montesquieu was an influential French political thinker who argued that a government's power should be divided among separate branches.

Montesquieu's most famous book was *The Spirit of Laws,* published in 1748. In this book, he described his theory of how governments should be organized.

Like John Locke, Montesquieu was concerned with how to protect political liberty. The best way to do this, he argued, was to divide power among three branches of government. In such a system, the legislative branch made the laws. The executive branch enforced the laws. The judicial branch interpreted the laws. In this way, no one branch would be too powerful. Montesquieu called this concept the **separation of powers**.

Montesquieu's theory reflected his admiration for the English government. In England, Parliament made the laws. The monarch enforced the laws, and courts interpreted them. Each branch of government checked, or limited, the power of the others. When powers were not separated in this way, Montesquieu warned, liberty was soon lost. Too much power in the hands of any one person is called **despotism**.

Montesquieu's ideas had a powerful impact on later thinkers. Among them were the men who wrote the U.S. Constitution. They made the separation of powers a key part of the American system of government.

34.6 Voltaire: Religious Tolerance and Free Speech

Francois-Marie Arouet was born in France in 1694. Under the pen name Voltaire, he became one of the most celebrated writers of the Enlightenment.

As a young man, Voltaire attended a Catholic college in Paris. After college, he settled on a career in literature. He soon earned fame as a writer and as a witty participant in Paris salons.

Voltaire believed passionately in reforming society in the name of justice and human happiness. He warned against what he saw as superstition, error, and oppression. With biting humor, he attacked the French court and the power of the Catholic clergy.

Like Montesquieu, Voltaire admired England's constitutional monarchy and separation of powers. In his view, the English were governed by law, not by the **arbitrary** wishes of a single ruler. To be governed by law, he said, was "man's most cherished right."

Voltaire was especially concerned with freedom of thought and expression. He championed **religious tolerance**. This means allowing people to practice religion in their own ways. Voltaire thought religious conflict was one of the main sources of evil in the world. He argued that no single religion possessed all the truth. At the same time, he held that there was a core of truth in all religions. This core was the "natural religion" that reason made available to everyone.

Voltaire also spoke out for the right of free speech. Once he wrote a letter to a man whose views he strongly opposed. He said that he would give his life so that his opponent could continue to write. A later writer expressed Voltaire's feeling in the words, "I disapprove of what you say, but I will defend to the death your right to say it."

Throughout his life, Voltaire criticized intolerance and oppression wherever he saw them. His outspokenness often led to conflicts with authorities. Twice, he spent time in prison. Several times, he was forced to flee to another city or country.

Voltaire's ideas about religious tolerance and free speech greatly influenced colonial American political thinkers, such as Thomas Jefferson. They demanded that freedom of religion and free speech be included in the U.S. Bill of Rights.

Voltaire was one of the main thinkers of the Enlightenment. His ideas about tolerance and free speech influenced the writers of the U.S. Bill of Rights.

religious tolerance the acceptance of different religious beliefs and customs

34.7 Cesare Beccaria: The Rights of the Accused

Cesare Beccaria (beck-kah-REE-ah) was born in Milan, Italy, in 1738. He was a pioneer in the field of criminology. His work stressed the rights of accused people to fair treatment.

The son of an aristocrat, Beccaria attended a Catholic school as a boy. In 1758, he received a degree in law from the University of Pavia. When he finished his studies, he returned to Milan. There he was soon caught up in the intellectual excitement of the Enlightenment.

In 1763, Beccaria began a study of the justice system. He was upset by the harsh practices that were common in his day. Torture was often used to force confessions from accused persons or statements from witnesses to a crime. People might have their thumbs crushed in a device called a thumbscrew. Or they might have their bodies stretched on a device called a rack until their joints were pulled apart.

Beccaria objected to other practices, as well. It wasn't unusual for trials to be held in secret. Judges were often corrupt. People found guilty of crimes were often sentenced to death.

Beccaria attacked these practices in a famous book called *On Crimes and Punishments*. He argued that laws exist to preserve security and order. Punishments, he said, should be designed to serve this purpose. Like other people, criminals made rational decisions. To stop people from committing crimes, punishment did not have to be brutal. It only had to be certain and severe enough to outweigh the potential benefits of the crime.

Cesare Beccaria argued against forms of punishment that had been in use for centuries, such as stretching a person on a rack.

Beccaria also argued for other specific rights. A person accused of a crime, he said, should receive a fair and speedy trial. Torture should never be used. In addition, it was wrong to punish some people more harshly than others for the same crime. Punishment, he said, should fit the seriousness of the crime. He also believed that capital punishment—putting someone to death—should be ended completely.

Beccaria's book encouraged the scientific study of crime. His ideas about rights and punishment influenced reform movements throughout Europe. In the United States, many laws concerning crime and punishment reflect his ideas.

34.8 The Impact of the Enlightenment on Government

Enlightenment thinkers proposed new ideas about human nature and the best forms of government. Let's take a look at the influence of these ideas in Europe and America.

Enlightened Rule A few European absolute monarchs tried to apply Enlightenment ideas in the 1700s. Among them were Frederick the Great of Prussia, Catherine the Great of Russia, and Joseph II of Austria. These rulers became known as "enlightened despots" or "benevolent despots." *Benevolent* means "to be kind; to do good for others."

Enlightened monarchs founded universities and scientific societies. They introduced reforms, such as greater religious tolerance and an end to torture and capital punishment. But these rulers pushed change only so far. They did not want to anger the noble classes, whose support they needed. Nor did they want to lose their own power.

The American and French Revolutions The ideas of the Enlightenment greatly influenced leaders of the American Revolution. English colonists in America shared the traditions of Magna Carta and the English Bill of Rights, as John Locke had. When the colonists rebelled in 1775, they pointed to the abuse of their rights by the English king. The Declaration of Independence echoed Locke's ideas on natural rights and the social contract.

The U.S. Constitution also contains ideas from the Enlightenment. The Constitution includes Montesquieu's idea of separation of powers. The Bill of Rights protects the freedoms of religion and speech championed by Voltaire. It also supports some of the rights promoted by Beccaria, such as the right to a speedy trial.

In 1789, a revolution broke out in France, and the absolute monarchy there was overthrown. France's National Assembly produced the Declaration of the Rights of Man and of the Citizen. This document proclaimed liberty and equality. It upheld the rights to own property and to resist oppression. It also guaranteed freedom of speech and religion. All these ideas grew out of the Enlightenment.

Enlightenment ideas greatly influenced the writing of the U.S. Declaration of Independence. From left to right, Benjamin Franklin, John Adams, and Thomas Jefferson work on drafting the document.

34.9 Women of the Enlightenment

The women of the 1700s did not enjoy the same rights or status as men. Yet a number of women played an important role in the Enlightenment. Some helped spread Enlightenment thinking by hosting salons, and in their thinking and published writing. Others extended ideas about rights and equality to women.

Madame Geoffrin One of the most prominent sponsors of salons was Madame Marie Thérèse Rodet Geoffrin (jhef-FRANH). Beginning in the mid-1700s, the brightest minds in Europe met in her home for lively talk about the latest ideas. Madame Geoffrin also gave financial support to the Encyclopedists, a group of men who put together the first encyclopedia.

At Madame Geoffrin's salons, princes and politicians mingled with artists, writers, and philosophers. Geoffrin led these gatherings with a firm hand. She reserved Mondays for artists and Wednesdays for writers and philosophers.

Abigail Adams was an influential and outspoken supporter of equal rights for women during the American Revolution.

Abigail Adams Abigail Adams firmly supported America's struggle for independence from England. She was married to John Adams, a leader of the American Revolution and the second U.S. president. During the war, she reminded John not to forget women's rights in the new American government. She wrote, "If particular care and attention is not paid to the Ladies, we are determined to foment [start] a Rebellion." Women, she went on, "will not hold ourselves bound by any Laws in which we have no voice." Abigail also spoke out for a woman's right to education.

Olympe de Gouges French Olympe de Gouges was the daughter of a butcher. Despite having little education, she became an important writer and social reformer. In 1791, she published the Declaration of the Rights of Woman and of the Female Citizen. This document was her answer to the National Assembly's Declaration of the Rights of Man and of the Citizen. De Gouges argued for women's equality in every aspect of public and private life. Women, she said, should have the right to vote, hold office, own property, and serve in the military. They should have equal power with men in family life and in the church.

Mary Wollstonecraft English writer Mary Wollstonecraft was another early leader in the struggle to gain equal rights for women. In an essay published in 1792, she argued that women deserve the same rights and opportunities as men. "Let woman share the rights," she wrote, "and she will emulate [imitate] the virtues of men, for she must grow more perfect when emancipated [freed]."

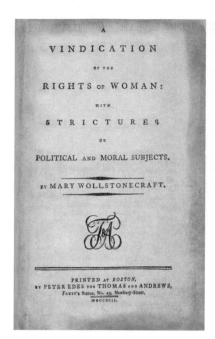

Writer Mary Wollstonecraft was an early reformer in the women's rights movment. She believed that access to education was necessary for women to achieve freedom and equality.

Wollstonecraft believed that education was the key to gaining equality and freedom. She called for reforms to give women the same education as men. In the 19th century, her ideas about equality for women inspired early leaders of the women's rights movement in the United States.

Chapter Summary

In this chapter, you learned about the Enlightenment, a new way of thinking that began in Europe in the late 1600s and became widespread in the 1700s.

The Roots of the Enlightenment The Enlightenment grew out of the Renaissance and the Scientific Revolution. Much Enlightenment thinking challenged accepted beliefs. Enlightenment philosophers wanted to apply the ideas and methods of the Scientific Revolution to problems of government and society.

Enlightenment Thinkers Thomas Hobbes used logic and his observations to reach conclusions about government. John Locke championed the rights to life, liberty, and property. Montesquieu argued for a separation of powers in government. Voltaire championed religious tolerance and free speech. Cesare Beccaria called for reform in criminal law to protect the rights of the accused.

The Impact of the Enlightenment on Government Modern views of government owe a great deal to Enlightenment thinkers. The Enlightenment influenced monarchs in Europe, especially "enlightened despots," and greatly affected revolutions in America and France.

Women of the Enlightenment Several women, such as Abigail Adams, Olympe de Gouges, and Mary Wollstonecraft, worked to extend ideas of liberty and equality to women.

Europe Enters the Modern Age

1492
Columbus Reaches the Americas
Christopher Columbus sails from Spain and reaches the Americas when he lands in the West Indies.

1519–1532
Spanish Conquer "New Spain"
Spanish conquistadors Cortés (below) and Pizarro conquer the Aztec and Inca empires. Wealth from the Americas helps Spain become one of the world's richest and most powerful countries.

1500s–1700s
Scientific Revolution
New thinking leads to the scientific method and tools such as the microscope that allow rapid advances in understanding nature.

1400	1450	1500	1550	1600

1500s
Asian Trade
Portuguese control of the Indian Ocean breaks the Muslim and Italian hold on Asian trade, lowering the price of goods, such as spices and silk, for Europeans.

1543
Copernicus's Heliocentric Theory
The heliocentric theory of the universe is published by Nicolaus Copernicus, changing scientific opinion about Earth as the center of the universe.

1588
Spanish Armada Defeated
The defeat of the Spanish Armada by England leads to declining Spanish power in Europe and abroad.

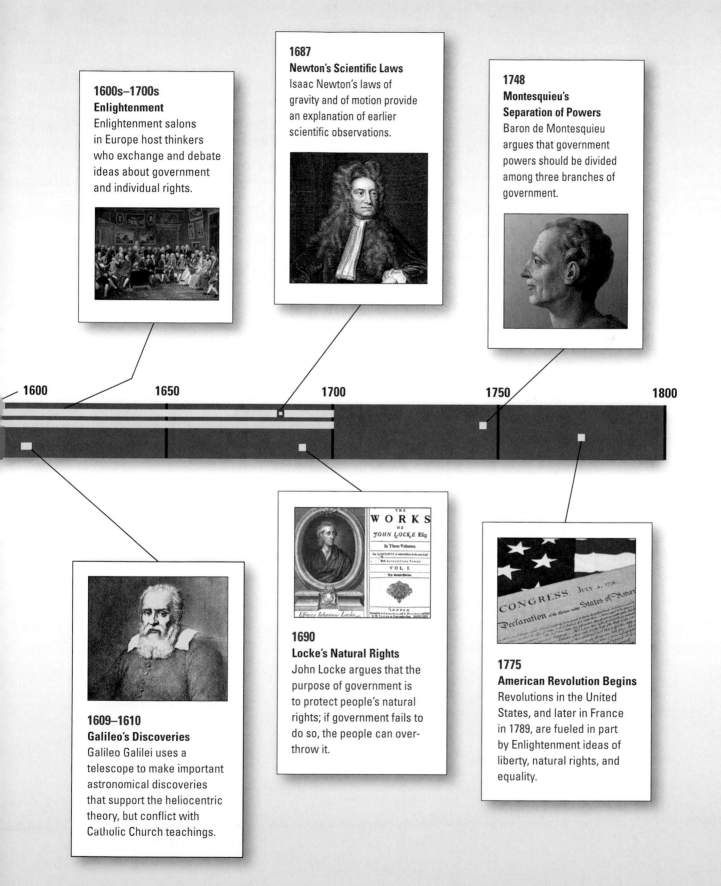

1600s–1700s
Enlightenment
Enlightenment salons in Europe host thinkers who exchange and debate ideas about government and individual rights.

1687
Newton's Scientific Laws
Isaac Newton's laws of gravity and of motion provide an explanation of earlier scientific observations.

1748
Montesquieu's Separation of Powers
Baron de Montesquieu argues that government powers should be divided among three branches of government.

1600   1650   1700   1750   1800

1609–1610
Galileo's Discoveries
Galileo Galilei uses a telescope to make important astronomical discoveries that support the heliocentric theory, but conflict with Catholic Church teachings.

1690
Locke's Natural Rights
John Locke argues that the purpose of government is to protect people's natural rights; if government fails to do so, the people can overthrow it.

1775
American Revolution Begins
Revolutions in the United States, and later in France in 1789, are fueled in part by Enlightenment ideas of liberty, natural rights, and equality.

Resources

The Strahov Library in Prague, Czech Republic, has thousands of books, prints, and manuscripts that date from the ninth to the eighteenth century.

Physical Features of the World

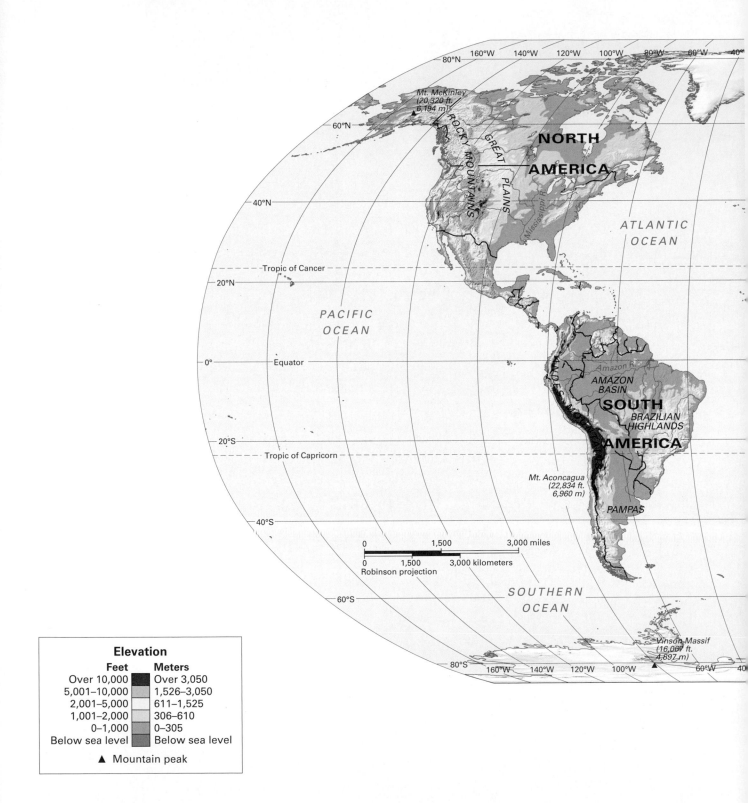

Mt. McKinley
(20,320 ft.
6,194 m)

ROCKY MOUNTAINS

GREAT
PLAINS

NORTH
AMERICA

Mississippi R.

ATLANTIC
OCEAN

80°N 160°W 140°W 120°W 100°W 80°W 60°W 40°

60°N

40°N

Tropic of Cancer

20°N

PACIFIC
OCEAN

0° Equator

AMAZON
BASIN

Amazon R.

SOUTH

BRAZILIAN
HIGHLANDS

AMERICA

20°S

Tropic of Capricorn

Mt. Aconcagua
(22,834 ft.
6,960 m)

PAMPAS

ANDES MTS.

40°S

0	1,500	3,000 miles

0	1,500	3,000 kilometers

Robinson projection

SOUTHERN
OCEAN

60°S

Vinson Massif
(16,066 ft.
4,897 m)

80°S 160°W 140°W 120°W 100°W 80°W 60°W 40°

Elevation

Feet		Meters
Over 10,000		Over 3,050
5,001–10,000		1,526–3,050
2,001–5,000		611–1,525
1,001–2,000		306–610
0–1,000		0–305
Below sea level		Below sea level

▲ Mountain peak

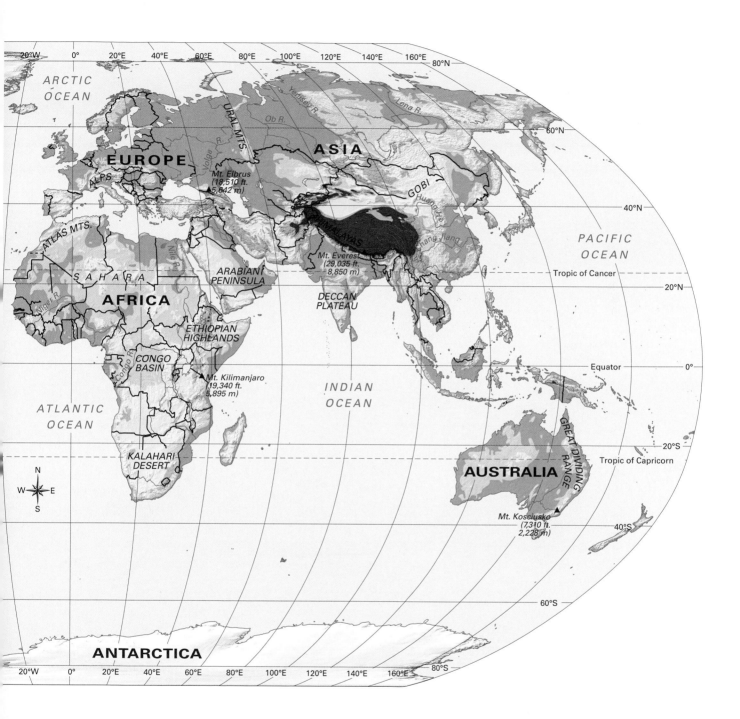

20°W 0° 20°E 40°E 60°E 80°E 100°E 120°E 140°E 160°E 80°N

ARCTIC OCEAN

EUROPE

ASIA

ALPS

URAL MTS.

Volga R.

Ob R.

Yenisey R.

Lena R.

60°N

Mt. Elbrus
(18,510 ft.
5,642 m)

GOBI

40°N

ATLAS MTS.

HIMALAYAS

Huang He

PACIFIC
OCEAN

SAHARA

Niger R.

ARABIAN
PENINSULA

Mt. Everest
(29,035 ft.
8,850 m)

Chang Jiang

Nile R.

Tropic of Cancer

AFRICA

DECCAN
PLATEAU

20°N

ETHIOPIAN
HIGHLANDS

INDIAN
OCEAN

Congo R.

CONGO
BASIN

Mt. Kilimanjaro
(19,340 ft.
5,895 m)

Equator

0°

ATLANTIC
OCEAN

KALAHARI
DESERT

AUSTRALIA

GREAT DIVIDING RANGE

Tropic of Capricorn

20°S

N
W E
S

Mt. Kosciusko
(7,310 ft.
2,228 m)

40°S

60°S

ANTARCTICA

80°S

20°W 0° 20°E 40°E 60°E 80°E 100°E 120°E 140°E 160°E 80°S

Political Boundaries of the World

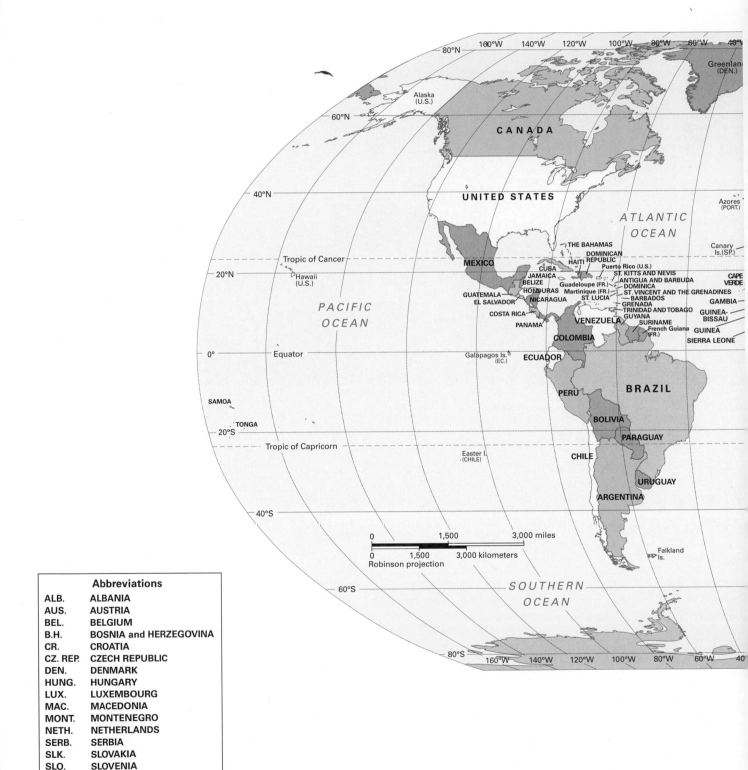

Abbreviations	
ALB.	ALBANIA
AUS.	AUSTRIA
BEL.	BELGIUM
B.H.	BOSNIA and HERZEGOVINA
CR.	CROATIA
CZ. REP.	CZECH REPUBLIC
DEN.	DENMARK
HUNG.	HUNGARY
LUX.	LUXEMBOURG
MAC.	MACEDONIA
MONT.	MONTENEGRO
NETH.	NETHERLANDS
SERB.	SERBIA
SLK.	SLOVAKIA
SLO.	SLOVENIA
SWITZ.	SWITZERLAND

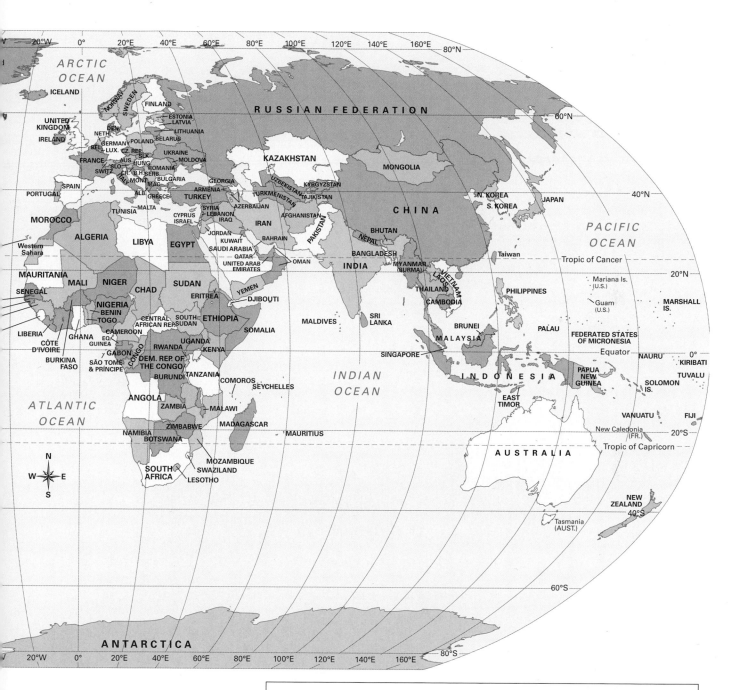

ARCTIC OCEAN

ICELAND

UNITED KINGDOM

IRELAND

NORWAY
SWEDEN
FINLAND

ESTONIA
LATVIA
LITHUANIA

RUSSIAN FEDERATION

DEN.
NETH.
GERMANY
BEL.
LUX.
CZ. REP.
FRANCE
AUS.
SWITZ.
SLO.
ITALY
MONT.
MAC.
POLAND
BELARUS
SLK.
HUNG.
ROMANIA
B.H. SERB.
BULGARIA

UKRAINE
MOLDOVA

KAZAKHSTAN

MONGOLIA

SPAIN

PORTUGAL

ALB.
GREECE
MALTA

GEORGIA
ARMENIA
TURKEY
AZERBAIJAN

UZBEKISTAN
TURKMENISTAN
KYRGYZSTAN
TAJIKISTAN

N. KOREA
S. KOREA

JAPAN

TUNISIA

CYPRUS
ISRAEL
LEBANON
SYRIA
IRAQ
JORDAN
KUWAIT

IRAN

AFGHANISTAN

CHINA

PACIFIC OCEAN

MOROCCO

ALGERIA

LIBYA

EGYPT

SAUDI ARABIA
QATAR
UNITED ARAB EMIRATES
BAHRAIN

PAKISTAN

NEPAL
BHUTAN

Taiwan

Tropic of Cancer

Western Sahara

OMAN

INDIA

BANGLADESH

MYANMAR (BURMA)

Mariana Is. (U.S.)

20°N

MAURITANIA

MALI

NIGER

CHAD

SUDAN

YEMEN

ERITREA

DJIBOUTI

THAILAND
LAOS
VIETNAM
CAMBODIA

PHILIPPINES

Guam (U.S.)

MARSHALL IS.

SENEGAL

NIGERIA
BENIN
TOGO

CENTRAL AFRICAN REP.
SOUTH SUDAN

ETHIOPIA

SRI LANKA

MALDIVES

BRUNEI

MALAYSIA

PALAU

FEDERATED STATES OF MICRONESIA

LIBERIA
CÔTE D'IVOIRE
GHANA
EQ. GUINEA
CAMEROON
GABON
CONGO
RWANDA
UGANDA
KENYA

SOMALIA

SINGAPORE

Equator

NAURU

KIRIBATI

BURKINA FASO
SÃO TOMÉ & PRÍNCIPE
DEM. REP. OF THE CONGO
BURUNDI
TANZANIA

COMOROS
SEYCHELLES

INDONESIA

PAPUA NEW GUINEA

TUVALU

SOLOMON IS.

ANGOLA
ZAMBIA

MALAWI

INDIAN OCEAN

EAST TIMOR

VANUATU

FIJI

ATLANTIC OCEAN

NAMIBIA
ZIMBABWE
BOTSWANA

MADAGASCAR

MAURITIUS

New Caledonia (FR.)

AUSTRALIA

Tropic of Capricorn

MOZAMBIQUE
SWAZILAND
SOUTH AFRICA
LESOTHO

N
W   E
S

NEW ZEALAND

Tasmania (AUST.)

ANTARCTICA

- Independent nations are printed in bold capital letters: **FRANCE**.
- Nations whose independence or governing rule is in dispute are printed in bold type: **Taiwan**.
- Territories, provinces, and the like governed by an independent nation are printed in bold type, with an abbreviation for the ruling nation: **French Guiana (FR.)**.
- Areas whose governing rule is in dispute are printed in nonbold type: Falkland Islands.
- Areas that are part of an independent nation but geographically separated from it are printed in nonbold type, with an abbreviation for the ruling nation: Hawaii (U.S.).

Physical Features of North America

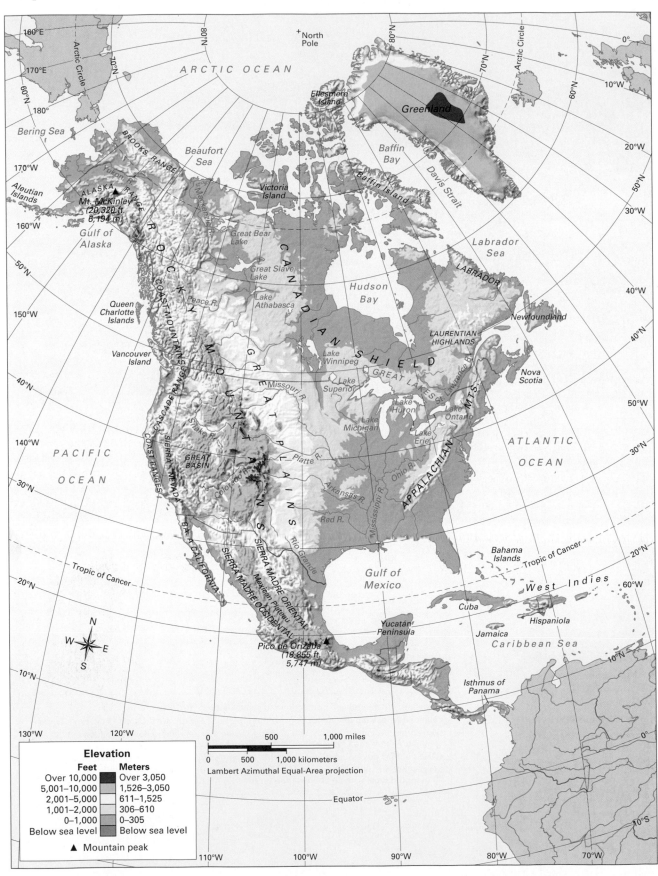

ARCTIC OCEAN

North Pole

Arctic Circle

Ellesmere Island

Greenland

Baffin Bay

Baffin Island

Bering Sea

Beaufort Sea

BROOKS RANGE

Aleutian Islands

ALASKA RANGE
Mt. McKinley
(20,320 ft.
6,194 m)

Gulf of Alaska

Victoria Island

Mackenzie R.

Great Bear Lake

Great Slave Lake

Davis Strait

Labrador Sea

LABRADOR

Queen Charlotte Islands

COAST MOUNTAINS

Peace R.

Lake Athabasca

Hudson Bay

CANADIAN SHIELD

LAURENTIAN HIGHLANDS

Newfoundland

Vancouver Island

Lake Winnipeg

Lake Superior

GREAT LAKES

St. Lawrence R.

APPALACHIAN MTS.

Nova Scotia

PACIFIC OCEAN

CASCADE RANGE

COAST RANGES

SIERRA NEVADA

GREAT BASIN

Snake R.

Colorado R.

Missouri R.

Platte R.

Lake Michigan

Lake Huron

Lake Erie

Lake Ontario

Ohio R.

ATLANTIC OCEAN

Arkansas R.

Mississippi R.

Red R.

Rio Grande

BAJA CALIFORNIA

SIERRA MADRE OCCIDENTAL

SIERRA MADRE ORIENTAL

Mexican Plateau

Gulf of Mexico

Bahama Islands

Tropic of Cancer

Cuba

West Indies

Hispaniola

Jamaica

Yucatán Peninsula

Pico de Orizaba
(18,855 ft.
5,747 m)

Caribbean Sea

Isthmus of Panama

Equator

N
W E
S

Elevation

Feet	Meters
Over 10,000	Over 3,050
5,001–10,000	1,526–3,050
2,001–5,000	611–1,525
1,001–2,000	306–610
0–1,000	0–305
Below sea level	Below sea level

▲ Mountain peak

0   500   1,000 miles
0   500   1,000 kilometers
Lambert Azimuthal Equal-Area projection

Political Boundaries of North America

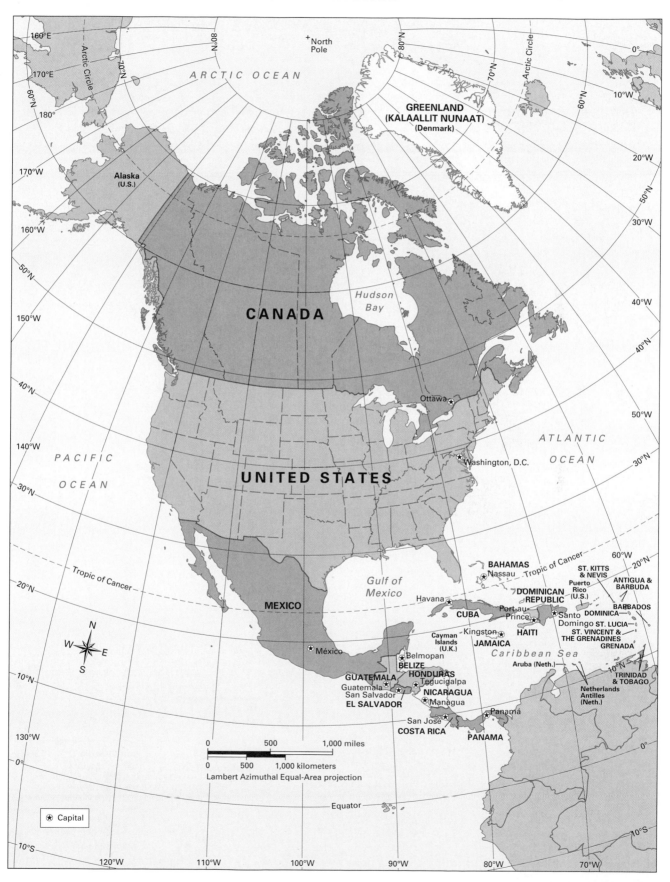

ARCTIC OCEAN

North Pole

GREENLAND
(KALAALLIT NUNAAT)
(Denmark)

Arctic Circle

Alaska
(U.S.)

CANADA

Hudson
Bay

Ottawa

UNITED STATES

PACIFIC
OCEAN

Washington, D.C.

ATLANTIC
OCEAN

Tropic of Cancer

Gulf of
Mexico

BAHAMAS
Nassau   Tropic of Cancer

MEXICO

Havana

CUBA

ST. KITTS
& NEVIS
Puerto
Rico
(U.S.)

DOMINICAN
REPUBLIC

ANTIGUA &
BARBUDA

BARBADOS

Port-au-
Prince

Santo
Domingo ST. LUCIA

DOMINICA

México

Cayman
Islands
(U.K.)

Kingston
JAMAICA

HAITI

ST. VINCENT &
THE GRENADINES

GRENADA

Caribbean Sea

Aruba (Neth.)

Belmopan
BELIZE

GUATEMALA

Guatemala
San Salvador
EL SALVADOR

HONDURAS
Tegucigalpa

NICARAGUA
Managua

Panamá

TRINIDAD
& TOBAGO

Netherlands
Antilles
(Neth.)

San José
COSTA RICA

PANAMA

0   500   1,000 miles

0   500   1,000 kilometers
Lambert Azimuthal Equal-Area projection

Equator

⊛ Capital

Physical Features of South America

Caribbean Sea

ATLANTIC OCEAN

LLANOS

Orinoco R.

GUIANA HIGHLANDS

AMAZON BASIN

Amazon R.

Equator

Galápagos Islands

PACIFIC OCEAN

ANDES MOUNTAINS

Lake Titicaca

São Francisco R.

BRAZILIAN HIGHLANDS

ATACAMA DESERT

Tropic of Capricorn

GRAN CHACO

Iguazú Falls

Mt. Aconcagua (22,835 ft. 6,960 m)

Paraná R.

Uruguay R.

PAMPAS

ATLANTIC OCEAN

Tropic of Capricorn

PATAGONIA

Laguna del Carbón (-344 ft. -105 m)

Strait of Magellan

Tierra del Fuego

Falkland Islands

Cape Horn

0   500   1,000 miles
0   500   1,000 kilometers
Lambert Azimuthal Equal-Area projection

N
W   E
S

Elevation

	Feet	Meters	
	Over 10,000	Over 3,050	
	5,001–10,000	1,526–3,050	
	2,001–5,000	611–1,525	
	1,001–2,000	306–610	
	0–1,000	0–305	
	Below sea level	Below sea level	

▲ Mountain peak

Political Boundaries of South America

Physical Features of Europe and Russia

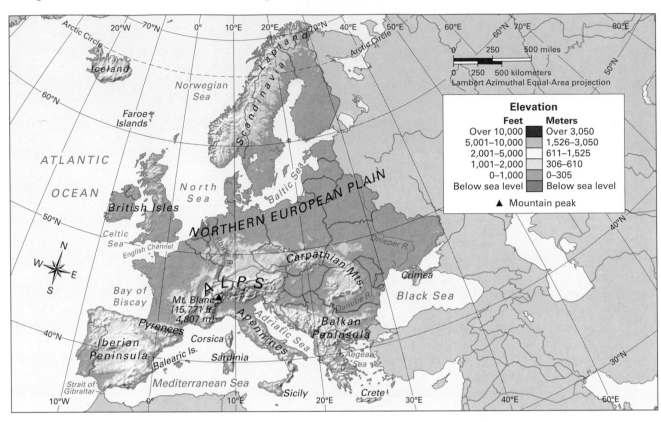

Elevation

Feet	Meters
Over 10,000	Over 3,050
5,001–10,000	1,526–3,050
2,001–5,000	611–1,525
1,001–2,000	306–610
0–1,000	0–305
Below sea level	Below sea level

▲ Mountain peak

Lambert Azimuthal Equal-Area projection

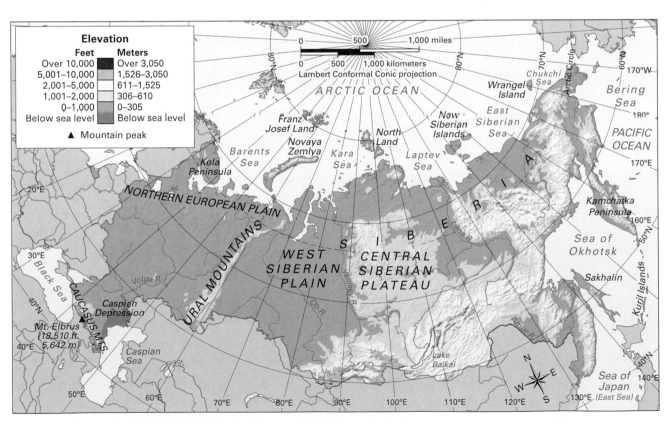

Elevation

Feet	Meters
Over 10,000	Over 3,050
5,001–10,000	1,526–3,050
2,001–5,000	611–1,525
1,001–2,000	306–610
0–1,000	0–305
Below sea level	Below sea level

▲ Mountain peak

Lambert Conformal Conic projection

Political Boundaries of Europe and Russia

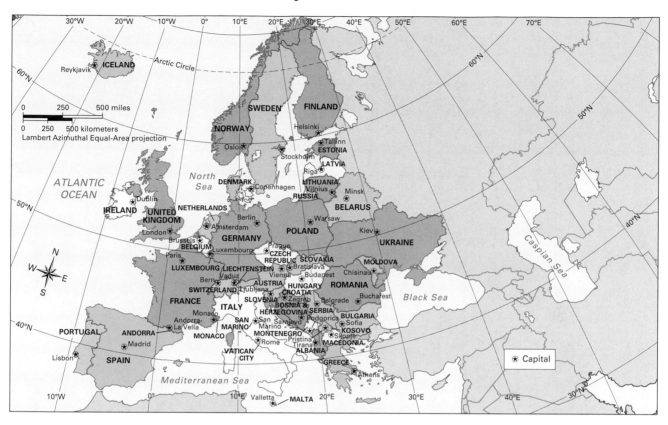

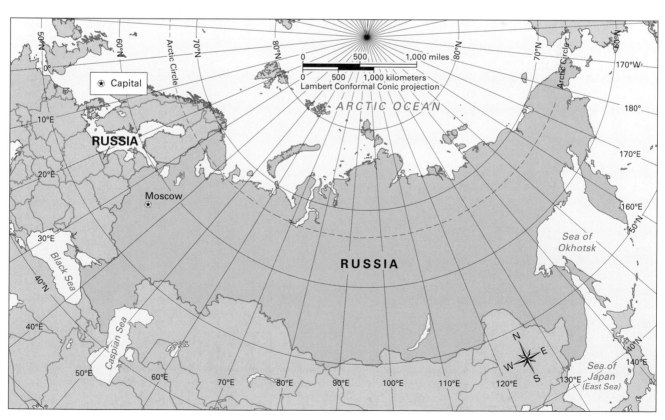

Physical Features of Africa

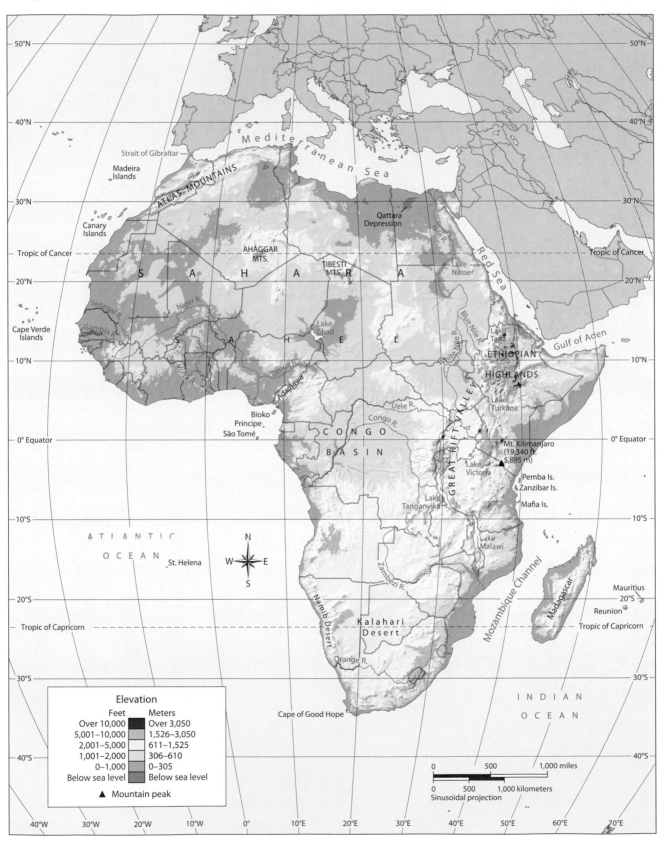

50°N

40°N

Strait of Gibraltar

Madeira Islands

ATLAS MOUNTAINS

Mediterranean Sea

30°N

Canary Islands

Qattara Depression

Tropic of Cancer

AHAGGAR MTS.

TIBESTI MTS.

S   A   H   A   R   A

Nile R.

Red Sea

Lake Nasser

Tropic of Cancer

20°N

Cape Verde Islands

Senegal R.

Niger R.

Gambia R.

Lake Chad

S   A   H   E   L

Blue Nile R.

Lake Tana

Gulf of Aden

10°N

Volta R.

Benue R.

Adamawa

White Nile R.

ETHIOPIAN HIGHLANDS

10°N

Bioko
Principe
São Tomé

Uele R.

Congo R.

C O N G O

Lake Turkana

0° Equator

B A S I N

GREAT RIFT VALLEY

Mt. Kilimanjaro
(19,340 ft.
5,895 m)

0° Equator

A T L A N T I C

Lake Victoria

Pemba Is.
Zanzibar Is.

O C E A N

St. Helena

Lake Tanganyika

Mafia Is.

10°S

N
W   E
S

Lake Malawi

10°S

Namib Desert

Zambezi R.

Mozambique Channel

Madagascar

Mauritius

20°S

Reunion

20°S

Tropic of Capricorn

Kalahari Desert

Tropic of Capricorn

Orange R.

30°S

I N D I A N

30°S

O C E A N

Cape of Good Hope

Elevation

Feet		Meters
Over 10,000		Over 3,050
5,001–10,000		1,526–3,050
2,001–5,000		611–1,525
1,001–2,000		306–610
0–1,000		0–305
Below sea level		Below sea level

▲ Mountain peak

0   500   1,000 miles

0   500   1,000 kilometers
Sinusoidal projection

40°W   30°W   20°W   10°W   0°   10°E   20°E   30°E   40°E   50°E   60°E   70°E

Political Boundaries of Africa

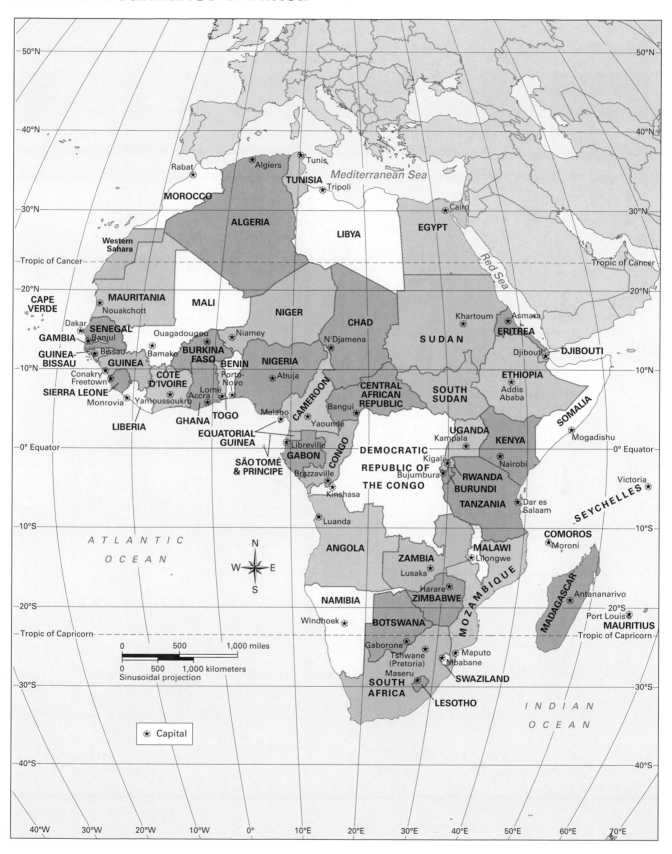

50°N

40°N

Rabat — MOROCCO
Algiers
Tunis — TUNISIA
Tripoli
Mediterranean Sea

30°N

ALGERIA
LIBYA
EGYPT
Cairo
Red Sea

Western Sahara

Tropic of Cancer

20°N

CAPE VERDE
MAURITANIA
Nouakchott
MALI
NIGER
CHAD
Khartoum
Asmara — ERITREA
Djibouti — DJIBOUTI

Dakar
SENEGAL
Banjul
GAMBIA
Bissau
GUINEA-BISSAU
Ouagadougou
Niamey
N'Djamena
SUDAN

Conakry
Freetown
GUINEA
BURKINA FASO
Bamako
BENIN
NIGERIA
Abuja
CENTRAL AFRICAN REPUBLIC
SOUTH SUDAN
ETHIOPIA
Addis Ababa

SIERRA LEONE
CÔTE D'IVOIRE
Porto-Novo
Lomé
Accra
Malabo
Bangui
SOMALIA

Monrovia
Yamoussoukro
CAMEROON
Yaoundé
UGANDA
Kampala
KENYA
Mogadishu

LIBERIA
GHANA
TOGO
EQUATORIAL GUINEA
Libreville
CONGO
DEMOCRATIC REPUBLIC OF THE CONGO
Kigali
RWANDA
Nairobi

0° Equator

SÃO TOMÉ & PRINCIPE
GABON
Brazzaville
Bujumbura
BURUNDI
Victoria
SEYCHELLES

Kinshasa
TANZANIA
Dar es Salaam

Luanda

10°S

ATLANTIC OCEAN
N W E S
ANGOLA
ZAMBIA
Lusaka
MALAWI
Lilongwe
COMOROS
Moroni

MOZAMBIQUE

Harare
ZIMBABWE
MADAGASCAR
Antananarivo

NAMIBIA
Windhoek
BOTSWANA
Port Louis
MAURITIUS

Tropic of Capricorn

0   500   1,000 miles
0   500   1,000 kilometers
Sinusoidal projection

Gaborone
Tshwane (Pretoria)
Maseru
Maputo
Mbabane
SWAZILAND

SOUTH AFRICA
LESOTHO
INDIAN OCEAN

⊛ Capital

40°S

40°W   30°W   20°W   10°W   0°   10°E   20°E   30°E   40°E   50°E   60°E   70°E

Physical Features of Southwest and Central Asia

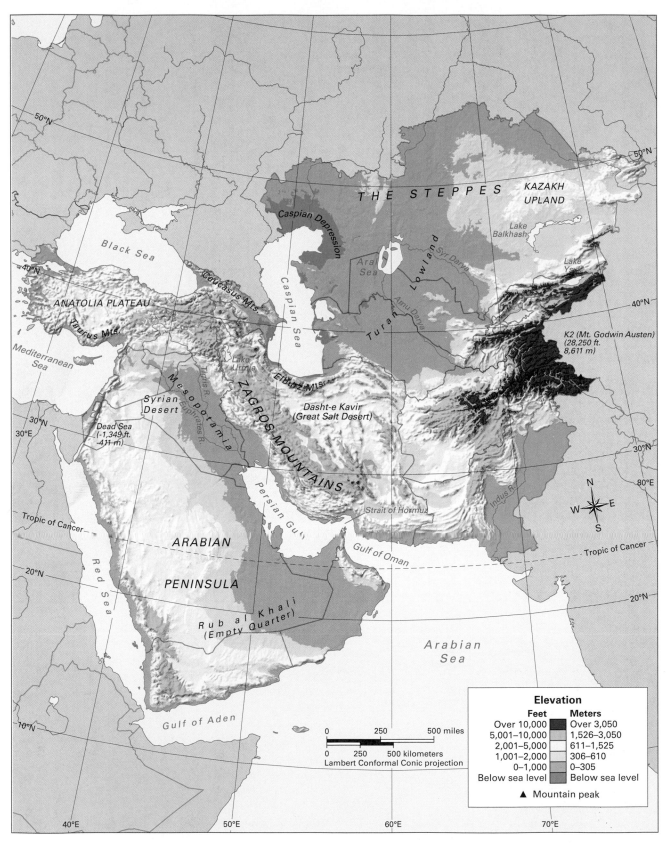

Black Sea

Caspian Depression

THE STEPPES

KAZAKH UPLAND

Lake Balkhash

Aral Sea

Caspian Sea

Turan Lowland

Syr Darya

Lake Y...

ANATOLIA PLATEAU

Caucasus Mts.

Taurus Mts.

Amu Darya

K2 (Mt. Godwin Austen)
(28,250 ft.
8,611 m)

Mediterranean Sea

Lake Urmia

Elburz Mts.

Tigris R.

Euphrates R.

Syrian Desert

Mesopotamia

ZAGROS MOUNTAINS

Dasht-e Kavir
(Great Salt Desert)

Dead Sea
(-1,349 ft.
-411 m)

Indus R.

Persian Gulf

Strait of Hormuz

ARABIAN

Red Sea

Tropic of Cancer

Gulf of Oman

Tropic of Cancer

PENINSULA

Rub al Khali
(Empty Quarter)

Arabian Sea

Gulf of Aden

N
W   E
S

0   250   500 miles

0   250   500 kilometers
Lambert Conformal Conic projection

Elevation

Feet	Meters
Over 10,000	Over 3,050
5,001–10,000	1,526–3,050
2,001–5,000	611–1,525
1,001–2,000	306–610
0–1,000	0–305
Below sea level	Below sea level

▲ Mountain peak

Political Boundaries of Southwest and Central Asia

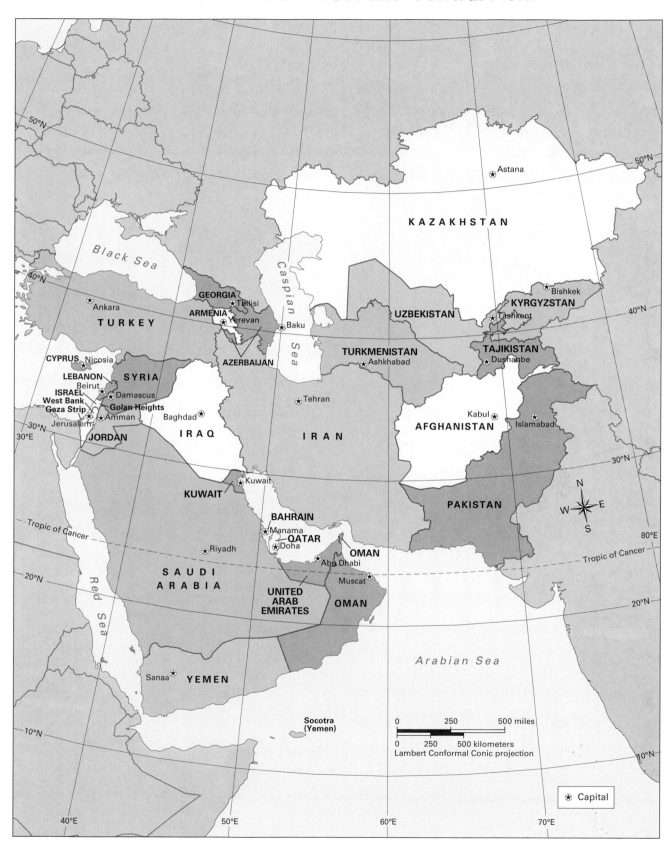

Black Sea

Caspian Sea

KAZAKHSTAN

★ Astana

★ Ankara
TURKEY

GEORGIA
★ Tbilisi
ARMENIA
★ Yerevan
★ Baku

UZBEKISTAN

★ Bishkek
KYRGYZSTAN

★ Tashkent

CYPRUS ★ Nicosia

LEBANON
Beirut ★
ISRAEL
West Bank
Gaza Strip
★ Jerusalem

SYRIA
★ Damascus
Golan Heights
★ Amman

AZERBAIJAN

TURKMENISTAN
★ Ashkhabad

TAJIKISTAN
★ Dushanbe

★ Baghdad

IRAQ

IRAN
★ Tehran

AFGHANISTAN
★ Kabul

★ Islamabad

JORDAN

30°E
30°N

KUWAIT
★ Kuwait

BAHRAIN
★ Manama
QATAR
★ Doha

PAKISTAN

N
W E
S

80°E

Tropic of Cancer

★ Riyadh

OMAN
★ Abu Dhabi
★ Muscat

Tropic of Cancer

**SAUDI
ARABIA**

**UNITED
ARAB
EMIRATES**

OMAN

20°N

Red Sea

Arabian Sea

★ Sanaa
YEMEN

Socotra
(Yemen)

0   250   500 miles

0   250   500 kilometers
Lambert Conformal Conic projection

10°N

40°E   50°E   60°E   70°E

50°N
40°N
30°N
20°N
10°N

★ Capital

Physical Features of South Asia, East Asia, and Southeast Asia

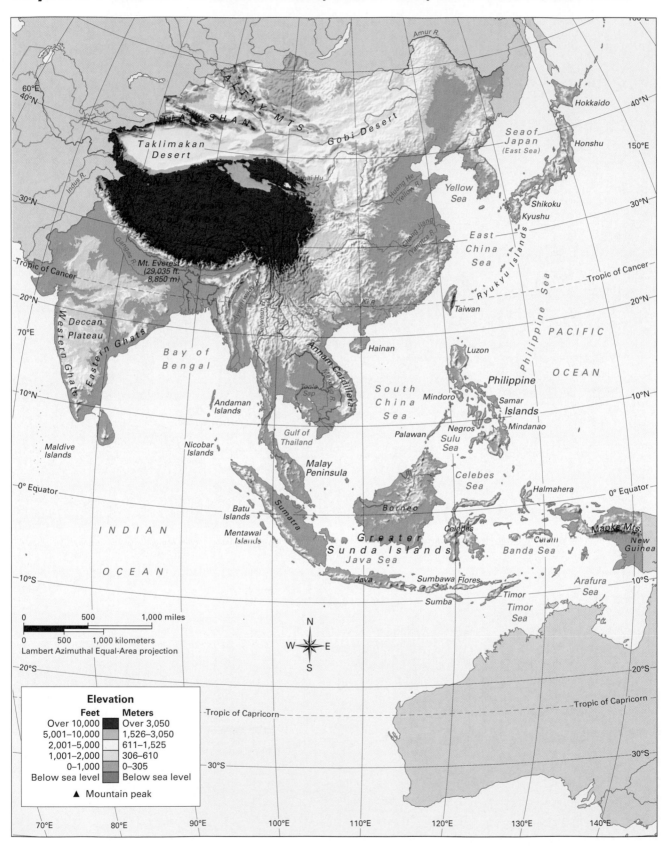

ALTAY MTS.

TIAN SHAN

Taklimakan
Desert

Gobi Desert

Amur R.

Hokkaido

Sea of
Japan
(East Sea)

Honshu

Qinghai Hu

Huang He
(Yellow R.)

Yellow
Sea

Shikoku

Kyushu

Plateau
of Tibet

Chang Jiang
(Yangtze R.)

East
China
Sea

Indus R.

Ganges R.

Mt. Everest
(29,035 ft.
8,850 m)

Tropic of Cancer

Brahmaputra R.

Salween R.

Ryukyu Islands

Taiwan

Tropic of Cancer

Deccan
Plateau

Western Ghats

Eastern Ghats

Bay of
Bengal

Annam Cordillera

Mekong R.

Hainan

South
China
Sea

Luzon

Philippine Sea

PACIFIC

OCEAN

Philippine
Islands

Mindoro

Samar

Andaman
Islands

Tonle
Sap

Gulf of
Thailand

Mindanao

Palawan

Negros

Sulu
Sea

Celebes
Sea

Halmahera

Nicobar
Islands

Malay
Peninsula

Maldive
Islands

0° Equator

Batu
Islands

INDIAN

Sumatra

Borneo

Celebes

Maoke Mts.

New
Guinea

0° Equator

Mentawai
Islands

OCEAN

Greater
Sunda Islands

Java Sea

Ceram

Banda Sea

Java

Sumbawa

Flores

Arafura
Sea

10°S

Sumba

Timor

Timor
Sea

Scale

0   500   1,000 miles

0   500   1,000 kilometers

Lambert Azimuthal Equal-Area projection

N
W   E
S

Elevation

Feet	Meters
Over 10,000	Over 3,050
5,001–10,000	1,526–3,050
2,001–5,000	611–1,525
1,001–2,000	306–610
0–1,000	0–305
Below sea level	Below sea level

▲ Mountain peak

Tropic of Capricorn

Tropic of Capricorn

Political Boundaries of South Asia, East Asia, and Southeast Asia

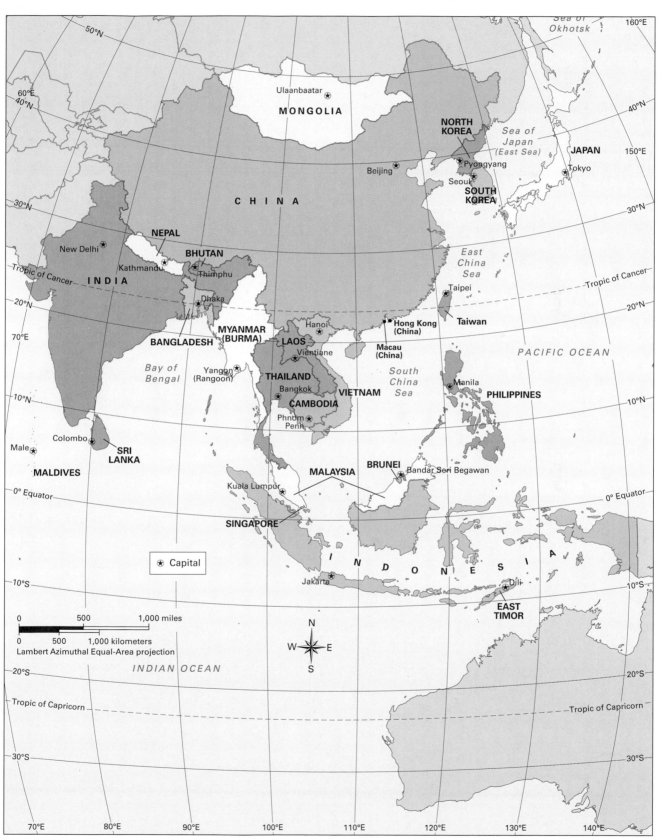

Physical Features of Oceania and Antarctica

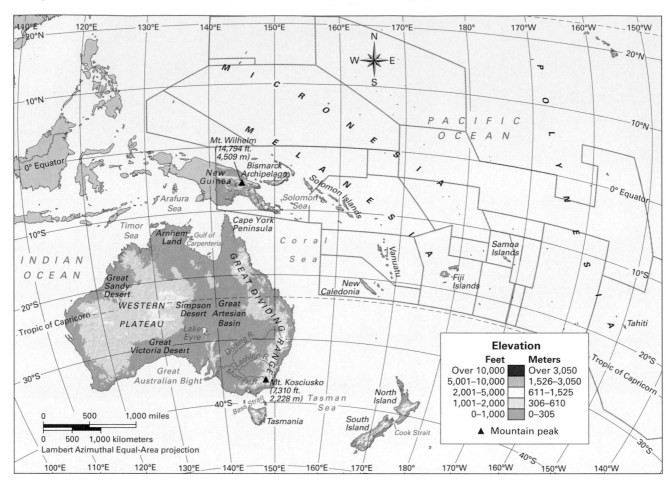

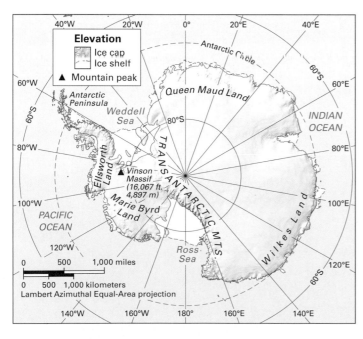

Political Boundaries of Oceania and Antarctica

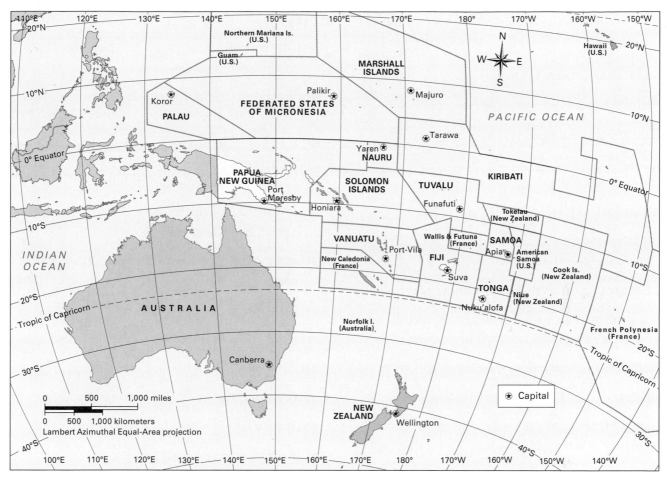

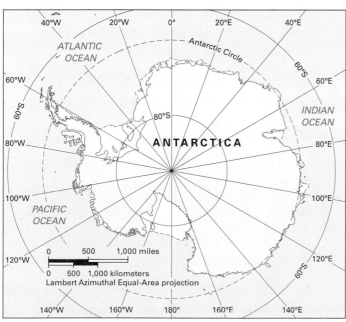

Glossary

Some words in this book have been respelled to help you pronounce them. Respelled words have been adapted from *Merriam-Webster's Collegiate Dictionary, Eleventh Edition; The American Heritage Dictionary of the English Language, Fourth Edition;* and *Random House Dictionary*.

Blue words are defined in the margins.

Black words are Academic Vocabulary terms.

A

abandon to leave something behind

absolute monarchy a monarchy in which the ruler's power is unlimited

abstract existing as an idea without physical form

accumulate to gather something over time, in greater and greater numbers or amount

acquire to come into possession of something

adapt to change to fit a new situation

adaptation a change made to an existing object or way or doing things

administer to manage and organize

Age of Exploration a period of European exploration and discovery that lasted from about 1418 to 1620

Alighieri, Dante a great Italian author of the Renaissance who wrote *The Divine Comedy*

alliance a group of countries, city-states, or other entities who agree to work together, usually for common defense or trade

alternative a choice that differs from another option

Amida Buddhism a form of Buddhism founded on the belief that all people can reach paradise by relying on the mercy of Amida Buddha

analyze to examine or think about carefully

Anglicanism a Protestant denomination of Christian faith founded by Henry VIII in England

anti-Semitism hostility or discrimination against Jews

appliqué a technique in which shaped pieces of fabric are attached to a background fabric to form a design or picture

apprentice a person who works for a master in a trade or craft in return for training

aqueduct a pipe or channel built to carry water over a long distance

arbitrary based on personal preference instead of reason

aristocracy a ruling class of noble families

aristocrat someone who holds a high social level

artifact an item left by an earlier culture

astronomy the study of the stars and planets

authority the power to influence or command

authorize to give official permission

available ready for use

ayllu an Incan clan (group of related families), the basic unit of Incan society

Aztecs a Mesoamerican people who built an empire in central Mexico that flourished from 1428 to 1519 C.E.

B

behalf something that is done for someone else

bill of rights a list of basic human rights that a government must protect

boycott a refusal to do business with an organization or group

bubonic plague a deadly contagious disease caused by bacteria and spread by fleas; also called the Black Death

bureaucracy a highly organized body of workers with many levels of authority

Bushido a samurai code that called on warriors to be honest, fair, and fearless

Byzantine Empire the name for the eastern Roman Empire, located at the crossroads of Europe and Asia; it lasted from about 500 to 1453 C.E.

C

call and response a song style in which a singer or musician leads with a call, and a chorus responds

Calvinism a Protestant denomination of Christian faith founded by John Calvin

capitalism an economic system based on investment of money for profit

capture to take control of a person or thing by force

cartography the science and art of making maps

causeway a solid earthen roadway built across water or low ground

ceremonial center a large plaza in a city center, surrounded by temples and palaces, where religious rituals and other public ceremonies took place

Cervantes, Miguel Spanish Renaissance author of the masterpiece *Don Quixote*

Charlemagne the leader of the Franks from 768 to 814 C.E., who unified most of the Christian lands of Europe into a single empire

charter a written grant of rights and privileges by a ruler or government to a community, class of people, or organization

chivalry the medieval knight's code of ideal behavior, including bravery, loyalty, and respect for women

Christianity the religion based on the life and teachings of Jesus

circulation the passing of something, such as money, from person to person

city-state an independent state consisting of a city and its surrounding territory

civil service examination a test given to qualify candidates for positions in the government

clarify to make understandable; to make clear

classical art art influenced by the styles and techniques of ancient Greece and Rome

clergy the body of people, such as priests, who perform the sacred functions of a church

collapse to fail suddenly and completely

colony a territory, often very large, under the political and economic control of another country

commerce the buying and selling of goods; business

common law a body of rulings made by judges or very old traditional laws that become part of a nation's legal system

communal shared by a community or group

communicate to exchange or share thoughts, feelings, or information using words, writing, or other methods

conduct a person's behavior, especially in front of other people

conflict a disagreement or fight caused by opposing points of view

conformity uniform behavior according to a set of social or cultural rules or beliefs

consequently as a result of

considerable a large amount

Constantine Roman emperor who, in 330 C.E., moved the capital to Byzantium and later renamed it Constantinople

Constantinople the city on the eastern edge of Europe, which Constantine made the capital of the Roman Empire in 330 C.E.

constitutional monarchy a form of government in which the monarch's power is limited by a basic set of laws

contradict to disagree, especially by saying the opposite

contrast a strong difference between two or more things

convert to change one's belief on something

cooperation the action of working together

corruption a pattern of illegal or immoral activities by government officials

cottage industry a small-scale business in which people produce goods at home

Counter-Reformation a movement of the Catholic Church, in reaction to the Reformation, in which Catholic leaders worked to correct abuses, to clarify and defend Catholic teachings, to condemn what they saw as Protestant errors, and to win back members

courtier a male member of a ruler's court

credibility worthy of being believed

Crusades a series of religious wars launched by European Christians to reclaim Jerusalem and other holy sites from the Muslims

cultural diffusion the spread of cultural elements from one society to another

currency the form of money used in a country

D

da Vinci, Leonardo a famous Renaissance artist, scientist, and inventor

daimyo a local lord in Japan in the era of the samurai

decline a slow breakdown or failure

dedicated assigned to a particular purpose

democratic rule by the people; available to the broad mass of people

denomination a particular religious group within a larger faith; for example, Lutheranism is one denomination within Christianity.

despotism rule by a single person with absolute power

detrimental something that does harm or damage

devoted to be completely committed to something; loyal

dialect a regional variety of a language

dispute disagreement

distinctive clearly different

distribute to give out or deliver

diverse a group of people or things with obvious differences between one another

divine related to or coming from a god or gods

doctrine a belief or set of beliefs, especially relating to religion

document a written work containing information

dominate to have control or power over something

Donatello a Florentine sculptor who was one of the first to use a realistic, lifelike style

dramatic noticeable and remarkable

drastic extreme or severe

dynasty a line of rulers descended from one family

E

Eastern Orthodox Church a Christian religion that developed out of early Christianity in the Byzantine Empire

economic relating to trade or money

economy a system of managing the wealth and resources of a community or region

edition a version of a printed text

efficient functioning in the best way, with very little or no waste

elaborate detailed and often complicated; carefully planned

elevate to raise

emancipate to free

emerge to appear or arise; to move from a low position to a higher one

emotional related to emotions or feelings

emperor the political leader of a territory containing several countries or groups of people

emphasis special importance

emphasize to call attention to or highlight the importance of something

empire a large territory in which several groups of people are ruled by a single leader or government

Enlightenment a period from the late 1600s to the late 1700s in Europe, in which people changed their outlook on life by seeing reason as the key to human progress

enlightenment the state of gaining spiritual knowledge and finding truth

enormous very large

epidemic an outbreak of a contagious disease that spreads quickly and over a wide geographic area

equation a mathematical statement in which the answer equals the statement

erode to slowly break down or destroy

error something that differs from what is correct

estimate a guess as to the value or size of something

evaporation the process in which a liquid, such as water, turns into a gas

evolution the slow process of change in plants and animals from simpler forms to more complex forms

evolve to slowly change over a long period of time

F

feudalism the economic and political system that developed in Europe during the Middle Ages

fief land granted by a lord to a vassal in exchange for loyalty and service

Five Pillars of Islam the most basic acts of worship for Muslims: declaration of faith, prayer, charity, fasting, and making a pilgrimage to Makkah

Florence an Italian city-state and leading cultural center during the Renaissance

folktale a story that is passed down orally and becomes part of a culture's tradition

formula a series of numbers or letters that represent a mathematical or scientific rule

foundation the basis from which an idea or situation develops

function the use or purpose of something

fundamental at the most basic level

G

genealogy an account of the line of ancestry within a family

geocentric theory a theory that Earth is the center of the solar system or the universe. *Geo* is Greek for "earth."

geometric one or a number of simple shapes, such as triangles, squares, or circles

Ghana a medieval civilization and empire in Western Africa

glyph a symbol for a word, idea, or sound in a hieroglyphic system of writing

golden age a period in a nation's past during which its culture and society attained the height of achievement and power

gravity the force of attraction between all masses in the universe

griot a talented poet-musician of the Mande people, who tells stories, sings songs, and recites poems to share history

guild an organization of people in the same craft or trade

gunpowder an explosive powder made of salt-peter and other materials

Gutenberg, Johannes a German inventor who, in about 1450, developed the first printing press with movable type in Europe

H

habeas corpus the legal concept that an accused person cannot be held in jail indefinitely without being charged with a crime

Heian period the cultural flowering in Japan that took place between the late 8th and the late 12th centuries

heliocentric theory a theory that places the sun at the center of the solar system with the planets, including Earth, revolving around it. *Helio* is Greek for "sun."

hereditary passed on from parent to child; inherited

heretic a person who holds beliefs that are contrary to a set of religious teachings

hierarchy a system of organization with lower and higher positions

hieroglyphic writing that uses pictures as symbols

Holy Land the area between Egypt and Syria that was the ancient homeland of Jews and the place where Jesus Christ had lived; also called Palestine

humanism a philosophy that tries to balance religious faith with an emphasis on individual dignity and an interest in nature and human society

humanities collectively, areas of study that focus on human life and culture, such as history, literature, and ethics

Hundred Years' War a series of battles fought by France and England between 1337 and 1453

hypothesis an idea or assumption to be tested in an experiment

I

identify to recognize something for what it is

illuminate to decorate a book with detailed designs and small pictures, especially using gold, silver, or bright colors

immortal able to live forever

imperial belonging or related to an emperor

import to bring in a product from another country to sell it

impressive causing admiration or awe

Incas people of a culture in the Andes Mountains of South America that arose in the 1400s C.E. and lasted until 1532

individualism the belief in the importance of an individual's achievements and dignity

indulgence a grant by the Catholic Church that released a person from punishment for sins

inferior lower in rank or quality

inflation a rise in prices, often due an increase in the supply of money

ingenious especially intelligent, creative, or clever

innovation something new; an improvement

inoculate to protect against disease by transmitting a disease-causing agent to a person, stimulating the body's defensive reactions

Inquisition a judicial body established by the Roman Catholic Church to combat forms of religious error

insight to see the inner nature of a situation; to understand

intellectual related to the interest in or study of ideas

intense strong effect or feelings; extreme

irrigation a means of supplying land with water

Islam the religious faith of Muslims; also the civilization based on the Islamic religion and the group of countries where Islam is the main religion

isolated set apart from other people or things

J

Jenne-jeno an ancient West African city built along the Niger River, which existed for 1600 years

jihad Muslims' struggle with challenges within themselves and the world as they strive to please God

K

kente a traditional form of cloth produced in West Africa

L

lens curved transparent material that, when looked through, changes the appearance of an object, often making it appear larger or smaller. The transparent material is often glass.

logic a way of thinking that uses reason

Luther, Martin a German priest who broke away from the Catholic Church to start his own religion, Lutheranism. His posting of the Ninety-Five Theses started the Reformation.

Lutheranism a Protestant denomination of Christian faith founded by Martin Luther

M

Machiavelli, Niccolò a Renaissance statesman and historian who wrote *The Prince*

Magna Carta a written legal agreement signed in 1215 that limited the English monarch's power

magnetic something that acts like a magnet. A magnet attracts iron or some other metals.

maintain to continue in the same way

Mali a West African empire ruled by the Mande that became a major crossroads of the Islamic world

Mansa Musa the first West African ruler to practice Islam devoutly

maritime relating to the sea

market economy an economy in which prices are determined by the buying and selling decisions of individuals in the marketplace

martial arts styles of fighting or self-defense, such as modern-day judo and karate, that began mostly in Asia

mass a measure of the amount of matter in an object

mass-produce to make quantities of an item by using standardized designs and dividing steps of production among the workers

matrilineal a family line traced through the mother

Mayas the people of an important Mesoamerican civilization that lasted from about 2000 B.C.E. to 1500 C.E.

meditation a spiritual discipline that involves deep relaxation and clearing the mind of distracting thoughts

mercantilism an economic policy by which nations try to gather wealth by controlling trade and establishing colonies

mercenary a professional soldier who is paid to fight for another country or group

meritocracy rule by officials of proven merit

Mesoamerica the region extending from modern Mexico through Central America

Michelangelo a Renaissance artist, renowned for his painting and sculpture

microscope an instrument used to make very small objects visible

Ming the dynasty that ruled China after the overthrow of the Yuan

Model Parliament a governing body created by King Edward I that included some commoners, Church officials, and nobles

momentum a force gathered over time

Mongols foreign rulers of China from Mongolia who established the Yuan dynasty

monotheism the belief in a single God

mosaic a picture made up of small pieces of tile, glass, or colored stone

mosque a Muslim house of worship

motive something that causes a person or people to act

movable type individual characters that can be arranged to create a printing job and then be used over again

Muhammad a man born in about 570 C.E. who taught the faith of Islam

Muslim a follower of the Islamic faith

mythical not real; imagined

N

nationalism the identification with, and devotion to, the interests of one's nation

natural law the concept that there is a universal order built into nature that can guide moral thinking

natural rights rights that belong to people "by nature," simply because they are human beings

New World the name given by Europeans to the Americas, which were unknown to most of Europeans before the voyages of Christopher Columbus

Niger River the longest river in West Africa, which was a kind of trading highway in ancient times

Nok a people living in West Africa in the 500s B.C.E. who mastered iron-making

O

oracle a person through whom a god or spirit is believed to speak about the future

oral tradition learning and cultural ideas passed down orally, from one generation to the next

orbit the path on which one object circles another

P

pagoda a tower-shaped structure with several stories and upturned, tiled roofs

patriarch in the Eastern Orthodox Church, the bishop of an important city

patrilineal descent from the father or the males in a family

persecute to cause a person to suffer because of his or her beliefs

philosopher a scholar, teacher, or thinker who seeks knowledge

philosophy the study of wisdom, knowledge, and the nature of reality

pictograph a drawing that stands for a word, phrase, or name

pilgrimage a journey to a holy site

plaza a public square or open area in a city where people gather

policy an overall plan, especially of a government

polygamy having more than one spouse at one time

polytheism belief in more than one god

predict to say what will happen in the future, based on experience or reason

process a series of actions that produce a certain result

proclaim to announce publically

prophet a person who speaks or interprets the words of God

proportion the relationship between amounts, numbers, or sizes

prosperous wealthy or successful

Protestant a Christian who separated from the Roman Catholic Church during the Reformation; today, any member of a Christian church founded on the principles of the Reformation

proverb a popular saying meant to express something wise or true

Puritans English Protestants who wanted to "purify" the Anglican Church of Catholic elements

Q

Qur'an the holy book of the religion of Islam

R

Ramadan the ninth month of the Islamic calendar, during which Muslims are required to fast

rational using reason and understanding

rationalism a belief in reason and logic as the primary source of knowledge

rebellious opposing or disobeying authority

reform to make change in order to bring about improvement

Reformation a religious reform movement from the early 1500s to the 1600s that led to the formation of new Christian groups

reign the period of time during which a king or other monarch rules

religion a set of spiritual beliefs, values, and practices

religious order a brotherhood or sisterhood of monks, nuns, or friars

religious tolerance the acceptance of different religious beliefs and customs

Renaissance a great flowering of culture, based on classical Greek and Roman ideas and art, that began in Italy in the Late Middle Ages and spread throughout Europe

republic a form of government in which citizens elect representatives to rule for them

require to have to do something based on a rule or command

resident someone who has lived in a place

response an answer to something that is done or said

restoration the return of a past state, situation, or ruler

restriction a limit or control placed on something

reveal to show or make known something that was hidden or secret

revolt a violent action in opposition to a government or law

ritual a set of actions that is always performed the same way as part of a religious ceremony

Roman Catholic Church the Christian church headed by the pope in Rome

Roman Empire an empire that, at its height, around 200 C.E., spanned the Mediterranean world and most of Europe

rural the countryside, as opposed to a city or town

S

sacrament a sacred rite of the Christian religion

sacrifice a gift of an animal for slaughter to honor the gods

Sahara large, hot desert in North Africa that covers about 3.5 million square miles

Sahel a zone of semidesert, south of the Sahara, where short grasses, small bushes, and a few trees grow

saint someone officially recognized as holy by the Catholic Church

samurai a member of a powerful warrior class in Japan

savanna a vegetation zone of tall grasses and scattered trees, with a long rainy season

scientific method a step-by-step method of investigation involving observation and theory to test scientific assumptions

Scientific Revolution a major shift in thinking between 1500 and 1700, in which modern science emerged as a new way of gaining knowledge about the natural world

scribe a person trained to write or copy documents by hand

secular relating to earthly life rather than to religious or spiritual matters

segment a part of something that is divided from the whole

segregation the forced separation of one group from the rest of a community

semidivine half-human and half-god

separation of powers the division of powers among branches of government

serf a peasant who could not leave the lord's land on which he or she was born and worked

shah a ruler in certain Middle East lands, especially Persia (modern-day Iran)

Shakespeare, William an English Renaissance poet and playwright whose plays show a deep understanding of human behavior

shari'ah the body of Islamic law based on the Qur'an and the Sunnah

Shinto a Japanese religion that expresses love and respect for nature

shogun the head of the military government of Japan in the era of the samurai

Shotoku (Prince) a Japanese ruler who encouraged cultural diffusion from countries on the Asian mainland

sibling a brother or sister

siege a military action in which a place is surrounded and cut off to force those inside to surrender

significant having meaning and importance

simony the selling and buying of positions in the Catholic Church

slash-and-burn agriculture a farming technique in which vegetation is cut away and burned to clear land for growing crops

smelting the process of melting ore to produce iron or other metals from it

social contract an agreement in which people give power to a government in exchange for its protections

social pyramid a social structure in the shape of a pyramid, with layers representing social classes of different rank

solar year the time it takes Earth to travel once around the sun

Songhai a people who broke away from the empire of Mali and eventually built their own vast empire in West Africa

sophisticated having experiences and knowledge, especially with culture and art

starve to suffer or die from lack of food

status the position of a person, either socially or professionally

stele a vertical stone slab or pillar with carvings or inscriptions

stimulate to encourage the growth or activity of something

successor the person who is next in line to hold a position

sultan the supreme ruler of a Muslim state

Sunnah the example that Muhammad set for Muslims about how to live

supreme the highest level

surplus more than is needed or used

survive to continue to exist

suspension bridge a bridge held up by cables anchored at each end

sustain to support or provide nourishment for

T

Tale of Genji a Japanese novel and Heian masterpiece, written by Murasaki Shikibu; considered one of the great works in world literature

technique a specialized method used to achieve a desired result

telescope an instrument used to view distant objects

Tenochtitlán the capital city of the Aztec Empire

terra-cotta a baked clay used to make pottery, tiles, and sculptures

territory a specific area of land

textile a woven cloth

texture the way a surface looks and feels

theocracy a government or state in which God is the supreme ruler, and religious officials govern in God's name

thesis an argument, often written, to support an idea

tolerance to be sympathetic and accepting of what others believe or do, even if those ideas differ from your own

traditional a belief, custom, or way of doing something that has existed for a long time

trans-Saharan trade trade between peoples north and south of the Sahara

transmit to pass something on to someone else

treaty a written agreement between two or more nations

trephination a type of surgery in which a hole is made in the skull

tributary a conquered country or territory that pays tribute to the conqueror

tribute payment made by one ruler or country to another for protection or as a sign of submission

U

unification the process of joining two or more things together

unique one of a kind

urbanization the growth of cities

V

verbal spoken, rather than written

vital necessary for the existence of something

vocabulary a collection of words that make up a language

W

ward a political unit within a city, often a neighborhood

warlord a military leader operating outside the control of the government

widespread spread out over a large area or among many people

Z

Zen Buddhism a form of Buddhism that stresses self-reliance and achieving enlightenment through meditation

Index

Page numbers followed by "c" indicate graphs, tables, or charts.

Page numbers followed by "m" indicate maps.

*Page numbers in **bold** indicate definitions.*

A

Abbasid dynasty, 101, 118
Abraham, prophet, 77–78, 80–81, 88, 90, 94, 156
absolute monarchy, **394**
Abu Bakr, Muslim ruler, 80, 83
Abu Talib, uncle of Muhammad, 79, 81
accused, rights of, 440–441
Acre, 120–121
Adams, Abigail (Mrs. John Adams), 442
Adams, John, 441
adaptation, **100**
Adoration of the Magi (Botticelli), 346–347
Africa, 132m, 133, 133m, 214m, 218, 408. *See also* North Africa; West Africa
Age of Exploration, 400–421, **404**
Age of Faith, 29
Age of Monarchs, 394
agriculture. See farms and farming
Ahmed, Muslim finance minister, 213
al-Jahiz, Muslim scholar, 103
al-Khwarizmi, Muslim scholar, 105
al-Kindi, Arab philosopher, 102
al-Mahdi, Ibrahim ibn, gourmet chef, 112, 114
al-Ma'mum, caliph, 102, 112–115
al-Mansur, caliph, 101
al-Mutawakkil, caliph, 115
al-Razi, Persian doctor, 106

al-Saheli, architect, 160–161
Alhambra palace, 98–99
Ali ibn Abi Talib, Muslim caliph, 84
Allah, 80, 90
alliance, **287**
Almoravid people, 151, 154
American Revolution, 441–442
Americas (Latin America). *See* Central America; Mexico; South America
Amida Buddha (sculpture), 243, 256
Amida Buddhism, **256**
Anatolia (Asia Minor), 118–120, 125–126
anatomy (science), 340, 347, 350–351, 361
Andes Mountains, 271, 303–304, 322
Anglican Church, 380–381, **388**–389
Ankara, Anatolia, 126
anti-Semitism, **124**
Appian Way, 4–5
appliqué, **168**
apprentices, **43,** 45
Apurimac River, 323, 325
aqueducts, **11,** 289
Aquinas, Thomas, 36, 424
Arab culture, 85
Arabia, 78, 83, 123, 125–126, 214m, 218–219
Arabian Nights, 107
Arabian Peninsula, 74m, 75, 78m
Arabic numerals, 99, 105
Arabic writing (calligraphy), 108–109, 161
Arc de Triomphe (Arch of Triumph), 11
architecture
    Aztec, 319
    Chinese/Japanese, 227, 230, 234
    Eastern Orthodox Church, 67

    Greco-Roman, 333
    Incas, 321
    legacy of Roman Empire, 10–11
    Mayan, 317
    Muslim, 98–99, 101, 105
    Renaissance, 340, 344–346
    Roman Catholic Church, 34–35
    West African, 160–161
aristocracy, 184, **184,** 229, 236–247
Aristotle, Greek philosopher, 36, 102, 423–426
armor (protective clothing), 25, 56, 251–252
Arno River, 343–344
art
    Aztec, 319
    Buddhist, 233
    Chinese, 211
    classical, 334
    Eastern Orthodox Church, 67
    Greco-Roman, 334
    Incas, 320
    Japanese, 243
    legacy of Roman Empire, 8–9
    Mayan, 317
    medieval, 335
    Muslim, 108–109
    Renaissance, 336, 346–348
    Roman Catholic Church, 34–35
    West African, 161–163, 168–169
artifacts, 135, **138,** 144, 168–169, 202–204, 233, 274, 277, 283–285, 314–315
artisans, 192, 203, 211, 277, 295
Asia. *See also* Southeast Asia
    bubonic plague, 54–55
    Byzantine Empire, 62–69
    medieval trade routes, 100m
    Mongol empire, 125–126, 181, 186

polygamy, **297**

polythesim, **78,** 280

Poor Clares, 39

popes, in Roman Catholic Church, 30–31, 68

population statistics, 192, 194, 230, 288, 304, 344, 413

porcelain, 202–203

Portugal, 121, 406–408, 407m

Praise of Folly, The (Erasmus), 377

prayer, 91, 156, 385

priests, 31, 67, 277, 281, 294, 300, 311

Prince, The (Machiavelli), 352

Principia (Principles) (Newton), 428

printing, 200–201, 356, 368–371, 380

Procession of the Magi, The (fresco), 352

Procopius, 65

prophet, **80**

Prophet's Mosque, Madina, 82

proportion, in art, 359, 366

Protestantism, 373, **377,** 378–381, 393–395

proverbs, **13,** 165

Ptolemy, Greek thinker, 405, 424–425

Puritan, **394**

pyramids, 268–269, 272–273, 280, 286, 288–289, 317

Q

Qin dynasty, 182c

Qin Shihuangdi (Prince Zheng), 182

quipus, 305, 321

Qur'an, **89**

  about, 81, 89

  art and decoration of, 108–109, 161

  on food and beverages, 114

  on hajj, 95

  on Jews and Christians, 84, 88

  on jihad, 95

  Ka'bah shrine, 78

  on learning, 103

  pictured, 77, 107

  on Ramadan, 92–93

  shari'ah and, 96

  in West Africa, 159

R

Rabi'a, Sufi poet, 107

Ramadan, **92**–93, 156

Raphael, 367

rationalism, **424**

recreation and leisure, 23, 48, 110, 300–301

Reformation, 331, 372–395, **376,** 434

religion, **30**

  Aztec, 287–289, 295, 300–301

  Buddist. *See* Buddhism

  Catholic. *See* Roman Catholic Church

  Christian. *See* Christianity and Christians

  Eastern Orthodox. *See* Eastern Orthodox Church

  Enlightenment period and, 434–435

  Incan, 310–311

  Islam. *See* Islam and Muslims

  Judaism. *See* Jews and Judaism

  Mayan, 276–277, 280–281

  Shinto. *See* Shinto

religious orders, in Roman Catholic Church, 38–39

religious tolerance, **439**

Renaissance, 9, 331–371, **334,** 434

republic, **339**

restoration, **260**

restrictions, 192, 213

rice, 99, 190–192

Richard I "the Lionheart," king of England, 120, 122

ritual, **277,** 291

roads and road building, 11, 303, 305, 320

Roman Catholic Church, **30**

  about, 29–31

  Anglicanism compared to, 388–389

  art and architecture, 34–35

  beliefs of, 32

  calls for reform, 376–377

  Calvinism compared to, 386–387

  Charlemagne and, 18–19

  conflict between East and West, 68–69

  conflict with humanist scholars, 341

  corruption in, 372–375

  Counter-Reformation, 382–383, 390–392

  Crusades, 33

  economic power of, 31

  education and, 29, 36

  friars, 39

  holidays, 37

  influence of, 28–39

  Inquisition, 121, 392, 427

  Joan of Arc, 57–61

  Latin language, 12, 31

  Lutheranism compared to, 384–385

  Luther's break from, 378–379

  missionaries, 391, 395

  monks, 38–39

  nuns, 38–39

  officials as members of Model Parliament, 53

  organization of, 30–31

  pilgrimages, 33

  political conflicts with European rulers, 375

  property ownership in feudal times, 20, 31

  reformers, 391

  sacraments, 32, 32c

  salvation, 32

  Thirty Years' War, 393

  weakening of authority, 373

Roman Empire, 5–15, **6**, 7m, 17–18, 334, 435

Roman numerals, 13

Rome, Italy, 331, 375

Royal Road, Inca empire, 303, 305, 322

rulers (kings). *See* monarchs

Rumi, Sufi poet, 107

S

sacraments, **32**, 32c, 379, 384–385, 387–389

sacrifices, **277**, 280–281, 291, 300, 311

Safavid empire, 126

Sahara Desert, 133, **136**

Sahel region, Africa, 133, **136**, 151

saints, 374, 377

Salah al-Din (Saladin), sultan, 120, 123, 125

salat (ritual prayer), 91, 156

salons, 433, 442

salt, trans-Saharan trade, 148–150

samurai (Japanese warriors), 248–265, **250**

Santa Maria (ship), 217, 398–399

Santa Maria del Fiore, Florence, Italy, 328–329, 343, 345–346

savanna, **136**

scholar-officials, in China, 180–181, 184–185, 187, 215

scholarship, 100–102, 158, 340–341

School of Athens, The (Raphael), 336

science, 100, 103, 316, 320, 347, 350–351

scientific method, 423, **429**, 429c

Scientific Revolution, 401, 422–431, **424**, 434

scribes, **12**, 31

sculpture, 8, 35, 168, 233, 243, 274, 319, 347–348, 357–358

Second Crusade, 120

Secret History (Procopius), 65

secular, **349**

segregation, **124**

Sei Shonagon, Japanese writer, 245

Seljuk Turks, 117–120, 125

semidivine, **294**

separation of powers, **438**

Sepúlveda, Juan Ginés, 421

serfs, **20**. *See* also peasants

Seventeen Article Constitution, 229

shah, **126**

shahadan (declaration of faith), 90

Shakespeare, William, **364**–365

shari'ah (Islamic law), **96**–97, 157

Shi'ah Muslims, 84, 126

Shikoku, Japan, 225

Shinran, Buddhist monk, 256

Shinto, 222–223, **230**, 234

ships and boats, 198–199, 216–217, 406

shogun, **250**, 260

Shotoku, Prince, Japanese ruler, 227–229, **228**, 231, 234

siege, **82**

Sijilmasa, 147

Silk Road, 54, 210, 210m, 212

simony, **374**

Sistine Chapel, 9, 357–358

Six dynasties (China), 182c

siyam (fasting), 92–93

slash-and-burn agriculture, **282**

slaves and slavery
    Aztec, 291, 295
    end of slavery, in West Indies, 418–421
    Mayans, 277
    Portuguese slaves, 408
    slave markets, 150
    Spanish slaves, 410–411, 418–421
    West African cultural legacy, 165–169

smelting, **138**

social contract, **438**

social pyramid, **276**

social structure, 17, 240–241, 276–277, 294–295, 306–307, 341

Society of Jesus (Jesuits), 383, 391–392, 395

Soga clan, 231

solar year, **316**

Song dynasty, 179m, 182c, 184–186, 189–200, 204–207, 211

Songhai people, 133m, 140–141, **156**

South America, 270m, 271, 271m, 326c–327c, 407–410. *See also* Incas

Southeast Asia, 127, 395

Spain
    explorers, 408–413, 410m, 412m, 418–421
    Islamic scholarship and learning, 102
    Muslims in, 85, 88, 99–100
    peasant revolts, 55
    Reconquista, 121
    Renaissance, 356, 362–363
    war with England, 415

Spirit of Laws, The (Montesquieu), 438

sports, 24–25, 48, 110, 242, 281, 301

Squier, Ephraim George, 325

St. Peter's Basilica, 367, 378

steles, **317**

Stoics and Stoicism, 14

Sufism, 107

sugar (al-sukkar), 99, 113, 115

Sui dynasty, 179m, 182c, 183

Suiko, empress of Japan, 227–228

sultan, **118**

Sun Stone (Aztec calendar), 318–319

Sundjata Keita, king of Mali, 169

Sunnah, **89**, 96

Sunni Ali, ruler of Songhai, 156

Correlations

California History Social Science Standards, Seventh Grade

Standards	Where Standards Are Addressed
7.1 Students analyze the causes and effects of the vast expansion and ultimate disintegration of the Roman Empire.	
1. Study the early strengths and lasting contributions of Rome (e.g., significance of Roman citizenship; rights under Roman law; Roman art, architecture, engineering, and philosophy; preservation and transmission of Christianity) and its ultimate internal weaknesses (e.g., rise of autonomous military powers within the empire, undermining of citizenship by the growth of corruption and slavery, lack of education, and distribution of news).	pp. 5–15, 30
2. Discuss the geographic borders of the empire at its height and the factors that threatened its territorial cohesion.	pp. 5, 6, 7
3. Describe the establishment by Constantine of the new capital in Constantinople and the development of the Byzantine Empire, with an emphasis on the consequences of the development of two distinct European civilizations, Eastern Orthodox and Roman Catholic, and their two distinct views on church-state relations.	pp. 6–7, 63–69 Online Resources: Ch. 6 Biographies
7.2 Students analyze the geographic, political, economic, religious, and social structures of the civilizations of Islam in the Middle Ages.	
1. Identify the physical features and describe the climate of the Arabian peninsula, its relationship to surrounding bodies of land and water, and nomadic and sedentary ways of life.	pp. 75, 78
2. Trace the origins of Islam and the life and teachings of Muhammad, including Islamic teachings on the connection with Judaism and Christianity.	pp. 77–85, 87–97
3. Explain the significance of the Qur'an and the Sunnah as the primary sources of Islamic beliefs, practice, and law, and their influence in Muslims' daily life.	pp. 80–81, 87–97
4. Discuss the expansion of Muslim rule through military conquests and treaties, emphasizing the cultural blending within Muslim civilization and the spread and acceptance of Islam and the Arabic language.	pp. 78, 81–85, 95, 99–101, 125–127, 153–161 Online Resources: Ch. 11 Biographies
5. Describe the growth of cities and the establishment of trade routes among Asia, Africa, and Europe, the products and inventions that traveled along these routes (e.g., spices, textiles, paper, steel, new crops), and the role of merchants in Arab society.	pp. 75, 78, 81, 85, 100–101
6. Understand the intellectual exchanges among Muslim scholars of Eurasia and Africa and the contributions Muslim scholars made to later civilizations in the areas of science, geography, mathematics, philosophy, medicine, art, and literature.	pp. 99–111 Online Resources: Ch. 11 Literature

Standards	Where Standards Are Addressed
7.3 Students analyze the geographic, political, economic, religious, and social structures of the civilizations of China in the Middle Ages.	
1. Describe the reunification of China under the Tang Dynasty and reasons for the spread of Buddhism in Tang China, Korea, and Japan.	pp. 182–183, 210–211, 227–228, 230–231 Online Resources: Ch. 15 Biographies
2. Describe agricultural, technological, and commercial developments during the Tang and Song periods.	pp. 189–195, 197–207, 210–211
3. Analyze the influences of Confucianism and changes in Confucian thought during the Song and Mongol periods.	pp. 184–186, 194–195
4. Understand the importance of both overland trade and maritime expeditions between China and other civilizations in the Mongol Ascendancy and Ming Dynasty.	pp. 212–215 Online Resources: Ch. 18 Primary Sources
5. Trace the historic influence of such discoveries as tea, the manufacture of paper, wood.	pp. 197, 198, 200–207
6. Describe the development of the imperial state and the scholar-official class.	pp. 181–187
7.4 Students analyze the geographic, political, economic, religious, and social structures of the sub-Saharan civilizations of Ghana and Mali in Medieval Africa.	
1. Study the Niger River and the relationship of vegetation zones of forest, savannah, and desert to trade in gold, salt, food, and slaves; and the growth of the Ghana and Mali empires.	pp. 132–133, 135–141, 143–151, 154–156 Online Resources: Ch. 13 Primary Sources
2. Analyze the importance of family, labor specialization, and regional commerce in the development of states and cities in West Africa.	pp. 137–141
3. Describe the role of the trans-Saharan caravan trade in the changing religious and cultural characteristics of West Africa and the influence of Islamic beliefs, ethics, and law.	pp. 146–151, 153–161
4. Trace the growth of the Arabic language in government, trade, and Islamic scholarship in West Africa.	pp. 158–159 Online Resources: Ch. 13 Biography
5. Describe the importance of written and oral traditions in the transmission of African history and culture.	pp. 164–165 Online Resources: Ch. 14 Literature

Standards	Where Standards Are Addressed
7.5 Students analyze the geographic, political, economic, religious, and social structures of the civilizations of Medieval Japan.	
1. Describe the significance of Japan's proximity to China and Korea and the intellectual, linguistic, religious, and philosophical influence of those countries on Japan.	pp. 227–235
2. Discuss the reign of Prince Shotoku of Japan and the characteristics of Japanese society and family life during his reign.	pp. 227–229 Online Resources: Ch. 19 Primary Sources
3. Describe the values, social customs, and traditions prescribed by the lord-vassal system consisting of shogun, daimyo, and samurai and the lasting influence of the warrior code in the twentieth century.	pp. 249–261, 262–265 Online Resources: Ch. 22 Literature
4. Trace the development of distinctive forms of Japanese Buddhism.	pp. 230–231, 256–257
5. Study the ninth and tenth centuries' golden age of literature, art, and drama and its lasting effects on culture today, including Murasaki Shikibu's *Tale of Genji*.	pp. 237–247 Online Resources: Ch. 20 Biographies
6. Analyze the rise of a military society in the late twelfth century and the role of the samurai in that society.	pp. 249–259 Online Resources: Ch. 21 Literature
7.6 Students analyze the geographic, political, economic, religious, and social structures of the civilizations of Medieval Europe.	
1. Study the geography of the Europe and the Eurasian landmass, including their location, topography, waterways, vegetation, and climate and their relationship to ways of life in Medieval Europe.	pp. 2–3, 42
2. Describe the spread of Christianity north of the Alps and the roles played by the early church and by monasteries in its diffusion after the fall of the western half of the Roman Empire.	pp. 18–19, 30–31, 38–39
3. Understand the development of feudalism, its role in the medieval European economy, the way in which it was influenced by physical geography (the role of the manor and the growth of towns), and how feudal relationships provided the foundation of political order.	pp. 17–27, 41–42, 44
4. Demonstrate an understanding of the conflict and cooperation between the Papacy and European monarchs (e.g., Charlemagne, Gregory VII, Emperor Henry IV).	pp. 18–19, 30–31
5. Know the significance of developments in medieval English legal and constitutional practices and their importance in the rise of modern democratic thought and representative institutions (e.g., Magna Carta, parliament, development of habeas corpus, an independent judiciary in England).	pp. 47, 52–53

Standards	Where Standards Are Addressed
6. Discuss the causes and course of the religious Crusades and their effects on the Christian, Muslim, and Jewish populations in Europe, with emphasis on the increasing contact by Europeans with cultures of the Eastern Mediterranean world.	pp. 33, 117–127 Online Resources: Ch. 10 Enrichment Essay
7. Map the spread of the bubonic plague from Central Asia to China, the Middle East, and Europe and describe its impact on global population.	pp. 54–55
8. Understand the importance of the Catholic church as a political, intellectual, and aesthetic institution (e.g., founding of universities, political and spiritual roles of the clergy, creation of monastic and mendicant religious orders, preservation of the Latin language and religious texts, St. Thomas Aquinas's synthesis of classical philosophy with Christian theology, and the concept of "natural law").	pp. 29–39
9. Know the history of the decline of Muslim rule in the Iberian Peninsula that culminated in the Reconquista and the rise of Spanish and Portuguese kingdoms.	pp. 121, 362–363 Online Resources: Ch. 10 Enrichment Essay
7.7 Students compare and contrast the geographic, political, economic, religious, and social structures of the Meso-American and Andean civilizations.	
1. Study the locations, landforms, and climates of Mexico, Central America, and South America and their effects on Mayan, Aztec, and Incan economies, trade, and development of urban societies.	pp. 270–272, 274–277, 282–283, 286–289, 304–305
2. Study the roles of people in each society, including class structures, family life, warfare, religious beliefs and practices, and slavery.	pp. 273–283, 290–291, 293–301, 306–313
3. Explain how and where each empire arose and how the Aztec and Incan empires were defeated by the Spanish.	pp. 274–275, 286–287, 290–292, 304–305, 312–313, 411–413 Online Resources: Ch. 25 Biographies
4. Describe the artistic and oral traditions and architecture in the three civilizations.	pp. 315, 316–317, 318–319, 320–321 Online Resources: Unit 6 Primary Sources; Unit 6 Literature
5. Describe the Meso-American achievements in astronomy and math-ematics, including the development of the calendar and the Meso-American knowledge of seasonal changes to the civilizations' agricultural systems.	pp. 315, 316–317, 318–319, 320–321

Standards	Where Standards Are Addressed
7.8 Students analyze the origins, accomplishments, and geographic diffusion of the Renaissance.	
1. Describe the way in which the revival of classical learning and the arts fostered a new interest in humanism (i.e. a balance between intellect and religious faith).	pp. 333–335, 340–341, 344–352
2. Explain the importance of Florence in the early stages of the Renaissance and the growth of independent trading cities (e.g., Venice), with emphasis on the cities' importance in the spread of Renaissance ideas.	p. 337–388, 343–353
3. Understand the effects of the reopening of the ancient "Silk Road" between Europe and China, including Marco Polo's travels and the location of his routes.	pp. 189, 212–213, 337–338 Online Resources: Ch. 18 Primary Sources
4. Describe the growth and effects of new ways of disseminating information (e.g., the ability to manufacture paper, translation of the Bible into the vernacular, printing).	pp. 356, 378–381
5. Detail advances made in literature, the arts, science, mathematics, cartography, engineering, and the understanding of human anatomy and astronomy (e.g., by Dante Alighieri, Leonardo da Vinci, Michelangelo di Buonarroti Simoni, Johann Gutenberg, William Shakespeare).	pp. 344–346, 357–361, 364–367, 404–405 Online Resources: Ch. 29 Investigating Literature
7.9 Students analyze the historical developments of the Reformation.	
1. List the causes for the internal turmoil in and weakening of the Catholic church (e.g., tax policies, selling of indulgences).	pp. 373–375
2. Describe the theological, political, and economic ideas of the major figures during the Reformation (e.g., Desiderius Erasmus, Martin Luther, John Calvin, William Tyndale).	pp. 376–381, 384–389
3. Explain Protestants' new practices of church self-government and the influence of those practices on the development of democratic practices and ideas of federalism.	pp. 392–395 Online Resources: Ch. 31 Enrichment Essay
4. Identify and locate the European regions that remained Catholic and those that became Protestant and explain how the division affected the distribution of religions in the New World.	pp. 392–395
5. Analyze how the Counter-Reformation revitalized the Catholic church and the forces that fostered the movement (e.g., St. Ignatius of Loyola and the Jesuits, the Council of Trent).	pp. 390–392
6. Understand the institution and impact of missionaries on Christianity and the diffusion of Christianity from Europe to other parts of the world in the medieval and early modern periods; locate missions on a world map.	pp. 392–395

Standards	Where Standards Are Addressed
7. Describe the Golden Age of cooperation between Jews and Muslims in medieval Spain that promoted creativity in art, literature, and science, including how that cooperation was terminated by the religious persecution of individuals and groups (e.g., the Spanish Inquisition and the expulsion of Jews and Muslims from Spain in 1492).	pp. 100–101, 108–109, 121, 362–363, 392–393
7.10 Students analyze the historical developments of the Scientific Revolution and its lasting effect on religious, political, and cultural institutions.	
1. Discuss the roots of the Scientific Revolution (e.g., Greek rationalism; Jewish, Christian, and Muslim science; Renaissance humanism; new knowledge from global exploration).	pp. 100–106, 424–425
2. . Understand the significance of the new scientific theories (e.g., those of Copernicus, Galileo, Kepler, Newton) and the significance of new inventions (e.g., the telescope, microscope, thermometer, barometer).	pp. 425–431
3. Understand the scientific method advanced by Bacon and Descartes, the influence of new scientific rationalism on the growth of democratic ideas, and the coexistence of science with traditional religious beliefs.	pp. 429
7.11 Students analyze political and economic change in the sixteenth, seventeenth, and eighteenth centuries (the Age of Exploration, the Enlightenment, and the Age of Reason).	
1. Know the great voyages of discovery, the locations of the routes, and the influence of cartography in the development of a new European worldview.	pp. 400–401, 403–415
2. Discuss the exchanges of plants, animals, technology, culture, and ideas among Europe, Africa, Asia, and the Americas in the fifteenth and sixteenth centuries and the major economic and social effects on each continent.	pp. 403–415 Online Resources: Ch. 32 Enrichment Essay
3. Examine the origins of modern capitalism; the influence of mercantilism and cottage industry; the elements and importance of a market economy in seventeenth-century Europe; the changing international trading and marketing patterns, including their locations on a world map; and the influence of explorers and mapmakers.	pp. 416–417
4. Explain how the main ideas of the Enlightenment can be traced back to such movements as the Renaissance, the Reformation, and the Scientific Revolution and to the Greeks, Romans, and Christianity.	pp. 433–435
5. Describe how democratic thought and institutions were influenced by Enlightenment thinkers (e.g., John Locke, Charles-Louis Montesquieu, American founders).	pp. 436–443 Online Resources: Ch. 34 Primary Sources
6. Discuss how the principles in the Magna Carta were embodied in such documents as the English Bill of Rights and the American Declaration of Independence.	pp. 437–438, 441

Historical and Social Science Analysis Skills

Chronological and Spatial Thinking

1. Students explain how major events are related to one another in time.

2. Students construct various time lines of key events, people, and periods of the historical era they are studying.

3. Students use a variety of maps and documents to identify physical and cultural features of neighborhoods, cities, states, and countries and to explain the historical migration of people, expansion and disintegration of empires, and the growth of economic systems.

Historical Research, Evidence, and Point of View

1. Students frame questions that can be answered by historical study and research.

2. Students distinguish fact from opinion in historical narratives and stories.

3. Students distinguish relevant from irrelevant information, essential from incidental information, and verifiable from unverifiable information in historical narratives and stories.

4. Students assess the credibility of primary and secondary sources and draw sound conclusions from them.

5. Students detect the different historical points of view on historical events and determine the context in which the historical statements were made (the questions asked, sources used, author's perspectives).

Historical Interpretation

1. Students explain the central issues and problems from the past, placing people and events in a matrix of time and place.

2. Students understand and distinguish cause, effect, sequence, and correlation in historical events, including the long- and short-term causal relations.

3. Students explain the sources of historical continuity and how the combination of ideas and events explains the emergence of new patterns.

4. Students recognize the role of chance, oversight, and error in history.

5. Students recognize that interpretations of history are subject to change as new information is uncovered.

6. Students interpret basic indicators of economic performance and conduct cost-benefit analyses of economic and political issues.

Notes

Chapter 1
5: John Henry Parker, *The Archaeology of Rome,* Vols. 1-3 (Oxford: J. Parker and Co., 1874), at www.books.google.com.

Chapter 2
18: Einhard, *Life of Charlemagne,* trans. Samuel Epes Turner (New York: Harper & Brothers, 1880), at www.books.google.com. Poet, in Robert MacHenry and Philip W. Goetz, eds., *The New Encyclopædia Britannica,* Part 3, Vol. 4 (Chicago: Encyclopædia Britannica, 1983).

Chapter 5
58: Joan of Arc, *Joan of Arc, Self Portrait,* trans. Willard Trask (New York: Stackpole Sons, 1936). **59:** Joan of Arc, in Mary Gordon, *Joan of Arc: A Life* (New York: Penguin Books, 2000). **60:** Joan of Arc, *Joan of Arc, Self Portrait.* **61:** Joan of Arc, *Joan of Arc: In Her Own Words,* trans. Willard Trask (New York: Turtle Point Press, 1996). Bishop Pierre Cauchon, in ibid. Joan of Arc, in ibid. Ibid.

Chapter 6
64: Geoffroi de Villehardouin, in Charles Diehl, *Byzantium: Greatness and Decline,* trans. Naomi Walford (New Brunswick, NJ: Rutgers University Press, 1957). **65:** Procopius, *The Secret History,* trans. Richard Atwater (New York: Cosimo, 1927).

Chapter 9
101: Historian, in Linda S. George, *The Golden Age of Islam* (New York: Benchmark Books, 1998). **102:** Muhammad, in ibid. **107:** Three lines of verse by Rabi'a from THE ILLUSTRATED WORLD'S RELIGIONS: A GUIDE TO OUR WISDOM TRADITONS BY HUSTON SMITH. Copyright ©1994 by Huston Smith. Reprinted by permission of HarperCollins Publishers. **113:** Anonymous, in Charles Perry, "Cooking with the Caliphs," *Saudi Aramco World,* July/Aug. 2006, at www.saudiaramcoworld.com.

Chapter 12
144: Historian, in A. Adu Boahen and Alvin M. Josephy, *The Horizon History of Africa,* Vol. 1 (New York: American Heritage, 1971).

Chapter 13
155: Al-Umari, in Patricia McKissack and Frederick McKissack, *The Royal Kingdoms of Ghana, Mali and Songhay: Life in Medieval Africa* (New York: Henry Holt, 1995). **157:** Ibn Battuta, in Editors of Time-Life Books, *Africa's Glorious Legacy* (Alexandria, VA: Time-Life Books, 1994).

Chapter 14
170: J. D. Considine and Michaelangelo Matos, "Biography: Youssou N'Dour," *Rolling Stone,* 2004, at www.rollingstone.com.

Chapter 15
181: Herbert Allen Giles, ed. and trans., *Gems of Chinese Literature* (B. Quaritch, 1884), at www.books.google.com.

Chapter 16
189: Marco Polo, *The Travels of Marco Polo, the Venetian* (Adamant Media Corporation, 2005). **194:** Marco Polo, in Patricia Buckley Ebrey, *The Cambridge Illustrated History of China* (Cambridge: Cambridge University Press, 1996).

Chapter 18
209: Joanna Waley-Cohen, *The Sextants of Beijing: Global Currents in Chinese History* (New York: W. W. Norton, 1999). **214:** Emperor Chengzu, in U.S.-China Peoples Friendship Association, U.S.-China Review, Vol. 28 (U.S.-China People's Friendship Association, 2004). **216:** Anonymous, in Laurence Bergreen, *Over the Edge of the World: Magellan's Terrifying Circumnavigation of the Globe* (New York: HarperCollins, 2003). Emperor Chengzu, in Zheng He, "Zheng He's Inscription," at www.hist.umn.edu. **218:** Ma Huan, in Gavin Menzies, *1421: The Year China Discovered America* (New York: HarperCollins, 2003 [first printed 2002, by Transword Pub.]). Zheng He, "Zheng He's Inscription," at www.hist.umn.edu. **219:** Zheng He, "Zheng He's Inscription," at www.hist.umn.edu.

Chapter 19
229: Prince Shotoku, in Frank Brinkley, *A History of the Japanese People from the Earliest Times to the End of the Meiji Era* (New York: The Encyclopædia Britannica Co., 1915). **231:** Japanese emperor (552 A.D.), in W. G. Aston, ed. and trans., *Nihongi: Chronicles of Japan from the Earliest Times to A.D. 697* Vol. 1 (London: Kegan Paul, Trench, Trübner and Co., 1896), at www.books.google.com. **233:** Japanese poet, in Edwin O. Reischauer and Albert M. Craig, *Japan: Tradition and Transformation,* rev. ed. (Cambridge, MA: Harvard University Press, 1989).

Chapter 20
240: Fujiwara Michinaga, in Ivan Morris, *The World of the Shining Prince: Court Life in Ancient Japan* (New York: Kodansha America, Inc., 1994 [originally published in 1964]). **245:** From *The Pillowbook of Sei Shonagon,* by Ivan Morris, trans. and ed. Copyright © 1991 Columbia University Press. Reprinted with permission from the publisher.

Chapter 21
250: Samurai writer, in Mikiso Hane, *Japan: A Historical Survey* (Charles Scribner's Sons, 1972). **255:** From FROM THE COUNTRY OF EIGHT ISLANDS by Hiroaki Sato and Burton Watson, copyright © 1981 by Hiroaki Sato and Burton Watson. Used by permission of Doubleday, a division of Random House, Inc. **262:** Anonymous, in Helen Craig McCullough, trans., *The Tale of the Heike* (Stanford, CA: Stanford University Press, 1988). Ibid. **263:** Ibid. **265:** Anonymous, in Chieko Irie Mulhern, ed., *Heroic with Grace: Legendary Women of Japan* (New York: M.E. Sharpe, 1991).

Chapter 23
285: Diego Durán, *The History of the Indies of New Spain,* trans. Doris Heyden (Norman, OK: University of Oklahoma Press, 1993).

Chapter 26
325: Ephraim George Squier, in John Noble Wilford, "How the Inca Leapt Canyons," *New York Times,* May 8, 2007, at www.nytimes.com. Helaine Silverman, in "Transcripts: Secrets of Lost Empires: Inca," airdate Feb. 11, 1997, at www.pbs.org.

Chapter 28
347: Giorgio Vasari, in Irene Earls, *Artists of the Renaissance* (New York: Greenwood Press, 2004).

Chapter 29
358: Titian, at www.getty.edu. Charles V, at www.getty.edu. **366:** King Phillip III, in Clifton Fadiman and John S. Major, *The New Lifetime Reading Plan* (New York: HarperCollins, 1997). **371:** Archbishop of Mainz, in Stephan Füssel, *Gutenberg and the Impact of Printing,* trans. Douglas Martin (Burlington, VT: Ashgate Pub., 2003 [first published 1999, by Insel Verlag Frankfurt am Main and Leipzig]).

Chapter 30
377: Martin Luther, in David S. Schaff, *John Huss: His Life, Teachings, and Death, After Five Hundred Years* (New York: Charles Scribner's Sons, 1915).

Chapter 31
384: Martin Luther, in Alister E. McGrath, *Historical Theology: An Introduction to the History of Christian Thought* (Malden, MA: Blackwell Pub., 1998). **386:** Martin Luther, *Luther's Large Catechism,* trans. John Nicholas Lenker (Minneapolis, MN: The Luther Press, 1908).

Chapter 32
403: Antonio Pigafetta, in Laurence Bergreen, *Over the Edge of the World: Magellan's Terrifying Circumnavigation of the Globe* (New York: HarperCollinss, 2003). **408:** Admiral Affonso de Albuquerque, in Craig Lockard, *Southeast Asia in World History* (New York: Oxford University Press, 2009). **418:** Lewis Henke, *The Spanish Struggle for Justice in the Conquest of America* (Dallas, TX: Southern Methodist University Press, 2002). **419:** Antonio de Montesinos, in ibid. Lewis Henke, *The Spanish Struggle for Justice in the Conquest of America.* **420:** Bartolomé de las Casas, in Francis Patrick Sullivan, *Indian Freedom: The Cause of Bartolomé de las Casas, 1484–1566: A Reader* (Kansas City, MO: Sheed and Ward, 1995). **421:** Juan Ginés Sepúlveda, in Rolena Adorno, *The Polemics of Possession in Spanish American Narrative* (New Haven, CT: Yale University Press, 2007).

Chapter 33
430: Antonie van Leeuwenhoek, in Robert Bingham Downs, *Landmarks in Science: Hippocrates to Carson* (Santa Barbara, CA: ABC-CLIO, 1982).

Chapter 34
433: Bernard de Fontenelle, in A. C. Grayling, *Britannica Guide to the Ideas That Made the Modern World* (London: Robinson, 2008). **436:** Thomas Hobbes, *Levianthan,* introduction by C. B. Macpherson (New York: Penguin Books, 1985 [first published 1651]). **439:** Voltaire, in Paul Edwards, ed., *The Encyclopedia of Philosophy,* Vol. 8 (New York: Macmillan, 1972). S. G. Tallentyre, *Friends of Voltaire* (New York: G. P. Putnam's Sons, 1907). **442:** Abigail Adams, in a letter to John Adams, Mar. 31, 1776, at www.thelizlibrary.org. Mary Wollstonecraft, *A Vindication of the Rights of Woman,* ed. Carol H. Poston (New York: Norton, 1988).

Photographs

Front Cover
Gina Marin/Getty Images

Title Page
Gina Marin/Getty Images

Unit 1 Opener
xiv–1: Rubberball/Getty

Chapter 1
4: Photos.com 5: Photos.com 6: North Wind Picture Archives 8BL: diane39/iStockphoto.com 8BR: New-York Historical Society, New York/The Bridgeman Art Library 9: Brenda Kean/Alamy 10: compassandcamera/iStockphoto.com 11TL: compassandcamera/iStockphoto.com 11TR: Royalty Free/Corbis 12: SEF/Art Resource, NY 13: Nancy Brammer/Shutterstock 14: iofoto/Shutterstock 15: AP Photo/Amy Sancetta

Chapter 2
16: Musée Condé, Chantilly/Réunion des Musées Nationaux/Art Resource, NY 18: Steven Wynn/iStockphoto.com 19: The Granger Collection, New York 20: The Art Archive/Real biblioteca de lo Escorial/Gianni Dagli Orti 21: Photos.com 22: Photos.com. 23: The Art Archive/Corbis 24: The Art Archive/University Library, Heidelberg, Germany/Dagli Orti 25: Photos.com 26: The Art Archive/Torre Aquila Trento/Dagli Orti 27: The Pierpont Morgan Library, New York/Art Resource, NY

Chapter 3
28: Granger Collection, NY 29: Steve Allen/Photodisc/Getty Images 30: Craig Lovell/Corbis 31: Bettmann/Corbis 32: The Art Archive/Bibliotheque Municipale de la Part-Dieu de Lyon/Kharbine-Tapabor/Coll. J. Vigne 33: Photos.com 34: Malcolm Freeman/Alamy 35TR: Monica Lau/PhotoDisc/Getty Images

35BL: From the Sketch book of Wilars do Honecort 36: Leonard de Selva/Corbis 37: Erich Lessing/Art Resource, NY 38: Bettmann/Corbis 39: Zvonimir Atletic/Shutterstock

Chapter 4
40: Bettmann/Corbis 41: nicoolay/iStockphoto.com 43: Stock Montage 44: The Bridgeman Art Library 45: Oster-reichische Nationalbibliothek, Vienna, Austria/Alinari/The Bridgeman Art Library 46: Bettman/Corbis 47: The Art Archive/Arquivo Nacional da Torre do Tombo Lisbon/Gianni Dagli Orti 48: The Art Archive 49: Bibliotea Estense, Modena, Italy/Giraudon/The Bridgeman Art Library

Chapter 5
50: Musée Condé, Chantilly/Réunion des Musées Nationaux/Art Resource, NY 51: Granger Collection, New York 52: Photos.com 53: The Granger Collection, New York 55: Bettmann/Corbis 56: Musée des Beaux-Arts, Orleans, France/Giraudon/The Bridgeman Art Library 57: Collection of the Earl of Leicester, Holkham Hall, Norfolk/The Bridgeman Art Library 58: Marek Slusarczyk/123RF.com 59: "Joan of Arc leads French army against the English defenders of Les Tourelles gate, during the siege of Orleans May 7th, 1429" (chromolitho), English School, (19th century)/Private Collection/Ken Welsh/The Bridgeman Art Library 60: "The Peasant Maid of Orleans in the Hands of the English," illustration from 'Hutchinson's History of the British Nation' (colour litho), Wheelwright, Roland (1870–1955) (after)/Private Collection/The Bridgeman Art Library 61: Photos.com

Chapter 6
62: Jean-Leon Huens/National Geographic Stock 63: PavleMarjanovic/Shutterstock 65: Granger Collection, NY 66: Terry Harris Just Greece Photo Library/Alamy 67: MFarling/Dreamstime.com 68: Faraways/Shutterstock 69: Bettmann/Corbis

Unit 1 Timeline
70TL: Pavle Marjanovic/123RF.com 70BL: DeliDumrul/Wikimedia 70TM: Dha, Wikimedia Commons 70BM:

B.S.Karan /Shutterstock 70TR: terry harris just greece photo library/Alamy 70BR: mountainpix/Shutterstock 71TL: stocksnapp/Shutterstock 71BL: Library of Congress 71TM: Photos.com 71BM: RF/Photos.com 71TR: RF/Photos.com 71BR: Roberto Castillo/Shutterstock

Unit 2 Opener
72–73: Digital Vision/Getty Images

Chapter 7
76: Private Collection/The Stapleton Collection/The Bridgeman Art Library 77: Eric Von Seggern/Shutterstock 78: World Stat International 79: "Bird's eye view of Mecca, 1784" (engraving), French School, (18th century)/Collection of Andrew McIntosh Patrick, UK/The Bridgeman Art Library 80: Nazli/Wikipedia 81: Marvin Newman/Woodfin Camp & Associates 82: Salem Alforaih/Shutterstock 83: The First Four Caliphs, plate 31 from Part III, Volume I of 'The History of the Nations', engraved by V. Raineri (aquatint), Italian School, (19th century) /Private Collection/The Stapleton Collection/The Bridgeman Art Library The Stapleton Collection 85: Glen Allison, PhotoDisc

Chapter 8
86: Jurnasyanto Sukarno/epa/Corbis 87: Mario Savoia/Shutterstock 88: Mikhail Levit/Shutterstock 89: Shezad Noorani/Woodfin Camp & Associates 90: Peter Sanders Photography 91: Aleksandar Kamasi/Shutterstock 92: Peter Sanders Photography 93: Peter Sanders Photography 94: Majedali/Dreamstime.com 95: The Art Archive/Museum of Islamic Art, Cairo/Dagli Orti 96: The Granger Collection, New York

Chapter 9
98: Paco Ayala/123RF.com 99: Irina Korshunova/Shutterstock 101: Yuliang/Dreamstime.com 102: The Art Archive/Topkapi Museum, Istanbul/Dagli Orti 103: Francisco Javier Gil Oreja/123RF.com 104: Jodie Coston/iStockphoto.com 105: Photos.com 106: Werner Forman Archive/Art Resource, NY 107: Jodi Jacobson/iStockphoto.com 108: R&S Michaud/Woodfin Camp & Associates 109: Bibliothèque Nationale, Paris/The Bridgeman Art Library 110: Photos.com 111: Courtesy of Museum of Maritimo